Taking Wrongs Seriously:
Apologies and Reconciliation

CULTURAL SITINGS

Elazar Barkan, Editor

CULTURAL SITINGS presents focused discussions of major contemporary and historical cultural issues by prominent and promising scholars, with a special emphasis on multidisciplinary and transnational perspectives. By bridging historical and theoretical concerns, cultural sitings develops and examines narratives that probe the spectrum of experiences that continuously reconfigure contemporary cultures. By rethinking chronology, agency, and especially the siting of historical transformation, the books in this series go beyond disciplinary boundaries and notions of what is marginal and what is central to knowledge. By juxtaposing the analytical, the historical, and the visual, this challenging series provides a venue for the development of cultural studies and for the rewriting of the canon.

Taking Wrongs Seriously

Apologies and Reconciliation

EDITED BY

Elazar Barkan
Alexander Karn

STANFORD
UNIVERSITY
PRESS

Stanford,
California

2006

Stanford University Press
Stanford, California
© 2006 by the Board of Trustees of the
Leland Stanford Junior University.

Printed in the United States of America
on acid-free, archival-quality paper

Library of Congress Cataloging-in-Publication Data

Taking wrongs seriously : apologies and reconciliation / edited by Elazar
Barkan and Alexander Karn.
    p.   cm. — (Cultural sitings)
   Includes bibliographical references and index.
   ISBN 0-8047-5224-9 (cloth : alk. paper)—
   ISBN 0-8047-5225-7 (pbk. : alk. paper)
   1. Interpersonal relations.   2. Apologizing—Social aspects.
3. Reconciliation—Social aspects.   I. Barkan, Elazar.   II. Karn,
Alexander.   III. Series.
HM1106.T35 2006
303.6′.9—dc22   2005027480

Typeset at TechBooks, New Delhi, in 10/13 Electra

Original printing 2006
Last figure below indicates year of this printing:
15   14   13   12   11   10   09   08   07   06

Contents

Contents

Contributors

ELAZAR BARKAN is Professor of History and Cultural Studies at the Claremont Graduate University. He specializes in modern European intellectual and cultural history, cultural property, imperialism, colonialism and post colonialism, history of anthropology, race and racism, and primitivism and modernism. Professor Barkan has recently coedited a volume for the Getty Research institute: *Claiming the Stones, Naming the Bones: Cultural Property and the Negotiation of National and Ethnic Identity*, with Ronald Bush. He is also the author of *The Guilt of Nations: Restitution and Negotiating Historical Injustices*, which addresses a topic on which he also organized a 1998 conference at Oxford University, and a recent international conference in Claremont. He is the author of *Retreat of Scientific Racism* and the coeditor, with Marie-Denise Shelton (Claremont McKenna College), of *Borders, Exiles, and Diaspora*, and with Ronald Bush, *Prehistories of the Future: Primitivism, Modernism and Politics*.

J.D. BINDENAGEL was appointed Special Envoy for Holocaust Issues with the rank of ambassador. Ambassador Bindenagel negotiated a $5 billion settlement with Germany for former World War II slaves and forced laborers as part of the United States Government negotiating team. In a year and a half of intensive negotiations, he won the trust of all parties and skillfully positioned himself to identify the compromises and tactics needed to keep the discourse civil and productive in reaching agreement. In addition, he crisscrossed Europe and the United States tirelessly, promoting the International Commission on Holocaust Era Insurance Claims, which resulted in a $300 million dollar settlement to pay insurance claims of the heirs of Holocaust victims. He was awarded the State Department Distinguished Honor Award, and the Commanders Cross of the Order of Merit of the Federal Republic of Germany.

ROY BROOKS is the Warren Distinguished Professor of Law, University of San Diego. Professor Brooks served as an editor of the Yale Law Journal, clerked on the US District Court in Philadelphia, and practiced law with Cravath, Swaine & Moore in New York City, before joining the faculty in 1979. He teaches and writes in the areas of civil procedure, civil rights, employment discrimination and critical theory, and is the author of numerous scholarly books, articles, and reviews. His publications include *Rethinking the American Race Problem* (University of California Press) and *Integration or Separation? A Strategy for Racial Equality* (Harvard University Press), both of which received the Gustavus Meyers Outstanding Book Award for civil rights. He is also the editor of *When Sorry Isn't Enough: The Controversy over Apologies and Reparations for Human Injustice* (New York University Press). He has been a professor of law at the University of Minnesota and has held the O'Connell Chair at the University of Florida College of Law. He is a member of the American Law Institute.

ALFRED L. BROPHY is professor of law at the University of Alabama. He is author of *Reconstructing the Dreamland: The Tulsa Riot of 1921-Race, Reparations, Reconciliation* (Oxford University Press, 2002) and *Reparations Pros and Cons* (Oxford University Press, 2006), as well as articles on such diverse topics as the transmission of seventeenth-century German law to North America, abolitionist legal thought, and property law during the Confederacy. His current research includes moral philosophy in antebellum colleges and courts, Progressives-era legal thought, and cemetery and monument law. Brophy teaches in the areas of property, wills and remedies.

DANIELLE CELERMAJER is a doctoral candidate in the department of political science at Columbia University. She studied philosophy, psychology, and social policy, before training and working as a community development worker and psychotherapist in Australia. She then moved into the field of human rights policy development, working for nine years in the field of Indigenous human rights. She spent seven years at the Australian Human Rights and Equal Opportunity Commission, for five of which she was the head of policy in the Indigenous Social Justice Unit. Her work there included monitoring Australia's compliance with domestic antidiscrimination law and international human rights obligations, and developing policy to address specific human rights issues facing Aboriginal people—such as water shortages, land rights, imprisonment, and health. During this time she also worked on the National Inquiry into the Separation of Aboriginal and Torres Strait Islander Children from their Families.

Since 1998, she has become involved in human rights and peace initiatives in Central America, specifically in the development of a theology of peace initiative bringing together Jews, Christians, and Mayans—and the North and the South, to develop models of peace work in the Americas.

DAVID CROCKER is Senior Research Scholar at the Institute for Philosophy and Public Policy and the Maryland School of Public Affairs (MSPA) at the University of Maryland. Dr. Crocker received three graduate degrees (M. Div., M. A., Ph.D.) from Yale University. He specializes in applied ethics and sociopolitical philosophy, international development ethics, transitional justice, and ethics of consumption. His courses at MSPA include Moral Dimensions of Public Policy, Development and Foreign Aid, Ethics and US Foreign Policy, and Ethics and Politics of Human Rights. While Professor of Philosophy at Colorado State University (1966–1993), Crocker wrote *Praxis and Democratic Socialism: The Critical Social Theory of Markovic and Stojanovic* (Humanities Press, 1983). He has been a visiting professor at the University of Munich and twice a Fulbright Scholar at the University of Costa Rica. After coming to the University of Maryland in 1993, Dr. Crocker has coedited (with Toby Linden) *Ethics of Consumption: The Good Life, Justice, and Global Stewardship* (Rowman and Littlefield, 1998). His most recent book, *Florecimiento humano y desarrollo internacional: La nueva ética de capacidades humanas* (Human Flourishing and International Development: The New Ethic of Human Capabilities) (Editorial de la Universidad de Costa Rica, 1998), analyzes and evaluates Amartya Sen's capabilities approach to development. Dr. Crocker has completed a manuscript entitled "Well-being, Capability, and Development: Essays in International Development Ethics." Recently, he has published several articles on transitional justice and is currently working on a book that defends and applies (to Argentina, Cambodia, Guatemala, South Africa, and Yugoslavia) a normative framework for reckoning with past political wrongs. He is a founder and current president of the International Development Ethics Association.

JULIE FETTE is Assistant Professor of French Studies at Rice University in Houston, Texas. She holds doctorates from the Institute of French Studies at New York University and the Ecole des Hautes Etudes en Sciences Sociales in Paris. In addition to her work on the role of public apology in coming to terms with the past, her research focuses on xenophobia, immigration, and women and work. She is writing a book about xenophobia in the medical and legal professions in twentieth-century France, tentatively titled *Professional Prejudice*. She teaches on contemporary French culture and society.

GEORGE IRANI is Professor of Conflict Analysis and Management at Royal Roads University. He was a Jennings Randolf Senior Fellow at the United States Institute of Peace in 1997–1998, where he conducted research on rituals of reconciliation as methods of conflict control and reduction. Between 1993 and 1997, Irani was assistant professor at the Lebanese American University in Beirut, Lebanon, where he taught courses on international relations and conflict resolution. In Lebanon, he organized two conferences on "Acknowledgment, Forgiveness, and Reconciliation: Lessons from Lebanon," and a seminar on "Reconciliation and the Displaced Communities in Post-War Lebanon." He is the author of *The Papacy and the Middle East* (University of Notre Dame Press, 1989), which was translated into Arabic, French, Italian, and Portuguese. Together with his wife, Laurie Elizabeth King-Irani, he has coedited a book entitled *Lessons from Lebanon: The Relevance of Acknowledgment, Forgiveness and Reconciliation to the Resolution of Protracted Inter-Communal Conflicts*. Irani holds a BA in Political Science from the Catholic University of Milan (Italy) and a Ph.D. in international relations from the University of Southern California.

ALEXANDER KARN is a doctoral candidate in the department of history at the Claremont Graduate University. He has been teaching in the department of history at California State University, Fullerton, and at California Polytechnic University, Pomona. He specializes in modern European history and nationalism studies. His dissertation examines property restitution and national identity in post-Communist Eastern Europe.

DANIEL LEVY is Assistant Professor in the Department of Sociology at the State University of New York, Stony Brook. Among his recent publications are: *Challenging Ethnic Citizenship: German and Israeli Perspectives on Immigration* (co-edited with Yfaat Weiss; Berghahn Books, 2002); *Old Europe, New Europe, Core Europe: Transatlantic Relations after the Iraq War* (co-edited with Max Pensky and John Torpey; Verso, 2005); and *The Holocaust and Memory in the Global Age* (together with Natan Sznaider; Temple University Press, 2005).

ROBERT ROTBERG is Director of the Program on Intrastate Conflict, Kennedy School, Harvard and President of the World Peace Foundation. He was Professor of Political Science and History at MIT, Academic Vice

President, Tufts University; and President, Lafayette College. He is the author of several dozen books on African, Asian, and Caribbean politics and history.

NATAN SZNAIDER is Professor of Sociology at the Academic College of Tel-Aviv, Yaffo. His recent publications include *The Compassionate Temperament: Care and Cruelty in Modern Society* (Rowman & Littlefield, 2001). He co-edited *Global America: The Cultural Consequences of Globalization* with Ulrich Beck and Rainer Winter (Liverpool University Press, 2003). He is the author of *The Holocaust and Memory in the Global Age* (together with Daniel Levy; Temple University Press, 2005).

RUTI TEITEL is the first Ernst C. Stiefel Professor of Comparative Law at New York Law School, where she teaches international human rights, comparative and constitutional law and chairs the Comparative Law and Politics Discussion Group. An author and frequent speaker in academia and the media, she has also served as the Senior Fellow at Yale Law School, 1999–2000 and 1996–1997. Her book, *Transitional Justice* (Oxford University Press, 1999), examines the twentieth century transitions from authoritarianism to democracy in many countries and offers a new paradigm for conceptualizing the role of justice in political change. Her extensive writings on comparative law, human rights and constitutionalism have been published in the country's leading scholarly journals, including the *Yale Law Journal* and the *Harvard Review*. She has contributed dozens of chapters to scholarly books. She is a member of the Council on Foreign Relations and Human Rights Watch Steering Committee Europe/Central America.

REBECCA TSOSIE is Professor of Law at Arizona State University, where she also serves as the Executive Director of ASU's Indian Legal Program. She serves as a Supreme Court Justice for Fort McDowell Yavapai Nation. She was appointed as the Lincoln Professor of Native American Law and Ethics in 2001. She joined the faculty of the ASU College of Law in 1993, after practicing with the law firm of Brown & Bain. Ms. Tsosie graduated from UCLA School of Law in 1990, and she clerked for then Vice-Chief Justice Stanley G. Feldman before joining Brown & Bain. Ms. Tsosie teaches in the areas of Indian law, Property, Bioethics, and Critical Race Theory and is the author of several articles dealing with cultural resources, environmental policy, and cultural pluralism. She is the coauthor of a federal Indian law casebook entitled: *American Indian Law: Native Nations and the Federal System*. She is admitted to practice in Arizona and

California. She is the recipient of the American Bar Association's "2002 Spirit of Excellence Award." Ms. Tsosie is of Yaqui descent.

VAMIK VOLKAN is Professor of Psychiatry at the University of Virginia and founder and Director of the Center for the Study of Mind and Human Interaction (CSMHI), University of Virginia School of Medicine, Charlottesville, Virginia. CSMHI studies large groups in conflict, and its multidisciplinary faculty includes psychoanalysts, psychiatrists, psychologists, historians, former diplomats, and political scientists. Dr. Volkan is a Training and Supervising Analyst at the Washington Psychoanalytic Institute, a former president of both the International Society of Political Psychology (ISPP) and the Virginia Psychoanalytic Society. He is the recipient of many awards, including: the ISPP's Nevitt Sanford Award for his work on political psychology (1994), the American Orthopsychiatric Association's Max Hayman Award for outstanding contribution to the psychology of racism and genocide (1995), the American Anthropological Association's L. Bryce Boyer Award for his study of post-Ceausescu Romania (1996), and the Margaret Mahler Literature Prize (1999) for his writings on clinical issues. In 2000, he served as an Inaugural Yitzhak Rabin Fellow at the Rabin Center in Israel. In 2001 he became a member of the ten-member Turkish-Armenian Reconciliation Commission. Dr. Volkan is the founder and editor of a quarterly journal, *Mind and Human Interaction*, which opens meaningful dialogues between the disciplines of history, culture, politics, and psychoanalysis. He is the author or coauthor of twenty-four books, including *The Need to Have Enemies and Allies, Bloodlines: From Ethnic Pride to Ethnic Terrorism, The Immortal Atatürk* (with Norman Itzkowitz), and *The Third Reich in the Unconscious* (with Gabriele Ast and William Greer), and the editor or coeditor of seven more books. His work has been translated into Dutch, German, Italian, Japanese, Romanian, Russian, Serbian, Spanish, and Turkish.

Acknowledgments

The majority of this volume is based on work that was originally presented at an inter-disciplinary conference, "Apologies: Mourning the Past and Ameliorating the Present," which was hosted at the Claremont Graduate University from February 8 to 10, 2002. The editors wish to thank, first and foremost, the contributors. We gratefully acknowledge the effort that all our authors mustered throughout the entire process of planning, composition, and revision.

We are also grateful to those who served as panel moderators: Patricia Easton (Claremont Graduate University); Julie Liss (Scripps College); Ann Taves (Claremont School of Theology); Paul Faulstich (Pitzer College); Rita Roberts (Scripps College); Michelle Raheja (University of California, Riverside); Zayn Kassam (Pomona College); and John Roth (Claremont McKenna College) as well as the conference participants, too numerous for individual mention, for their enthusiasm and endurance, and for the insights they brought to this important topic.

Additional thanks go to the following for their help in organizing and hosting this three-day event. From the Claremont Graduate University, Sara Patterson and Amy Donnelly were instrumental in all phases of conference planning and organization, as were Elysabeth Flores Griffith and Holly Domingo. Patricia Easton, Dean of the Claremont Graduate University's School of Arts and Humanities, supported our efforts greatly and helped to make funding available for the conference. Likewise, we owe a debt of gratitude to David Lloyd from the Scripps College Humanities Institute, our co-host and co-sponsor for much of the conference program, and to his assistant, Claire Bridges, who helped to coordinate our cross-campus planning. A number of student volunteers also assisted us during the conference. Our sincere thanks to: Rosemary Clark, Rob Dechaine, Sarah Metcalf, and Michelle Ladd.

One of the highlights of the "Apologies" conference was a special screening of *Long Night's Journey into Day* (2000), an award-winning documentary study of South Africa's Truth and Reconciliation Commission; and we were honored to have the film's directors, Frances Reid and Deborah Hoffman,

Acknowledgments

on hand to take questions from our audience. We wish to thank the staff at Iris Films in San Francisco, California, for the use of this extraordinary film and for helping to coordinate the attendance of the directors.

Finally, we would like to thank the staff at Stanford University Press for taking on this project and for the countless hours of work that went into the production of this volume. In particular, we extend our thanks to Norris Pope, Director of Scholarly Publishing, Angie Michaelis, Assistant Editor, and John Feneron, Production Editor.

E.B.
A.K.

PART I

An Ethical Imperative: Group Apology and the Practice of Justice

CHAPTER 1

Group Apology as an Ethical Imperative

ELAZAR BARKAN AND ALEXANDER KARN

1. The Practice of Justice: An Ethical Imperative

In his *Republic*, Plato flirts with the notion that humans are diverted into the path of justice only by coercion and force of law. Given the opportunity to commit injustice and avoid punishment, reasonable humans choose to act in their own interest, because that is what nature deems good. Rehearsing the tale of Gyges, who one day finds a magic ring which confers on him the power of invisibility, Plato (as Glaucon) concludes "that a man is just, not willingly or because he thinks that justice is any good to him individually, but of necessity, for wherever any one thinks that he can safely be unjust, there he is unjust."[1] Although we may praise in public the individual who exhibits self-restraint when presented with an opportunity to live "like a God among men," privately, Plato suggests, we regard this character as "a most wretched idiot." We do not—indeed, cannot—expect to see justice practiced voluntarily, since humans, unless confronted by the possibility of exposure and punishment, are unwilling either to speak truthfully or pay their debts (for Plato, the twin hallmarks of justice).

Of course, Plato (as Socrates) ultimately rejects Glaucon's proposition, arguing instead that humans submit freely to justice and law because they profit by doing so. There are ample rewards for those who restrain themselves in the face of temptation and make amends in the case of transgression. Justice, in this scheme, represents more than a middle road—as Plato's Thrasymachus characterizes it—between what is best (that is, to do evil and escape punishment) and what is worst (that is, to suffer injustice without remedy). Instead, the practice of justice becomes a certifiable good, an exercise in right behavior, inextricably linked for an idealist like Plato to the unfolding and refinement of history and reason. Philosophers, having identified the nexus between justice and right, need only to map its terrain for their fellow citizens in order for society to blossom fully and prosper. In the ideal state, sapient humans, well taught by the philosophers who govern them, *hope* to be punished for their trespasses and *wish* to be set on the path of justice:

> He who is undetected only gets worse, whereas he who is detected and punished has the brutal part of his nature silenced and humanized; the gentler element in him is liberated, and his whole soul is perfected and ennobled by the acquirement of justice and temperance and wisdom, more than the body ever is by receiving gifts of beauty, strength and health, in proportion as the soul is more honorable than the body.[2]

Here, Plato suggests that humans, given proper instruction and opportunity, will gladly accept censure and punishment in cases where they have lapsed into injustice. In the ideal state, humans are conditioned to feel the injuries of others as their own and are motivated to do whatever is in their power to repair these wounds because they view the exercise of care as an avenue to self-improvement and social perfection. Freely chosen in the first instance, the practice of justice rises steadily in Plato's perfect world to the level of *ethical imperative*. As long as our faculties are undisturbed and our wits intact, we cannot help but practice justice; for Plato, it is in our nature to do so.

Outside the pages of the *Republic*, humans, not up to the standards of the philosopher-king, are often less than perfect. We retain a capacity for acts of immense irrationality (not to mention cruelty and callousness), and we adapt ourselves readily to the moral disorder which Plato once hoped to eliminate from the world. We humans, it seems, can get used to anything, bending our practice and shifting our allegiances to enhance our chances for fulfillment and self-gratification. And yet, in spite of this moral elasticity, we retain a commitment to the practice of justice, even for injuries suffered generations ago. There is an impulse in us which flies in the face of Glaucon's cynicism and refuses the uncertainty of the postmodern age. Our striving for justice, however naïve or idyllic it appears in the light of rational skepticism, nevertheless is rooted deeply in our conscience so that we find ourselves bothered even by distant episodes of injustice to which we are not directly party. This sneaking but persistent sense of guilt is particularly intriguing in light of the centrality attributed to *Realpolitik*. So, what is the relationship between justice and the politics of everyday existence?

International law and conventions reveal the depth of our political idealism and manifest in part our aspirations for a global *Republic*. Aiming to legislate good will and political justice, these international instruments reach for higher moral ground, but often fail miserably as pragmatic guides. This volume aims to explore in a comparative and interdisciplinary framework the role and function—as well as the limitations—that apology has in promoting dialogue, tolerance, and cooperation between groups confronting one another over past injustices. The essays collected here seek to explain how and to what degree apology injects an idealist component into realist political discourse; or, to put it in another way, how apology manages to accommodate both perspectives at once. It seems clear now that a one-sided approach to the subject is too narrow. By bringing our moral aspirations to the "old-fashioned" negotiations and bargaining of national and international politics, are we moving closer to a global *Republic* as a result? The borders of our ideal *Republic* have been enlarged not only geographically, but also temporally, and we direct our aspirations for justice to the past as well as to the future. As the desire for equanimity is directed to history, and we attempt in our narratives of the past to accommodate minority voices, a picture emerges that is also more tangled and recriminating. Every example of past cruelty and injustice becomes a potential contemporary political topic for denizens of the *Republic*. The growing list of historical cases that demand our attention and emerge as candidates for compensatory measures is a testimony to the expansiveness of the moral *Republic*, as well as to its concrete, political impact. However, not all cases receive equal public attention; the details and nuances are the subject of the following essays.

After the end of the Cold War, and especially during the last fifteen years, the human need to amend immoral wrongs has been expressed in political discourse as a propensity to apologize for acts of past injustice. Nicholas Tavuchis was among the first scholars to take up the subject of these political apologies, and his text *Mea Culpa: A Sociology of Apology and Reconciliation* still serves as a historical starting point for the field.[3] Tavuchis regarded apology as one of the "deep truths" of social life and as a "moral expedition" which could repair damaged social relations and allow the parties to past injustices to go on with their lives. As the middle component of a "moral syllogism," the apology, in Tavuchis's scheme, bridged a linguistic and psychological gap between the victim's need for acknowledgment and the perpetrator's desire to reclaim his humanity. The passage of time since Tavuchis' publication is indicative of the shift in the public significance of apologies. Where Tavuchis once asked, "How do these apologies, which appear both magical and mundane, do their work?" he referred to apologies as an exceptional phenomenon. Today, the inquiry engages the center of the political dynamic.[4]

This propensity to apologize, the frequency of these delicate "speech acts" and the window which they offer into the realm of ethics, suggests that we ought to "take wrongs seriously," just as Ronald Dworkin once urged us to with respect to our rights, if we want to produce a nuanced theory of justice.[5] Group apology represents a new and compelling iteration of our commitment to moral practice. Despite new tensions and escalating hostilities associated with what some view as the new world disorder, apology remains a powerful trend in global politics. Even as cycles of violence propagate in some spots, in others we see rival groups willing to put their troubled histories in the service of justice and peace. Indeed, we have witnessed during the past two decades an increased willingness on the part of perpetrators to engage the demands of their victims.[6]

The critics of group apology have been vocal. By dredging the past for episodes of injustice, they claim, we divide and unsettle communities trying to forge a common future. They argue that we cannot judge history fairly against the standards of the present. They warn that we overlook the problems of today, as well as those looming ahead, by focusing too much on the past. They characterize apology as lip service and empty rhetoric, or as overly idealistic window dressing for hard-nosed legal and political negotiation. Even where it may be warranted, the critics argue, apology turns out to be a cheap and easy way for perpetrators and their descendants to assuage their guilt. On the other hand, even among those who do regard history and memory as a source of contemporary identity, there are some who reject apology as an act of erasure and a dangerous step down the slippery slope of forgetting. The complexity of life ensures that there is some truth in these perspectives, as well as the need for critics to address the popularity of apology, which despite compelling arguments against it, continues to have enormous appeal in an age of supposed political amorality.

A wave of apology continues to work its way through global politics. In September 2003, the presidents of Croatia and Serbia-Montenegro unexpectedly exchanged apologies for "all of the evils" perpetrated by their countries.[7] Likewise, the Irish Republican Army surprised many of its supporters and critics in July 2002 by offering "sincere apologies and condolences" for the deaths and injuries of noncombatants during thirty years of sectarian violence.[8] In California, Governor Gray Davis apologized to more than 20,000 individuals involuntarily sterilized under a state-mandated eugenics program which operated until 1964.[9] In Canada, the provincial government in British Columbia apologized to those who suffered severe emotional and sexual abuse while living in state-chartered homes for the developmentally disabled.[10] In Japan, controversy erupted when researchers discovered among the papers of Emperor Hirohito a letter of apology for Japanese aggression during the Second

World War.[11] The letter, drafted in 1948 but never published or delivered publicly, expresses "deep shame" for what Hirohito terms acts of "immorality," though it is addressed, to the consternation of many, to the Japanese people rather than the victims of Japanese aggression. An apology offered by leaders of Japan's Zen Buddhist community for acts of wartime complicity was also charged by intense emotion.[12] A statement issued by leaders of Myoshin-ji (one of Japan's main Zen temples) in September 2002 apologizes for lending religious credence to a militaristic regime bent on the destruction of "twenty million precious lives" and, more directly, for providing funds used by the Japanese imperial government to purchase military hardware. Apologies pry open the chapters of history which some prefer to remain closed. The Japanese examples reveal the difficulty of translating the western rhetoric of apology into terms consistent with non-Western culture. This challenge was particularly acute in the dispute over the appropriate Japanese governmental response to victims of sexual slavery during World War II.[13]

In the best cases, the negotiation of apology works to promote dialogue, tolerance, and cooperation between groups knitted together uncomfortably (or ripped asunder) by some past injustice. A sincere expression of contrition, offered at the right pitch and tenor, can pave the way for atonement and reconciliation by promoting mutual understanding and by highlighting the possibilities for peaceful coexistence. Practiced within its limits, apology can create a new framework in which groups may rehearse their past(s) and reconsider the present. By approaching their grievances through a discourse of repentance and forgiveness, rivals can explore the roots and legacies of historical conflict as a first step toward dampening the discord and frictions that they produce. It is possible, of course, to overstate the effectiveness of apology, but the psychological attraction it has for perpetrators, victims, and those who live in the shadow of historical injustice seems empirically undeniable. Especially at the *group level*, apology has emerged as a powerful negotiating tool for nations and states eager to defuse tensions stemming from past injustices.

Other well-known examples of the apology phenomenon include: Pope John Paul II acknowledging the role played by the Catholic Church in fomenting anti-Semitism; the determination of ordinary Australians to observe a "National Sorry Day" in commemoration of the injustices suffered by the indigenous Aboriginals and Torres Strait Islanders; President Bill Clinton's apology to survivors of the Tuskegee Syphilis Study; President Jacques Chirac's public meditation on France's collective responsibility for Vichy and the deportation of Jews to Nazi death camps; Kevin Gover (himself a Pawnee) apologizing on behalf of the Bureau of Indian Affairs in September 2000 for "efforts to annihilate Indian cultures" and a pattern of negligence in federal policy which has produced widespread poverty, disease, and disenfranchisement among many of the Native American tribes; Bishop Desmond Tutu's stewardship of the Truth and Reconciliation Commission (TRC), an organ established in 1995 to help South Africa overcome the most damaging legacies of apartheid; and, finally, the "superfund" established by a consortium of Swiss banks in 1997 to compensate Holocaust survivors and their heirs for lost wages, assets, and incalculable suffering. These are some of the best examples in a long string of apologies, which dates back to the early- and mid-1990s.[14]

Although each case entails its own unique problems and complexities, the overall willingness of these individuals and groups to engage in what we may call *negotiated history* is remarkable. Through a process of open dialogue, victims and perpetrators can exchange perspectives, combine their memories, and recover their lost dignity. As they allow themselves to become enmeshed in each other's stories, historical adversaries uncover new possibilities for self-definition and fresh avenues for cooperation. Apology can unlock the door to a more peaceful and secure future. Whether or not groups choose to take advantage of these openings is a different matter.

2. Amending the Past: Ethical and Political Considerations

The age of apology is distinguished by its unparalleled commitment to remove the past as an obstacle to productive and peaceful intergroup relations. Although they obviously do not erase or undo what has already happened, apologies can *amend the past* so that it resonates differently in the present for those who feel aggrieved by it or responsible for it. In cases of intrastate conflict, for example, where the origins and causes of the conflict are often disputed, apology can create a possibility for closure and can assist in effecting successful transition and reconciliation. Robert Rotberg explores this potential in his work on apology, truth commissions, and intrastate conflict. He writes:

[S]ince the utterance of apology is capable of muting recrimination and reducing bitterness, public acts of contrition are able to assist, accelerate, or commence the process of post-traumatic reconciliation in a manner that enables a nation-state to build or rebuild. Without the conferring of apology, a post-conflict nation-state may remain no more than a collective of contending sections and groups in search of a whole.

8

Not only can apology reconstitute relations between communities ripped apart by conflict, but it can also lay a foundation for unity even where ethnonational rivals have historically lived apart, for example, in the case of South Africa following the abolition of apartheid. Groups that have endeavored, even violently, to maintain their autonomy and keep themselves sequestered can be welded more closely to their rivals, where peace and practical considerations (for example, economic efficiency) support such a partnership, as long as group members on both sides are willing to negotiate an apology which adjusts the boundaries of their collective identity. The German-Czech Declaration on Mutual Relations and Their Future Development, concluded in January 1997, illustrates this point. In their bilateral agreement, Germans acknowledged responsibility for the crimes of National Socialism, while Czechs expressed regret for the expulsion of Sudeten Germans immediately after the Second World War. These negotiations cleared the way for fresh economic cooperation and significantly enhanced the candidacy of the Czech Republic for accession to the European Union.[15] According to the terms of the Declaration:

Both sides agree that injustice inflicted in the past belongs in the past, and will therefore orient their relations towards the future. Precisely because they remain conscious of the tragic chapters of their history, they are determined to continue to give priority to understanding and mutual agreement in the development of their relations, while each side remains committed to its legal system and respects the fact that the other side has a different legal position. *Both sides therefore declare that they will not burden their relations with political and legal issues which stem from the past.*[16]

Of course, historical injustice can be an imposing obstacle where adversaries hold tightly to the experience (and identity) of victimization as bargaining leverage. For example, it is precisely because Greek Cypriot leaders and their Turkish Cypriot counterparts do not or cannot imagine themselves as co-nationals or "fellow countrymen" that no apology has emerged from either camp in Cyprus.[17] Neither group can let go of the notion that its members have endured exceptional hardships and suffered grave injustices. What this suggests, skeptics of apology contend, is that (implied) wrangling over identity must be conducted *before* any apology can take shape. In other words, apology is often the result, and always a part of the process of reconciliation, but in itself is no magic potion.

Indeed, uncoerced offers of apology, like the one Belgium made in 2002 for its role in the assassination of Congolese Prime Minister Patrice Lumumba, suggest that apology can *set the stage* for rapprochement between estranged groups and for substantive reformulations of group identity.[18] The real significance of the Lumumba apology, one could argue, is not Belgium's admission of guilt or the expression of regret—received rather coolly by the Congolese public—that accompanied it; rather, it is the process of inter-rogation and self-examination which has begun in Belgium in accordance with the apology. For instance, an exhibition held in January 2005 at the Royal Museum for Central Africa, outside Brussels, offered a compelling reinterpretation of Belgium's colonial past.[19] As the museum's director, Guido Gryseels, explains, the exhibition was assembled to examine the museum's holdings in a new light: "[W]e have very fine collections, but the museum [...] remained unchanged for over forty years. So it need[ed] all sorts of change, first of all the message, which [was] still very colonial and [...] not very much related to the Africa of today."[20] The historical facts (or, in this case, artifacts) remained mostly unchanged in the new exhibition, but the context in which they were displayed, and the message that they helped to communicate, were both revised. For example, a large statue at the museum's entrance, which shows a white colonial standing above two kneeling Africans (inscribed: *Belgium brings civilization to the Congo*), was re-described in the museum's catalog as one of a number of "allegorical or 'ethnographic' sculp-tures [which] represent the philosophy in vogue during the colonial era."[21] This important shift, from triumphalism to contextualization, suggests that apology can acknowledge and correct ethical blind spots that linger in the popular imagination by initiating an earnest and open confrontation with the past.[22] Given relief from the strategic preoccupations of the Cold War, and still enjoying considerable economic prosperity, the global community has elevated its moral aspirations and committed itself to a higher standard of justice.

At the same time, the flaccidity of apology in the face of entrenched injus-tices and atrocities can be sobering, as critics rightly note. For those who refuse to engage their enemies because they cannot move themselves to a place of forgiveness or cannot make room for the expectations of such moral idealism, sorry is never enough. Nor should it be. David Crocker's essay on "Punish-ment, Reconciliation, and Democratic Deliberation" reminds us that apology alone may not be sufficient for those who want to reckon with past wrongs as a way of promoting a thorough transition to democracy. Crocker argues that restorative justice and the logic of reconciliation, though well intentioned, cannot fully replace retributive justice and the logic of punishment. There is a point at which too much emphasis on apology and forgiveness helps to promote an environment of impunity, which can only encourage new incidences of injustice or a self-perpetuating cycle of violence. In the case of South Africa's Truth and Reconciliation Commission (TRC), Crocker worries that excessive emphasis on forgiveness puts unrealistic and unfair burdens on the victims of apartheid, who may not want (or need) to exonerate the people who treated them inhumanely. Although apology does not necessarily require forgiveness, Crocker argues that there was an implicit suggestion with the TRC that the former should elicit the latter. The TRC put South Africans on a forced march toward reconciliation, which Crocker views as incompatible with the principles of democratic deliberation and civic participation. By requiring forgiveness, the TRC imposed a "minority" view of the future on South Africans who might have wanted to offer other formulations of justice for consideration and debate. No matter what the intention, even if it aspires to noble ends, the apology model quickly becomes oppressive when foisted on groups and individuals not interested in experimenting with it (or not yet psychologically prepared to do so), and so Crocker prefers to see apology deployed in concert with other tools from the retributive arsenal such as criminal trials, international tribunals, and reparations. Justice in a racially divided state, Crocker concludes, will require a careful "division of labor."

Crocker alerts us to the danger of overloading apology with expectations of forgiveness and reminds us that distinct tools are appropriate for different jobs. Still, apology has great flexibility and potential when considered as part of a larger framework of transitional justice, as the notable lack of mass violence in South Africa would seem to suggest. Ruti Teitel explores the ways apology can serve as an important demonstration of public accountability as new regimes endeavor to generate political legitimacy. By mediating between past and present, apology can create the conditions for forgiveness and cement credibility for new regimes struggling to put painful legacies of the past behind them. What Teitel calls the "transitional apology" is typically situated in the state's chief executive and is derived, historically, from the powers of that office to grant clemency and pardons when they are deemed appropriate, and to shape foreign policy in accordance with professed values. In this light, Willy Brandt's "executive apology" for Germany's Nazi past—symbolized by his historic visit to the Warsaw Ghetto Monument in December 1970— becomes a "foundational narrative" for the Federal Republic of Germany and more recently, perhaps, for a united and morally resolute Europe. It is interesting to note that Gerhard Schröder deliberately rekindled the memory of Brandt falling to his knees during his own visit to Warsaw in December 2000 (on the thirtieth anniversary of Brandt's dramatic gesture of apology) just

11

before heading to Nice for summit talks on European Union (EU) enlargement. "Without Willy Brandt and his 'Eastern Politics' [*Ostpolitik*], without his vision of a free Europe," Schröder told a crowd in Warsaw, "I would not be standing here."[23] Despite the fact that aspirations for public morality sometimes outpace the possibilities for implementation, Teitel's work on apology reminds us that we can still speak seriously of moral progress even in moments of intense geopolitical uncertainty. The continued usefulness of apologies like Brandt's (in both Germany and Poland) suggests not only that things in the past *might have been different* (that is, a higher standard of moral vigilance could have prevented certain injustices), but also that intergroup relations *can still be amended* for those who live in the shadows of past injustices. The power of transitional apology is further enhanced, according to Teitel, when it is "the culmination of democratic investigation." Applying Teitel's analysis to the South African TRC, one could argue that the narrative offered by the Commission (that is, the executive body) became the new identity of the Apartheid regime. The public requests for amnesty—the perpetrators' explicit and implied apologies—came to constitute the national memory. The TRC acted as the negotiator of national identity rather than the arbiter of retributive justice.

This "negotiation" is effective, in part, because it operates in a gray zone of uncertainty, where it may chart a new direction (for example, the TRC) or implement a traditional role in an arbitrary manner (for example, clemency, grace). This plenary power operates within legal constraints, but without a binding precedent. The uncertainties involved in granting clemency or issuing an apology, the need of the individual to make the decision, to carry out a policy, yet not be accountable in a regular sense for the decision, does and should create a sense of caution. These personal attributes, however, also embed in the apology a kind of *gravitas*, which it may not have enjoyed otherwise.

3. Negotiating Intergroup Apologies: Preparing to be Heard

The German-Polish reconciliation and the final report of the TRC inspire optimism, but obstacles abound, especially when adversaries confront each other across the divide of religion. When the IRA apologized in July 2002 to victims of sectarian violence in Northern Ireland, Protestants regarded the statement with suspicion and sometimes scorn. Ulster leader David Trimble bristled, "I wonder if this apology might possibly have been prompted by the investigative pieces that several journalists were working on about

Bloody Friday, and the names of those involved."[24] Colin Parry, who lost his twelve-year-old son in a 1993 IRA bombing, railed: "[L]ike everything they seem to do, it is as late and as little as they can possibly get away with. This apology is not hugely significant for those who lost loved ones over the past thirty years. Nothing can lessen the damage the IRA did to my family. A blanket apology like this has no effect on me whatsoever." The IRA statement came at a delicate moment in the peace process, just as unionists were calling for the removal of Sinn Fein ministers from Northern Ireland's coalition government. Given this context, many victims came to view the apology as a crude political calculation, and some publicly challenged the IRA to back its statement with monetary compensation. Although the British and Irish governments tried to lend the apology greater political substance, many of those touched directly by the violence rejected it outright. Victims of the attacks could not "hear" the IRA apology, while their wounds remained psychologically and spiritually unhealed. This underscores a significant distinction in the work apologies perform: the immediate victims are often less seduced than the general public. The rejection of the apology by the victims may, in part, be motivated by their assumption that there is a reciprocal demand for forgiveness. And yet, despite these misgivings, apology might still offer important benefits after all.

Vamik Volkan offers thoughtful observations on the process of mourning and its relationship to apology and forgiveness. Groups locked in conflict experience a cycle of rapprochement and subsequent withdrawal until they manage to fully accept their losses. This "accordion effect" offers periodic opportunities for dialogue, which mediators must recognize and exploit if the conflict is to be resolved. "Realistic negotiations can be carried out when the alternating between distance and togetherness (the squeezing and pulling apart of the accordion) is no longer extreme and each can easily hold on to their group identities. It is at such times that forgiveness, and apology also, can be considered realistically." Volkan explores this complex dynamic in his psychoanalytic investigation of public monuments and their role in group mourning. Victims build monuments to recall their traumas and honor their dead, Volkan explains, but these "linking objects" may function unconsciously to prolong the process of mourning (that is, to defer the deepest experience of loss). In the Republic of Georgia, for example, where major ethnic conflict erupted after the collapse of the USSR, South Ossetians have developed a unique and complex relationship to the *Crying Father* monument erected in Tskhinvali to commemorate the killing of three schoolboys during a 1991–1992 siege. The monument serves as a "concrete symbol" of unfinished mourning and is frequently recalled in mediated dialogues between Georgians and South Ossetians. Volkan explains in gripping detail how the monument disrupts efforts to promote peace by fueling the desire of South Ossetians for revenge against the Georgians; however, he notes progress in cases where Georgians offer to visit the *Crying Father* and pay their respects to the victims alongside their South Ossetian counterparts. Despite the duality, the positive response of South Ossetians to this gesture of acknowledgement suggests that apology can transform the process of mourning, especially where it is complicated and prolonged by trauma. While trauma may diminish the ability of victims to "hear" an apology in its fullness, a potential for reconciliation still exists as long as adversaries can manage to communicate their sorrow and remorse effectively. It will be interesting to see now whether Georgia's new leadership can move the process forward.[25] The fact that the ouster of Eduard Shevardnadze unfolded bloodlessly offers some reason for hope, as do the repeated calls for national unity made by the newly elected President, Mikhail Saakashvili. On the other hand, separatists in Abkhazia have so far refused to take up Tbilisi's olive branch, and Saakashvili has at times found it difficult to navigate between Washington and Moscow. Just as Volkan suggests, the question of timing will be crucial. If the political fallout of the "Rose Revolution" overwhelms or suffocates the possibilities for dialogue and remembrance in South Ossetia, then the window for a transformative apology could remain closed for many years. So far, however, the new President has managed to keep that window propped open. On the eve of his inauguration, Saakashvili visited the tomb of Georgia's founder, King David the Builder, demonstrating not only the profound symbolic power of public monuments, but also his determination that Georgia pays its debts to the past.

Finding the right "language" is critical in any effort to overcome injustice. Words and deeds often matter as much as (or even more than) the sentiments behind them. Where cultural difference and theological idioms interfere with the peace process, it may be necessary for rivals to craft a "bridging discourse."[26] This discourse offers a cross-cultural vocabulary that enables groups with "sacred" convictions to find common ground and cooperate in the wake of conflict and injustice. Mediators ought to help rivals find a mode of discourse which allows them to negotiate and make themselves heard without giving up their unique religious claims. The nature of religious differences is such that sacred spaces are exclusive and are not open to compromises. Without a bridge between the sacred and the secular, groups separated by religious difference talk past one another, making apology and reconciliation impossible. In order to build a culture of tolerance and nonviolence, religious communities must develop a language which connects them to their particular notion of the sacred, while still permitting intercultural communication. Reconciliation can be achieved more easily if peace is couched in terms of holy work and moral obligation rather than the rhetoric of human rights and multicultural pluralism, since these abstractions are essentially meaningless to fundamentalists. A good example of bridging discourse is the notion of *ubuntu* which Bishop Desmond Tutu has worked to develop in South Africa.[27] Derived from South African indigenous culture, *ubuntu*, though difficult to render in English, comes across in the proceedings of the TRC as a deeply spiritual appeal to the shared humanity and essential unity of all peoples. White South Africans who testify before the TRC accept the notion of *ubuntu* because it closely resembles the Judeo-Christian doctrine of universal brotherhood which is recognizable to them. Black South Africans, for their part, accept *ubuntu* because it offers a spiritual conception of justice untainted by the legacies of European imperialism. The two groups are equally at home on territory both consider morally relevant, and so they can effectively communicate their grievances and regrets. Apology and forgiveness are feasible under conditions of parity where each side can recognize its own principles being validated. A bridging discourse helps to smooth over markers which might otherwise be viewed as partial and one-sided.

Cultural specificity clearly shapes the terms of reconciliation and negotiation. The need in South Africa to refer to the African tradition is crucial if parity is to be established. Likewise, in the Middle East, where there have been numerous attempts to impose imported models of conflict management, the choice of specific concepts must also be based on appropriateness and familiarity; all sides must find a way to identify with the terms of peace. Yet, given the heralded cultural clash between the West and Islam, it might be the very adoption of Islamic traditions that facilitates an entry point for reconciliation. Increased sensitivity to local traditions and indigenous rituals could help to allay the suspicions of Arab Muslims who view the current peace process and its various "road maps" as externally imposed and, therefore, unacceptable. As George Irani explains in his work on "Rituals of Reconciliation," a new course may be charted by moving beyond the formal boundaries of a "punitive peace" to ensure that parties on both sides feel empowered by the process rather than denigrated by it. Instead of focusing on high-level diplomacy, which rarely trickles down to the grassroots communities who observe these conversations from a distance, mediators might consider adopting rituals with a longer history in the region such as *suhl* (settlement) and *musalaha* (reconciliation). These practices promote acknowledgement, pardon, and forgiveness where blood feuds and other conflicts have destabilized the community, and both work in "traditional symbolic vocabularies" which enjoy broad-based legitimacy. Although it might be difficult to make these rituals acceptable outside of Arab-Muslim circles, Irani notes that close parallels to the practice of *suhl* exist in Christian and Jewish custom. Mediators could take advantage of this overlap to build a peace process which appeals to grassroots communities by engaging the language and rituals which they know and accept already. Ample room also exists to integrate this "cultural" approach to apology with the "bridging discourse." The Arab-Muslim traditions of conflict resolution might be analogous to the role played by *ubuntu* in South Africa. Indeed, the cease-fire achieved in the summer of 2003 between Israel and the Palestinian Authority was based in part on the idea of *hudna*, a concept that originates in the Koran. Although the term has been malleable, in its interpretation as a "truce without loss of honor," *hudna* might yet serve to create space in the political process. Although culture in the current context can be quickly drowned out by violence, it is not impossible that the prospects for a durable peace in the region might benefit from the ability and willingness of Palestinians and Israelis to share creative concepts of reconciliation such as *hudna*, *suhl*, and *musalaha*, not only with each other, but also within their own groups. Even if high-level negotiations eventually work to pry from the disputed territory a two-state solution, friction at the borders seems inevitable unless parties on both sides perform some of the work required for a mutual apology.

4. Case Studies: Confronting the Past Through Apology

The core principles of apology are further illuminated in a comparative framework. The case studies treated in this volume underscore a rich process of reconciliation which offers more than a mere reenactment of standard diplomacy with different terminology. At the heart of the process, a set of real and symbolic transactions unfolds to challenge the limitations of high-level diplomacy. Indeed, these are cases where new public resources are identified that suggest the novelty and potential of apology.

A good starting point is Danielle Celermajer's examination of the Australian apology for evidence of a deep "grammatical" structure. Despite the refusal of their Prime Minister to make an official apology to members of the so-called "Stolen Generation," ordinary Australians devised a number of creative ways to demonstrate their contrition for social policies enacted by their government against the Aboriginal and indigenous peoples. Celermajer's essay on "Re-covenanting the National Imaginary" nudges readers away from the traditional view of apology (that is, the apology as an expression of regret and remorse) toward a more complex and richer view of apology as a "performative act of [ethical] recommitment." Australians have apologized for the past in order to exercise and redefine the moral principles of their community; in doing so, they deploy an expanded conception of social responsibility. Those who have subscribed to the apology do not necessarily accept causal responsibility for the moral lapses of the past (indeed, many were not alive when these injustices occurred). Instead, the apologists acknowledge that they live as members of a nation in whose name these misdeeds were committed. Celermajer writes, "Apologizing in this mode is not a way of compensating for wrongdoing, but [is] rather an expression of shame, where shame marks a recognition of ethical flaws in the identity of the collective, or rather its failure to live up to its ideal self as defined in its constitutional principles." In this formulation, apology becomes an act of *rehabilitation for the perpetrators* and their descendants rather than the victims. Apology allows Australians to acknowledge a "breakdown of norms" which enabled their government to pursue an objectionable and immoral policy, and it restores "active fidelity" to the ethical principles which members of the national community consider "essential to their identity." Australians who attached themselves to the apology movement: (1) accepted that the policy toward Aboriginals was radically out of keeping with constitutive principles of Australian identity; (2) felt that the policy was executed in the name of all Australians; and (3) sought a public ritual by which they could purge the sense of shame they felt and, at the same time, "renew [. . .] the idea of human rights as a legitimate and authoritative source of order and law."

The apology to Native American tribes on behalf of the Bureau of Indian Affairs (BIA) is more problematic. Whereas, in the Aboriginal case, tens of thousands of Australians made public display of their shame and contrition, in the case of the BIA, the apology came from a single (and most unlikely) individual. When Kevin Gover, a Pawnee Indian, was appointed Assistant Secretary for Indian Affairs in 1997, few could have imagined the stir he would create just a few years later. At an event held on September 8, 2000, to commemorate the 175th anniversary of the BIA, Gover opened the ceremonies with a thoughtful apology for the "historical conduct of this agency." In a formal statement, Gover rehearsed the policies and programs which the

ELAZAR BARKAN AND ALEXANDER KARN

BIA had pursued to "destroy all things Indian." He then closed with a pledge which moved many in the audience to tears:

Never again will we attack your religions, your languages, your rituals, or any of your tribal ways. Never again will we seize your children, nor teach them to be ashamed of who they are. Never again. We cannot yet ask your forgiveness, not while the burdens of this agency's history weigh so heavily on tribal communities. What we do ask is that, together, we allow the healing to begin: As you return to your homes, and as you talk with your people, please tell them that the time of dying is at its end. Tell your children that the time of shame and fear is over.[28]

Despite its poetic and emotional appeal, however, the grassroots response to Gover's apology was mixed. Along with other tribal leaders, Lyle Marshall, Chairman of the Hoopa Valley Tribe of California, has called the Gover apology inadequate, primarily because it came from the wrong person.[29] For Marshall, a Native person simply cannot apologize for offenses committed against the Native tribes. Not only was the apology "hollow," but it was also offensive, because it was not accompanied by substantive action to remedy the injustices that it cited. Until the Department of the Interior (which oversees the BIA) undertakes a serious campaign to support Indian self-sufficiency and sovereignty (for example, by working to reconcile the Indian Trust Accounts that it has badly mismanaged), it is unlikely that many Indian tribes will see an apology as sufficiently just or meaningful.[30] The survival of American Indian culture may well depend on the conscience of ordinary Americans and their insistence that the federal government be held accountable for its past actions and policies. Apology, in this case, helps to underscore the insufficiency of contemporary policies.

On the other hand, Rebecca Tsosie, the Executive Director of the Indian Legal Program at Arizona State University, supports the Gover apology and considers it a useful first step. For her, the apology allows for interrogation of American mythology, offers an opportunity for self-reflection, and "begin[s] a dialogue about what must be done to heal the past." Although problematic in certain respects, the apology is significant for "its effort to acknowledge the truth of history and accept responsibility for that history and its commitment to a dynamic, inter-group process of healing." Also important is the fact that Gover "does not prescribe the manner in which healing should occur." Instead, Tsosie suggests: "Native nations will have to reach their own understandings of what the healing process must entail, at both the internal and external levels." Her emphasis on negotiation here lends additional flexibility to the apology and clears the way for a reassessment of moral responsibility. Like Celermajer, Tsosie believes that group members inherit some remnant of the injustices committed in their name. Without being "guilty" of the trespasses committed against the Native tribes in any direct sense, Americans are nevertheless compromised by them as long as the victims and their descendants are left unaided. Gover's apology, therefore, "indicates that current representatives of an institution are in privity with their predecessors, and thus, they share in the moral responsibility for past wrongs." Though we arrived after the BIA had endeavored to "destroy all things Indian," as the "current representatives" of that institution, we are invited to reimagine and recollect the suffering of the tribes as a first step toward reconciliation and substantive healing. By underlining the moral debt owed by the United States, the apology issues a direct challenge to those who still see Native Americans as "wanting it both ways" (that is, seeking federal "assistance," while rejecting interferences in self-government). Here, Tsosie and Marshall seem to be in perfect agreement: the process of healing for Native communities requires a renewed *moral commitment* to the old promise of self-determination.

There has been no official apology to date for slavery in the United States, though a number of headline-grabbing reparations cases have made their way into the American courts already.[31] By comparison, the European Union included a statement of apology for slavery and colonialism in the final declaration of the United Nations World Conference Against Racism, convened at Durban, South Africa in early September 2001, and abandoned while still in progress by delegates from the United States.[32] While some claim that the war on terror has squashed the prospects for serious political dissent in the United States, Roy Brooks believes that the current climate of patriotism provides an excellent opportunity for those who might want to question the government and the private sector about their roles in the slave trade. This is because the terrorist attacks in New York City, Washington, D.C., and elsewhere, have prompted many Americans to closely examine the notion of national identity and the political ideals to which they aspire. This wave of civic soul-searching, Brooks thinks, could help to support an apology or some other corrective measure as a way for Americans to reassure themselves that their nation is morally decent and worth defending. In fact, the more embattled and threatened Americans feel, the higher their capacity for justice, Brooks seems to suggest, since mobilization for war and the threat of a "demonic" enemy have, historically, worked to give Americans a more urgent sense of moral purpose, something crucial if the reparations movement is to make headway.

At the same time, Brooks worries that the wrong kind of apology might emerge from these circumstances because the focus of current legal cases seems to be on winning monetary compensation, while the public and private sectors cope with the double-blow of terrorism and economic uncertainty. This helps to explain the emphasis Brooks puts on virtue and "moral apology" as opposed to what he calls "political apology." A moral apology, for Brooks, has no price tag attached to it. Instead, he writes:

Apology is the virtuous act of honoring the lives of the millions of dead slaves who contributed to the economic development of this country without so much as receiving a pay check. If it is virtuous to construct a memorial to mourn the death of 3,000 innocent people who perished in the World Trade Center and the Pentagon at the hands of terrorists, then it is surely virtuous to pay similar tribute to the millions of slaves who died in service to this country.

These essays, all focused on racial minorities, provide for apology a spectrum of possibilities and limitations, aspirations and contradictions. Brooks and Marshall, for example, aspire to polarized ends: whereas apology, for Marshall, lacks substance unless it is backed by monetary compensation and economic justice, Brooks seems to suggest the opposite here; that is, apology loses its meaning when overshadowed by financial considerations. The significance of their divergence is fundamental to our understanding of apology: it illustrates the massive extent to which apology is *context-dependent*. One possible interpretation for this distinction might stem from power-relations. Apology might be regarded differently by a group which feels its survival is immediately threatened (that is, Native Americans) compared to a group which regards itself as undervalued and underrepresented, but not faced with imminent extinction (that is, African Americans). The key would be to promote an open exchange between victims and potential apologists so that an apology can be rendered in terms acceptable to both sides. The BIA apology, from Marshall's perspective, does not pass this important test, while Tsosie sees it as a useful foundation for subsequent negotiations. With respect to Brooks and the African American case, there is so far very little evidence to indicate that this community is on the verge of gaining an apology of any kind, let alone one that would be acceptable to a substantial number of its members. The Australian case is also instructive, both for its wide public support and for its notable failures in the upper echelons of government. The political fortunes of the nation overshadow the specifics of the domestic apology, which was eclipsed by other dominant political issues in the national elections. The American and Australian cases highlight differently the clash between politics and civil society, where the place of the indigenous peoples in the nation's identity and the local politics determine the specific outcome. In the United States, despite the low political profile of the apology discourse, the bureaucratic constellation of the BIA allowed a formal apology to emerge, while in the Australian case, the stakes (for the Prime Minister, at least) were much higher as was the subsequent political resistance.

Local claims for reparations from the African American community have so far gathered mixed results. Survivors of the Rosewood Massacre (1923) won a two million dollar settlement from the state of Florida in 1994, twelve years after their story was broadcast nationwide to an audience of the news program *60 Minutes*. On the other hand, the Oklahoma legislature has so far declined to compensate victims or apologize for the Tulsa Race Riot (1921) despite the recommendations of a state-sponsored historians' commission that such measures be taken. Alfred Brophy, a historical consultant to the Tulsa Race Riot Commission and author of *Reconstructing the Dreamland*, a carefully documented account of the Tulsa Race Riot, suggests that apology and reparations will depend on the ability of historians to suggest a new narrative to replace the widespread conception that Tulsa's black residents were to blame for the violence that killed as many as 300 people and left thirty-five blocks of the city's Greenwood district in charred ruins. A successful claim for redress will transform the way the riot is remembered and treat the city's refusal to aid in the process of rebuilding. In other words, those who favor apology and reparations should work to circulate a richer, more comprehensive history of the riot, which can "re-apportion moral culpability" as well as educate and inform. This is precisely what it means to put history in the service of justice. As one member of the Riot Commission said in 1997, there "may be other things more important—more appropriate—things [than cash payments] like public statements, public proclamations, [and] publicly hearing from people who survived the devastation."[33] As this statement suggests, historical inquiry can serve as an effective way to frame apology, and the work that historical commissions perform can provide a useful tool for those committed to conflict mediation and management. Moreover, the failure of the Riot Commission to convince Oklahoma legislators to adopt its recommendation for reparations demonstrates that political obstacles remain where the historical enterprise and its emphasis on negotiation are misunderstood or thought to be too risky. Apologies for historical injustice not only have to contend with the rewriting of history and the attendant challenge of enlightening the current generation about the wrongs of the past, but they also must engage the contemporary political discourse to turn a moral view into political action. This requires a fresh coalition of actors with which we have very little experience at present. The people engaged in the rewriting of history are, after all, not likely to be the ones who can move the political machine, therefore effective interest groups and civic activism are indispensable. The opponents of apology have a much easier task because it nearly always takes much greater effort to enact change than to block it. A good illustration of this point is Oklahoma, where one state senator who did not participate on the Riot Commission complained during his appearance on a nationally syndicated radio talk-show that the investigation into the riot "just makes black people hate white people and *vice versa*."[34] The refusal to offer an apology in this case exemplifies the gravity of apology for those who reject it. Clearly, these are not mere words for the parties who feel vulnerable in the face of the past. Apologies cut to the core of our political and moral identity. The instances of resistance also suggest that supporters of apology should not limit their own actions to holding the moral high ground, but may have to plunge directly into the political process, which means they must be prepared to respond to the opposition and rally public opinion. What the Tulsa Commission and others working in a similar vein need to decipher now, as preparations are being made to launch a large-scale restitution campaign for slavery, is what kind of historical descriptions are most effective in eliciting a moral response. What narrative strategies and documentary techniques awaken and activate the ethical striving which characterizes the age of apology? Those who wish to take wrongs seriously will need to represent and depict historical injustice in a manner that evinces both moral indignation and the political will to undertake corrective action.

This process has received increased public attention and has evoked what supporters of apology and restitution might view as progressively higher standards of morality. For example, the Holocaust continues to work on the conscience of Europeans, who seem, in general, more determined than ever to assist its victims and to guard against possibilities for repetition. Far from creating a spiral of closure or forgetting, apologies elicit more apologies in a pattern of concentric and commemorative circles. In France, for instance, a flurry of apologies for various anti-Semitic measures enacted under the Vichy regime shows that the state can act as a powerful catalyst in efforts to come to terms with the past. Julie Fette illustrates how an "official" apology for Vichy in 1995 penetrated many segments of French civil society and promoted a new atmosphere of openness regarding the past. Members of various professional associations and public institutions openly confronted their organizations' darkest chapters after President Jacques Chirac legitimized a counter-narrative which qualified popular myths of national resistance. On July 16, 1995, while visiting a cycling stadium in Paris where French police had fifty-three years earlier rounded up and deported 13,000 Jews, Chirac departed from official protocol and the policy of his predecessors by pronouncing that "France, land of the Enlightenment and of human rights, land of hospitality and asylum, France, on that day, committed the irreparable."[35] Chirac's commemorative address, in a sense, embedded and made actionable what was already known about Vichy. Whereas tales of French complicity previously had circulated without direct political implications (that is, as plain fact rather than as pronounced ethical failure), Chirac's apology recast these stories in a stark narrative of national shame which disturbed the self-image of many French citizens and, in doing so, prompted numerous declarations of repentance. The analogy between the French and Australian cases may suggest the similarity in civic activism, as well as the difference a head of government makes. Neither Chirac nor Australian Prime Minister John Howard was elected based on their attitude to apology (nor, in all likelihood, would they have been if presented that way on the ballot). The fact that France's prime minister was able to embrace an apology, while Australia's did not, is in large measure due to the politics of the involved personalities. Individual personalities and leadership make an important difference; the apology discourse cannot be understood properly if it is treated as an impersonal phenomenon.

J. D. Bindenagel shifts our attention to the implementation of moral policies in the formal and semiformal relations between states. Addressing the crimes of the past is most challenging in severe cases of historical trauma. Bindenagel brings the perspective of practitioner from his time as Special Envoy for Holocaust Issues during the Clinton administration. As Ambassador, Bindenagel helped steer critical negotiations conducted between 1999 and 2000 with German business leaders, politicians, and the victims of Nazi slave labor, which led to a "future-oriented" settlement worth more than five billion dollars.[36] In addition to the much needed financial support which it provided for labor camp survivors scattered throughout Eastern Europe, the settlement established a $325 million endowment for education and remembrance and included a pledge on behalf of the United States government to assist in helping German firms achieve legal peace. The settlement also included an apology by the German President, Johannes Rau, emphasizing acknowledgement and repentance rather than money. In the end, the reparative/restorative approach and the legal/political approach reinforced each other, illuminating the complex interplay between idealist and realist positions. A "moral syllogism" provided both sides the security they needed to move forward. Rau addressed his apology to an audience, which included Holocaust survivors:

I know that for many it is not really the money that matters. What they want is for their suffering to be recognized as suffering and for the injustice done to them to be named injustice. I pay tribute to all those who were subjected to slave and forced labor under German rule, and, in the name of the German people, beg forgiveness. We will not forget their suffering.[37]

Again, the apology and the executive agreement that encompasses it succeed because they balance pragmatism and idealism in a package both sides see as tenable and morally substantive. While the apology speaks of the ideals of justice, democracy, and human decency, the settlement also resolves sticky financial and legal matters to ensure that "loose ends" do not haunt future interactions. Each facet of the negotiations reinforces the other. Although there are still mountains to climb before we can claim to have "defeat[ed] the scourge of hatred," group rights, human rights, and the prospects for a reinvigorated liberal-democratic future all have received an important boost from the age of apology.

This last point requires amplification. Although the cases linked to World War II suggest that a "precise inventory" of misconduct can generate the feelings that lead to apology, it remains to be seen whether apology has sufficient power to entrench and sustain the ethical norms that would prevent future incidences of injustice. It may be too much (or too early) for us to claim, as Fette does in the case of France, that these apologies allow society to move on from the tragedies of the previous century "in a repaired and cleansed way." Indeed, the age of apology does not absolve us of the guilt we carry for past transgressions; instead, apology makes our guilt operational and useful by constructing a new language and norms to deal with the notion of responsibility. The apologies treated in this volume clearly show that there can be a practical benefit in taking a moral inventory of the past. The discourse of apology allows its participants to transform their ethical striving into substantive political action and makes the world—however scarred and bruised—a bit more like the one we want to live in.

5. Conclusions: Taking Wrongs Seriously

One of the most compelling arguments for the apologies treated in this volume is the recognition which they afford to cultural groups and ethno-national collectives. The "age of apology" is born, in part, out of a demand that group identity be given the legitimacy and protections which the individual is granted already (in principle) under most liberal-democratic regimes. Group apology is an extension and deepening of a liberal conception of right behavior which focuses on the individual as the agent and victim of injustice. In an era of rapid globalization, as the boundaries and sovereignty of the nation-state are challenged and the role of multinational and transnational corporations expands, these apologies remind us that individuals have a "group life" for which they demand (and deserve) consideration. As long as history serves as a wellspring of identity, references to past injustice will cement the individual to his/her community and the desire for justice will play itself out at the level of the group. The "double-identity" of the individual (as autonomous agent and as a member of the group) need not be regarded as a conflict, but rather as a useful complement to the overidealized conception of the "liberal" agent. As Daniel Levy and Natan Sznaider put it, "[B]esides the principle that 'all men are created equal and share a common sense of humanity' there is [another] principle that views 'every individual as unique and irreplaceable.'" What reconciles these apparent opposites is an "ethics of responsibility," which we have characterized in an age of apology as an ethical imperative. Formulations of justice will need to be "group-sensitive" as long as ethno-national and ethno-cultural conceptions of identity continue to capture the imagination, and apology does a suitable job of treating strongly attached group members in the terms they prefer. Historical injustices, unlike conventional instances of criminal trespass, leave their mark on history and memory precisely because they entail the identity of groups as both victims and perpetrators. This becomes increasingly clear when forgiveness is examined in the light of past atrocities and mass human rights abuses. Forgiveness, in these instances, becomes its own "bridging discourse." Victims who restore to their tormentors the humanity which they lost in the commission of barbarous acts do not forget (or reverse) the "radical evil" to which they were once subject. Instead, they create a link between what Levy and Sznaider see as "two worlds of the sacred and profane." In the sacred realm, the past is nonnegotiable, and perpetrators pay for their crimes in perpetuity. In the realm of the profane, perpetrators and victims exchange apologies (and frequently money) for forgiveness so that both sides can again attend to the practical matters of everyday existence. As Levy and Sznaider have suggested, the age of apology seems to demonstrate that "we do not want to be prisoners of the past, because only our radical openness to the future makes political action possible." Mourning the past makes sense only insofar as it prepares and allows us to ameliorate the future. To wallow in the authenticity of "deep" victimization serves nobody well. This is something that critics of apology might stop to consider. For those who question whether we should revisit the injustices of the past: we undertake the exercise in the hope of releasing ourselves from the grip of history. We go back in order to go forward with resolve and purpose.

Committed liberals rightly chafe against the notions of collective guilt and collective punishment, but apology will have an enduring appeal because it navigates between the extremes of orthodox individualism and romantic collectivism. It simply is not the case (*pace* Tutu) that we are all equally guilty for the injustices that transpire in our communities, but, then, the apologies treated in this volume do not make this kind of claim. Instead, the apologies recognize that the individual is, to a significant degree, folded into the communities and groups with which she/he identifies and, further, that group members have a responsibility for the actions of others who identify (or have identified) themselves in the same way. As Celermajer reminds us, the appeal of apology for ordinary Australians (many of whom never knew until very recently about the forced removal of Aboriginal children from their families and homes) is that it restores fidelity and confidence to the principles and ideals which they take to be fundamental to their group identity.

Obviously there are limits to group responsibility: it makes very little sense to suggest, for example, that ordinary Iraqis are to blame for the gassing of ethnic Kurds by the Ba'thist regime in 1988. On the other hand, it seems reasonable to suggest that the prospects for multiethnic democracy in Iraq will depend to some degree on Kurdish-Arab reconciliation and that apology could play a significant role here. Prosecuting the architect of Iraq's chemical weapons program, General Ali Hassan al-Majid, will of course mark an important step toward the reestablishment of the rule of law; however, sanctions against one individual (or even against a full "deck" of perpetrators) seem on their own insufficient to repair a rift between large ethnic groups. Kurdish survivors of the gas attacks, many of them resolved (or resigned) to coexistence within the state of Iraq, count their losses as both personal and communal, which makes an extrajudicial remedy like apology both appropriate and substantive. This leads to a second point concerning apology and its relation to group identity.

Critics of group apology often creatively misconstrue these expressions of contrition as for the most part useless (or worse), while embittered rivals still wrangle over questions of identity and responsibility. If apologies emerge only at the end of the day, these critics assert, when adversaries have already channeled their hostility and resentment through the traditional avenues of retributive justice, how can these expressions of guilt and remorse rightfully be thought of as tools for conflict mediation? But as we know, this simply is not the case. The question of timing is a difficult one, as Volkan's essay on mourning and reconciliation illustrates. Although victims in some instances do view the apology as "too little, too late," it is also clear that apology often can help to move along the process of mourning where other vocabularies and discourses encounter resistance. For therapists, the challenge lies in recognizing these instances of avoidance and pressing victims to confront their losses (including their loss of victim status). For mediators, the difficulty is analogically complex. The proponents of apology must work to expand the imaginations of groups (and group members) locked in conflict so that new articulations of identity will have a chance to take hold. Again, this should not be regarded as a special obligation or an additional task for victims of injustice. Unless perpetrators can also expand the limits of their imaginations and learn to express themselves in a symbolic vocabulary that is considered nonthreatening, then apology is unlikely to have any of the restorative effects described here. In certain cases, like the Israeli-Palestinian conflict, the mediator's biggest challenge is to instill a notion of co-responsibility and to reapportion guilt so that it weighs more equally on the two parties. Apology, in this sense, represents an opportunity to reimagine identity, not to change the past, but to change the way groups and their members stand in relation to it. Yet it also underscores its own shortcoming: apology in many cases may be premature or impossible. The cases above suggest the potential for reconciliation based on apology, as well as some of the limitations. Apology, in this sense, is very much a measure of *realpolitik*, not merely a performance of teary-eyed innocence. The creative application of apology as a tool for mediation is at present more likely than ever before. The age of apology suggests that groups can reposition themselves with respect to the past without abandoning either their moral compass or the objective rationalism derived from the enlightenment. Apology teaches that we can wiggle and negotiate in good faith without having to give up our claims to truth.

Notes

1. [Plato], *The Republic*, translated by Benjamin Jowett, 1986, part II, chap. 5, p. 360c (Buffalo: Prometheus).

2. Ibid., part IV, chap. 38, p. 591b.

3. Nicholas Tavuchis, 1991, *Mea Culpa: A Sociology of Apology and Reconciliation* (Stanford: Stanford University Press).

4. For more recent work on the topic, see John Torpey, 2003, *Politics and the Past* (Lanham, MD: Rowman and Littlefield) and Janna Thompson, 2002, *Taking Responsibility for the Past: Reparation and Historical Injustice* (Cambridge: Polity Press).

5. Ronald Dworkin, 1978, *Taking Rights Seriously* (Cambridge: Harvard University Press).

6. For a broad survey of the new international morality and a sampling of recent restitution cases, see Elazar Barkan, 2000, *The Guilt of Nations* (New York: Norton).

7. *Los Angeles Times*, September 11, 2003. Dusan Janjic of the Forum for Ethical Relations welcomed the apologies as "symbol[s] of a new culture."

8. *The Washington Post*, July 16, 2002. Responses to the IRA apology were mixed. Although the British and Irish governments both welcomed a statement of contrition, David Trimble, leader of the Ulster Unionist Party, blasted the apology, urging that the Blair government do more to punish republican breaches of the Good Friday Agreement and ceasefire. Families of victims were also divided in their assessments of the apology, one parent claiming that it marked a "tremendous stride," another that sorry "was just a word."

9. *Los Angeles Times*, March 12, 2003. Davis's apology followed that of South Carolina Governor Jim Hodges for the involuntary sterilizations performed in his state under a statute which remained in the books until 1985.

10. *The Vancouver Sun*, May 31, 2003. In addition to the apology it offered, British Columbia's provincial government established a $2 million dollar fund to provide support and counseling for survivors.

11. *Chicago Sun-Times*, June 12, 2003.

12. *New York Times*, January 11, 2003.

13. With respect to Japan, Ruth Benedict has developed an interesting dichotomy between shame (Japanese) and guilt (Western); however, this distinction may be overstated in light of the numerous public displays of remorse that have arisen there. See Barkan, *The Guilt of Nations*, p. 63.

14. The apology trend accelerates at this time, thanks in large part to the sudden end of the Cold War. The emphasis on morality in international and intergroup relations, however, dates back even further to the Nuremberg (1945–1946) and Eichmann (1961) trials and, in particular, to the reparations settlement (1952), which provided aid to individual Holocaust survivors and the state of Israel via the Conference on Jewish Material Claims Against Germany. For more on the Claims Conference and the German-Jewish dialogue, see Ronald W. Zweig, 1987, *German Reparations and the Jewish World: A History of the Claims Conference* (Boulder: Westview Press).

15. Prior to the Czech Republic's entrance to the European Union in 2004, public debate over the Beneš decrees and the expulsion of the Sudeten flared up again. A reiteration of the mutual apology included in the 1997 Czech-German Declaration calmed the waters and highlighted, once again, the

practical benefits that apology offers to parties determined to build and maintain relationships uncompromised by past traumas.

16. Emphasis added. A transcript of the German-Czech Declaration is available online at: http://law.gonzaga.edu/library/ceedocs/cz/decz.htm; Internet, accessed July 16, 2003.

17. Although a great deal has been made over the peace talks which began in February, 2004, significant opposition at the grassroots level has threatened to undermine high-level diplomacy. A poll of Greek Cypriots revealed deep concern and skepticism. Asked whether the plan backed by the United States, the United Nations, and the European Union ensured a lasting settlement, 67 percent of respondents said "no." See "Cyprus Reunification Talks Face Challenges," *Associated Press*, February 20, 2004.

18. *Agence France Presse*, February 5, 2002. The 1961 assassination was carried out, according to a report commissioned by the Belgian Parliament, to avoid losing control over resources in the former colony.

19. According to the Museum's web site, the exhibit will offer "[a] new look at the colonial past in which not only the European, but also the African players take their part." Organizers hope that the exhibit can serve as a "stimulus for reflection" and as an "encouragement for an open dialogue with today's Africa."

20. *The New York Times*, September 21, 2002.

21. See http://www.africamuseum.be/museum/permanent; Internet, accessed July 23, 2003.

22. Not all Belgians agree with this assessment. The exhibition was criticized from the beginning by individuals who maintained that Belgium's imperial legacy should be viewed in positive terms. According to Gryseels, the Museum received numerous calls of complaint from former colonial administrators and functionaries. Maurice Lenain, for one, who served as principal administrator in the Congo's northeast province from 1945 to 1960, continued to defend the policies of the past: "The Belgian colonial officials shouldn't be ashamed of what they did in Congo. The millions who are supposed to have died—didn't exist." *Deutsche-Welle*, October 7, 2003

23. *Die Süddeutsche Zeitung*, December 7, 2000.

24. *The Washington Post*, July 16, 2002. "Bloody Friday" refers to the multiple IRA bombings on July 21, 1972, which killed nine and injured 130.

25. While it brings the Soviet era to an official close, the so-called "Rose Revolution" which took place in November 2003 also leaves Georgia to dangle over the political gulf between Washington and Moscow.

26. See R. Scott Appleby, 2000, *The Ambivalence of the Sacred: Religion, Violence, and Reconciliation*, p. 293 (Lanham, MD: Rowman and Littlefield).

27. Ibid., p. 199.

28. A transcript of Gover's speech is available at http://www.doi.gov/plw/octnov2000/culture.htm; Internet; accessed July 23, 2003.

29. The discussion that follows is based on remarks made by Lyle Marshall on February 9, 2002 at a conference on apologies hosted by the Center for the Arts and Humanities at the Claremont Graduate University. Marshall appeared on a panel alongside two other Native American tribal leaders, former Assistant Secretary for Indian Affairs Ada Deer (Menominee) and Rachel Joseph (Lone Pine), both of whom, like Marshall, responded critically to the Gover apology.

30. A federal justice ruled in June 2003 that the Department of the Interior must shut down its Internet systems—the second such order—to prevent hackers from accessing more than $1 billion in Indian money under its management. The same court ruled in September 2002 that Interior Secretary Gale Norton had committed fraud by failing to fix or reveal failures in her department's accounting methods. For more details, see *The Associated Press*, June 27, 2003.

31. One of the largest cases, a class-action suit filed in New York, seeks compensation for profits generated through slave labor and the slave trade. The suit names three firms, Fleet Boston, Aetna, and CSX, and promises to explore the role that "private institutions and government played during slavery and the era of legal racial discrimination that followed." See "Litigating the Legacy of Slavery," *The New York Times*, March 31, 2002.

32. *Associated Press*, September 7, 2001. The declaration reads as follows: "The World Conference Against Racism further notes that some have taken the initiative of regretting, or expressing remorse, or presenting apologies, and calls on those who have not yet contributed to restoring the dignity of the victims to find appropriate ways to do so, and to this end we appreciate those countries who have done so."

33. *Tulsa World*, August 17, 1997.

34. The interview aired on Pacifica Radio's "Democracy Now," February 8, 2000.

35. *Agence France Presse*, July 16, 1995.

36. An overview of the negotiations and settlement appears in *The Washington Post*, December 16, 1999.

37. News of Rau's apology first appeared in the international press. See *Deutsche Presse-Agentur*, December 17, 1999.

PART II

Amending the Past: Conceptual
Approaches and Impediments

CHAPTER 2

Apology, Truth Commissions, and Intrastate Conflict

ROBERT I. ROTBERG

Apology can usefully create the possibility of closure in post-conflict transitions. Where victors and losers have emerged in the aftermath of intrastate hostilities, and where the causes of civil strife remain in dispute, with blaming a preponderant form of discourse, then the delivery of apology from a dominant side to an aggrieved minority, or from each or all of the contenders mutually, can calm long roiled waters and greatly assist in effecting a successful transition. Equally, since the utterance of apology is capable of muting recrimination and reducing bitterness, public acts of contrition are able to assist, accelerate, or commence the process of post-traumatic reconciliation in a manner that enables a nation-state to build or rebuild. Without the conferring of apology, a post-conflict nation-state may remain no more than a collection of contending sections and groups in search of a whole.

The voicing of contrition ought to be easy. "We apologize for our attacks on our fellow countrymen. On behalf of my predecessors, as president of the newly reunited republic, I apologize for doing what we did when we were striving for total dominance. We harmed our fellow nationals. Ethnic cleansing was wrong. We cannot make up for what we the dominant party did, but at least I can apologize."[1]

Yet, the Greek-speaking Republic of Cyprus has never apologized to its Turkish-speaking island mates for the years of conscious extirpation that preceded the coup and invasion of 1974. Turkey itself neither acknowledges nor could conceive of apologizing for the Armenian genocide. Nor have Hutu and Tutsi in Rwanda and Burundi apologized to each other for decades of brutal attempts (not just the 1994 genocide) to eliminate each other en masse. Neither President Omar al-Bashir nor any of his Sudanese colleagues have apologized to the Zaghawa or other dark-skinned indigenous Muslims for the Arab-perpetrated genocide in Darfur in 2003–2004. Although President Frederik W. de Klerk uttered a halfway apology in 1992 and a prominent Dutch Reformed Church preacher tried to commit his denomination to a broad form of apology, Afrikaners have never apologized, per se, for apartheid in South Africa.[2] Other than the Belgians, descendants of foreign and indigenous conquerors and subjugators have not apologized for physical as well as mental exploitation of the inhabitants of the developing world. Mobutu Sese Seko never apologized for destroying the Congo and immiserating his own people. Saddam Hussein has never apologized for gassing and poisoning thousands of his own Kurdish Iraqis.

For politicians, offering apology has many uses. Indeed, apology sometimes fulfills episodic, idiosyncratic, and banal needs. In the recent history of the proliferation of apology in South Africa, for example, Transport Minister Dullah Omar apologized to African rail commuters for a communications mistake causing trains to run very late (the commuters had burned down a rail station). Education Minister Kadar Asmal apologized to Christians for calling a very large rally against the African National Congress (ANC) "sectarian and divisive." Safety and Security Minister Steve Tshwete apologized to prominent alleged plotters for accusing them of organizing a cabal to oust President Thabo Mbeki.[3] Surely, apology has its everyday political value at this level, but this essay sharply separates apologies for misspeaking, for speaking in a way offensive to a constituency or interest group, for making what turns out to be a political error, and for speaking the truth at an inopportune time, from a higher and more serious form of apology for wrongs against a class of citizenry, a division of the body politic, ethnic or religious groups, or other sections of a nation.

Contrition comes easily when it serves to limit damages or close off debate, but in larger contexts it is most effective only when the perpetrators of outrages or their lineal successors are ready to admit to the commission of wrongs (not just mistakes). Only in the theatre of the absurd would we have expected Saddam to confess and apologize, and often it is conceptually difficult for contemporary leaders to apologize in any effective manner for injustices and attacks perpetrated over many earlier decades by previous regimes. Nevertheless, a pope has done so on behalf of the Church, and Japanese statesmen have expressed sorrow for their national atrocities during World War II. (But Japan has never formally apologized to China or the Chinese for atrocities in the 1930s and 1940s.) In late 2002, Prime Minister Junichiro Koizumi went to North Korea to apologize for Japan's thirty-five-year colonization of the Korean peninsula. (In response, Kim Jong-Il unexpectedly apologized for kidnapping Japanese citizens and spiriting them to North Korea.) Thus, where there is the possibility of diplomatic or economic gain, where new evidence has emerged to embarrass a nation-state or a government, or where a leader has a domestic political need, apologizing often proves graceful, comparatively easy, necessary, and forward-looking. At a certain point, an apology is cost-free, and loss of face minimal.

Nevertheless, apologizing often bears, or is thought to bear, danger to the apologizer. Apologies are resisted when confessions of previous guilt might confer negotiating disadvantages, when aggrieved parties might demand onerous reparations, or (especially in East Asia) when a perceived and profound loss of "face" might occur. Until such time as the Turkish-speaking and Greek-speaking Cypriots ultimately settle their outstanding differences, and agree definitively on a joint or a separate future, giving an apology can be construed as a weakening of one side's bargaining leverage. Doing so certainly strengthens the side receiving the apology; its specific or general grievances will thus have been recognized and accepted. Alternatively, in the case of Cyprus and many other troubled and divided polities (such as Bosnia, Nigeria, Sri Lanka, the Sudan, Fiji, the Solomon Islands, and Papua), the positive and voluntary admission of error or guilt through apology can paradoxically alter the shape and tenor of negotiating endeavors by depriving the weaker side of its sense of grievance, and of its need to cast blame.

Apology is sometimes easy, but it may not be cheap. Giving apology has its political risks for the giver, especially if (as in Cyprus) there is still no settlement, and the two sides technically remain at war, with numerous Turkish soldiers guarding the north. If the government of Sri Lanka were to apologize for marginalizing Tamils from the late 1940s to the onset of civil war in 1983 (and beyond), doing so would clear the air. But it might complicate the government's attempt to arrange a permanent cessation of hostilities with the Liberation Tigers of Tamil Eelam. If Indonesia apologized for mistreating Papuans since the annexation of Papua in 1963 (with a fake referendum in 1969), the Papuans would surely demand autonomy, even secession. And what about Aceh? Furthermore, in all of these cases and in many others, the domestic political basis for an apology has not been established. There is no national consensus that the government or the dominant side should apologize. It is not yet established domestically in so many of these cases (even in Japan) that the horrors perpetrated by predecessor regimes or governments were in fact wrongs deserving of apology and of some form of restitution. (Belgium apologized for King Leopold's rule of the Congo Independent State from 1884 to 1908, not for Belgium's own period of colonial suzerainty from 1908 to 1960.)

There are various kinds of societal apology, all well meant and well intended, but some are more solidly grounded and therefore much more effectively utilitarian. The usual form of apology is that articulated by a national executive during a state visit. Any such expression of executive contrition, say President Clinton's personal apology to Rwandans or that of Japanese leaders to Korean comfort women, has value, but a national apology that flows out of meaningful investigation and careful research has stronger moral and practical claims. Thus, because a commission had recently reviewed past misdeeds and reported accordingly, when President Olusegun Obasanjo apologized to the Nigerian people on behalf of his predecessors for collective human rights violations, his speech of contrition conveyed a substantial moral and political message.[4] In the context of post-conflict healing, apologies that thus derive from broad inquiry arguably accomplish more healing, and provide a more durable basis for societal reconciliation.

Apologies that arise out of a detailed forensic examination of the bloody grievances and charges and countercharges that typify intrastate conflict in the modern world are more powerful than mere executive utterances in preparing the ground for reconciliation and in helping the peoples of a traumatized nation-state to move forward together in some kind of harmony. When a post-conflict society has investigated itself and subjected the recent past to searching interrogation, a subsequent official apology need not seem perfunctory or expedient. If the interrogation has been democratic and deliberative—if peoples from opposing as well as ruling tendencies have been able to air their views—it will help to lay the national groundwork for a public acknowledgement of suffering in the form of a meaningful apology.

Naked apologies are not unhelpful. But apologies deeply founded on exhaustive analyses of the old hurts—of the causes of deep fissures in divided societies—carry more moral and depositive weight even as they doubtless risk reopening national wounds long plastered over. Such kinds of apology are more influential in the accomplishment of societal reconciliation for, if evidentially based, they implicitly convey the powerful message of *Nunca Mas*—never again! Cambodians still seek an acknowledgement by those in power—through a tribunal and/or via a powerful apology—that the Khmer Rouge atrocities were wrong and that no leaders will ever impose themselves in that way again.[5]

If the underlying processes of retrospective scrutiny are deliberative and conducive to truth telling (that is, if a successor regime has truly broken with the past and its members harbor no responsibility for previous atrocities), then the apologetic stance can reflect what the once riven society has learned about itself, and not just the offerings of an executive. If the apology can be owned by all components of the post-conflict state, victor and defeated alike, then it will possess a transcendent power to promote reconciliation. It will also constitute a deep-veined form of apology that fully embraces the aggrieved and moves far beyond acknowledgement and contrition to demonstrate a magnanimous extension of empathy.

In order to accomplish this higher order of apology, a post-conflict investigative phase is required. That imperative coincides with the need, in countries emerging from civil war or other forms of internal conflict, for discovery, for cleansing, and for the uncovering of truth. Whether or not perfect truth is attainable, in order to move ahead—in order for the once oppressed to be restored and reconciled to the former oppressors in their midst—truth has to be sought through traditional forms of retributive justice (as in the special court for crimes against Rwanda, sitting in Arusha); through ad hoc tribunals like those at the village level in Rwanda; through the employment of a historical clarification commission; or through the practice of restorative justice—the impaneling of a truth commission.

The practice of restorative justice contributes strongly to the possibility of reconciliation by enabling victims to confront perpetrators and learn exactly how and when atrocities occurred. Because it is not encumbered by lengthy methods of discovery and burdened by detailed forms of procedure, restorative justice works well when achieving broad redress for vast numbers would overwhelm the courts, and when proof beyond reasonable doubt can be achieved through public interrogation and confession. Restorative justice emerges from the desire to reconstruct a just society. Better than punishment alone for perpetrators through retributive justice is a public accounting of violations, a confronting of wrongdoers by victims, and an emphasis on personal motivations. That is the theory of restorative justice. It claims that such a method of truth finding and truth telling helps to achieve reconciliation and societal reorientation, and generates apology by action.[6]

This approach begs the somewhat chronology-dependent complex question of whether some societal wounds should never be opened up, for fear of rending a social fabric that has been repaired, or at least been patched. President Joaquim Chissano of Mozambique believed firmly that a truth commission process would have marred the successfully mediated peace seeking that ended his country's civil war in 1992. Speaking twelve years later, he said that Mozambique had crafted a peaceful answer to war through the political process. To have rehashed the war in a truth commission exercise either in the early 1990s or later, would have risked opening up bandaged wounds. The proof of that observation was demonstrated for him by the three national elections that have occurred since the end of the civil war and the thorough peace that permeates Mozambique.[7]

Retributive justice is capable of ascertaining truth or falsehood, and calibrating degrees of responsibility. When guided by effective and impartial judges, trial proceedings can provide firm foundations for an apologetic posture. Blame can be fixed, once and for all, and the extent of one side's culpability decided by a series of proceedings, cross-examinations, confessions, and evasions. But, especially in post-conflict states where there are shortages of well-trained court-related personnel, and where trust in a new system of governance is limited, retributive justice is ponderously slow as well as being excessively expensive. Because proper trials take months and years (witness Prime Minister Slobodan Milosovic's trial at The Hague), accumulating knowledge sufficient for a serious form of apology takes almost forever. The sample becomes too small, as well, for courts can only hear so many defendants. Thus, the truth that is a requisite precursor to reconciliation can never be compiled with sufficiently thick description. Retributive justice, with all of its necessary procedural safeguards, provides too few solid bases for effective apology.

Traditional courts are no better. Whatever the claims for post-genocidal *gacaca* (decisions by local notables) court proceedings in Rwanda and village- or rural-based hearings elsewhere in Africa and Asia, the thorough and dispassionate evaluation of the available evidence of guilt and innocence of individuals and groups cannot be one. Fairness can never be demonstrated, one way or the other. Such courts can process the criminals accused at a much faster clip than can modern courts, with their elaborated respect for and attention to fundamental rights, but since their judgments cannot be tested and standards maintained, traditional courts offer no definitive basis on which to propose a conclusive apology.

Historical clarification commissions, a variant of truth commissions, are not common. Although in theory they are constituted and operated differently from truth commissions, in practice the differences to date have been excessively subtle. Clarification commissions review all kinds of evidence — written, oral, legal, forensic (to the extent that bodies may be exhumed) — relating to specific events or a chain of occurrences in the past. On the basis of such a review, a historical clarification exercise can provide a dispassionate, or at least an agreed upon view of the past. Historical clarification can decide whether there in fact was genocide in Turkey in 1915, and its dimensions. It can decide who did what to whom in Cyprus from 1955 to 1974. It can determine each side's responsibility for loss of life in the Sudan, or the exact steps that led to the chaos of the 1990s in Sierra Leone.

Historical clarification commissions ideally comprise reputed judges, lawyers, or historians, not all of whom need be nationals, accustomed to sifting retrospective evidence, to removing barriers to truth, and to uncovering long-buried facts. These commissions may or may not proceed by taking public testimony. In the case of Cyprus, many witnesses are dead and disputes may exist not over what happened, but in what sequence, and why. In other cases, for example Sri Lanka, there may be more disagreement over the impact of national policy decisions than over what they were and why they were introduced. A clarification commission in Fiji could quickly report on the coups of 1987 and 1999, but would then have a difficult time putting together an accurate account of the exact roles of all of the key actors, and their real motives. In the case of Fiji, participants would need to be interrogated carefully as to their actions, whereas in the Sudan the record of brutalities may not require that it be based on interviews with perpetrators.

Historical clarification commissions can establish chains of culpability, offer support to or refutation of accusations about the perpetuation of atrocities, suggest plausible causality, and single out groups or individuals for criticism. Such commissions can thus provide unimpeachable grounds for apology. Furthermore, they can become markers of collective memory. If their work is regarded as fair and legitimate, and if their proceedings are transparent, then the very gravity of their respective undertakings will command the kind of respect that could form the solid basis for a substantive apology. Anything less, anything ad hoc and potentially shoddy, provides a less effective platform from which to proffer apologies in states emerging from civil war or other internal hostilities.

Some thoughtful critics argue that historical clarification commissions ought to be mandated to go beyond neutral fact-finding and documentation of past atrocities to negotiate a mutually acceptable national past. That is, such commissions could consciously set out to interpret and construct a new narration of past conflicts, thus "mediating" and reformulating the past in ways that will, presumably, be helpful for reconciliation and effective transitions. In this manner, such commissions could explain why one ethnic group targeted another, place controversies and atrocities in context, focus (as Chissano would have wanted) on the coming together rather than the pulling apart, and develop the basis for an acceptable rendering of a difficult period in a nation-state's history when hard-edged conflict manifested itself, and one ruling group disadvantaged the then weaker side. But to proceed in any such manner would vitiate a commission's moral authority. A historical clarification commission's legitimacy depends entirely on its ability to sift the often contentious and muddled record objectively. Such commissions fail their mission if they offer political or prescriptive reports rather than scrupulously researched reports of times of turmoil. If their opinions are programmatic rather than abundantly factual, they cannot be relied upon to undergird a successful form of apology.

The subtle theoretical differences between an historical clarification commission and a truth commission are implicit in their titles. Historical clarifiers interrogate the ledgers and graves of the past; truth commissioners cross-examine contemporary victims and perpetrators in order to learn what really happened when individuals vanished, or when violent incidents and massacres occurred. Were the missing people killed, and why? Who assassinated those who disapppeared, who tossed victims out of airplanes, and on whose orders? Historical clarifiers can and do ask some of the same questions, but usually of documents rather than the actual victims and perpetrators. Historical clarifiers more often are attempting to assign blame to a government agency, a military group, or an insurgency unit, not to individuals. Truth commissions work more generally with individuals. Both forms of post hoc review can provide a detailed, nearly complete, record of past or recent injustice, meticulously documented. Both methods hence can inform the basis of well-grounded apology. Depending on the quality of a commission's research and hearings, and their integrity, such reports provide a morally defensible basis for apology. The reports may also make apologies (and/or prosecutions) imperative.

The post-conflict societies that through 2005 had actively chosen the commission (usually the truth commission) route to retrospective understanding and possible reconciliation, were actively considering creating a commission, or needed to establish such a body to come to terms with the realities of their pasts through a commission-type undertaking, were numerous. Their ranks included: Afghanistan, Angola, Bosnia, Burma, Burundi, Chad, Colombia, Congo, Cyprus, Fiji, Haiti, Indonesia, Kenya, Kosovo, Liberia, Malawi, Nigeria, Paraguay, Peru, Serbia, Sierra Leone, the Solomon Islands, Sri Lanka, the Sudan, Uganda, Zambia, and Zimbabwe.

Each of these polities possesses one or more unsavory chapters in its postindependence past. Some or all of these governments have massacred minorities, indulged in ethnic cleansing, bombed their own citizens, pillaged, invited or facilitated coups, were complicit in orgies of corruption, refused to provide political (public) goods to citizens, denied the existence of or failed to deal with the consequences of scourges such as HIV/AIDS, and ruled irresponsibly. Oppositions and insurgents have likewise attacked innocent civilians and used reprehensible methods to gain military advantage. In order for these war-torn nation-states to restore a minimal sense of comity; in order for the events that divided ethnic, religious, and linguistic groups within one country to be consigned to memory and not continue to fester; and in order for these nation-states to begin to construct a new future, they have to come to terms with and assign responsibility for the destructive elements in their mutual past. (Admittedly, sometimes, as President Chissano argued, it is best for societal peace not to mount a truth-type commission.[8] Sometimes the time is not ripe. Other negotiations are taking place that would be interrupted. Both the former and present rulers are complicit and want to avoid any post hoc investigations of earlier conduct. Truth commissions are not always the best recipe for a creating a soufflé of post-conflict harmony.)

The argument for assigning responsibility by means of a truth-type commission, which then permits the articulation of contrition on a meaningful basis, is compelling. There have been several kinds of truth commission, depending on their origins and mandates, but also on the quality and character of their leaderships.

Too many of the early truth commission efforts were inconsequential.[9] Many of the first commission efforts (for example, Uganda [1974], Bolivia [1982], Zimbabwe [1985], Uruguay [1985], and Nepal [1990]) were political exercises. Either they dared not hear too much testimony in public for fear that it would be inflammatory or arouse retaliation from ousted military officers (who were still in uniform) or their patrons, and/or their reports were never allowed to be published. In at least one case (Haiti), a commission disbanded before writing a report.

The more effective truth commissions attempted to discover precisely what happened to persons who disappeared during regime-sponsored attacks on alleged opponents and random civilians. These clinical commissions about disappearances took testimony behind closed doors and, only belatedly in their published (sometimes unpublished) reports, and, given the constraints under which they operated (lack of cooperation or downright hostility from oppressive regimes still in office, or lack of funding), gave as accurate an accounting of the disappeared as possible. The Argentinean (1983) and Chilean (1990–1991) commissions were greatly hindered by the military menace that overhung their work and by the consequent need to act quietly and privately. Nevertheless, the conclusions of both efforts at truth finding had dramatic short-term and even more consequential long-term impacts on their societies.

As heralds of apology, the Argentinean and Chilean commissions stand out. Despite the baleful contexts in which they operated, both commissions managed to distinguish wrong from right, pinpoint injustice, apportion blame, and—if anyone wanted to apologize—to provide firm evidentiary foundations for a well-founded and well-rounded articulation of regret.

In other clinical commission cases (in Haiti [1994–1996] and Sri Lanka [1994–1997], among others), there was little attempt to go beyond recitations of the bare facts. There was no desire to examine the moral and historical underpinnings of the crimes committed. It was enough, they believed, to answer a limited set of specific questions rather than to be too precise about affixing blame.[10]

Another category of commission was born circumscribed because of bargains struck between an outgoing regime and its successor, or between contemporary governments and the United Nations and/or nongovernmental human rights organizations. The Guatemalan and El Salvadoran commissions were limited by agreement and mandate, for example. The Guatemalan three-man Commission to Clarify Past Human Rights Violations and Acts of Violence that Have Caused the Guatemalan People to Suffer, known as a historical clarification commission (1997–1999), was prohibited from naming names and apportioning blame directly. The UN-sponsored Commission on the Truth in El Salvador was given a mere eight months to hear testimony from 2000 victims and witnesses and to exhume a massacre burial site.

Despite such restrictions, both commissions produced devastatingly critical reports. The thoroughly international El Salvadoran commissioners and their expatriate staff worked throughout 1992 to investigate military and opposition abuses against each other and against civilians during the country's post-1980 civil war. The Commission's forthright report—*From Madness to Hope*—pinned responsibility for 95 percent of atrocities on the government and government forces, but, instead of embracing the report and acting accordingly, the government of the day legislated a blanket amnesty for perpetrators, and allowed the military publicly to deny the report's veracity. The Guatemalan commission issued a very strong report describing extreme acts of cruelty; 93 percent of the violations documented were ascribed to the national military or their confederates. Both commissions operated without cooperation from the military officers who were suspected of ordering or allowing their soldiers to brutalize and kill innocent as well as opposition nationals of Amerindian descent. Both commissions were foisted on outgoing military regimes as conditions of a peace agreement; both operated quietly, and out of public view. Nevertheless, in the Guatemalan case, a wily German chair managed to produce a nine-volume report that found the national army responsible for 200,000 deaths and disappearances during thirty-six years of civil war. It detailed 626 massacres by the army and thirty-two by the rebels.

The paradigm for twenty-first century truth commissions (and in many ways for future historical clarification commissions as well) in method, organization, and output is the South African Truth and Reconciliation Commission (TRC), 1995–1999. Apartheid was unique in its brutality, but not without similarities to the victimization, ethnic cleansing, and disappearances in other developing world societies. Partially because of the duration and epistemology of apartheid, however, it made sense in the post-conflict period to avoid blanket amnesties (unlike the situations in Argentina, Chile, and El Salvador) and to provide a mechanism which could lay bare the truth of apartheid, could account for mysterious deaths, and could bring closure to forty years of misery while simultaneously moving South Africa's peoples forward in harmony—"reconciled" to their collective past. This was a tall order, but revenge was impolitic and the usual process of retributive justice would have taken too long, been too expensive, and been too problematic in producing salutary results (as the first big post-apartheid trials were to demonstrate).[11]

The TRC was created by the South African parliament with a broad official mandate to unmask the stark, squalid facts of apartheid, to report to South Africa and the world, and to trade amnesty, where necessary, for information about the atrocities and other events of the past. The broad mandate—the TRC was empowered to investigate everything and anything after 1964—was innovative and of critical importance, for it enabled the TRC to avoid the compromises and constraints of the commissions in Argentina, Chile, and Guatemala, among others. The TRC also interpreted its mandate to report creatively. Previous commissions had published reports, which the TRC was eventually to do, too. But the TRC decided to be completely transparent, to encourage the televising and broadcasting of all of its victim hearings (more than 21,000 victims ultimately appeared before it), to encourage daily press coverage, and to ensure that no South African could escape the import of and the facts revealed by the hearings. The TRC went public, from the beginning, so that all South Africans could relive the apartheid drama through the eyes of victims, and also of perpetrators (who were compelled to testify).

The TRC solved the problem that had so bedeviled its predecessor commissions—how to force testimony. In addition to subpoena power, which the TRC possessed but used infrequently, it was empowered to offer amnesty only in exchange for full testimony. The TRC indeed grew out of an elaborate political compromise that rejected the outgoing white regime's demand for blanket amnesty and impunity in exchange for a modality, the TRC, that could grant amnesty for acts committed for political reasons or according to the political calculations of superiors. Ultimately, the TRC could send unresolved cases to prosecutors, and recommend retributive justice.

The TRC was constituted to and chose to unearth the past and condemn apartheid not on the basis of theory or generality, but as a result of the accumulation of facts about a collection of individual victimizations and atrocities. Aggrieved next of kin would ask questions; so would the TRC's prosecutors and commissioners. The perpetrators would be summoned and, if they believed that they could obtain amnesty from prosecution, they would offer accounts and explanations. Of the approximately 7000 persons seeking amnesty before the TRC, only 2500 were approved. The denials came when acts were insufficiently political, or when the persons seeking amnesty were not believed to be telling all.

The TRC was a powerful example of accumulated truth building sufficient to approximate apology. It was democratic, accessible, open, and fearless, despite worries about a backlash from the Afrikaners who had been ousted from power. Whereas the excellent commissions in Argentina, Chile, and Guatemala (and others) were compelled to operate largely out of public view, the TRC insisted on a public presence. Its internal debates were largely open. Its disputes with the old and the new governments were public. Its commissioners and staff were outspoken. Moreover, the TRC operated relentlessly.

Consciously or not, the TRC's operations continuously reaffirmed the notion that there was such a thing as truth (about the apartheid past), that *that* truth could be ascertained best through an iterative, repetitive process of thousands of informal but disciplined hearings and testimonies, and that the devastation of apartheid could best be demonstrated by facts, not sermons. The story of apartheid was not just one story, moreover, but a collection of myriad perceptions of what had been revealed before the commission and argued back and forth between those charged with disclosing what and why, and the victims, who wanted nothing but raw knowledge. By this accumulation of testimony, post-conflict South African society could begin consciously to reconstruct itself. As the TRC proceedings revealed more about what had happened, they piled on layer after layer of apartheid atrocity. Although a commissioner believed that the TRC's report could "not tell the story of apartheid as a whole, but only the story of its abuses of bodily integrity," its hearings were able to disclose more and more of the terror and inhumanity of the nation's past in ways that the more limited commissions elsewhere could but envy.[12]

At the center of the TRC's *raison d'etre*, at least in the mind of Archbishop Desmond Tutu, its Nobel laureate and charismatic Chair, was the massing of material sufficient to elicit or demand apology from the former regime. He shared with others on the commission the strong sense that a society could only move forward after it came to terms with its collective angst. In the South African case that meant coming to terms with the brutalities committed by whites against Africans, by Africans against other Africans, by Africans against whites, and by the African National Congress (ANC) against its own members, as well as with whites coming personally to terms with the evils of four decades of apartheid. Tutu directly asked whites to apologize—to take responsibility for their actions during the apartheid era. Is there no leader of "some stature and some integrity in the white community," he pleaded, who will admit that whites "had a bad policy that had evil consequences?"[3] No one embraced Tutu's challenge.

Tutu simultaneously sought through the sessions of the TRC to achieve societal and individual forgiveness and atonement. To him, those objectives were at one with apology, and together served the overarching goal of reconciliation. But, not all students of the truth commission endeavor agree. Whether realizable or not, forgiveness could erase wrongdoing, and thus be a submission to wrongdoing. "It is morally objectionable," wrote Crocker, "as well as impractical for a truth commission...to force people to agree about the past, forgive sins committed against them, or love one another."[4] Bhargava suggested that imposing forgiveness was morally inappropriate for a truth commission. To forgive was not always appropriate or virtuous. Bhargava wanted forgiveness, if any, to be made "consistent with the dignity and self-respect of the victim." Moreover, perpetrators could not be forgiven "if they neither acknowledge nor repent a crime."[5] Although apology and forgiveness are not at all congruent, some of the same objections are worth hearing when the value of personal and societal apology is considered.

Achieving reconciliation was another of the foremost aims of the TRC (and was included in the titles of the Chilean and Peruvian commissions also); its relationship to apology is tight. Tendering apology is intended to promote reconciliation among old adversaries as well as to excuse error. Alternatively, formal apologies permit informal arrangements between former antagonists to become open and acknowledged. Within states, apology may be the handmaiden of reconciliation. Where enduring interaction is inevitable and unavoidable, the act of apology reduces friction and enables hitherto torn societies to move forward toward some reasonable sense of equilibrium.

Many of these same assumptions motivated the TRC. The TRC operated as if societal reconciliation were possible, even in a country plundered and antagonized by the long brutal years of apartheid—the economic misfortunes, the removals, the terrible injustices, the crazy illogic of the homelands, the abrogation of human rights, and the denial of educational and health services. The TRC functioned as if the mere retailing of the truths of the deepest and nastiest machinations of apartheid—the culpability of its highest leaders and its mad-doctor schemes of biological and chemical warfare against Africans— would somehow set the new South Africa free to forge a successful post-conflict multiracial society. If that society became at least partially reconciled, an apology would strengthen the process of reconciliation.

Unfortunately, as much as truth commission investigations are essential for reconciliation, and effective apology, the truth commission process does not necessarily, or always, lead to societal reconciliation. Opinion polls in South Africa imply that as much as the effective publicizing of the TRC hearings inoculated all South Africans against ignorance about apartheid, reconciliation was not necessarily a product.[16] Tutu asserted that the TRC would create reconciliation, but he was almost alone among the TRC commissioners and the Chilean commissioners in believing that the revealing of "truth" necessarily led to reconciliation. Minow argues that the "truth" arrived at through the commission method, through restorative justice, contributes more to reconciliation than does the trial method, retributive justice. She also suggests that if the goal of healing individuals and society in post-conflict settings is elevated morally and practically, truth commissions are better at those functions than are trials. Indeed, trials dehumanize victims. For the provision of a public acknowledgement of what happened and who did what to whom—the very basis of apology—a truth commission provides a safe and effective setting for positing a mutually developed sense of the truth of the past.[17]

The TRC process further restored to victims of gross human rights violations their civil and human dignity. Arriving at the "truth" set victims and kin of victims free. It importantly destroyed a culture of impunity on the part of the perpetrators. All of these results lay the groundwork for apology. So did the nature of the victims' hearings of the TRC, and the fact that they were broadcast and reported widely, constitute a public shaming of violators of human rights norms. Exposure was punishment.

Nevertheless, those who argue that reconciliation is available through truth have to posit a range of questionable assumptions to prove their case. According to Tomuschat, the leader of Guatemala's commission, "no one can today insure that [the] immense challenge of reconciliation through truth can be met with success. In order to do so, the historic facts must be recognized and assimilated into each individual consciousness and the collective consciousness [of a nation]."[18]

Apology acts in a vacuum if there is no investigative underpinning to anchor and support such contrition. Truth commissions or historical clarification commissions can provide that information. The more rigorously such information is obtained, the more effective apologies can be. The conclusions of a commission process may, as in the South African case, moreover be based on a larger sample of cases than could ever be obtained in courts of law. In post-conflict contexts, one of the many virtues of restorative justice is its ability to enable conclusions to be made on the basis of numerous cases. Proceedings like the TRC are also capable of strengthening the new civil society precisely because restorative justice is simultaneously investigative, judicial, political, educational, and therapeutic. Admittedly, such a process is morally ambitious. Sachs calls it "moral, cultural, psychological, and human rather than . . . solely legal or instrumental"—"the creation of a nation."[19]

Those who elevate restorative justice over retributive justice suggest that it offers the best method, perhaps coupled with a large measure of apology, of reconstructing both a new nation and a just society. Indeed, punishment alone for perpetrators, in line with prosecutions and the requirements of an arms length criminal system, hinders the achievement of restorative justice and, hence, reconciliation. The better path is forgiveness (and apology) preceded by a full accounting of violations, the confrontation of perpetrators by victims, reparations, and an emphasis on personal motivation and transformation. The truth commission process is individual-centered. Truth commissions are also more supple and constructive than court proceedings and enable the creation of a new, tolerant society to be imagined, if not realized.[20]

Additionally, post-conflict nation-states have "unfinished business" that can only be addressed by a wide-ranging, powerful, and transparent public investigatory commission capable of extraordinary truth telling and truth finding. Only the deliberations of such a body—and the same assertions would hold true for a historical clarification commission in a war-torn society like Cyprus—can restore a fractured nation's moral order. Nuremberg-like trials would prevent a peaceful transition. Punishment alone does not heal or reconcile.

The many utilitarian advantages of truth commissions are easy to assert. But are they just? Do they offer justice as well as truth? Answers to this question turn on whether restorative (also called transitional) justice is an acceptable substitute for, or even a better alternative to, traditional justice. Many argue that the commission process produces quantitatively more, and more rapidly achieved, justice than traditional justice. It provides good accountability, which is essential to any form of justice. There are gains in justice in identifying offenders, even if retribution is imperfectly delivered and some offenders go free through amnesties. Indeed, amnesty is expedient, not moral. It assists the pursuit of justice as does plea bargaining, but it cannot be considered completely just. So restorative justice is cathartic in a way that retributive justice can never be, but retributive justice is more certain, given obedience to careful procedural rules.

Some of those who objected in South Africa to the truth commission process preferred the traditional system, with its protection against self-incrimination, its endless delays, its appeal process, and the difficulties of presenting convincing evidence of long-past events. Others, partial to victims, protested that amnesty was unjust and unforgivable. "It stinks to high heaven," wrote a prominent black editor. "To imagine that after confessing, these people who committed the most horrendous crimes will then be patted on the shoulder ... The TRC is a denial of justice. Without justice, how can victims feel healed?"[21]

The commission process has flaws. But in considering how most effectively to apologize, and on what basis apology can be proffered, the societal dissection that is inherent in the best of the commission endeavors is an essential underpinning. Apologies are more compelling if they arise out of thoroughly democratic investigations, as in South Africa, if they follow a consensus developed by a commission's work, and if they reflect the findings of a thorough commission. Nothing less is so powerful.

Notes

1. This essay consciously leaves the discussion of reparations to others. The author is grateful to Mary Kay Magistad for her very helpful suggestions and criticisms, and to Mitsi Sellers, Maria Koinova, and Gwendolyn Young for good ideas and systematic research.

2. For de Klerk, see *The Guardian*, October 10, 1992; for the DRC, see *The Guardian*, November 8, 1990.

3. For Omar, *Africa News Service*, June 24, 2002; for Tshwete, *Africa News Service*, December 5, 2001; for Asmal, *Global News Wire*, March 30, 2001.

4. Obasanjo apologized on Democracy Day, following the report of the investigative commission, *Africa News Service*, May 29, 2002.

5. Mary Kay Magistad makes this point powerfully (private communication, October 4, 2002).

6. Robert I. Rotberg, 2000, "Trust Commissions and the Provision of Truth, Justice, and Reconciliation," in Robert Rotberg and Dennis Thompson, eds., *Truth v. Justice: The Morality of Truth Commissions*, pp. 10–11 (Princeton: Princeton University Press).

7. President Chissano, in oral remarks at the Kennedy School of Government, Harvard University, September 19, 2004.

8. For a discussion of this issue in several larger contexts, particularly Palestine/Israel, see Henry Steiner, ed., 1997, *Truth Commissions: A Comparative Assessment* (Cambridge, MA: Harvard University Press).

9. Priscilla B. Hayner, 2001, *Unspeakable Truths: Confronting State Terror and Atrocity* (New York: Routledge) contains the history of truth commissions.

10. This and some of the material in the following paragraphs draw on Rotberg, "Truth Commissions and the Provision of Truth, Justice, and Reconciliation," pp. 4–18, and on Hayner, *Unspeakable Truths*, pp. 35–68.

11. The alleged apartheid-driven perpetrators of the notorious Trust Feeds massacre in South Africa were brought to trial at the same time as the South African Truth Commission began meeting. After a lengthy court process, the high level accused were acquitted, thus demonstrating to many observers how imperfect retributive justice could be in bringing the architects and operatives of apartheid attacks to justice.

12. Mary Burton, summary (p. 16) of a meeting in Somerset West between the contributors to Rotberg and Thompson, *Truth v. Justice*, and the members of the TRC, May 1998.

13. Quoted in the *Boston Globe*, August 7, 1998.

14. David Crocker, "Truth Commissions, Transitional Justice, and Civil Society," in *Truth v. Justice*, p. 108.

15. Rajeev Bhargava, "Restoring Decency to Barbaric Societies," in Ibid., pp. 62–63.

16. See Rotberg, "Provision of Truth," p. 19.

17. Martha Minow, "The Hope for Healing: What Can Truth Commissions Do?" in *Truth v. Justice*, pp. 235–255.

18. Christian Tomuschat, quoted in *New York Times*, February 26, 1999. See also Breyten Breytenbach, 1999, *Dog Heart: A Memoir*, p. 21 (New York).

19. Albie Sachs, 1995, quoted in Alex Boraine and Janet Levy eds., *The Healing of a Nation?* p. 103 (Cape Town); Sachs, 1994, quoted in Alex Boraine, Janet Levy, and Ronel Scheffer eds., *Dealing with the Past: Truth and Reconciliation in South Africa*, p. 146 (Cape Town).

20. Elizabeth Kiss, "Moral Ambition Without and Beyond Political Constraints: Reflections on Restorative Justice," in *Truth v. Justice*, pp. 79–93.

21. Mdu Lembede, quoted in *Boston Globe*, February 20, 1999.

CHAPTER 3

Punishment, Reconciliation, and Democratic Deliberation

DAVID A. CROCKER[1]

From Chile, to Cambodia, to South Africa, to the United States—societies and international institutions are deciding how they should reckon with past atrocities(including war crimes, crimes against humanity, genocide, rape, and torture)that may have been committed by a government against its own citizens, by its opponents, or by combatants in an international armed conflict.

In deciding whether and how to address these political crimes, it is commonly believed that trials and punishment, on the one hand, and reconciliation, on the other, are fundamentally at odds with each other, whether a nation must choose one or the other, and whether reconciliation is morally superior to punishment. For example, in *No Future without Forgiveness*,[1] Archbishop Desmond Mpilo Tutu evaluates the successes and failures of the South African Truth and Reconciliation Commission (TRC). The chair of the TRC, Tutu defends the Commission's granting of amnesty to wrongdoers who revealed the truth about their pasts, and he lauds those victims who forgave their abusers. While recognizing that a country must reckon with its past evils rather than adopt "National Amnesia," (p. 13) Tutu nevertheless rejects what he calls the "Nuremberg trial paradigm" (p. 19). He believes that victims should not press charges against those who violated their rights, and the state should not make the accused "run the gauntlet of the normal judicial process" (p. 19) and impose punishment on those found guilty.

Tutu offers practical and moral arguments against applying the Nuremberg precedent to South Africa. On the practical side, he expresses the familiar view that if trials were the only means of reckoning with past wrongs, then proponents of apartheid would have thwarted efforts to negotiate a transition to democratic rule. The South African court system, moreover, biased as it was toward apartheid, would hardly have reached just verdicts and sentences (pp. 24, 180). Tutu points out that trials are inordinately expensive, time-consuming, and labor-intensive—diverting valuable resources from such tasks as poverty alleviation and educational reforms. In the words of legal theorist Martha Minow, prosecution is "slow, partial, and narrow."[2] Rejecting punishment, Tutu favors the TRC's approach in which rights violators publicly confess the truth, while their victims respond with forgiveness.

Powerful practical reasons may explain the decision to spare oppressors from trials and criminal sanctions. Tutu, however, offers two *moral* arguments to justify rejection of the "Nuremberg paradigm." The first, which I call the "argument against vengeance," is a non-consequentialist argument that identifies punishment with retribution, rejects retribution, and concludes that punishment is morally wrong. Tutu's second argument, which I call the "reconciliation argument," is consequentialist: it contends that punishing human rights violators is wrong because it only further divides former enemies and impedes social healing. Tutu contends that "reconciliation" — the restoration of social harmony — is best promoted when society grants amnesty and victims forgive their abusers.

This article assesses Tutu's two arguments.[3] First, I argue that retribution, properly conceived, not only is one appropriate aim of punishment, but it also differs significantly from vengeance. Second, I distinguish three ideals of reconciliation, argue for a democratic conception over Tutu's social harmony view, and contend that regardless of the meaning given to reconciliation, in reckoning with past wrongs, a society must be wary of *overestimating* the restorative effect of amnesty and forgiveness as well as *underestimating* the reconciling power of justice. In the paper's concluding section, I contend that although punishment and reconciliation do "pull in different directions"[4] and sometimes clash, when adequately conceived, they are both morally urgent goals that often can be combined in morally appropriate ways. When such combining is not possible, decisions concerning trade-offs should be arrived at through public deliberation and democratic choice.[5]

1. The Argument Against Vengeance

In his argument against vengeance, Tutu offers three premises for the conclusion that—at least during South Africa's transition—legal punishment of those who violate human rights is morally wrong. The premises are: (i) punishment is retribution, (ii) retribution is vengeance, and (iii) vengeance is morally wrong.

Although Tutu understands that forgiveness may be appropriate for any injury, at one point he claims that amnesty provides only a *temporary* way for South Africa to reckon with past wrongs. He provides no criteria, however, to determine at what point punishment for crimes should be reinstated, and he also offers no reasons that punishment is justified in normal times. Further, one might wonder on what grounds Tutu would deny exoneration for those who committed human rights violations *after* the fall of apartheid and who now wish to exchange full disclosure of their wrongdoing for amnesty.[6]

2. Is Punishment Retribution?

Consider the first of Tutu's three premises in his argument against punishment. While Tutu assumes that punishment is no more than retribution, he fails to define what he understands by "punishment." He does not, for example, explicitly identify legal punishment as state-administered and intentional infliction of suffering or deprivation on wrongdoers.[2] Tutu also says almost nothing about the nature and aims of legal punishment. He fails to distinguish court-mandated punishment from therapeutic treatment and social shaming, among other societal responses to criminal conduct. Tutu does not consider the various roles that punishment may play—such as to control or denounce crime, isolate the dangerous, rehabilitate perpetrators, or give them their "just desserts"—and whether these roles justify the criminal sanction. He does at one point say that the "chief goal" of "retributive justice" is "to be punitive" (p. 54). Tutu apparently takes it as given that "punishment" means "retribution" and that the nature of legal punishment is retributive.

Tutu does at times concede that trials have two other aims, at least during South Africa's transition: vindicating the rights of victims, and generating truth about the past. Again and again, Tutu states that victims of past wrongs have the right—at least a constitutional right and perhaps also a moral one—to press criminal charges against and seek restitution from those who abused them (pp. 51, 144, 147, 211). He also extols the "magnanimity" of individuals who, like former South African President, Nelson Mandela, (pp. 10, 39), have not exercised this right but are willing to forgive and seek harmony (*ubuntu*) with their oppressors. These statements suggest that Tutu regards legal punishment not merely as a means to retribution, but also as a way to affirm and promote the rights of victims.[7]

Tutu also endorses the credible threat of punishment as a social tool to encourage perpetrators to tell the truth about their wrongdoing. The TRC did not grant a blanket amnesty to human rights violators or pardon all those convicted of rights abuses committed during apartheid. Instead the TRC offered amnesty to *individual* perpetrators *only if* (i) their disclosures were complete and accurate, (ii) their violations were politically motivated, and (iii) their acts of wrongdoing were proportional to the ends violators hoped to achieve. According to Tutu, individuals who fail to fulfill any of the three conditions have a strong incentive to apply for amnesty and reveal the whole truth. It is precisely because violators are threatened with trial and eventual punishment that they realize that making no application for amnesty or lying about their wrongdoing is too risky. Without such a threat of trial and punishment, the TRC is unlikely to have had the number of perpetrators who did come forward to confess gross wrongdoing.

But Tutu cannot have it both ways. He cannot both reject actual punishment and still defend the threat of punishment as efficacious in dispelling lies and generating truth. Hence, Tutu's acceptance of a "threat to punish" practically commits him to a non-retributive and consequentialist role for punishment, because without occasionally making good on the threat to punish, such a threat loses credibility.

Tutu does not bring enough precision to the term "retribution." He seems, at points, simply to identify retribution with legal punishment. Instead, one must understand retribution as one important *rationale* or *justification* for, and a constraint upon, punishment. Proponents of the retributive theory of punishment offer a variety of competing accounts, but all agree that any retributive theory minimally requires that punishment must be "backward looking in important respects."[8] That is, justice requires that a crime is punishable as, in the words of lawyer and legal theorist Lawrence Crocker, "a matter of the criminal act, not the future consequences of conviction and punishment."[9] These future consequences might comprise such good things as deterrence of crime, rehabilitation of criminals, or promotion of reconciliation. For the proponent of retributivism, however, the infliction of suffering or harm, something normally prohibited, is justified because of—and in proportion to—what the criminal *has done antecedently*. Only those found guilty should be punished, and their punishment should fit (but be no more than) their crime.

Some supporters of the retributive theory of punishment, assert, moreover, that only (and perhaps all) wrongdoers *deserve* punishment, and the amount or kind of punishment they deserve must fit the wrong done.[10] Philosopher Robert Nozick explains "dessert" in terms of both the degree of wrongness of the act and the criminal's degree of responsibility for it.[11] Retribution as a justification for punishment requires that wrongdoers should get no more than (and perhaps no less than) their "just desserts."[12]

3. Is Retribution Vengeance?

The second premise in Tutu's argument against punishment–that retribution is (nothing but) vengeance or revenge—is flawed as well. Given Nozick's understanding of retribution as "punishment inflicted as deserved for a past wrong,"[3] is Tutu right to treat retribution and revenge, or vengeance, as equivalent? Both retribution and revenge share, as Nozick puts it, "a common structure."[3] They inflict harm or deprivation for a reason. Retribution and vengeance harm those who in some sense have it coming to them. Following Nozick's brief but suggestive analysis, I propose that there are at least six ways in which retribution differs from revenge.

Retribution Addresses a Wrong

First, as Nozick observes, "retribution is done for a wrong, while revenge may be done for an injury or slight and need not be done for a wrong."[14] I interpret Nozick to mean retribution metes out punishment for a crime or other wrongdoing, while revenge may be exacted for what is merely a slight, an unintended injury, an innocent gaze, or shaming in front of one's friends.

Retribution is Constrained

Second, Nozick also correctly sees that in retribution there exists some "internal" upper limit to punishment, while revenge is essentially unlimited.[15] Lawrence Crocker concurs: "an absolutely central feature of criminal justice" is to place on each offense "an upper limit on the severity of just punishment."[16] This limitation "is the soul of retributive justice."[17] It is morally repugnant to punish the reluctant foot soldier as severely as the architects, chief implementers, or "middle management"[18] of atrocities. Retribution provides both a sword to punish wrongdoers and a shield to protect them from more punishment than they deserve.[19] In contrast to punishment, revenge is wild, "insatiable," and unlimited. After killing his victims, an agent of revenge may mutilate them and incinerate their houses. As Nozick observes, if the avenger does restrain himself, it is done for "external" reasons having nothing to do with the rights or dignity of his victims. His rampage may cease, for instance, because he tires, runs out of victims, or intends to exact further vengeance the next day.[20]

Notably, Martha Minow and others subscribe to a different view. Minow suggests that retribution is a *kind* of vengeance, but curbed by the intervention of neutral parties and bound by the rights of individuals and the principles of proportionality. Seen in this light, in retribution vengeful retaliation is tamed, balanced, and recast. It is now a justifiable, public response that stems from the "admirable" self-respect that resents injury by others.

While Minow's view deserves serious consideration, Nozick, I think, gives us a picture of vengeance — and its fundamental difference from retribution — that better matches our experience. Precisely *because* the agent of revenge is insatiable, limited neither by prudence nor by what the wrongdoer deserves, revenge is not something admirable that goes wrong. The person seeking revenge thirsts for injury that knows no (internal) bounds, has no principles to limit penalties. Retribution, by contrast, seeks not to tame vengeance, but to excise it altogether. Retribution insists that the response not be greater than the offense; vengeance insists that it be no less and if possible more. Minow attempts to navigate "between vengeance and forgiveness," but she does so in a way that makes too many concessions to vengeance. She fails to see unequivocally that retribution has essential limits.[21] Vengeance has no place in the courtroom or, in fact, in any venue, public or private.

Retribution is Impersonal

Third, vengeance is personal in the sense that the avenger retaliates for something done antecedently to her or her group. In contrast, as Nozick notes, "the agent of retribution need have no special or personal tie to the victim of the wrong for which he exacts retribution."[22] Retribution demands impartiality and rejects personal bias, while partiality and personal animus motivate the "thirst for revenge."

The figure of Justice blindfolded (so as to remove any prejudicial relation to the perpetrator or victim) embodies the commonplace that justice requires impartiality. Justice is blind — that is, impartial — in the sense that she cannot distinguish between people on the basis of familiarity or personal ties. This not to say, however, that justice is impersonal in the sense that she neglects to consider an individual's traits or conduct relevant to the case. Oddly, Tutu suggests that the impartiality or neutrality of the state detracts from its ability to deal with the crimes of apartheid. He defends the TRC because it is able to take personal factors into account. He writes:

One might go on to say that perhaps justice fails to be done only if the concept we entertain of justice is retributive justice, whose chief goal is to be punitive, so that the wronged party is really the state, something impersonal, which has little consideration for the real victims and almost none for the perpetrator (p. 54).

Although justice eliminates bias from judicial proceedings, it may be fair only if it takes certain personal factors into account. Because Tutu confuses the impersonality or neutrality of the law with an indifference to the personal or unique aspects of a case, he insists that judicial processes and penalties give little regard to "real victims" or their oppressors.

It is true that if victims are called to testify, defense attorneys may treat them disrespectfully. In a deeper sense, however, the trial affirms the dignity of the victim, because the judicial proceeding is the proper forum to denounce the violation of the victim's humanity and vindicate his/her rights. The state, with its impersonal laws, has pledged to protect, vindicate, and restore the rights of a human being. Further, the impersonal rule of law applies to wrongdoers as well. If and when the accused is found guilty, verdicts and sentencing should take into account reasonable excuses or mitigating circumstances. Hence, retribution's shield protects the culpable from overzealous prosecution and overly severe punishment. There is also room for leniency and even mercy when a judge (or executive), to the extent permitted by law, either reduces the perpetrator's punishment to better match his degree of culpability, or takes into account personal conditions as advanced age, dementia, or illness.[23] Fair trials and just punishments, then, consider relevant personal factors. At the same time, however, fairness demands that bias must be eliminated from judicial proceedings themselves.

Retribution Takes No Satisfaction

A fourth distinction between retribution and revenge concerns the "emotional tone" that accompanies—or the feelings that motivate—the infliction of harm. Agents of revenge, claims Nozick, get pleasure, or we might say "satisfaction," from their victim's suffering. Agents of retribution may either have no emotional response at all, be distressed by having to inflict pain ("this hurts me more than it hurts you"), or take "pleasure at justice being done."[24] Adding to Nozick's account and drawing on the work of political theorists Jeffrie Murphy and Jean Hampton, I add that a "thirst for justice" may—but need not—arise from moral outrage over and hatred of wrongdoing.[25]

Retribution is Principled

Fifth, Nozick claims that what he calls "generality" is essential to retribution but may be absent from revenge. By this term, Nozick means that agents of retribution who inflict deserved punishment for a wrong are "committed to (the existence of some) general principles (prima facie) mandating punishment in other similar circumstances."[26] If I am a Kosovar committed to retributive justice, I believe that an Albanian who violates the rights of a Serb deserves the same upper limit of punishment—if the act and culpability is the same—as the Serb who violates the rights of a Kosovar. In contrast, the Kosovar seeking revenge is committed to no principles and is motivated solely by the desire to retaliate without limit against his Serbian foe. He has no moral reason to avoid double standards or to urge prosecution of his fellow Kosovars for atrocities committed against Serbs.[27]

Retribution Rejects Collective Guilt

Nozick, I believe, helpfully captures many of the contrasts between retribution and revenge. To these, I add a sixth distinction. Mere *membership* in an opposing or offending group may be the occasion of revenge, but not of retribution. Retributive justice differs from vengeance, in other words, because it extends only to individuals and not to the groups to which they belong. In response to a real or perceived injury, members of one ethnic group might, for instance, take revenge on members of another ethnic group. However, a state or international criminal court could properly mete out retribution only to those *individuals* found guilty of rights abuses, not to *all members* of the offending ethnic group.

In undermining the notion of collective guilt, just retribution has the potential to break the cycle of revenge and counter-revenge. As Neier observes:

Advocates of prosecuting those who committed crimes against humanity in ex-Yugoslavia have argued that the effect is to individualize guilt. What they have in mind, of course, is criminal guilt. Some of the strongest voices advocating this—all strong supporters of the tribunal—have come from inside the former Yugoslavia. They and others have maintained that in a territory where violent ethnic conflict has taken place three times in the twentieth century, it is crucial to break the cycle of the collective attribution of guilt. Serbs, as a people, did not commit mass murder, torture, and rape in Croatia and Bosnia; rather, particular Serbs, and also particular Croats and Muslims, committed particular crimes. If those directly responsible are tried and punished, the burden of blame will not be carried indiscriminately by members of an entire ethnic group. Culpability will not be passed down from generation to generation. Trials will single out the guilty, differentiating them from the innocent.[28]

No trial, of course, can guarantee that it will find the innocent to be innocent and the guilty to be guilty. Although Tutu finds adversarial cross-examination callous and disrespectful to victims called to testify, such procedures minimize the risk that the innocent are convicted and maximize the probability that the guilty receive their just desserts. Only then is justice truly done. Because collective guilt has no place in an understanding of retributive justice, revenge and retribution should not be conceived as equivalent. Tutu makes precisely this mistake.

Following the Hegelian dictum "first distinguish, then unite," Nozick promptly concedes, as he should, that vengeance and retribution can come together in various ways. Particular judicial and penal institutions may combine elements of retribution and of revenge. The Nuremberg trials, arguably, were retributive in finding guilty and punishing some Nazi leaders, punishing some more than others, and acquitting those whom it found not guilty as charged. But Tutu is right to say that the Nuremberg precedent was contaminated, compromised by revenge or "victor's justice." As he notes, Nuremberg used exclusively allied judges and failed to put any allied officers in the dock. However, Tutu neglects to affirm the achievements of Nuremberg: it vindicated the notion of individual responsibility for crimes against humanity, and defeated the excuse that one was "merely following orders." One reason that Nuremberg is an ambiguous legacy is that it had both good (retributive) and bad (vengeful) elements.[29]

Customary practices also may combine both retribution and revenge. Consider, for example, those killings in the Balkans that are said to be due to "blood and vengeance"[30] and are regulated by a medieval honor code or kanun.[31] In some of these cases, one or more members of one group (an extended family or ethnic group, for instance) inflict harm on some member(s) of another group in retaliation for an earlier harm. On the one hand, it seems that the notion of collective guilt motivates vengeful retaliation. For instance, Leka Rrushkadoli, an Albanian villager, explains why he avenged the death of his father by in turn killing the son of his father's killer: "By the kanun, any of the Lamthis were equal, just so long as one of them paid. I saw Shtjefen first, so he paid."[32] On the other hand, this same honor code does constrain or limit—albeit in ways that appear excessive—the number and kinds of injuries permissibly inflicted on members of an offending group. For example, Leka Rrushkadoli's two sons assert their interpretation of the kanun's requirements: "By the kanun, the very worst crime is to kill someone inside your house, no matter the circumstances or how it started. [. . .] For killing our father inside their house, they [the Lamthis] owe us three deaths."[33]

Likewise, both the thirst for retribution and the thirst for vengeance also may motivate those who impose judicial penalties. Suppose a black South African judge, committed to just desserts, correctly finds an Afrikaner defendant guilty of a human rights violation. Then, yielding to vengeance, he unfairly metes out an excessively severe punishment. This is not a case in which the motive "giving what is coming to the wrongdoer" failed to be "curbed" by the rule of law.[34] Rather, the judge's commitment to (and desire for) just desserts was not as strong as his thirst for revenge. It is all too common, of course, for the talk of retributive justice to disguise vengefulness.

From these various mixtures of retribution and revenge it does not follow that there is no distinction between the two. Judges, juries, and others responsible for justice must exercise virtue, and judicial and penal institutions must be shaped in ways that minimize opportunities to take revenge.

4. Is Vengeance Morally Wrong?

What of Tutu's third premise that vengeance is morally wrong? When I shift the focus from vengeance to the agent of revenge, I accept Tutu's premise. Unlike the agent of retribution, the agent of revenge does wrong, or at least he is morally blameworthy. He retaliates and inflicts an injury without regard to what the person impartially deserves. If the penalty *happens* to fit the crime, it is by luck; the agent of revenge is still blameworthy since he gave no consideration to dessert, impartiality, or generality.[35] If, as is more likely given the limitless nature of revenge, the penalty is more excessive than the crime, the agent of revenge is not only culpable, but also his/her act is morally wrong. Nonetheless, Tutu's overall argument against vengeance is unsound since two of its premises are not acceptable.

5. The Reconciliation Argument

Tutu proposes a second moral argument against the "Nuremberg trial paradigm" for South Africa's transition and others like it. Tutu rejects judicial justice not only because he alleges it is vengeful and revenge is intrinsically wrong, but also because punishment, he claims, prevents or impedes reconciliation. He understands reconciliation as "restorative justice," the highest if not the only goal in South Africa's reckoning with past wrongs. Tutu defends amnesty and forgiveness as the best means to promote reconciliation. In this consequentialist argument, I address both the moral desirability of the end and the practical efficacy of the two sets of means—amnesty and forgiveness, on the one hand, and trial and punishment, on the other.

6. Three Concepts of Reconciliation

Ubuntu

What does Tutu mean by the vague and not infrequently contested term "reconciliation" and its synonym "restorative justice?" Tutu explicitly defines restorative justice (in contrast to retributive justice) as reconciliation of broken relationships between perpetrators and victims:

> We contend that there is another kind of justice, restorative justice, which was characteristic of traditional African jurisprudence. Here the central concern is not retribution or punishment. In the spirit of *ubuntu*, the central concern is the healing of breaches, the redressing of imbalances, the restoration of broken relationships, a seeking to rehabilitate both the victim and the perpetrator, who should be given the opportunity to be reintegrated into the community that he has injured by his offense (pp. 54–55).

Although Tutu in this passage uncharacteristically leaves room for punishment, he understands the "central concern" of restorative justice as the reconciliation of the wrongdoer with his victim and with the society he has injured. The wrongdoing has "ruptured" earlier relationships or failed to realize the ideal of "ubuntu." *Ubuntu*, a term from the Ngunui group of languages, refers to a kind of "social harmony" in which people are friendly, hospitable, magnanimous, compassionate, open, and non-envious (p. 31).[36] Although Tutu recognizes the difficulty of translating the concept, it seems to combine the Western ideal of mutual beneficence, the disposition to be kind to others, with the ideal of community solidarity. Each benefits when others do well; each "is diminished when others are humiliated or diminished [...] tortured or oppressed, or treated as if they were less than who they are" (p. 31).

Tutu regards "social harmony" or "communal harmony" as the *summum bonum*, or highest good. He concedes that South Africa must in some way "balance" a plurality of important values — "justice, accountability, stability, peace, and reconciliation" (p. 23). Whatever "subverts" or corrodes social harmony, however, "is to be avoided like the plague" (p. 31). Presumably, whatever maximizes social harmony is morally commendable and even obligatory.

Tutu may believe that *ubuntu* presents so lofty an ideal that no one would question its justification or importance. In any case, he offers little argument for its significance or supremacy. He does seek to support it by calling attention to its African origins. He also remarks that, while altruistic, *ubuntu* is also "the best form of self-interest," for each individual benefits when the community benefits.

As it stands, neither defense is persuasive. The evil character of apartheid, also a South African concept, is not dependent on its South African origins. Similarly, the geographical origin of *ubuntu* does not ensure its reasonableness. Further, although individuals often benefit from harmonious community relationships, the community also at times demands excessive sacrifices from individuals. Moreover, dissent or moral outrage may be justified even though it disrupts friendliness and social harmony.

Recall that Tutu offers practical objections—as well as moral ones—to seeking retributive justice against former oppressors. He does not consider the practicability of *ubuntu,* however, as a goal of social policy. He does not discuss, for example, what to do with those whose hearts cannot be purged of resentment or vengeance. Nor does he explain how society can test citizens for purity of mind and heart—how it can determine who has succeeded and who has failed to assist society toward this supreme good.

Nonlethal Coexistence

Tutu's concept of reconciliation can be compared critically to two other versions of social cooperation: (i) "non-lethal coexistence" and (ii) "democratic reciprocity." In the first, reconciliation occurs just in case former enemies no longer kill each other or routinely violate each other's basic rights. This thin sense of reconciliation, attained when ceasefires, peace accords, and negotiated settlements begin to take hold, can be a momentous achievement. In Kosovo following NATO intervention, for example, observers agreed that the best that could be hoped for, at least as a medium-term goal, was not a socially harmonious "'multiethnic society' but 'peaceful coexistence' among largely separated communities."[37] Achieving even this minimal goal in Kosovo in 2000, given both Albanian and Serb thirst for revenge (and counter-revenge) and the complete absence of "an effective structure of law, judges, courts, and prisons,"[38] was extraordinarily difficult.[39]

Reconciliation as nonlethal coexistence—however difficult to achieve—demands significantly less and is easier to realize than Tutu's much "thicker" ideal that requires mutuality and forgiveness. Societies rarely, if ever, choose between harmony and mere toleration. Historically, societies have to choose between toleration among contending groups and the war of each against all.

Democratic Reciprocity

A more demanding interpretation of reconciliation—but one still significantly less robust than Tutu advocates—is "democratic reciprocity."[40] In this conception, former enemies or former perpetrators, victims, and bystanders are reconciled insofar as they respect each other as fellow citizens. Further, all parties play a role in deliberations concerning the past, present, and future of their country. A still-divided society will surely find this ideal of democratic reciprocity difficult enough to attain—although much easier than an ideal defined by mutual compassion and the *requirement* of forgiveness. Some would argue, for instance, that there are unforgivable crimes or point out that a government should not insist on or even encourage forgiveness, since forgiveness is a matter for *victims* to decide.[41]

Not only is Tutu's ideal of social harmony impractical, but it is also problematic because of the way it conceives the relation between the individual and the group. Tutu's formulation of *ubuntu* either threatens the autonomy of each member, or unrealistically assumes that each and every individual benefits from the achievements of a larger group. Sometimes individuals do benefit from social solidarity. But life together is often one in which genuinely good things conflict, such as communal harmony and individual freedom, my gain and your gain. In these cases, fair public deliberation and democratic decision making are the best means to resolve differences. A process that allows all sides to be heard, encourages all arguments to be judged on their merits, and forges policies that no one can reasonably reject—such a process respects public well being, individual freedom, and a plurality of values.[42]

This analysis of alternative conceptions of reconciliation not only shows that Tutu's ideal is unrealistic but also that it pays insufficient attention to individual freedom, including the freedom to withhold forgiveness. In making social harmony the supreme good, Tutu unfortunately subordinates—without argument—other important values, such as truth, compensation, democracy, and individual accountability. In some contexts, social harmony—if it respects personal freedom and democratic deliberation—should have priority. In other contexts, society may pursue other equally important values, for example, justice, which might require a society to indict, try, sentence, and punish individuals who violated human rights. If social harmony is judged to have priority over other values, then that judgment should emerge not from a cultural, theological, or philosophical theory, but from the deliberation and democratic determination of citizens.

7. Means of Reconciliation

Tutu claims that in South Africa amnesty and forgiveness have maximized the *summum bonum* of reconciliation as social harmony, while trials and punishment would only have thwarted reconciliation. Even stronger, as the title of his recent volume suggests, without forgiveness (coupled with amnesty), not only is there no reconciliation, but there is also "no future." Unless victims offer—and their abusers accept—forgiveness, former enemies will destroy each other and their society. Can these empirical claims stand up to scrutiny?

To answer this question, it is important first to consider the South African tool of amnesty and also what Tutu means by "forgiveness." Many Latin American governments guilty of human rights abuses have granted unconditional immunity to many of their leaders, military personnel, and police. South Africa's Truth and Reconciliation Commission (TRC) has operated under a different model. The TRC's Amnesty Committee has awarded amnesty to very few human rights violators. Recall that the TRC granted amnesty if, and only if, the applicant has shown that his act(s) of commission or omission fulfill three conditions: (i) the act was chosen to advance a political objective (for instance, defense of apartheid or destruction of apartheid); (ii) the means employed were proportional to the end; and (iii) the perpetrator fully disclosed to the TRC the truth about the act. The applicant need not express remorse, confess moral guilt, or request to be forgiven.

An (alleged) human rights perpetrator—whether free, in hiding, indicted, sentenced, or serving time—had two options. He could have chosen not to face the TRC, a choice made by many suspected or imprisoned perpetrators. However, he then ran the risk that he would be implicated by the testimony of others and either face prosecution and possible imprisonment, or, if already imprisoned, an even longer prison term. Alternatively, a wrongdoer could have applied for amnesty. Regardless of whether amnesty was granted or refused, his appearance before the TRC would likely have resulted in some kind of social opprobrium. If he lied to the TRC or failed to fulfill one of the other two conditions, then he risked denial of amnesty and the possibility of prosecution and litigation. If, however, the TRC judges that the wrongdoer met all conditions, he would go free (if already imprisoned) and/or receive legal protection from future legal proceedings.

The TRC's Amnesty Committee received 7,112 amnesty applications, many from police but disappointingly few from political leaders or military personnel. By November 1, 2000, the Committee had refused amnesty to 5,392 applicants (77 percent) and granted it to only 849 (12 percent). (248 applications were withdrawn, fifty-four partly refused, thirty-seven were duplicates, 142 are in chamber, and eighty-eight are scheduled for decision).[43] In its report, the TRC recommended: "prosecution should be considered" for those persons who had not applied for amnesty or were denied amnesty.[44]

Consider now the second element in the "amnesty-forgiveness" complex. Tutu understands personal "forgiveness" in relation to a Reformation concept of divine grace. For him, forgiveness is completely unconditional; the wrongdoer's desert or merit—contrition, pleas for forgiveness, making amends, and transformation—is entirely irrelevant. Forgiveness is also supererogatory. The victim who forgoes his legal rights to press claims and instead grants forgiveness, expresses, according to Tutu, the virtue of "breathtaking magnanimity" (p. 10) and "remarkable generosity of spirit" (p. 145). Tutu repeatedly marvels at those—especially Nelson Mandela—who have willingly waived their right to make legal claims, setting aside their great personal suffering and freely offering the gift of forgiveness. Finally, drawing a distinction between the (divine) hate of the sin but redeeming love for even the worst sinner, Tutu maintains that there are no unforgivable perpetrators, for each has the potential to accept forgiveness.

Given the South African policy of amnesty and Tutu's ideal of forgiveness, one can ask the extent to which the South African combination of amnesty and forgiveness has contributed to reconciliation. Further, one wonders whether South Africa would have thwarted or advanced reconciliation if it had relied more on trial and punishment and less on the TRC. If South Africa prosecutes those who either never applied for amnesty or were refused it, one can only speculate about what effects such efforts will have on reconciliation. Finally, one wonders if reconciliation is best achieved by granting amnesties, or whether national or international tribunals are the better course of action.

These questions are difficult to answer for at least three reasons. First, the empirical evidence with respect to South Africa has been largely anecdotal; little systematic data examines the TRC's use of amnesty and forgiveness in promoting reconciliation. More generally, few empirical studies compare the effects in different countries of the various types and forms of tools—including amnesties, truth commissions, museums, and trials—for reckoning with past wrongs. Second, one must remember that just because repaired relationships might have followed *after* forgiveness was offered and prosecution forgone, this does not prove that forgiveness without trials somehow *caused* whatever healing occurred. Further, because the TRC granted relatively few applications for amnesty and in its report urged prosecution of those denied amnesty, one cannot know the effect the *threat* of future prosecution may have in achieving reconciliation. If victims believe that there is a good chance that justice will be done rather then ignored or denied, they are more open to reconcile with their abusers. Third, to assess—albeit provisionally and speculatively—the relative impacts of amnesty-forgiveness and trial-punishment on reconciliation, we must do so in relation not only to *ubuntu* but also to the two other senses of reconciliation: peaceful coexistence and democratic reciprocity.

Means to Peaceful Coexistence

If reconciliation is conceived as no more (and no less) than peaceful, non-lethal coexistence, then the TRC's amnesty device clearly had some initial success. Without the negotiators' agreement on amnesty, the transition from an apartheid government to democratic elections and an African National Congress (ANC)-controlled successor government likely would not have occurred. If negotiations had broken down and violence had ensued, it was, as Tutu argues, reasonable to suppose that a "blood bath" or "comprehensive catastrophe" (p. 20) would have resulted. Most observers believe that the agreement on conditional amnesty (in exchange for truth) contributed to averting such nightmare scenarios and, perhaps, when coupled with forgiveness, ushered in the "miracle" of South Africa's relatively peaceful and democratic transition.

The story, however, is more complicated. Although Tutu describes cases in which confessed violators asked for and received amnesty and victims in turn granted forgiveness, he provides no evidence that these strategies themselves reduced racial and class conflict. Furthermore, even if one grants the pacifying effects of amnesty-forgiveness, these beneficial consequences may prove short-lived. If either side comes to believe that the other lied in its testimony or was insincere in offering or accepting forgiveness, social peace will deteriorate.

One may question, however, whether the many people *other* than those who offered and received forgiveness ultimately were satisfied. Even Tutu reluctantly admits that many people on both sides of the apartheid divide believe that the state's failure to achieve retributive justice increases animosity, and even justifies taking justice into one's own hands. Private acts of vengeance are particularly likely when victims or their families believe that justice has not been done. As Richard Goldstone reminded the delegates at the 1998 Rome Conference (which agreed to establish a permanent international criminal court), "only by bringing justice to victims could there be any hope of avoiding calls for revenge and that their hate would sooner or later boil over into renewed violence."[45] Although the high crime levels in South Africa undoubtedly have many sources—including extreme and widespread poverty—it is plausible that amnesty coupled with forgiveness has helped to *undermine* peaceful coexistence. When victims, bystanders, and perpetrators believe that killers neither deserve to be forgiven (at least until after they are punished and make reparation) nor maintain their positions of social privilege, then amnesty-forgiveness may deepen social polarization rather than reduce it. By contrast, if perpetrators of human rights violations get something of what they have coming to them, then former enemies have a reason to renounce vengeance and live together peaceably. Aryeh Neier, President of the Open Society Institute, summarizes some evidence from Bosnia:

> Peaceful coexistence seems much less likely if those who were victimized see no one called to account for their suffering. In such circumstances the victims or their ethnic kin may take revenge themselves, in the same way victims of an ordinary crime might respond if they see no effort by the state to prosecute and punish the criminal . . . Justice provides closure; its absence not only leaves wounds open, but its very denial rubs salt in them. Accordingly, partisans of prosecutions argue, peace without justice is a recipe for further conflict.[46]

It is important to stress that the reconciling power of justice occurs not as a result of just any trial and punishment, but only when both trial *and* punishment are seen as fair. Although international affairs scholar Gary Jonathan Bass, in his recent *Stay the Hand of Vengeance: The Politics of War Crimes Tribunals*, argues that although the causes of a defeated Germany's transition (after World War II) to a unified democracy and reintegration into the world community were complex, the procedurally fair Nuremberg Tribunal was an important factor.[47] In contrast, following World War I, the Allied-mandated but locally run war-crime trials in Leipzig and Constantinople whitewashed, respectively, alleged German war criminals and Turks accused of massacring Armenians. The Allies rejected both tribunals as farces, while Germans and Turks resented the trials as expressions of their enemies' vindictiveness. The trials contributed to an anti-Allies backlash that only deepened the bitterness between former enemies.[48] The lesson is clear: only when its means and ends are fair does penal justice have the power to reduce conflict.

A more general rejoinder to Tutu's optimism about amnesty coupled with forgiveness is worth mention. When wrongdoers receive amnesty and are offered forgiveness instead of being justly punished, the effect is likely to strengthen what Latin Americans call a "culture of impunity."[49] The deterrent effect of prosecution and punishment is weakened when people believe they can break the law and get away with it.[50] In Africa, this lesson has had calamitous consequences. In July 1999, the United Nations, seeking to end the civil war in Sierra Leone, arranged peace accords that included amnesty and high government positions for Foday Sankoh, leader of the main rebel group, and three of his lieutenants. Sankoh's forces are responsible for such horrendous crimes as mutilations, gang rape, and forcing children to massacre their own families. This award of amnesty, as Peter Kakirambudde of Africa Human Rights Watch remarks, "shook the concept of accountability to the core"[51] and paved the way for the worst kinds of atrocities. His prediction is dire: "For the rest of Africa, where there are rebels in the bush, the signal is that atrocities can be committed—especially if they are frightening atrocities. The lesson to other rebels is that half measures will not do."[52]

Sankoh himself learned the lesson well. When Sierra Leone's coalition government collapsed ten months after the amnesty, Sankoh—emboldened by impunity—resumed the slaughter of his countryman and took 500 UN peacekeepers hostage, killing seven of them. Sierra Leone, the United Nations, and the United States have only begun to learn their own lesson. Acknowledging that amnesty only encouraged Sankoh to recommence and widen his atrocities, Sierra Leone's new government arrested him, and the United Nations approved an international criminal tribunal for Sierra Leone. Yet Sierra Leone's instability continues. We have not yet seen the end of the damage ensuing from an ill-advised amnesty.

Those contemplating crimes against humanity are deterred—if at all—only when they know such acts seriously risk severe punishment. And such results occur only when the international community establishes stronger ad hoc criminal courts or, even better, a permanent international criminal court, as Bass recognizes:

At a minimum, long-run deterrence of war crimes would require a relatively credible threat of prosecution: that is, a series of successful war crimes tribunals that became so much an expected part of international affairs that no potential mass murderer could confidently say that he would avoid punishment. The world would have to set up tribunals significantly more intimidating than the UN's two current courts for ex-Yugoslavia and Rwanda. The proposed ICC would likely help, but only if it somehow receives political support from the same great powers who have largely neglected the ex-Yugoslavia and Rwanda tribunals for so long.[53]

Neier argues that although amnesty (and forgiveness) may bring about some healing, it is on a moral par with acceding to the demands of terrorists. Giving in to such demands may save many lives, but acquiescing to terrorist demands "only inspire[s] more terrorism."[54] He concludes: "the way to stop terrorists is to ensure that they derive no profit from their acts."[55] The best way to diminish the possibility of a repetition of atrocities is to ensure that perpetrators are punished for their wrongdoing.

Tutu tries to counter this sort of argument with a marital analogy to argue for unconditional forgiveness. A victimized spouse, maintains Tutu, should forgive the unfaithful spouse when the latter is contrite and asks for forgiveness (p. 151). Yet even or, perhaps, especially, in the domestic case, I would argue, this sort of grace is too easy unless the adulterer makes amends and reforms his ways. Undemanding forgiveness encourages a repetition of infidelity. Similarly, for the state simply to offer amnesty to perpetrators and for victims unconditionally to forgive them, is to compromise the message of "never again" and promote a culture of impunity.

Tutu might respond to this argument as follows. It is true that people sometimes resort to violence when they perceive that justice has not been done, but this unfortunate fact does not count against the view that amnesty-forgiveness is the best way to reconciliation, because these new wrongdoers would be expressing a morally defective motive (vengeance) and, hence, the proponents of amnesty-forgiveness can ignore the lethal effects of revenge.

Two rejoinders are appropriate. First, those who thwart peaceful coexistence might do so not from revenge, but (at least partly) from moral outrage that justice has been denied. Although, as I have discussed above, hybrid cases exist in which both motives are present, surely some acts that imperil peaceful coexistence are done from a sense of deserved justice rather than vengeance or reprisal. This is particularly true when the existing judicial system fails to hold the guilty accountable or to punish them appropriately. A second response to the above argument takes a different tack. Even if it were solely vengeance that motivated all acts that destroyed peaceful coexistence, such acts would have to be part of any consequentialist accounting that compared amnesty-forgiveness, on the one hand, and "prosecution-punishment" on the other. What matters is the comparison of the relative effectiveness of these two tools in advancing (and hindering) peaceful coexistence and not merely the motives with which either tool is employed.

Means to Democratic Reciprocity: "Reconciliation as Democratic Reciprocity"

One also can doubt whether South Africa's amnesties coupled with forgiveness contributed to reconciliation in a second and "thicker" sense of "democratic reciprocity." In this conception, reconciliation goes beyond peaceful coexistence to include the give-and-take of deliberation and democratic decision making. One could argue that South Africa's negotiated settlement and amnesty provision made elections possible and thus contributed to democratic reciprocity. Moreover, the TRC, which helped implement the transition from apartheid, employed internal democratic processes and achieved broad-based popular participation.

It is unclear, however, that South Africa's victims were democratically represented *initially* in the negotiations; more importantly, they might not have agreed freely to an arrangement that gave even the worst rights violators the opportunity to exchange amnesty for truth. Tutu argues that the negotiated agreement should be taken as the will of the victims of apartheid, since many of the negotiators were themselves victims, and the ANC gained a resounding victory in the initial (and subsequent) national election (pp. 56–57). But these arguments are flawed.

The fact that some of the negotiators were themselves victims does not guarantee that the victims excluded from the negotiations would have agreed to the same amnesty provisions. As has been the case in Latin America, opponents negotiating a peace accord might postpone the question of amnesty or, were that not possible, exclude particularly heinous crimes or categories of rights violation from the amnesty option.[56] Even the 1990 agreement between Chile's Pinochet government and its opponents excluded from the self-amnesty law (which the Pinochet government had passed in 1978) those who took part in a 1976 car bombing in Washington, D.C., which killed former Chilean ambassador Orlando Letelier and his American assistant.[57] Moreover, ANC electoral success does not imply endorsement by victims of the amnesty provision. The ANC might have received even *more* support had provisions for individual amnesty *not* been part of the negotiated agreement, or if conditions for amnesty had been limited even further. Moreover, given the other electoral options, some voters might have voted for ANC candidates, but not endorsed the amnesty provision. Although the parents of the brutally murdered Steve Biko may well have voted for the ANC, they also brought an unsuccessful court challenge against the amnesty provision, forcefully arguing that Biko's murderers be brought to trial.

One can also ask how successfully the strategies of amnesty-forgiveness, on the one hand, and prosecution–punishment, on the other, promote the *process* of democratic reciprocity in contrast to whatever *outcomes* issue from deliberative procedures. Again, little empirical evidence is available, and one must rely on anecdote and hypothesis. One can plausibly believe that seeing the guilty escape punishment, let alone resume their official—even judicial— positions diminishes the credibility of a new democracy and reduces citizen commitment to it. Moreover, fair judicial processes and deserved punishment would sharply distinguish past injustice and present justice—with the result that most people would strengthen their commitment to democratic institutions that instituted fair prosecutions and sanctions.

Means to Ubuntu

One wonders whether the South African amnesty mechanism and private acts of forgiveness actually promoted reconciliation in Tutu's preferred sense of social healing and harmony. Results so far are mixed. On the one hand, Tutu recounts wonderful stories of hardened killers who confessed their crimes, expressed remorse, and asked for (and received) forgiveness (pp. 150–51). In all likelihood, when confessions are sincere, the granting of forgiveness helps repair personal relationships, especially in cases where perpetrators undergo an inner transformation or voluntarily pay restitution to their victims. On the other hand, one should be skeptical about how widespread such transformed personal relationships have been. Notably, Nielsen-Market Research Africa found that two-thirds of the 2,500 South Africans questioned believed that the TRC had caused a deterioration of race relations in South Africa.[58]

What might have been the effects on *ubuntu* if the TRC had given a more robust role to prosecution and punishment? Might not national healing be furthered if South Africa conducts trials of those who were denied (or never applied for) amnesty when these individuals are suspected of planning or executing the most egregious crimes? Many hold the view of philosopher Jean Hampton, among others, that a broken relationship cannot be healed until the perpetrator, who arrogantly violated his victim's dignity, is "humbled," and the victim, who has been degraded, returns to something approaching his/her proper status.[59] Judicial processes, punishment, and the payment of reparations can both bring down rights abusers and properly elevate their victims. An act of forgiveness that ignores proper rectification results in a relationship in which at least the victim—if not the offender—feels that the new relationship is not deserved. Hence, genuine forgiveness may require trial, penalty, and restitution if strong reconciliation among persons is to be achieved.[60]

Moreover, one can find increasing evidence that *fair* indictments, trials, sentences, and punishments "stay the hand of vengeance," diminish the likelihood of a cycle of reprisals, and thereby both reduce the polarization between adversaries and help unify the nation. Since Pinochet's arrest in England, threatened extradition to Spain, return to Chile, and possible trial in Chile, more than twenty-five of Pinochet's former officers have been arrested for kidnapping. Former Chilean political prisoners, not blocked by something like South Africa's amnesty agreement, have filed more than 177 criminal complaints accusing Pinochet of torture and kidnapping. Not only did complaints and (prospective) prosecutions *not* undermine Chile's January 2000 presidential campaign and election, but both candidates—including Joaquín Lavín, a former official in Pinochet's government—also said prior to the election that Chilean courts should have jurisdiction over Pinochet and justice should be done. As a *New York Times* editorial observed: the fact that "none of this has disturbed Chile's fledgling democracy [...] suggests that those who feared the destabilizing power of justice underestimated its healing effect."[61] Seven months after the election, the Chilean Supreme Court (voting 14–6) stripped Pinochet of his senatorial immunity from prosecution. Although a small band of Chileans desperately search for a strategy to keep him out of the dock, most Chileans believe prosecuting Pinochet would help unify a divided nation as well as consolidate Chile's democracy.

It is undeniable that national or international trials—because of insufficient resources and/or a lack of will to arrest those indicted (Yugoslav and Rwandan tribunals), scapegoating (US trials after the My Lai Massacre), politicization (Leipzig, Constantinople, Republika Srpska), or overly ambitious prosecutions (Argentina)—have not always had such healing effects.[62] In reckoning with past wrongs, trials must be combined with other tools, such as truth commissions, reparations, and judicial reform, to achieve success— and even then the beneficial results will not come quickly. Nuremberg, however, shows that reasonably fair trials and deserved punishment of those most responsible for atrocities help dissolve bitterness and rehabilitate a nation.

It might be argued, of course, that the sort of healing that the *Times* editorialist extols or that Nuremberg achieved is not that of the mutual love and social solidarity enjoyed by family members. Instead, the healing achieved may be the mutual respect and tolerance of fellow citizens who together deliberated and decided on the common good. This kind of reconciliation is a tremendous accomplishment nonetheless. Amnesty—especially conditional amnesty that is democratically approved—and personal forgiveness may play a role in achieving and sustaining this important goal. Yet, as I have argued, in reckoning with past wrongs, a society must be wary of *overestimating* the restorative effect of amnesty and forgiveness, as well as *underestimating* the reconciling power of justice.

8. Conclusions

If my assessments of Tutu's arguments and possible counter arguments are sound, several conclusions follow concerning judicial justice and reconciliation. First, Tutu correctly distinguishes the goal of reconciliation in a fledgling democracy from the goal of penal justice. However, since Tutu inadequately conceptualizes both, they are for him unalterably at odds. For Tutu, punishment is nothing more than vengeful getting even for the wrongdoer's past wrong, while reconciliation requires that the wrongdoer be immune from punishment and unconditionally forgiven for his past wrong. The only prospects, at least for South Africa, were retribution and "a society in ashes," on the one hand, and amnesty combined with forgiveness and reconciliation, on the other. In contrast, I have argued that punishment and reconciliation not only are distinct, but that they are also intrinsic goods that may reinforce each other.

One can view legal punishment, the state's or international tribunal's intentional imposition of some deprivation, as justified, among other reasons, because it is prima facie just—or, at least, not unjust—to punish the wrongdoer in a way that does not exceed his crime, apart from whatever good consequences also might occur. Further, both moral and practical reasons exist that justify defining reconciliation not as a social harmony—which might threaten individual rights—but as peaceful coexistence or "civic friendship" (these words are John Rawls'). Through public deliberation fellow citizens respect each other's rights, are tolerant of differences, and try to reduce disagreements and arrive at compromises that all (or most) can reasonably accept.

Considered in this way, each goal also can instrumentally promote the other. Former enemies can agree to live together nonlethally under the rule of law and reduce their remaining differences through public deliberation. This kind of reconciliation can lead to further agreement that it is not wrong to prosecute and punish at least those *on both sides* who are most guilty of the worst crimes. Likewise, punitive justice can have reconciling power in the sense that upon getting (no more than) what they deserve, perpetrators have set things right and can be reintegrated into society. (This rectification may include—as part of and not a substitute for the punishment—court-ordered restitution of victims.)

Furthermore, societies and the international community should design institutions in which the ideals of both just punishment and reconciliation are realized simultaneously in various institutions and tools. Fair trials and just punishments not only mete out what wrongdoers deserve and reject a culture of impunity; but they also may bring people together as fellow citizens. Unfair trials, unjust verdicts, or excessive punishment, of course, do just the opposite. Adequate truth commissions not only provide the occasion for a society to deliberate about its past, but also to recommend prosecution and provide evidence to judicial authorities.

The goals of penal justice and reconciliation, then, can reinforce each other and be jointly realized in, or affected by, the same tools. At the same time, these two goods can also create tensions, because (among other things) morally justified punishment is partially oriented toward the past, while reconciliation is an ideal for creating a better future. Unfortunately, in this as in many other cases, all good things do not always go together, and morally costly choices must be made.

At least four ways exist to address clashes of these two ideals. First, the creation of new tools can promote the *joint* realization of just punishment and reconciliation. One example, arguably, is the Spanish indictment and request for the extradition of Pinochet, leading to his subsequent house arrest in England, extradition to Chile, and indictments of Pinochet in Chile. Even if Pinochet never stands trial in his native land, the Spanish, British, and Chilean actions have (i) brought him to "moral ruin,"[63] (ii) shown that "even former heads of state do not enjoy impunity for crimes against humanity, and may be tried outside the country where the crimes were committed,"[64] and again (iii) helped liberate Chileans from some of their former divisions as well as deepened their fragile democracy.

A second way to resolve the clash of ideals is by a division of labor. For example, trials and truth commissions can work cooperatively, each responsible for emphasizing one of the two ideals—punishment and reconciliation—but not completely ignoring the other. It is better if neither tool is overloaded with functions that the other can perform better. For example, the International Criminal Tribunal for the Former Yugoslavia has indicted, is trying, and is punishing some middle-level implementers, some high (not yet the highest) military commanders, former Yugoslav president Slobodan Milosevic, and other alleged planners of atrocities in Bosnia. In contrast, a proposed truth and reconciliation commission, comprised of representatives of the Serb, Croat, and Muslim communities, could investigate and deliberate together concerning the truth about the past. This kind of investigation and a resultant authorized report would partially settle accounts with the great number of rank-and-file rights violators. Such a report would also go beyond the scope of judicial processes—recognize and applaud those from all sides who found ways to aid their ethnically diverse and endangered neighbors.[65]

The relations of trials and truth commissions can be complementary in a stronger sense, because each body may enhance as well as supplement the other. Fair trials and punishment may contribute to the reconciliation and truth sought by truth commissions. On the one hand, if victims believe that their testimony might be used by national or international tribunals to bring perpetrators to justice, this knowledge can also satisfy the thirst for justice and lead to healing. Moreover, as Hayner argues, "prospects that its documentation could be used for international prosecutions could add weight to a commission's work, focus its targeted investigations, and help shape or clarify its evidentiary standards."[66] On the other hand, the evidence that truth commissions unearth may have a positive role to play in judicial proceedings. Moreover, truth commissions, after evaluating the fairness and independence of a country's judicial system, might recommend judicial reform or argue that an international tribunal should have jurisdiction.[67]

Similarly, a third way to deal with a clash of the two ideals is to embody them sequentially. Among other things, reconciliation was most prominent in the initial stages of both Chile's and South Africa's transitions to democracy. Since 2000, however, the time has been ripe for Chile to prosecute Pinochet's chief lieutenants, if not Pinochet himself.[68] Similarly, subsequent to the work of the TRC, one can be hopeful that in the near future South Africa will vigorously indict and bring to trial those who were denied (or never applied for) amnesty.[69]

Each of these approaches avoids a clash and establishes a reasonable and balanced approach to the goals of just punishment and reconciliation. Notably, Tutu himself justifies South Africa's foregoing of justice by an appeal to the ideal of balance: "We have had to balance the requirements of justice, accountability, stability, peace, and reconciliation" (p. 23). The trouble is that the balance that Tutu advocates for South Africa and other societies virtually disregards justice. Even with respect to P. W. Botha, the intransigent and unrepentant former South African president, who defiantly rejected a court order to appear before the TRC, Tutu disagreed with those who wanted to see "the leaders of the old dispensation getting a dose of retributive justice" (p. 250).

What should be done when no resolution of the clash of values seems possible? Perhaps there are cases when (civil) conflicts cannot end or democratization begin unless or until some sort of amnesty agreement is reached in peace accords or the formation of a new government. Perhaps plans for trials may have to be postponed, abandoned altogether, or restricted to those suspected of the worst crimes. Perhaps non-retributive considerations such as reconciliation or stability will be the basis for imposing less than the punishment deserved. Under circumstances in which a clash of good ends cannot be deferred or avoided, societies and international bodies in a variety of venues should engage in democratic and public deliberation and decide on the best balance or trade off in that particular situation.

The choices are not merely between, as Tutu assumes, the immoral world of politics on the one hand and the moral/religious realm of forgiveness and love on the other. Politics can be a sphere in which fellow citizens reason together and make costly choices when it is clear that, at least for now, all good things do not go together. As *Washington Post* editorialist Jim Hoagland observes: "There is no more important new subject on the international agenda than the necessity of balancing the human need for justice and retribution with the state's interest in stability and reconciliation."[70] I would amend Hoagland's point to say that in reckoning with past evil, nations and the international community must strive to realize (among other things) both penal justice and reconciliation, and balance them in morally appropriate ways.

Notes

1. I am grateful to Alex Boraine, Cory Briggs, Lawrence Crocker, Richard J. Goldstone, Pablo De Greiff, David Dyzenhaus, Jason Marsh, Verna Gehring, and Mark Sagoff for helpful comments on earlier versions of all or parts of this essay. I also owe thanks to the following universities and host institutions, where I was invited to give portions of the paper: Conference on "Apologies: Mourning the Past and Ameliorating the Present," Claremont Graduate University, Claremont, California; Conference on "Justice, Memory, and Reconciliation," Munk Centre for International Studies, University of Toronto; Inaugural Lecture, Human Rights B. A. Program, Carleton University, Ottawa, Canada; Departmental Colloquium, Department of Philosophy, Colorado State University; and Workshop, Committee on Politics, Philosophy, and Public Policy, University of Maryland; Symposium on Ethics and Global Issues, Department of Philosophy, College of Wooster; Eastern Division Meeting, American Philosophical Association; Carnegie Council on Ethics and International Affairs; Central Division Meeting, American Philosophical Association; and V Diálogo Mayor de la Universidad del Rosario, Bogotá, Colombia. A shorter version of the paper's first section appeared in *Report from the Institute for Philosophy & Public Policy*, vol. 20, no. 1: (Winter/Spring, 2000), pp. 1–6. A shorter version of the second section appeared in *The Responsive Community*, vol. 11, no. 2 (Spring 2001), pp. 32–42. A Spanish translation (by Carlos Parales) of the first two sections appeared in Adolfo Chaparro Amaya, ed., *Cultura, política y perdón*, pp. 173–191 (Bógota, Colombia: Centro Editorial Universidad del Rosario). The complete paper appeared in a special issue, "Democracy and Punishment" of the *Buffalo Criminal Law Review*, vol. 5, no. 2: (2002), pp. 509–549.

2. Lawrence Crocker, "The Upper Limits of Punishment," *Emory Law Journal*, 41 (1992): p. 1063; cf. Geoffrey Cupit's definition of (both legal and nonlegal) punishment: "To punish is intentionally to make suffer, intentionally to inflict something

disadvantageous, burdensome, and unwelcome." (*Justice as Fittingness* p. 139 [Oxford: Clarendon Press, 1996]).

3. Nozick, *Philosophical Explanations*, p. 366.

1. Desmond M. Tutu, 1999, *No Future without Forgiveness* (New York: Doubleday). Citations from Tutu's volume will appear within parentheses in the text.

2. Martha Minow, 1998, *Between Vengeance and Forgiveness: Facing History after Genocide and Mass Violence*, p.9 (Boston: Beacon Press). See also Paul van Zyl, 1999, "Evaluating Justice and Reconciliation Efforts," *Perspectives on Ethics and International Affairs* 1, pp. 17–20. "Justice Without Punishment: Guaranteeing Human Rights in Transitional Societies," in Charles Villa-Vicencio and Wilhelm Verwoerd, eds., 2000, *Looking Back, Reaching Forward: Reflections on the South African Truth and Reconciliation Commission*, pp. 42–57 (Cape Town: UCT Press/London: Zed Books).

3. My focus on Tutu's views and arguments does not mean that I assume that other members of the TRC shared his ideas. In comments on an earlier version of the present paper, Alex Boraine, Deputy Chair of the TRC, remarked that Tutu's personal contribution to the TRC was enormous and even indispensable, but Tutu's own opinions should not necessarily be taken to represent the TRC or the opinions of its other members ("Comments," Carnegie Council on Ethics and International Affairs, New York City, March 2, 2001.) Although Boraine seems to agree with Tutu when Boraine says the African ideal of *ubuntu* includes the concrete principle that "the adjudication process must be conciliatory in order to restore peace, as opposed to an adversarial approach which emphasizes retribution," Boraine also says: "while broadening the concept of justice, the TRC model does not contradict retributive justice" (Alex Boraine, 2000, *A Country Unmasked: Inside South Africa's Truth and Reconciliation Commission*, pp. 425, 427–428 (Oxford and New York: Oxford University Press).

4. David Little, 1999, "A Different Kind of Justice: Dealing with Human Rights Violations in Transitional Societies," *Ethics and International Affairs* 13, p. 79.

5. In earlier papers I formulated eight principles or goals to evaluate reckoning with past wrongs and employed them in assessing the merits of various tools, such as trials and truth commissions. These goals, which I merely list here, are: truth; a public platform for victims; punishment; rule of law; compensation to victims; institutional reform and long-term development; reconciliation, and public deliberation. See David A. Crocker, 1999, "Civil Society and Transitional Justice," in Robert Fullinwider, ed., *Civil Society, Democracy, and Civic Renewal* (Lanham, Md.: Rowman & Littlefield); "Reckoning with Past Wrongs: A Normative Framework," *Ethics & International Affairs* 13 (1999): pp. 43–64; "Truth Commissions, Transitional Justice, and Civil Society, " in Robert I. Rotberg and Dennis Thompson, eds., 2000, *Truth v. Justice: The Morality of Truth Commissions* pp. 99–121 (Princeton and Oxford: Princeton University Press). In the present paper I focus on three of the eight goals: punishment, reconciliation, and public deliberation.

6. See Ronald C. Slye, "Justice and Amnesty," in the Villa-Vicencio and Verwoerd anthology, pp. 174–183; "Amnesty, Truth, and Reconciliation: Reflections on the South African Amnesty Process," in the Rotberg and Thompson, eds., *Truth v. Justice*, pp. 170–188.

7. Some retributive theories of punishment or mixed theories with a retributive component emphasize respect for the victim and his or her rights. See, for example, Aryeh Neier, 1998, *War Crimes: Brutality, Genocide, Terror, and the Struggle for Justice*, pp. 83, 222 (New York: Times Books).

8. Lawrence Crocker, "Upper Limit," p. 1061.

9. Ibid.

10. Mandatory retributivism contends that all and only wrongdoers should be punished and that the punishment should be no less than and no more than what the wrongdoer deserves; limited or permissive retributivism contends that only wrongdoers should be punished and that the punishment should not be more—but may be less—than what is deserved. I owe this distinction to Lawrence Crocker, "A Retributive Theory of Criminal Justice" (unpublished mss.). Many critics of retributivism unfortunately tend to identify retributivism with the mandatory form. See Carlos Nino, "The Duty to Punish Past Abuses of Human Rights Put into Context," *Yale Law Journal* 100 (1991): p. 2620; and T. M. Scanlon, 1999, "Punishment and the Rule of Law," in Harold Hongju Koh and Ronald C. Slye, eds., *Deliberative Democracy and Human Rights*, p. 258 (New Haven and London: Yale University Press).

11. Robert Nozick, 1981, *Philosophical Explanations*, p. 363 (Cambridge, MA: Belknap Press).

12. Urgently needed, but beyond the scope of the present paper, is a detailed analysis and evaluation—in relation to "transitional justice"—of recent attempts to defend retributivism or a retributive dimension of a mixed theory of punishment. These efforts, for example, appeal to intuition (Michael Moore) or employ higher order principles such as fittingness (Geoffrey Cupit), reciprocity (L. Crocker), communication (Jean Hampton, Robert Nozick) or fair distributions of benefits and burdens (Herbert Morris, George Sher, James Rachels). In addition to other essays cited in this article that defend a form of retributivism, see Michael Moore, 1997, *Laying Blame* (Oxford: Clarendon Press); Jean Hampton, "The Moral Education Theory of Punishment," *Philosophy and Public Affairs* 13 (1984): p. 208, 238; Herbert Morris, "Persons and Punishment," *Monist* 52 (1968): pp. 475–501; George Sher, 1987, *Desert* (Princeton, NJ: Princeton University Press); James Rachels, 1997, "Punishment and Desert," in Hugh LaFollette, ed., *Ethics in Practice: An Anthology* (Cambridge, MA and Oxford: Blackwell). Important criticisms of retributivism include Richard W. Burgh, "Do the Guilty Deserve Punishment?" *Journal of Philosophy* 79 (1982): pp. 193–213; David Dolinko, "Some Thoughts on Retributivism," *Ethics* 101 (1991): pp. 537–559; Carlos Nino, "A Consensual Theory of Punishment," *Philosophy and Public Affairs* 12 (1983): pp. 289–306; T. M. Scanlon, "Punishment and the Rule of Law."

13. Ibid., p. 368.

14. Ibid., p. 366.

15. Ibid., p. 367.

16. L. Crocker, "Upper Limit," p. 1060.

17. Ibid.

18. Bill Berkeley, "Aftermath: Genocide, the Pursuit of Justice and the Future of Africa," *Washington Post Magazine* October 11, 1998, pp. 14, 28.

19. L. Crocker, "Upper Limit," p. 1061.

20. Steve Coll, "Peace without Justice: A Journey to the Wounded Heart of Africa," *Washington Post Magazine* January 9, 2000, pp. 8–27.

21. Minow rightly claims that "retribution needs constraints" but leaves an open question whether these come from the ideal/practice of retribution itself or from "competing ideals such as mercy and moral decency" (*Between Vengeance and Forgiveness*, p. 12). That only wrongdoers should be punished and that they should get no more than they deserve, builds constraint right into the retributive idea. On the basis of consequentialist and other considerations, such as protecting a fledgling democracy from a military coup, punishment might be further limited, delayed, and even set aside.

22. Nozick, *Philosophical Explanations*, p. 367.

23. Martha Nussbaum, 1999, *Sex and Social Justice*, pp. 153–183 (Oxford and New York: Oxford University Press).

24. Nozick, *Philosophical Explorations*, p. 367.

25. See, Jeffrie G. Murphy and Jean Hampton, 1988, *Forgiveness and Mercy* (New York: Cambridge University Press). Jeffrie G. Murphy, 1991, "Retributive Hatred: An Essay on Criminal Liability and the Emotions," in R.G. Frey and Christopher W. Morris, eds. *Liability and Responsibility* (Cambridge: Cambridge University Press).

26. Nozick, *Philosophical Explorations*, p. 368.

27. See below for the way in which traditional Balkan honor codes may present mixed cases of collective guilt and reprisals calibrated to earlier harms.

28. Aryeh Neier, *War Crimes*, p. 211. See also Minow, *Between Vengeance and Forgiveness*, p. 40.

29. See David Luban, 1994, "The Legacies of Nuremberg," in *Legal Modernism*, pp. 335–378 (Ann Arbor: University of Michigan Press); Neier, *War Crimes*, pp. 15–18; Mark J. Osiel, 1999,*Obeying Orders: Atrocity, Military Discipline and the Law of War* (New Brunswick and London: Transaction).

30. Chuck Sudetic, 1998, *Blood and Vengeance: One Family's Story of the War in Bosnia* (New York: W. W. Norton).

31. Scott Anderson, "The Curse of Blood and Vengeance," *New York Times Magazine* December 16, 1999.

32. Ibid., p. 15.

33. Ibid.

34. Minow, *Beyond Vengeance and Forgiveness*, pp. 10, 12.

35. In the film *Eye for an Eye* (Paramount, 1996) the character played by Sally Field takes justice into her own hands when a court dismisses (incorrectly, she believes) the case against a man whom she (and we) believe is guilty of raping and killing her teenage daughter. When the police make clear that they have no case against the suspect, even after he rapes and kills again, Field lures the (suspected) rapist-murderer to break into her house and then kills him in an act of staged—and then real—self-defense. As we assess the moral character of the agent, we are at least uneasy about her private vengeance and perhaps hold her blameworthy. She has taken justice into her own hands and, by killing the suspect, has perhaps gone beyond the upper limit of punishment. And yet we also judge that the slain killer deserved severe punishment—if not death—or at least that the "pay back" was not wrong. We find the outcome fitting not only because the killer will not kill again, but also because severe punishment probably coincides with what the court should have decided. Although not uncomplicated, the case illustrates the idea that an agent of revenge might be morally blameworthy and yet—*pace* Tutu—the vengeful act not clearly wrong.

36. Discussing the sources of Tutu's theology and the meaning of *ubuntu*, in *A Country Unmasked* (p. 362) Boraine cites the following words of Anton Lembede, the founding president of the ANC Youth League: "[The African] regards the universe as one composite whole, an organic entity, progressively driving towards greater harmony and unity whose individual parts exists merely as interdependent aspects of one whole realising their fullest life in the corporate life where communal contentment is the absolute measure of values. His philosophy of life strives towards unity and aggregation, towards greater social responsibility" (quoted in Peter Dreyer, 1980, *Martyrs and Fanatics, South African and Human Destiny*, p. 154 [New York: Simon and Schuster]).

37. Ash, "Kosovo," p. 50.

38. Ibid.

39. A hopeful sign that reconciliation as peaceful coexistence may be giving way to reconciliation as democratic reciprocity, occurred in the Kosovo elections of November 2001, when a surprising number of Serbs voted and an Albanian was elected, who is committed to a pluralistic society.

40. See D. Crocker, "Civil Society and Transitional Justice," "Reckoning with Past Wrongs: A Normative Framework," and "Truth Commissions, Transitional Justice, and Civil Society; James Bohman, 1996, *Public Deliberation: Pluralism, Complexity, and Democracy* (Cambridge: MIT Press); Amy Gutmann and Dennis Thompson, 1996, *Democracy and Disagreement* (Cambridge: Harvard University Press); Amy Gutmann and Dennis Thompson, "The Moral Foundations of Truth Commissions," in the Rotberg and Thompson , eds., *Truth v. Justice*, pp. 22–44; Amy Gutmann and Dennis Thompson, 2000, "Why Deliberative Democracy Is Different," in Ellen Frankel Paul, Fred D. Miller, Jr., and Jeffrey Paul, eds., *Democracy* (Cambridge:

Cambridge University Press); James Bohman and William Rehig, eds., 1999, *Deliberative Democracy: Essays on Reason and Politics* (Cambridge: MIT Press).

41. See Minow, *Beyond Vengeance and Forgiveness*, pp. 20–21, 115, 155, n. 65.

42. A fourth and "epistemological" ideal of reconciliation should also be mentioned, one that like Tutu's model "social harmony" threatens individual freedom. Susan Dwyer ("Reconciliation for Realists," *Ethics and International Affairs*, 13 (1999): pp. 81–98) argues that what we should mean by reconciliation and what a society in transition should aim for is a consensual narrative that settles accounts with past evil by forging a single narrative about what happened and why. Truth commissions, historians, and even judicial processes might contribute to such a "reconciliation" with the past. While such interpretative agreement is arguably desirable and might be aspired to, it is unlikely to be realized unless promoted by morally problematic means such as coercion or indoctrination. The most that democratic reciprocity may be able to achieve is an agreement to disagree on certain matters and a mutually respectful compromise on others.

43. See TRC website, http://www.truth.org.za/PR/1999/pr991209a.htm, and Margaret Popkin and Nehal Bhuta, "Latin American Amnesties in Comparative Perspective: Can the Past be Buried?" *Ethics and International Affairs* 13 (1999), p. 120.

44. Ibid. See also Truth and Reconciliation Commission, *Final Report* October 29, 1998, vol. 5, chap. 8, p. 309.

45. Richard J. Goldstone, 2000, *For Humanity: Reflections of a War Crimes Investigator*, p. 130 (New Haven: Yale University Press).

46. Neier, *War Crimes*, pp. 212–213.

47. Gary Jonathan Bass, 2000, *Stay the Hand of Vengeance: The Politics of War Crimes Tribunals*, pp. 147–205 (Princeton and Oxford: Princeton University Press).

48. Ibid. pp. 37–146.

49. Comisionado Nacional de los Derechos Humanos, *El difícil transito hacia la democracia: Informe sobre derechos humanos, 1996* (Honduras: Comisionado Nacional de los Derechos Humanos, 1996), pp. 20–21.

50. See Cynthia Arnson, 2000, "Introduction," in Arnson, ed., *Comparative Peace Processes in Latin America*, pp. 10–11; Ramón Romero and Leticia Salomón, *La reforma judicial: Un reto para la democracia* (Tegucigalpa: CEDOH-ASDI).

51. Cited in Steve Coll, "Peace without Justice," p. 27.

52. Ibid.

53. Bass, *Stay the Hand of Vengeance*, p. 295.

54. Neier, *War Crimes*, p. 107.

55. Ibid.

56. For a comparative discussion of various ways in which Latin American countries have limited amnesty for past perpetrators, see Popkin and Bhuta, "Latin American Amnesties."

57. Recently the Chilean courts have further limited the 1978 amnesty law. Those who ordered—including Pinochet himself—the "disappearance" of hundreds of Chileans are liable to prosecution today for torture, because in 1998 Chile signed the International Torture Convention and Chilean courts have ruled that the torture of those still unaccounted for continues into the present.

58. "Only Half of People Feel TRC is Fair and Unbiased: Survey," South Africa Press Association, March 5, 1998. Quoted in Priscilla B. Hayner, 2001, *Unspeakable Truths: Confronting State Terror and Atrocity*, p. 156 (New York and London: Routledge). See also Hayner, *Unspeakable Truths*, pp. 30, 37, as well as the important research of the Centre for the Study of Violence and Reconciliation, for example Brandon Hamber et al., Survivors' Perceptions of the Truth and Reconciliation Commission and Suggestions for the Final Report (1998), at http://www.cvsr.org.za/papers/papkhul.htm (accessed May 9, 2002); Hugo Van der Merwe and Lazarus Kgalema, The Truth and Reconciliation Commission: A Foundation for Community Reconciliation? at http://www.csvr.org.za/articles/artnch&1.htm (accessed May 9, 2002).

59. Hampton, "The Retributive Idea." For a view of forgiveness that captures some elements in the retributive idea, see David Little, "A Different Kind of Justice."

60. Hamber et al., "Survivors' Perceptions of the Truth and Reconciliation Commission and Suggestions for the Final Report", pp. 5, 7, 11–14.

61. "New Twist in the Pinochet Case," *New York Times* January 15, 2000, p. A18.

62. See Bass, *Stay the Hand of Vengeance*.

63. Isabel Allende, "Pinochet without Hatred," *New York Times Magazine* January 17, 1999, p. 24.

64. "New Twist in the Pinochet Case."

65. See Neil J. Kritz and William A. Steubner, "A Truth Commission for Bosnia and Herzegovina: Why, How, and When?" paper presented at the Victimology Symposium, Sarajevo, Bosnia, May 9–10, 1998.

66. Hayner, *Unspeakable Truths*, p. 211. This complementarity, of course, is not automatic; for, as Hayner demonstrates, there are "potential areas of tension" as well, for example, the award of amnesty limits the reach of criminal trials and civil litigation. See Hayner, *Unspeakable Truths*, pp. 206–212, especially p. 208. For a review of Hayner's fine book, see David A. Crocker, review of *Unspeakable Truths* by Hayner and *Transitional Justice* by Ruti G. Teitel, *Ethics & International Affairs* 15, 2 (2001): pp. 152–154.

67. Ibid., p. 210.

68. Pablo DeGreiff has objected that this sequencing of the ends of retribution and reconciliation might be embraced retrospectively, but runs into problems as a matter of forward-looking policy. DeGreiff remarks, "Announcing to former perpetrators that they will not be prosecuted now, but rather in five years, will not do much to make prosecutions more acceptable to them" or, we might add, to their supporters. (Pablo DeGreiff, e-mail message, February 15, 2000). This point is indeed worrisome because

it seems to be changing the rules of the game during the match as well as keeping a potential indictee in limbo with respect to whether or not she/he will be indicted and tried. There are two possible strategies to meeting this objection. Authorities could either refrain from adopting sequencing as public policy ("first reconcile and then try"), but later seize it when politically feasible, especially if political will is determined by democratic deliberation. Alternatively, the sequencing of reconciliation-retribution could be democratically agreed to *as a matter of policy*, as arguably occurred in South Africa's policy of making those refused amnesty vulnerable to judicial processes.

69. Of deep concern is the possibility that the South African government will have insufficient funds or political will to carry through with the judicial processes called for upon the TRC's denial of applications for amnesty. I owe this point to discussions with Alex Boraine and David Dyzenhaus.

70. James Hoagland, "Justice for All," *Washington Post* April 19, 1998, p. C7.

Forgive and Not Forget: Reconciliation Between Forgiveness and Resentment

DANIEL LEVY AND NATAN SZNAIDER

"Who, after all, is left to remind the winners that someone else once owned these houses, worshipped here, buried their dead in this ground."
—Ignatieff 1997, p. 177

Thus wrote Michael Ignatieff in connection with ethnic cleansing and its effect of eradicating the truth of the past. It speaks about a broader issue that has become a pervasive feature of both domestic and international politics. Namely, whether forgiveness, in light of state-sponsored mass atrocities and other severe human rights abuses, can be uttered in meaningful ways, both on a personal and a collective political level. This essay explores the theoretical underpinnings and manifestations of forgiveness against the backdrop of an emerging Human Rights regime, and memories of historical injustices in the second half of the twentieth century. A brief discussion of state-sanctioned restitution measures serves to highlight the ambiguous meanings forgiveness can assume, depending on the political and moral context within which it is articulated.

Most current debates about forgiveness start from an unquestioned as-sumption: namely, that forgiveness is the morally superior sentiment; resent-ment is atavistic, archaic, leading to revenge and renewed cycles of violence. On the one hand, uttering the truth about historical injustice and doing this in conjunction with the former enemy will set us free. Truth commissions, in particular, are said to have these redemptive qualities, but it is very much part of other forms that are celebrated because of their reconciliatory usages. History and politics are turned into trauma laboratories. Rather than presup-posing these "healing effects," we analyze these underlying assumptions by situating them in their respective philosophical and historical traditions.

In this paper we address the conceptual roots of forgiveness and how they relate to emerging conceptions of restitution. Who can tell what the right relation is between memory and forgetting, between punishment, revenge, and forgiveness? And what about those who do not want to forgive, who demand and insist on their right to resentment and retribution? The literature on these subjects has by now become a specialized field of its own, fusing moral and normative arguments. Sociological thinking counters the belief that politics should be guided by theoretical doctrine, universal principle, and appeals to abstract rights. On the other hand, it is this metaphysical zeal, which lies at the heart of the contemporary project of global justice. We seek to overcome this discrepancy by focusing on the politico-theoretical thoughts found in various works of Hannah Arendt. Expanding upon Arendt, we argue that the political significance of forgiveness is contingent upon a set of historical and institutional circumstances that condition the respective meanings forgiveness can (or cannot) assume.

1. Forgiveness as a Form of Politics?

Forgiveness constitutes the implied and often explicit background on which issues of restitution, the politics of memory, and other reactions to the un-covering of historical injustices are debated. It confronts us with difficult questions. Should we privilege memory over forgetting, punishment over amnesty, and resentment over forgiveness? Does it privilege former victims or does it abdicate the perpetrators? These and other questions have triggered a rich literature, which in the aftermath of the Holocaust and against the global backdrop of the Balkan conflicts during the 1990s, received renewed attention. At its core stand different perceptions of forgiveness. But behind all of them lies the alleged power to undo what has been done, that is, "the pos-sible redemption from the predicament of irreversibility" as Hannah Arendt had already put it in the late 1950s (Arendt 1958, p. 236). It implies freedom for political action, to liberate oneself from the prison of time, to be born anew in politics. As she puts it, the opposite of forgiveness is vengeance, and vengeance can be predicted; it runs its due course, people acting as they were supposed to act, the past determining the present and the future. Forgiveness, on the other hand, is unpredictable; it is undetermined action, therefore, in Arendtian terms, true political action and an expression of political liberty (Ibid.). The alternative to it is punishment and trials, and Arendt shortly ex-plores this connection by stating that "men are unable to forgive what they cannot punish and they are unable to punish what has turned out to be un-forgivable" (Ibid., p. 241). Here, Arendt claims that such offenses can neither be punished nor forgiven and that they are outside of human affairs. As we shall see below, this view is somewhat modified when situated in the context of "Crimes against Humanity," where it might be exactly the "unforgivable," which seeks to be forgiven.

Here the problem of the right mixture between what Max Weber called "*Verantwortungsethik*" (ethics of responsibility) and "*Gesinnungsethik*" (ethics of ultimate ends) sets in. Forgiveness might actually be a bridge between the two worlds of the sacred and the profane, and as such, it has the potential to become a recipe against Arendt's aforementioned dictum of "irreversibility." We do not want to be prisoners of the past because only our radical openness to the future makes political action possible. Political forgiveness is one path to this. Arendt emphasized that this political forgiveness should not be based on Christian Love, but on Greek Respect. It is highly political and not sentimental. Arendt does not care about how people feel in that process. She is against authenticity. And this is an important point, because many of the debates regarding political forgiveness are framed around the notion of whether people really meant and mean it. The debates regarding "*Wiedergutmachung*," the monetary compensation the Federal Republic of Germany provided to Israel and the Jewish people, to be discussed below, are a good example of how intentions and actual consequences do not always mix. Accordingly, for Arendt, it is the moral equality between the forgiver and the recipient of forgiveness that matters. It is the sharing of a common world between two sides that voluntarily agree to break out of their prisons of the past (Digeser 2001). However, Arendt qualifies her view on forgiveness insofar as she relates it to the judicial and the political. Deeds, which are not punishable, cannot be forgiven. What she called "Radical Evil" needs to be excluded from the politics of forgiveness. Perpetrator and victim needed to share a common world, to be "at home in the world" in the words of Arendt. This living in plurality makes "politics" possible. "Radical Evil" (and even the "banality of evil") destroys plurality and therefore politics. And it is clear that she was referring to the Holocaust when she wrote about "radical evil." Former victims and perpetrators have stopped sharing the same world. Taking Arendt seriously poses a huge conceptual problem for theorists and activists of reconciliation.

What then has pushed forgiveness to the forefront of public and political attention? It is Christian morality, or rather its secular embodiments, which have raised forgiveness to the status of supreme, even constitutive value (for a development of this argument, see Heyd 2001). Not only has Christianity emphasized internal transformative capacities, but it has also put suffering and its redemption at the core. The cultural code of Christianity has also been diffused throughout the world through processes of cultural globalization. However, forgiveness as a cultural code does not need its Christian roots by now. As Arendt put it: "The fact that he [Jesus of Nazareth] made this discovery [of forgiveness] in a religious context and articulated it in religious language is no reason to take it any less seriously in a strictly religious sense (Arendt 1958, p. 238). This is especially true in global times where increased processes of universalization are at the same time processes of secularized Christianity.

Thus, in the late 1950s, Arendt already believed that a new politics could be constructed out of the Christian roots of forgiveness. It seems that she thought that as long as people understood Christianity in the correct political (and Greek) way, the roots do not matter. For her that meant first of all to de-privatize forgiveness and to make it public. Decisive for her was Jesus's insistence that it is not true that only God has the power to forgive. For Arendt, what shocked people the most in Jesus's message was that he believed in people's "power to forgive" (Ibid., p. 239). Arendt, in an interesting turn, takes Kant's rejection of moral sentiments like forgiveness and gives it a Kantian bent. Forgiveness is not moral sentiment for her, but part of politics and justice. One just has to look again at her criticism of Jaspers' "On German Guilt" to see this clearly. Karl Jaspers, Arendt's dissertation supervisor and long time friend, tried to deal in the first semester after Nazi Germany's defeat with the "Question of German Guilt" (1946). This text can be read as a "founding text" for the new West German collective identity (Diner 2000, p. 219).

Jaspers' distinction between criminal, political, moral, and metaphysical guilt is crucial for the issue at hand here. Especially "moral guilt," where individuals subordinate their conscience to the demands of the state, seems problematic (Rabinbach 2001). It stipulates that *that* guilt demands to be for-given after the deed, and it does not demand punishment. To place moral and metaphysical guilt outside the sphere of legal punishment individual-izes crimes, which were conducted as a collective. This poses almost insur-mountable problems for reconciliation. Locating "moral guilt" somewhere beyond judicial control shifts it into the realm of memory, of a dark shadow lying on the conscience of the former perpetrators—at least in the hope-ful optimism of Jaspers in 1945, right after the German defeat; an optimism he soon came to abandon. He did reject the notion of "collective guilt," and his attempts to outline different notions of guilt individualized (and humanized) the problem. However, the crimes we are dealing with here, crimes connected to historical injustice, even crimes against humanity and genocide, are crimes committed by political groups, by collectives, against other members of groups. The question remains open if guilt serves to extirpate responsibility. Since the 1970s, Germany's official public culture seeks to distinguish between guilt and responsibility by refusing the former's collective character and insisting on its collective responsibility. Arendt seemed to be already aware of that problem in 1945 (see also Fine 2000). Guilt (and with it forgiveness) seems to be about inner attitude, while responsibility (and an Arendtian political notion of forgiveness) is about the outer sphere, the political public space. This problem seems to be amplified because, according to Arendt, in Germany one could not distinguish anymore between a "secret hero" and a "mass murderer" (Arendt 1945, p. 125). But Arendt enlarges the problem beyond its German boundaries: "For many years now we have met Germans who declare that they are ashamed of being Germans. I have often felt tempted to answer that I am ashamed of being human" (Ibid., p. 131). She accepts Jaspers' notion of moral and metaphysical guilt, but wants to politicize these notions. In clearly foreboding contemporary global politics she closes her essay: "For the idea of humanity when purged of all sentimentality, has the very serious consequence that in one form or another men must assume responsibility for all crimes committed by men and that all nations share the onus of evil committed by all others" (Ibid., p. 131). From here to the notion of "Crimes against Humanity," the way is short.

2. Resentment and Retribution: Antidotes of Forgiveness

This point will be made even clearer by studying two voices rejecting forgiveness and reconciliation. Expressions of national atonement, fiscal compensation, and other redemptive matters do not necessarily imply forgiveness. A look at the writings of especially Jean Améry and Vladimir Jankélévitch, both refusing forgiveness, both insisting on the moral worth and virtue of resentment, underscores this point. Their views express that the passage of time should be resisted and deny to time the power of moral and legal absolution. They want retribution not forgiveness. Are they wrong? It is clear that personally forgiving the people that murdered your family or put you to inhumane torture is a rare and heroic act that should not be expected of anyone. Another dimension of Améry and Jankélévitch's refusal to forgive is that it takes place completely within an individual perspective — it is about feelings. It has nothing to do with politics, because no punishment could possibly be enough. So if all punishment is meaningless and therefore all reconciliation is also meaningless, then there is only the feeling of resentment and the memory it keeps warm. The best that can be done in these circumstances is legal justice, even though both are very much aware that justice cannot be done anymore. Jankélévitch wrote his essay in the midst of the French debate regarding the imprescriptability of Nazi Crimes. For him, pardon is equal to forgetting. Crimes against Jews are truly Crimes against Humanity, against the human essence. They cannot be pardoned. He also does not believe in German repentance: "German Repentance, its name is Stalingrad . . . it's name is defeat" (Jankélévitch 1996, p. 566). For all these reasons, it may have nothing to do with reconciliation in the sense we use the term today, which is understood entirely in a social and political perspective that is completely independent of personal feelings. No one expects the victims to forgive anyone, but the social process of receiving restitution and processes of political forgiveness can still legitimately be considered part of a reconciliation process. However, Améry and Jankélévitch seem to be lonely voices in a global trend moving toward forgiveness and reconciliation. They insist on their resentment and their inability to settle the past: "Today when the Sophists recommend forgetfulness, we will forcefully mark our mute and impotent horror before the dogs of hate; we will think hard about the agony of the deportees without sepulchers and of the little children who did not come back. Because this agony will last until the end of the world" (Ibid., p. 572).

These voices represent resistance to a trajectory, defined by Jeffrie Murphy, a philosopher of forgiveness, as "the overcoming, on moral grounds, of the feeling of resentment, and it is particularly important in allowing human relations to continue that otherwise would be disrupted by resentment." (Murphy 1988, p. 20). This view is echoed in Archbishop Desmond Tutu's view of forgiveness as a civic sacrament as the basis for the South African Truth and Reconciliation Commission (2000).

Jacques Derrida's essay "On Forgiveness" (2001) addresses similar problems. However, he puts forgiveness outside of politics and articulates it in the formula "forgiveness forgives only the unforgivable" (Ibid., p. 32 and passim). For Derrida, it is unconditional forgiveness and it must forgive the guilty as *guilty* without a reference to a request for forgiveness, without transforming the guilty into the innocent. It seems that Derrida is oblivious to the difference of legal guilt and moral responsibility. Or as put by Thane Rosenbaum in an article dealing with German attempts to memorialize the Holocaust: "Guilt is a legal term; responsibility is a moral one. Acknowledgment, truth, and apologies are moral imperatives; forgiveness is not, precisely because it suggests starting over with a clean slate, which, in this case, only the ghosts are empowered to grant" (Thane Rosenbaum, *New York Times*, November 8, 2003).

However, for Derrida forgiveness is not a system of exchange. And it has nothing to do with reconciliation. And he refuses, of course, to accept Jankélévitch's point that "forgiveness died in the camps." Derrida wants to bring back "radical evil" to dimensions where forgiveness is possible. It tries the impossible, namely to reconcile the universal and the particular, and the public and the private. It is salvation translated into politics. But if it lies outside political action, what is it good for? Are we just playing deconstructive games? Or even messianic ones? In Derrida's world, we base ourselves on some transcendent human substance that needs to be saved. "A Dream for Thought" (Derrida 2001, p. 60) in his own words. In this sense, he wants to politicize even more than Arendt the Christian roots of forgiveness. Arendt's strict political separation between private sentiments and public action is being put away by Derrida. The demarcation line between the private and the public spheres is abolished. Private and public forgiveness become the same.

But then, what is it we are trying to nurture and preserve? If we are now dealing with de-centered quasi-subjects of which no one can definitively say what they are or what they ought or want to be, then what is the inviolate essence our institutions should be set up to protect? On what grounds can we guarantee that we will not be hauled off, tortured, and killed? Just on the grounds of humanity? Is that enough? The abolishment between the private and the public does away with the demarcation between the particular and the universal as well. Humanity and particular human groups are being collapsed into the same conceptual framework.

This puts us into the classical modernist's problem of which forgiveness has to give an account. It revolves around notions of individuality and collectivity, and thus is about modern politics. Political forgiveness acknowledges that all are equal and therefore share a common sense of humanity. That seems to be the unconditionality—even the metaphysical—Derrida talks about. The transcendental—or even religious part of our human existence—explicates why, according to Derrida, "forgiveness" is Abrahamic, because it is connected to the notion of "One God," which makes the "human" possible. Thus, "Crimes against Humanity" is basically a religious-sacred conception in which—as Derrida puts it—we accuse ourselves of crimes against ourselves—but without the notion of the sacred—humanity could not be the subject of crimes—but only a specific group of people (which again makes it conditional). But besides the principle that "all men are equal and share a common sense of humanity" there is the other principle that views "every individual as unique and irreplaceable." Here starts the reconciliation between the two principles. They do not need to contradict. But this reconciliation is in need of a mechanism connecting the two through an "ethics of responsibility." Thus, although both principles are logically exclusive, their opposition is constantly overcome in our lives. Here, we are again closing in on the limits of universal forgiveness.

This tension between individuality and collectivity is also mirrored in the emerging legislative language of international law, especially if it comes to crimes against humanity (references from our sovereignty article). The individual autonomy is taken away from victims of genocide and other atrocities where people are targeted because of their group (that is, not individual) characteristics. Ironically, their subsequent attempts to redeem their individuality also involve a collective approach (for example, class action suits, which place the emphasis on that which is collective and categorical). This in turn leads to the recognition of the individual and the abstraction of the crimes and the ensuing processes. And that is why the "law" is so problematic in that respect. How can judicial procedures deal with big questions like "humanity" and crimes against it? This is a concern echoed in many of Arendt's deliberations.

This concern also leaves open the precise nature of the transition from forgiveness to restitution. Legislation (and profanization) of matters indicates such a shift. It may start with forgiveness and end up with restitution, possibly leaving the alleged paradox between the individual autonomy and the moral conscience intact, insofar as the act of forgiveness becomes secondary. In effect, it is the victim giving forgiveness, while restitution is provided by the perpetrator. This is the translation from the metaphysical level to the mundane one. This is how forgiveness is translated into money. Even looking at crimes against humanity directly, one can argue that there is the event—may be beyond understanding, beyond witnessing—when only the dead could have known what happened—and then there is representation. Derrida talks about the crimes against humanity as crimes "we" committed against ourselves, meaning we are all responsible. Thus, again, the crimes and the victims are individualized. The victims are "humanity" and not the "Jews," for instance. What does this mean for forgiveness and testimony? The relationship of testimony and representation is mutually constitutive. Questions of truth or authenticity are secondary, especially since the impact of representation on recreated memory and testimony in no way implies that they are untrue.

However, ultimately the various constraints and opportunities forgiveness imposes on both collective and individual practices cannot be determined in a metaphysical vacuum, but are greatly shaped by historical junctures and how they are collectively remembered. Here, the Holocaust in particular posed a challenge to the universal Enlightenment premises of reason and rationality. Paradoxically, the Holocaust functioned simultaneously as the source for a critique of Western universalism and the foundation for a cosmopolitan desire to propagate human rights universally. The central question here is whether the Holocaust is part of modernity or the opposite, a return to barbarism, representing the breakdown of modernity—a question that connects to the broader debate about whether barbarism constitutes a separate breakdown of civilization or whether it is very much part of modern rationalization and bureaucratization itself. According to Theodor Adorno and Max Horkheimer's study of the "Dialectic of Enlightenment" (1944), barbarism is an immanent quality of modernity, not its corruption. In their view, civilizational ruptures inhere, at least potentially, in the processes of rationalization and bureaucratization that characterize modernity.

For Arendt, however, the Nazis represented the breakdown of the Enlightenment and democracy, of critical judgment and of reason. The ambivalence between the above-mentioned frames of civilization and barbarism remained the primary organizing principle for her thoughts on the Holocaust. Nazism, for her, was nothing particularly German, but rather a manifestation of totalitarianism. Universalizing the phenomenon did not preclude her from recognizing its singular features. She perceived the uniqueness of the Holocaust not only to consist in the scope and systematic nature of the killings, but also in the very attempt to deny humanity as such. Conventional categories of crime become irrelevant, a view that was later incorporated into the legal canon through the concept of "crimes against humanity" (Levy and Sznaider, 2004).

3. The Politics of Restitution

One symptom of these developments relates to the emergence of a discourse about restitution measures that are no longer confined to relations between states but also involve individuals. This is exactly what Crimes against Humanity mean. Individuals and not states are turned into legal subjects. Questions of restitution stand at the intersection of memory, forgiveness, and justice. Whether restitution (especially for individuals) could serve as an adequate matter in the moral equation of victim and perpetrator has remained a thorny issue. A paradigmatic case is the abovementioned German-Israeli story of "*Wiedergutmachung*" (Barkan 2000). Although it is now often mentioned as an exemplary case for the healing effects of restitution measures, the respective reactions the agreements caused in Germany and Israel are instructive for our argument about the difficulty to disentangle the reconciliatory effects generated by official forgiveness and its actual connection to intentions (by the perpetrators) and willingness to accept (by the victims). Controversial at the time, a mere seven years after the Holocaust, the agreement almost caused a Civil War in Israel (Segev 2000). Moreover, the measure was highly un-popular among the German population and Germany's chancellor, Konrad Adenauer, put his political career at stake by pushing the measures through.

In Israel, the opponents often used the notion of "blood money" when talking about it. On a deeper level, there seems to be a problem with money and reconciliation. However, principles of market society do not have to contradict moral concerns (Sznaider 2000). The German Jewish agreements can serve us to see how money can have a meditative function in the new equation of moral equivalency. Moreover, it serves also as the limiting case for forgiveness and restitution and should be a cautious reminder for those who take it as a model case for other historical contexts.

4. Honor and Money

There is a reason for this widespread opposition between morality, often connected with honor and money. Honor and money, like fire and water, cannot exist together. They are the circulatory media of two very different systems of behavior that are distinguished in both our historical memory and in social theory. Economic behavior is supposed to be self-regarding, rational, and calculative. Honorable behavior is supposed to be undertaken without thought of gain, to be based on intrinsic values, and to be other-regarding. In common parlance, to act honorably is to override one's personal interest and to act on principle. But restitution, by its very nature, must mix the two together.

Honor is appropriate to a world of social hierarchies, which no longer exist. Its attraction lives on even though the world it once regulated is dead. But it is important to emphasize how the concept of honor is inextricably linked to inequality. Charles Taylor makes this point quite clearly in his ex-tended analysis (Taylor 1992). For some to have honor, it is necessary that others must not have it. The bourgeois concept that is analogous to honor is the concept of "dignity." Unlike honor, it applies to everyone. Everyone can have it, everyone can lose it, and everyone can fight for it. It is an egalitarian concept, and is therefore compatible with democratic society. And it is a uni-versalistic concept that is, therefore, compatible with money. Money makes very different things equal. That is the whole point. But it is also exactly what romantics of the left and right hate about it.

However, there is another tradition in social theory, which tries to come to terms with money from a completely different angle. It was Georg Simmel who, in his *Philosophy of Money* (1900), identified money as the means and expression of social abstraction. The abstraction of personal relations results in the much wider nexuses of impersonal relations. Historically, money has been a universal solvent that has replaced personal obligations with services purchased in the market, and thereby freed individuals from particular others by making them more dependent on the whole. This replacement of one large, unbreakable bond by a thousand little bonds is real freedom. It is the history of an increase in the individual's scope of action. At the same time, the extension of the money economy tends to erode inequality through the same process of making people substitutable. It is hard to maintain the ideal of inequality—with some people born to rule, and others born to serve— when people are functionally interchangeable. Money, therefore, tends to extend the concept of equality, insofar as the legitimacy of inequality was based upon a perception of essential differences in the person.

The hatred of the bourgeoisie and its spirit was clear in the works of conservative and leftist thinkers. They denounced the modern world as a world of strangers. Simmel characteristically turned their idea on its head and defended strangerhood as one of the most positive features of the modern world. He thought indifference was a great cultural and historical achievement, and thought that strangership made a positive contribution to the social order. And this brings us straight to the modern global world. When people are strangers, each person gives signs to the others to let them know that he has recognized their existence, but signs which also makes clear in the same instant that the other person is not a special target of curiosity or design. But we only need to add that concept of "civil society" to see what an epochal turning away this is from warrior society. Now we are in a world where people are constantly, without thinking about it, assuring each other of their non-hostile intentions. And this might just be the cultural and social underpinning of the current reparation movement.

At the level of states and ethnic collectivities, money is exchanged for forgiveness. Legal and politically consequential forgiveness are distinct from feelings of forgiveness. And at the level of individuals, the act is one of closure. Money symbolizes the irrevocable admission that a crime has been committed. As Marcel Mauss had already stated in 1925 in his analysis of *The Gift*, symbolic exchanges are relations between people as much or more than they are relations between objects. In the case of restitution, the acceptance of the money symbolizes the acceptance of the giver. And that is an acceptance that would never be possible on the basis of personal relations. Who can forgive the murderer of his grandparents?

5. Forgiveness in Transitional Justice

The question of forgiveness takes on different meanings when situated in the context of state practices. Despite, or maybe because of the pervasive trend for public apologies and forms of national introspection, we need to differentiate the political circumstances under which these practices take place. The relative success of restitution measures greatly depends on particular regime constellations. Especially countries (most prominent are the post-communist cases) under conditions of transitional justice and faced with the daunting task of becoming stable democracies, frequently need to strike a balance between the search for justice and the need for civil and political stability (Mansfield and Snyder, 1995; Snyder and Vinjamuri, 2003). The example of post-war Germany underscores how official restitution attempts did have little effect on preventing former Nazis to play a part in rebuilding the country. It was only later, during the late 1960s, when successful reconstruction and political stability were achieved, that the pervasive failure to punish former Nazis became unacceptable. And it took another two decades before the historical spotlight focused directly on the deeds of the perpetrators (as opposed to the routinized official ritual of mourning its victims).

The political expediency of this development is not confined to Germany or the post-war context. Discussing the recent initiative to create a "Museum of Baathist Crimes" in Iraq, Elizabeth Cole writes: "Numerous studies have shown that reconciliation—the rebuilding of deeply damaged relations between nations, peoples, or faiths—can begin only when peace and stability have been achieved. Once the right conditions are in place, a nation can begin to debate its past. Countries acquainted with difficult transitions can provide expertise on the traditional tools of reconciliation, from the establishment of truth commissions (South Africa, Guatemala), to the creation of documentation centers (Cambodia) on the years of violence [...] In the early days of reconstruction, might Iraq in fact be better off focusing on its distant rather than recent past?" ("Shop of Horrors," *New York Times*, October 21, 2003). There is, in other words, another memory practice, namely that of "restorative forgetting" (Booth 2001).

Thus the question shifts from a quest for absolute justice to one in which states look for the best outcome possible at a given time and in light of available resources. With "best" being measured only against the alternatives, and not in terms of how far they fall short of ultimate goals like "human rights" or justice. There is no internal contradiction between humanitarian goals and the principles of *Realpolitik*, but there could be one between human rights and *Realpolitik*. They may be at antipodes. Human rights are an absolutist framework whose principles admit of no compromise. It provides a set of standards against which all governments can be measured, and against which all will fall short. Arguably, that is appropriate and effective in its proper context. But it is completely inappropriate to the context of providing peace and stability. This could be one of the fundamental reasons why the successor government must always be made out of at least some preexisting elements. The basic strategy will almost always be to back some horses, make acceptable compromises with others, and arrest and exclude entirely a small minority that make compromise impossible. This last group must by definition be small or the operation cannot possibly be accomplished in a limited period of time. Thus, at times, amnesties appear as the right political choice.

The de facto amnesty granted to Nazi officials after the war cannot possibly be squared with the demands of justice, and of course, always looms in the background of such processes. Again, this needs to be decided case by case. Adam Michnik and his fellow activists, who engendered the transformation in Poland, operated with the slogan "Amnesty Yes. Amnesia No" (Michnik and Havel, 1993). Current debates in Argentina (and Peru) about the acceptable balance of memory and prosecution are ultimately decided under the requirements of social and political stability. Amnesties will always contain groups and members of the former regime that are seriously tainted in human rights terms. And this is also where forgiveness as a political principle may come in. A human rights framework that knows no compromise or that sees any trade-off as a damnable dilution of its principles is completely unsuited to apply such a strategy. This is especially important in ethnic struggles all over the globe today. Human Rights principles, we should not forget, are principles of truth. And like the truth, these principles are indivisible.

Could it be that states after transition will grant amnesties and forgive political criminals in the name of peace and stability? Should we allow these decisions to be overturned by an international tribunal? Here one faces the fundamental Hobbesian situation, where civil peace is often more important than morality—where it is often the only precondition that would make real morality possible. This is fundamentally the opposite perspective to that of human rights, which essentially assumes civil peace can never be endangered by its activities—that any amount of mobilization, polarization, and condemnation will never bring about a complete breakdown of the state, but always only purify it. The ultimate reality of the situation is the needs of peace,which means the realities of power. And this is why we need flexible principles, whose essence is to find the best solution given the limits of the situation, and the possibilities at any point of making things worse or not lasting. These principles are designed to lead to the best compromise. They are the right principles to guide our choices even when we are trying to reach humanitarian goals, that is, a society in which people live better, safer, freer, less fearful lives. They are the right principles to organize our thought on such matters. Human rights principles, which are not designed for compromise, may not be. This also leads to a tentative solution to the problem of saving what is good in the human rights tradition, while purifying it of what is often wrong and abused.

6. The Mnemonics of Forgiveness

By the early 1990s, the Nuremberg principles were looming large in both the international reaction to mass atrocities as well as their legal inscription in the International Criminal Court (Levy and Sznaider, 2004). However, the broader significance of these trials and the emerging legalism cannot be reduced to its adjudicatory functions. For Jankélévitch and Améry, trials are not arenas of forgiveness, but a forum where "justice and memory resist the passage of time and deny to it any power of moral/legal absolution" (quoted in Booth 2001, p. 779). In this view, "justice becomes the memory of evil, and it fights a desperate battle against the oblivion that always threatens to engulf it, that gives sanctuary to the perpetrators and a victory to injustice" (Ibid.).

In many ways legal manifestations of forgiveness are but one facet. No less important are memories of justice. W. James Booth suggests that "justice is, in part, a form of remembrance: Memory occupies a vital place at the heart of justice and its struggle to keep the victims, crimes, and perpetrators among the unforgotten" (Ibid., p. 777). In this view, "justice as the institutionalized remembrance of the past is seen here, as in other truth commissions, as a duty to the dead and as a condition of reconciliation" (Ibid., p. 778). Contrary to those who view memory as merely ephemeral, Booth argues "that this memory-justice at once informs core judicial practices and ranges beyond them in a manner that leaves judicial closure incomplete. It reminds us of a duty to keep crimes and their victims from the oblivion of forgetting, of a duty to restore, preserve, and acknowledge the just order of the world" (Ibid., p. 777).

This view is evidenced in the "mnemonic turn" that we observe during the last decade or so. New concepts began floating into the discourse about forgiveness. Concepts like healing, reconciliation, restitution, peace, and truth. Trauma and its overcoming, take over the place of justice and its administration. Memory is turning into a key-organizing concept of those processes. Political and legal theory has done a decisive Freudian turn (Teitel 2003). Truth commissions, public debates, and restitution claims, and not the courtroom alone, became models for this process. Let us briefly elaborate on the relationship between law and memory as it casts an important light on the possibilities of justice and forgiveness.

Elsewhere we have discussed in detail the seminal role of Holocaust representations and the emergence of what we call "cosmopolitan memories" (Levy and Sznaider, 2002, 2005). We analyzed the distinctive forms that collective memories take in the age of globalization, focusing on the transition from national to cosmopolitan memory cultures. Cosmopolitanism refers to a process of "internal globalization" through which global concerns become part of local experiences of an increasing number of people. Global media representations, among others, create new cosmopolitan memories, providing new epistemological vantage points, and emerging moral-political interdependencies. We traced the historical roots of this transformation through an examination of how the Holocaust has been remembered in different countries. Nothing legitimizes human rights work more than the slogan "Never Again!" And behind that imperative is the memory of the Holocaust. It is a mark of just how deeply that memory has saturated our everyday consciousness that the phrase "Never Again" does not require any further specification for us to know what it refers to. The very notion of these rights grew directly out of what was then considered its worst breach, namely the crimes of the Nazis. Hence, the United Nations Universal Declaration of Human Rights from the year 1948 says in its preamble: "whereas disregard and contempt for human rights have resulted in barbarous acts which have outraged the conscience of mankind . . . " And this connection between Human Rights and the Holocaust, especially in the European and American contexts, poses problems of compromise and power politics. Judicialism will, therefore, face the problem of being part of politics and be part of morality at the same time. The Rule of Law might not be the last answer.

It is precisely the abstract nature of "good and evil" that symbolizes the Holocaust, we argue, which contributes to the extraterritorial quality of cosmopolitan memory. The historical details of this development cannot be discussed here. What matters, for our purpose, is to direct attention to how the Holocaust has been remembered through institutions and the ritualistic power of criminal trials. These memories, based on a shared negative sentiment of the catastrophe, are not only able to produce despair at the modern world, but also actually help enlightened ideas to come to the fore (Rorty 1993). It is a sentiment based on a universality that is not derived from reason, but rather based on common experiences of human wrongs. "Human wrongs are everywhere; all societies find it easier to recognize and agree upon what constitute wrongs elsewhere than they do rights; wrongs are universal in a way rights are not" (Booth 1999, p. 62), and as such they are "a new, welcome fact of the post-Holocaust world" (Rorty 1993, p. 115).

At this point, the Holocaust has been reconfigured as a de-contextualized event. Memories of the Holocaust shape the articulation of a new rights culture. Once this new rights culture is in place, it no longer needs to rely on its original articulation (in this case, the memory of the Holocaust), but it assumes strong normative powers. The Holocaust memory and the new rights culture are, in other words, mutually constitutive. To be sure, this is not by necessity but as the result of particular historical conjunctures (the end of the Cold War, the Balkan wars of the 1990s, as well as the failed attempts by this new human rights regime to prevent acts of ethnic cleansing and genocide). The term Holocaust has passed from an abstract universal, to a set of very particularistic and/or national meanings, back to what we have elsewhere referred to as cosmopolitan memories. The Holocaust is now a concept that has been dislocated from space and time precisely because it can be used to dramatize any act of injustice, racism, or crime perpetrated anywhere on the planet. The anti-Communism that justified intervention during the Cold War had to be replaced with something after its end. And in this new context, human rights seem to be fitting the bill. The idea of genocide contains the admonition that a moral world cannot stand idly by, while others are destroyed.

7. Conclusion

Despite its European origins and a western dominance, it would be erroneous to conceive of these developments as a new form of "moral Imperialism." Judging by the multitude of experiences in different parts of the world, global discourse about forgiveness and restitution does not seem to be based on an absolute universalistic ethic. It is the product of negotiations with the respective other. The recent case of Rwanda is a case in point. It shows that even an internationally established tribunal, such as the International Criminal Tribunal for Rwanda, recognizes the need to adjust to local jurisprudence, as is evidenced in recognizing the decision of the Rwandan government to work together with civil society on the implementation of the informal "gacaca" courts. Ultimately, this entails the coexistence of local and global standards of jurisdiction.

This dialogue, therefore, entails a reassessment of prevalent dichotomies such as the local and the global or the juxtaposition of the universal and the particular. Forgiveness and debates about restitution do not presume a universally valid legal or normative notion, but it is the mutual recognition that provides the basis for reconciliation and the foundation for a shared experience. In other words, it is not a universal morality, but instead we are witnesses to a global genesis of conditions of forgiveness that are shaped through the dialogue with the local. It is, oftentimes, an ad hoc conception of justice that incorporates a globalized Human Rights culture into respective local and particular negotiations.

References

Améry, Jean. 1977. "Ressentiments." In *Jenseits von Schuld und Sühne. Bewältigungsversuche eines Überwältigten*. Stuttgart: Klett-Cota.

Arendt, Hannah. 1945. "Organized Guilt and Universal Responsibility." In *Essays in Understanding*, 121–132. New York: Harcourt, 1994.

Arendt, Hannah. 1958. "Irreversibility and the Power to Forgive." In *The Human Condition*, 236–243. Chicago: Chicago University Press.

Barkan, Elazar. 2000. *The Guilt of Nations*. New York: Norton.

Booth, W. James. 1999. "Communities of Memory: On Identity, Memory and Debt." *American Political Science Review* 93 (1999): 249–263.

Booth, W. James. 2001. "The Unforgotten: Memories of Justice." *American Political Science Review* 95, 4: 777–791.

Cole, Elizabeth. 2003. "Shop of Horrors." *New York Times*, October 21.

Derrida, Jacques. 2001. *On Cosmopolitanism and Forgiveness*. London: Routledge.

Digeser, Peter. 2001. *Political Forgiveness*. Ithaca: Cornell University Press.

Diner, Dan. 2000. "On Guilt Discourse and Other Narrations." In *Beyond the Conceivable: Studies on Germany, Nazism, and the Holocaust*. Berkeley: University of California Press.

Fine, Robert. 2000. "Crimes Against Humanity: Hannah Arendt and the Nuremberg Debates." *European Journal of Social Theory* 3, 3: 293–311.

Heyd, David. 2001. "The Charitable Perspective: Forgiveness and Toleration as Supererogatory." *Canadian Journal of Philosophy* 31, 4: 567–586.

Ignatieff, Michael. 1997. *The Warrior's Honor: Ethnic War and the Modern Conscience.* New York: Metropolitan Books.

Jaspers, Karl. 1946. *Über die Schuldfrage.* München: Piper, 1986.

Jankélévitch, Vladimir. 1996. "Should We Pardon Them?" *Critical Inquiry* 22, 3: 552–572.

Levy, Daniel and Natan Sznaider. 2005. *Memory in the Global Age: The Holocaust and Memory in the Global Age.* Philadelphia: Temple University Press.

Levy, Daniel and Natan Sznaider. 2004. "The Institutionalization of Cosmopolitan Morality: The Holocaust and Human Rights." *Journal of Human Rights* 3, 2: 143–157.

Levy, Daniel and Natan Sznaider. 2002. "Memory Unbound: The Holocaust and the Formation of Cosmopolitan Memory." *European Journal of Social Theory* 5, 1: 87–106.

Mansfield, Edward D., and Jack Snyder. 1995. "Democratization and the Danger of War." *International Security* 20, 5: 5–38.

Mauss, Marcel. 1925. *The Gift: The Form and Reason for Exchange in Archaic Societies.* New York: Norton, 2000.

Michnik, Adam and Vaclav Havel. 1993. "Justice or Revenge?" *Journal of Democracy* 7, 4: 20–27.

Murphy, Jeffrie G. 1988. "Forgiveness and Resentment." In J.G. Murphy, and J. Hampton, eds., *Forgiveness and Mercy.* Cambridge: Cambridge University Press.

Rabinbach, Anson. 2001. *In the Shadow of Catastrophe. German Intellectuals between Apocalypse and Enlightenment.* Berkeley: University of California Press.

Rorty, Richard. 1993. "Human Rights, Rationality and Sentimentality" In S. Shute and S.Hurley, eds., *On Human Rights.* New York: The Oxford Amnesty Lectures, Basic Books.

Simmel, Georg. 1900. *Die Philosophie des Geldes.* Frankfurt: Surhkamp, 2001.

Segev, Tom. 2000. *The Seventh Million. The Israelis and the Holocaust.* New York: Owl Books.

Snyder, Jack, and Leslie Vinjamuri. 2003. "Principle and Pragmatism in Strategies of International Justice." *Paper presented at the Conference on Promises and Pitfalls of International Courts,* Bellagio, Italy.

Sznaider, Natan. 2000. *The Compassionate Temperament: Care and Cruelty in Modern Society.* Boulder, CO.: Rowman & Littlefield.

Taylor, Charles. 1992. *Multiculturalism and the Politics of Recognition.* Princeton: Princeton University Press.

Teitel, Ruti. 2003 "Humanity's Law: Rule of Law for the New Global Politics." *Cornell International Law Journal* 35, 2: 355–387.

Tutu, Desmond. 2000. *No Future Without Forgiveness.* New York: Doubleday.

Weber, Max. 1958. "Politics as a Vocation." In H. H. Gerth and C. Wright Mills, trans., and ed., *From Max Weber: Essays in Sociology,* 77–128. New York: Oxford University Press.

CHAPTER 5

The Transitional Apology

RUTI TEITEL

My book, *Transitional Justice*,[1] explores the question of the relationship between various forms of accountability to the prospects for transition to more
liberal regimes. At the time of the book's writing, I focused only briefly on the
role of apologies; therefore, I welcome the opportunity to explore further this
particular form of response. I want to pursue here the significance of what I
term the "transitional apology."

To begin, consider some of the comments made by Elazar Barkan and
Alexander Karn in their introduction regarding the extent to which we now
find ourselves in a period that could be characterized as reflecting a "political
discourse of apology." Toward the end of the last century, and in the beginning
of the new millennium, it is evident that we are in a period of heightened
political transition: of political liberalization and regime change.[2] In many
regions, the contemporary period has been accompanied by an extraordinary
explosion of apologies: unprecedented World War II-related apologies by the
Presidents of Switzerland[3] and Austria,[4] the Prime Ministers of Belgium[5] and
Japan;[6] by the Polish President for actions taken against its Jewish citizens; by
England's Queen for the excesses of imperialism, by the Church for colonialism, by President Clinton for American involvement in Central America,[7]
and for noninvolvement in Africa.[8] The list is extensive. At present, there
is an evident social demand for apologies, which only seems to accelerate.
Although I shall elaborate on some of these further on, here I only want
to provide a flavor of the breadth of the contemporary transitional apology,
which culminates years of political discourse.

In what follows, I shall explore the meaning of what I here term the
"transitional apology." The central claim that I shall elaborate is that the
transitional apology constitutes a leading ritual of political transformation.
While in my prior book, *Transitional Justice*, I discussed various alternative
modalities chiefly in the law: trials, constitutions, reparations, and historical
accountings—the apology, too, merits independent attention for its role in

mediating regimes; in enabling a response to the past, while, at the same time, offering a path to a changed future. Like other practices discussed in my book as transitional responses, the apology is also a public statement that can advance transformation in the collective.

I shall discuss four dimensions of the transitional apology here: first, the apology as an exercise of executive power, elaborating upon the vesting of the apology powers in the state's chief political actor; second, the distinctive role of the apology in, and its connection to, periods of political transition; third, the transitional apology's association with political liberalization, that is, this response's distinctive contribution to advancing the path to democracy; and finally, the contemporary transitional apology's relation to a politics of globalization.

1. The Executive Apology

First, I shall argue here for recognition of the modern transitional apology as an independent political power, which is generally situated in the state executive, its top political actor. Historically, the apology can be seen to be a power belonging to the monarch. The historical connection between the king and the exercise of the apology lays the foundation for the modern executive apology power. As discussed in historical work, this relationship dates back to the Middle Ages and to the medieval understanding of the relationship the king bears to the body politic.[9]

The executive apology power, which I shall explicate here, relates to other more clearly defined executive powers: such as, the power of execution of justice; the pardon power, and the foreign policy making power (that is, including treaty and war powers). The apology power, it is contended here, even if not explicitly recognized in prevailing constitutional authority, can arguably be implied from these other powers. The apology power lies at the convergence of these three executive powers. These powers come together in the executive apology during political transitions. Clearly then, the presidential apology, building upon the pardon power, reflects the idea of perfecting justice. Consider that the transitional apology incorporates the notion of general binding law, while at the same time offering the possibility of the transcendence of the law. Moreover, the transitional apology, building upon the executive pardon powers, creates the conditions for forgiveness within the justice system. The transitional apology's complex dimensions—as both within and beyond justice—clarifies the distinctive executive role in the exercise of foreign policy making.[10]

The executive has special competence regarding these twin aspects of transition in the pursuit of justice in periods of political flux: not only for the law's execution, and its enforcement, but also, beyond the law, in the service of the broader aims of justice.

A core dimension of the executive apology power goes to its performance, and to the way this power is embodied, quintessentially so, in a unitary political entity with multiple representative, performative, and symbolic functions. In this regard, there is a historical nexus between the king and his country, the executive power, and the modern state.

Last, I will discuss instances of the exercise of the modern apology and, in particular, distinctions between the apology's historical, monarchical, and democratic uses in contemporary politics.

2. Apology as a Ritual of Transition

I now turn to explore dimensions of the performance of these apologies. Consider the nexus between the monarchical and the presidential apology. Within the common law, the king was conceived as having two bodies.[11] This concept informed both legal and political conceptualizations of the state and its justice system. In common-law England, the leading legal advisor, Blackstone, wrote about this idea, interpreting medieval theory in terms of the body of the monarch as reflecting the political collective.[12] Perhaps, the most famous historical example was epitomized in the reign of King Richard. So, Shakespeare wrote of King Richard and his performance of an act of contrition, "undoing" his political authority. Richard states:

> Now mark me, how I will undo myself; / I give this heavy weight from off my head / And this unwieldy scepter from my hand, / The pride of kingly sway from out my heart; / With mine own tears I wash away my balm, / With mine own hands I give away my crown, / With mine own tongue deny my sacred state, / With mine own breath release all duty's rites: / All pomp and majesty I do foreswear; / My manors, rents, revenues I forego; / My acts, decrees, and statutes I deny: / God pardon all oaths that are broke to me!"[13]

Consider the trial of King Charles I as an instance of the performance of justice on the body of the king, while also allowing continuity in the body politic.[14] Incorporation of the political collective—through the body of the executive—offers a significant potentiality in transition, as the idea of a dual body can help to mediate between regimes.

The modern apology builds on these historical forms. More and more, the executive apology constitutes a symbol of the construction of transition. Like the king, the president can be conceived in terms of two bodies: Through this legal and political fiction, when the executive apologizes, it can perform more than one function—it is for himself in his natural mode; or, on behalf of the political body.

Consider here the role of the presidential apology for the body politic, as a distinctive exercise of executive powers and, in particular, in the construct of his twin bodies, the private and the political. The executive enables performance of the exercise of the apology power. Through his apology as speech act,[15] the executive mediates the state's past and present, and allows the construction of a line in political time. Transitional apologies allow for both discontinuity and continuity in the body politic. Through the apology, the president can perform a symbolic defrocking and, at the same time, a diminishment of political authority associated with the predecessor regime in order to reestablish, and re-legitimate the political regime.

The executive apology offers a useful tool of political transformation. Exercise of the official apology relates primarily to political offenses, which have been used, largely, in periods of political flux. As a matter of political practice, what emerges in such periods is the dynamic connection between the apology power contended for here, and the hitherto recognized pardon power.[16] Indeed, the authority granted for the pardoning power was historically intended precisely for such transitional periods.[17] Thus, to illustrate, going back to the American founding, Alexander Hamilton wrote that the most fertile time for the exercise of the executive pardon power was in periods of transition.[18] Moreover, the executive associated with the successor regime was conceived to be the preeminent political actor for the exercise of the pardon power. So, for example, Reconstruction, the United States' post-Civil War period, illuminates the greatest exercise of the presidential pardoning power, whereby successor presidents embarked on a policy of pardon of the predecessor Confederate regime, despite the gains of the Union, as part of the spirit of a conciliatory political transition.[19] An analogy can be seen in the modern transitional presidential apology.

The emerging power, which I characterize here as the "apology power," shares with the pardon power the idea of a political dimension constituting a norm that exists beyond established legal processes. The political exercise of these powers contributes a certain flexibility in transitional justice, particularly important in periods of political change. Understanding this transitional practice is facilitated by the conception of the executive's two bodies, which allows for the differentiation of treatment of actions considered, in principle, as private, from those deemed to belong to the public domain. In this regard, one might reflect upon former United States President Clinton's exercise of the apology power. Despite his general reluctance to apologize for private behavior, there was a contrasting willingness to apologize in the political realm.

If we were to examine the extraordinarily rich survey of apologies in the last decade, we would note the distinctive form in which the executive may debase or degrade his body as a performative symbol of political contrition. Consider what constitutes perhaps the most memorable of the historical political apologies. This comes from Willy Brandt, the "Peace Chancellor," and his attempts to produce reconciliation with the East through the Moscow treaty, and also between Germany and Poland through the Warsaw treaty.[20] In the context of the treaty signing, Brandt visited the Warsaw ghetto in Poland, where he apparently spontaneously fell to his knees. Because of the form it took, this executive apology became instantly mediatized. In Brandt's memoirs, he wrote, "I had not planned anything [...] the feeling that I must express the exceptional significance of the ghetto memorial from the bottom of the abyss of German history under the burden of millions of victims of murder, I did what human beings do when speech fails them."[21] According to a reporter's account: "Then he who does not need to kneel knelt, on behalf of all who do need to kneel but do not—because they dare not, or cannot, or cannot dare to kneel."[22]

"Then he who does not need to kneel knelt," captures something of the symbolic significance of the apology of the chancellor, and, perhaps, more particularly, of the role of the executive. After this landmark apology, Brandt went on to sign the Warsaw treaty, initiating the beginnings of unification with East Germany. This initiative toward the goals of peace and reconciliation would later be recognized in the Nobel Prize. The apology stands out as a preeminent example of its kind. Later on, in a similar gesture, Germany's President Johannes Rau visited Israel's Parliament and asked for his nation's forgiveness for the Holocaust.[23] Next, Rau went to the hills of Marzabotto, Italy, the site of a World War II massacre, to ask for forgiveness once more for German atrocities.[24] In a more contemporary illustration, Indonesia's President Abdurrahman Wahid, while laying a wreath at the Santa Cruz cemetery site of the 1991 massacre, apologized for the country's occupation of East Timor.[25]

Another illustration of the performance of an executive apology, in its modern monarchical form, occurred at the time of Queen Elizabeth's long-deferred visit to India. Despite longstanding demands for recognition of England's imperial role, it would not be until 1997, when the Queen, for the first time, would pay homage at the site of a colonial massacre (Amritsar), which had occurred almost ninety years before. Some political leaders found the action absurd, because, as they put it, "the Queen had played no part in the event."[26] Nevertheless, representatives of the victims of the massacre reported feeling vindication in the Queen's speech and in her ceremonial role in representing the body politic.[27] At the very least, the apology was understood to perform limited accountability in a symbolic function.

To date, there are ninety-four instances of Pope John Paul's apologies[28] regarding, among other things, the Inquisition, the Crusades, the persecution of Jews, the religious wars, and the treatment of women.[29] Through this ritual the Pope had performed contrition and had sought to enable "transition" in the public perception of the institution of the church. In spring 2000, a sweeping papal apology pleaded for repentance for the Church's errors over the last two millennia.[30] In this "millennial" apology, the Pope was accompanied by several cardinals and bishops who cited the key lapses, which included a great variety of injustices to indigenous peoples, women, immigrants, and the poor.[31] The apology was made a part of the Lenten service, thus building upon a preexisting ritual of sacrifice and constituting a symbolic form of degradation of authority, aimed at forgiveness and reconciliation.

Thus, from diverse quarters, there is a surge in transitional apologies.

3. Democracy's Turn

Above, I have discussed diverse executive apologies, which appear to reflect a form of political transformation. However, hitherto, these were discussed without much differentiation in the character of the political regime in the represented collective. Therefore, I shall now endeavor to develop further the relationship of the apology to the political body characterized by the contemporary democratic state.

Here, I seek to trace the historical development of the apology power from its monarchical provenance to its modern form. In particular, I examine the apology's core political dimension in modern democracies as well as in transitions between hierarchic and more democratic arrangements. What becomes evident is the flexibility of the apology as a transitional mechanism. A core distinction in the modern executive apology power is that, while the authority of the monarchical pardon and the related apology power historically derived from the sense of the king's innate superior ability to perfect justice, in the contemporary moment, the executive power reflects, instead, the recognition of the executive's authority in the delegation of democratic processes. Accordingly, in its modern form, the apology process necessarily depends on the prior action of other political actors involved in processes of investigation, laying the foundation for the apology's exercise. Thus, over the last ten to fifteen years, the role of the executive in transitions has been to ratify findings arrived at by diverse truth commissions, historical commissions, and preexisting established commissions of governmental accountability. The apology power, as it is exercised by the modern presidency, implies a complex interaction with other political actors, institutions, and processes involved primarily in the justice system. In its final phases, the executive performs the political ritual of exercise of the apology power.

There are many contemporary examples of this gradual process. The leading one in the United States concerns the World War II-related Japanese-American internment. The inquiry into this history, and its civil rights abuses, was long delayed, and was brought to the country's attention only through journalistic investigation, the organization and advocacy efforts of the Japanese-American community, and, ultimately, congressional hearings. Only at the end of this process, in 1988, was an apology called for on behalf of the people of the United States.[32] That apology would be performed by the executive, in a series of administrations,[33] of President George Bush,[34] and, subsequently, of Bill Clinton.[35] Both presidents expressed an apology, in their own terms, but on the country's behalf.[36] Further, the Civil Liberty Act amendments of 1992, with its commitment to reparations, accompanied every letter to the internees, which also included an executive apology clarifying the significance of the payments in their political context.[37]

Transitional presidential apologies build on a predicate of historical governmental investigations. Through the transitional apology, the executive's role is to ratify and affirm the democratic findings of the people. Beyond this, what will constitute the "critical facts" underlying the exercise of the apology will depend in large part on the political nature of the repression in any given regime. In a leading illustration, that is, post-military junta Chile, the relevant information found by the truth commission there concerned the finding that, contrary to the prior regime's political propaganda, the victims were not "enemies of the state," but instead, unarmed civilians. This finding became a critical part of President Patricio Aylwin's apology, which was performed within the very stadium where the political detainees had previously been held.[38] This geographical juxtaposition was used to create a critical "inversion," the "undoing" of prior repression, performed through the presidential apology.

In recent decades, with the fall of authoritarian and communist rule, there are many other illustrations of this sort of transitional apology following the reopening and investigation of these questions in a host of transitions, from Central America to Africa. There was fairly explicit endorsement by President Clinton regarding the findings of the Guatemala Commission concerning the role of the United States in that region. The South African Truth and Reconciliation Commission (TRC) triggered a rather weak presidential apology. After new research and the revelations of a book documenting the World War II massacre of hundreds of Jews in 1941, Poland's President, Aleksander Kwasniewski, apologized for the actions of his people.[39] On a visit to the National Holocaust Museum, Argentine President Fernando De La Rua apologized for that country's historical World War II-related behavior supportive of the Nazi-regime. He declared that his act of contrition would be critical to the prevention of other forms of xenophobia and racism.[40] Whether or not it would have that prospective liberalizing effect, the apology's significance at the time derived from its having been the first time Argentine leadership acknowledged its historical behavior toward its minority (Jewish) community.

The instances discussed above reflect the provenance of the modern apology deriving from a more extended democratic process, involving other representative bodies, which exercise apology-related investigatory powers often delegated by the executive. In the process of the execution of the law regulating the apology, investigative powers may well be delegated to a historical or investigatory commission, but, ultimately, competence is often returned to the executive to engage in the exercise and performance of the political apology.

4. The Apology Goes Global

This last part discusses the contemporary apology, in its contemporary manifestation, where it has taken the form of what I term the "global apology." The most contemporary role of the transitional apology proposed here concerns its relation to new globalizing practices. Recent phenomena reflect that the contemporary apology's role transcends the purposes and parameters of the nation-state. These transnational apologies reflect the new global interdependencies and the reality of shared responsibility for contemporary political catastrophes. By extension, these apologies also illuminate this political practice's constructive potential to the attribution of political responsibility and, similarly, sovereignty. An illustration is afforded in former President Bill Clinton's apologies, as well as those of Secretary General Kofi Annan for the United Nations. Both actors' apologies display dimensions of the modern apology's global character and its role in the construction of political responsibility in contemporary global politics. In particular, these apologies related to the present status and power, even where foregone, and therefore implied responsibility of the United Nations and the United States as two players with the potential for substantial humanitarian intervention through military action with the aim of reconciliation and peacemaking. In their global variant, the new apology powers transcend the traditional monarchical notion of the political body, as well as that of the more modern executive president, representing a body politic with dominion over a certain territory and its sovereign constituencies. By contrast, the global apology extends not only to the representation of a particular state's citizenry, but also to nonnationals and to other peoples for actions taking place extraterritorially; that is, for political conduct, which is deemed to somehow implicate transnational responsibility. The apology constitutes a sign of a new understanding of political responsibility, namely, of "effective control,"[41] a de facto recognition that, in global politics, political sovereignty and, therefore, responsibility are becoming de-territorialized, and therefore, no longer exclusively, or even primarily, associated with the contiguity of state borders.

There are numerous illustrations of the contemporary global apology proposed here. Thus, for example, President Clinton's apologies well reflect the role of his presidency in supporting a range of political democratization, contributing to his being perceived as a president of transition. For instance, following the Guatemalan commission report, Clinton declared: "for the United States it is important that I state clearly that support for military forces or intelligence units which engage in violence and fights for repression of the kind that is described in the report, was wrong and the United States must not repeat that mistake."[42] This was the first clear acknowledgment from the top of the political echelon of the fact of American involvement in repression in Latin America. Moreover, the apology was coupled with a Presidential call for forward-looking change in foreign policy, an area in the executive prerogative. Finally, President Clinton went on to commit $25,000,000, to processes of peace and reconciliation, a form of reparations complementing the apology.

The global apology's potential in the construction of political responsibility is plainly seen in statements regarding the Rwandan genocide, concerning the failure of intervention in an area not often considered to be a traditional domain for the United States. Therefore, it was significant to have the then president make the statement: "that the killings were not spontaneous or accidental,"[43] but, rather, occasioned in part as a result of negligence in the international community. The apology's language recognized that, after the killing began, together with the international community, the United States did not act quickly enough. Beyond its backward-looking dimension, the President's apology was also forward-looking, as it directed his administration, together with the international community, to improve its capacity to identify genocide, so that there could be a greater awareness of impending threats. Further, there was a commitment to remedy the effects of the genocide in Rwanda, to address the justice system, and to advance the International Tribunals for the former Yugoslavia, and for Rwanda.[44] There are reported admissions of negligence around the world, and a brief reference to the ongoing neglect of the entire region of Africa.[45] In a time of globalization, primarily but not exclusively in the economy,[46] former President Clinton was early to recognize the political fallout of economic globalization; and more specifically, the implied responsibility attendant to promoting market change throughout the world, through the contemporary global apology. That the new balance of power is clarified through these practices suggests the assumption of responsibility in these ways and is a form of expression of de facto "effective" control.

The apology's globalization is further illustrated in United Nations Secretary General Kofi Annan's apologies on behalf of the leading international body.[47] Annan was the first to call for an independent inquiry into the actions of the United Nations during the 1994 genocide in Rwanda.[48] At the conclusion of this inquiry, and building on its findings, Secretary-General Annan apologized on behalf of the United Nations. Similar statements were made concerning the Srebrenica massacre, where so many died because of the absence of adequate protection at the so-called "safe havens," ostensibly in the care of the United Nations.[49] Annan also referred to the absence of political will in the international community, as well as the lack of adequate United Nations resources, and a failure by the United Nations system as a whole. In his forward-looking statement, Annan called for the need to improve the United Nations system.[50] Ultimately, Annan would use these instances to call for a new doctrine of humanitarian intervention, recognizing the changed responsibility of the United Nations and the international community, in an age of political fragmentation and global politics.[51]

5. Conclusion

To conclude, the pervasiveness of transitional apologies in the last two decades of transition appears to recognize the avertability of contemporary political violence, and that policy making, however erroneous, is at stake. Accordingly, these contemporary apologies represent the notion that, somehow, action, whether by individual or collective actors, could have changed the course of history: that, somehow, something could have been done. The liberal line implicitly being recognized is that, at this moment, from the vantage point of history, there is a hope that things will be different. It is this core belief that lies at the crux of the connection between the transitional apology power, and a liberalizing politics.

Notes

1. See Ruti Teitel, 2000, *Transitional Justice* (Oxford University Press).

2. Id. at pp. 229–230.

3. See Associated Press, "Swiss Admit Guilt for Rejecting Jews Fleeing Nazis,"*Chicago Tribune*, May 8, 1995, at p. N16 (formal apology by President Kaspar Villiger).

4. See Associated Press, "Austria Issues an Apology for Holocaust Role,"*Toronto Star*, November 16, 1994, at p. A21 (Austria's Presidential apology for the country's role in the Holocaust).

5. See MATP, "PM Apology to Jews," *The Daily Telegraph*, October 8, 2002 at p. 19 ("Prime Minister Guy Verhofstedt made country's first official apology").

6. On the fiftieth anniversary of World War II, at the Yakasuni Shrine, holding the ashes of the war dead, Japanese Prime Minister Tomiichi Murayama apologized for his country's conduct, expressing his "feelings of deep remorse." See Charles A. Radin, "Japan Makes First Apology for Conduct in WWII," *The Boston Globe*, August 15, 1995, at p. 1.

7. See John M. Broder, "Clinton offers his Apologies to Guatemala," *New York Times*, March 11, 1999, at p. A1.

8. See*Public Papers of the Presidents*, "Remarks at the Kisowera School in Mukono, Uganda," 34, *Weekly Comp. Pres. Doc.* 490, March 24, 1998 (regarding Uganda); see also*Public Papers of the Presidents*, "Remarks Honoring Genocide Survivors in Kigali, Rwanda," 34, *Weekly Comp. Pres. Doc.* 495, March 25, 1998 (regarding inaction in Rwanda).

9. See infra note 10.

10. On the moral and political significance of political acknowledgement in transitions see Thomas Nagel in "State Crimes: Punishment or Pardon, Papers and Report of the Conference," November 4–6, 1988, WYE Center, Maryland 93 (Alice Henkin ed., Aspen Institute, 1989).

11. See Ernst H. Kantorowicz, 1997, *The King's Two Bodies: A Study in Medieaval Political Theology* (Princeton University Press).

12. See William Blackstone, *Commentaries on the Laws of England: In Four Books* (Clarendon Press 4th ed., 1770) (1765).

13. See William Shakespeare, "Richard II." In Stanley Wells and Gary Taylor, eds., 1988, *William Shakespeare: The Complete Works: Compact Edition* 388 (Clarendon Press).

14. See David Lagomarsino and Charles Tiwood, 1989, *The Trial Of Charles I: A Documentary History* (Hanover, N.H.: University Press of New England).

15. See Judith Butler, 1997, *Excitable Speech: A Politics of the Performative* (Routledge Press).

16. See, e.g., United States Constitution. Art. II, § 2.

17. Presented as periods of insurrection, see*The Federalist No. 74* (Alexander Hamilton).

18. Id.

19. For discussion of the role of pardons in periods of transition see Ruti Teitel, 2000, *Transitional Justice*, pp. 152–154 (Oxford University Press); see also Jonathan T. Dorris, *Pardon and Amnesty Under Lincoln and Johnson: The Restoration of the Confederates to Their Rights and Privileges 1861–1898* (WestPoint, Conn.,: Greenwood Press, 1953) 1997.

20. Warsaw Treaty, December 7, 1970, F.R.G.-Pol., 830 U.N.T.S. 327.

21. See Willy Brandt, 1992, *My Life In Politics* (Hamish Hamilton Press).

22. Id.at p. 200.

23. See Rebecca Trounson, "German President Visits Israel, Seeks Forgiveness,"*Los Angeles Times*, February 17, 2000, at p. A13 ("with the people of Israel watching, I bow my head in humility").

24. See Bruce Johnston and Toby Helm, "Germany Says Sorry for Italian Massacre,"*The Daily Telegraph*, April 18, 2002, at p. 16.

25. See Joanna Jolly, "Wahid Apologises for Massacres in East Timor,"*The Independent* (London), March 1, 2000 at p. 16; see also*Asiaweek*, "Living Together," March 17, 2000, available at http://www.asiaweek.com/asiaweek/magazine/2000/0317/ed.living.html ("we as a nation have made mistakes").

26. See John F. Burns, "In India, Queen Bows Her Head Over a Massacre in 1919," *New York Times*, October 15, 1997, at p. A6.

27. Id.

28. Mary Ann Glendon, "Public Acts of Contrition in the Age of Spin Control," *Tertium Millenium*, N.3/July 1997 at p. 26, available at http://www.vatican.va/jubilee_2000/magazine/documents/ju_mag_01071997_p-2_en.html.

29. Id.

30. See Alessandra Stanley, "Pope Asks for Forgiveness for Errors of Church over 2,000 Years," *NewYork Times*, March 13, 2000, at p. A1.

31. Id. Pope John Paul's first message over the Internet was an apology. Via e-mail, the pope sent an apology to victims of sexual abuse, as well as for the excesses for evangelization, and, finally, to the aboriginal community. Consider that this recognition of shameful injustice was performed in a medium that tends to render nontransparent the trappings of authority.

32. Katherine Bishop, "Day of Apology and 'Sigh of Relief'," *New York Times*, August 11, 1988, at p. A16.

33. *Public Papers of the Presidents*, "Remarks on Signing the Bill Providing Restitution for Wartime Relocation and Internment of Civilians," 24, *Weekly Comp. Pres. Doc.* 1034, August 10, 1988; see also *Public Papers of the Presidents*, "Statement on the Dedication of the National Japanese-American Memorial," 36, *Weekly Comp. Pres. Doc.* 2834, November 9, 2000.

34. Civil Liberties Act Amendments of 1992, H.R. 4551 1992, 102 H.R. 4551, Pub.L. No 102–371, 106 Stat. 1167.

35. *Public Papers of the Presidents*, "Statement on the Dedication of the National Japanese-American Memorial," 36, *Weekly Comp. Pres. Doc.* 2834, November 9, 2000.

36. Compare the Letter from George Bush, President of the United States of America, to Japanese Americans incarcerated during World War II (October 1990), available at http://www.imdiversity.com/villages/asian/Article_Detail.asp?Article_ID+3267; with the Letter from Bill Clinton, President of the United States of America, to Japanese Americans incarcerated during World War II (October 1990), available at http://www.imdiversity.com/villages/asian/Article_Detail.asp?Article_ID+3267.

37. Civil Liberties Act Amendments of 1992, H.R. 4551 1992, 102 H.R. 4551, Pub.L. No. 102–371, 106 Stat. 1167.

38. See Ruti Teitel, 2000, *Transitional Justice* at p. 84 (Oxford University Press).

39. See Marcin Grajewski, "Poland Apologizes for WWII Pogrom,"*The Jerusalem Post*, July 11, 2001, at p. 1.

40. See*Spanish Newswire Services, De La Rua Pide Disculpas por Relacion de Argentina con Nazis*, June 13, 2000.

41. See "Draft Statute for the International Criminal Court," UN Doc. A/Conf.183/2/Add.1 (1998) art. 25, available at http://www.un.org/icc/index.htm.

42. See "Guatemala Memory Of Silence: Report of the Commission for Historical Clarification Conclusions and Recommendations" (Guatemalan Commission for Historical Clarification, February 25, 1999), available at http://shr.aaas.org/guatemala/ceh/report/english/.

43. See supra regarding Rwanda, note xliv.

44. "Statute of the International Tribunal for the Prosecution of Persons Responsible for Serious Violations of International Humanitarian Law Committed in the Territory of the Former Yugoslavia Since 1991," S.C. *Res.* 827, *UN SCOR*, 48th Sess., 3217th mtg., UN Doc. S/25704, Annex (1993), as amended by S.C. *Res.* 1166, UN SCOR, Annex, UN Doc. S/RES/1166 (1998), reprinted in 32 ILM 1192 (1993), Statute

of the International Tribunal for Rwanda, *S.C. Res.* 955, UN SCOR, 49th Sess., 3453rd mtg., UN Doc. S/RES/955 (1994), reprinted in 33 I.L.M. 1598 (1994). Statute of the International Tribunal for Rwanda, *S.C. Res.* 955, UN SCOR, 49th Sess., 3453rd mtg., UN Doc. S/RES/955 (1994), reprinted in 33 I.L.M. 1598 (1994).

45. See supra regarding Uganda, note 4.

46. Id.

47. See Serge Schmemann, "Nobel Peace Prize is Awarded to Annan and U.N.," *New York Times*, October 13, 2001, at A1; see also "Kofi Annan and the United Nations: Nobel Peace Prize Laureates," October 13, 2001, for rising "to such new challenges as HIV/AIDS and international terrorism, and brought about more efficient utilization of the United Nation's modest resources."

48. See Judith Miller, "Annan Asks Security Council For Inquiry on Rwanda Horrors,"*New York Times*, March 24, 1999, at p. A5; see also Press Conference on Report of Rwanda Inquiry Team (December 16, 1999), available at http://www. fas.org/man/dod-101/ops/war/docs/19991216-rwanda.htm; see also "Report of the Independent Inquiry into the Actions of the United Nations During the 1994 Genocide in Rwanda," (December 15, 1999), available at http://www.ess.uwe.ac.uk/documents/ RwandaReport1.htm.

49. See Ruti Teitel, "Bringing the Messiah through the Law," in Carla Hesse and Robert Post, eds., 2000,*Human Rights in Transition: from Gettysburg to Bosnia.*

50. See Kofi A. Annan, "Millennial Vision," *New York Times*, Editorial, April 9, 2000, section 4 at p. 16; see also "The Nobel Lecture given by The Nobel Peace Prize Laureate 2001, Kofi A. Annan," (December 10, 2001), available at http://www.nobel.no/ eng_lect_2001b.html.

51. See Kofi Annan, "The Legitimacy to Intervene: International Action to Uphold Human Rights Requires a New Understanding of State and Individual Sovereignty," *Financial Times*, Editorial, December 31, 1999, available at http://www.globalpolicy. org/secgen/interven.htm (last visited September 15, 2003); see also Judith Miller, "The World: Checkered Flags; Sovereignty Isn't so Sacred Anymore," April 18, 1999, section 4 at p. 4.

CHAPTER 6

What Some Monuments Tell Us About Mourning and Forgiveness

VAMIK D. VOLKAN

1. Introduction

Because of several well-publicized apologies in the political arena, such as German chancellor Willy Brandt's apology to Jewish people for the Holocaust during his 1971 visit to a monument at the former site of the Warsaw ghetto, and the then Soviet leader Mikhail Gorbachev's 1990 apology to Polish people for the Katyn Forest Massacre during World War II, apology and forgiveness have become concepts that interest practitioners and scholars dealing with international relations. The work of South Africa's Truth and Reconciliation Commission (TRC) — begun in the 1990s as a way to deal with atrocities committed during apartheid — involved victims telling their stories and "forgiving" their victimizers, who had apologized for, or at least confessed, their deeds. This work further brought these concepts to our attention. In some circles, the idea of acquiring the perceived perpetrator's apology and even strongly encouraging such a perpetrator to apologize through a third, "neutral" party, began to be considered a significant element in the resolution of ethnic, national, religious, or ideological large-group conflicts. Thus, the practice of "apology and forgiveness" that exists in the practice of some religions began to be promoted also as a diplomatic/political practice. Meanwhile, an estimated twelve "imitations" of the TRC's activities appeared in various parts of the world. The problems faced by those attempting to recreate the TRC's work, and their failures, suggest a closer examination of when and how reliance on apology and forgiveness is useful and when it is not. Furthermore, observations from dialogue series between representatives of enemy groups in the presence of a neutral third party show that parties in conflict cannot reach an agreement on making an apology, accepting it, and forgiving the other without controversy; mostly, they cannot reach such an agreement at all.

Over two decades, I have been involved in dialogue series between representatives of Arab and Israeli, Russian and Estonian, Turk and Greek, Turk and Armenian, Serb and Croatian, and Georgian and South Ossetian groups. When representatives of enemies come together for a series of dialogues for unofficial negotiations, usually meeting every three months over some years, they evolve as spokespersons of their large-group's shared sentiments. During these meetings, I noted that sentiments close to concepts of apology and forgiveness are related to what I named an "accordion phenomenon" (Volkan 1987, 1997, 1999). This phenomenon refers to opposing participants suddenly experiencing a rapprochement that is followed by a sudden withdrawal from one another. This pattern repeats throughout the dialogue series. This phenomenon resembles the playing of an accordion. The groups "squeeze" together and then pull apart.

Derivatives of aggression within the participants from the opposing groups, even when they may be denied, underlie this phenomenon. Each party brings to such meetings its mental representations of historical injuries and each experiences conscious or hidden feelings of aggression toward the "enemy." Initial distancing is thus a defensive maneuver to keep aggressive attitudes and feelings in check, because, if the opponents were to come close, they may harm one another—at least in fantasy—or in turn become targets of retaliation. When opposing parties are confined together in a meeting room with a third "neutral" party and are sharing conscious efforts for a civilized negotiation, they tend to deny their aggressive feelings as they press together in a kind of illusory union. After a while, this closeness threatens each party's large-group identity. The groups have a need to preserve their identity as one separate from their enemies. Therefore, the closeness occurring in these meetings induces anxiety; it feels dangerous, and as a result, a distancing occurs. It is during times of squeezing together that participants become directly interested in ideas or feelings that can be related to concepts of apology and forgiveness. But, as I stated, when the accordion phenomenon is at work in the dialogue process, giving and accepting apology and forgiveness is illusory. When the accordion is pulled apart, preoccupations with such efforts disappear. Realistic negotiations can be carried out when the alternating between distance and togetherness (the squeezing and pulling apart of the accordion) is no longer extreme and each can easily hold on to their group identities. It is at such times that forgiveness, and apology also, can be considered realistically. However, on their own, they have no magical powers; they are useful only when they are part of a multilevel effort toward reconciliation.

Similarly, outside of the meeting rooms for unofficial dialogues and on the international scene, expressions of apology and corresponding feelings of forgiveness also have not always been followed by positive outcomes. Some such apologies were experienced as genuine, while others were perceived as empty gestures. Thus, we need to be curious about why Willy Brandt's apology had a seemingly positive outcome and why Saddam Hussein's apology to the Kuwaiti people in early December 2002, when the Iraqi leader was facing pressure from the United Nations and threats of war initiated by the United States, was perceived as a joke. The arts of apology and forgiveness should not be considered to have magical diplomatic and political consequences. Willy Brandt's apology was a factor in making the German–Israeli interactions better not because it was a single act, but because it was included in slowly developing diplomatic and political attitudes backed by multiple factors, including providing compensation for the survivors.

Furthermore, the concepts of apology and forgiveness cannot be fully understood without considering an involuntary human condition: mourning over losing people, possessions, land, prestige, and so on. Indeed, we mourn the loss—and sometimes the threat of loss—of objects in which we invest considerable emotion (Volkan 1981; Volkan and Zintl, 1993). Thus, it does not surprise us that we also mourn the loss of objects that have been the target of our hate: the enemy, for example. The relation of mourning to apology and forgiveness is the focus of this chapter. I will start with a description of the process of mourning in an individual.

2. Individual Mourning

For an individual, in general, there are two types of mourning: developmental and concrete. As we develop mentally, we must mourn what is left behind each time we climb a step higher in our mental growth. For example, an infant has to leave behind his or her mother's breast in order to crawl around and get to know his or her environment; a "loss" is followed by a "gain." An adolescent has to mourn the parental images of his or her childhood in order to expand his or her relationships with others in a large world. The adolescent's mourning is included in what is popularly known as the "adolescent crisis" (Blos 1979). The second type of mourning refers to concrete losses, such as losing loved ones, possessions, prestige, or ideals. In general, an adult who has been successful in handling his or her developmental mourning is better equipped to respond to concrete losses, since in the human mind, concrete losses are always unconsciously intertwined with developmental losses.

Mourning occurs because the human mind does not allow the reality of a significant loss to be accepted without an internal struggle. When I speak of the process of mourning here, I am not referring to the *acute grief* of people in shock and/or in pain, who may experience crying spells, frustration, anger, numbness, and withdrawal from their environment. Rather, I am referring to a *slow process* of internally reviewing our real or wished-for relationship with the lost person or thing again and again until the reality of the loss or change is emotionally accepted. Thus, "normal" mourning comes to a practical end after a year or so (if there is no complication) when the image of the deceased (or the lost thing) becomes "futureless" (Tähkä 1984). When completed, the mourning process ushers in an adaptive liberation from old burdens and from being preoccupied with persons or things long gone and no longer available to respond to our internal wishes. The image of a lost person or thing thus becomes a "memory" (Tähkä 1984). It is through the process of mourning and its conclusion, for practical purposes, that we accept changes (losses) in reality and become able to face more realistically the disappointments of our wishes, hopes, and aspirations. Thus, a "normal" mourning process leads to an eventual freeing of one's energy so that it can be invested into new persons or things and into one's new post-mourning identity.

Because the occurrence of loss in anyone's life is inevitable, we can easily imagine that complications in dealing with loss frequently arise. There are many circumstances that can interfere with the "normal" work of mourning. For example, a person may be too dependent on someone who is lost; the mourner then will have difficulty letting this lost person "die." And while there is a certain degree of "normal" anger that accompanies our response to losses, if a death is due to suicide or murder, the mourner's "normal" anger may unconsciously be contaminated with the violence that caused the death of the loved one. In these cases, the mourning process may become complicated.

Let me stay with the individual mourning and further examine its relationship with an individual's ability to accept an apology and grant forgiveness. Obviously, not all losses are perceived or experienced as results of other's activities. For example, people die because of old age or illness and due to natural disasters like floods or earthquakes. But there are many situations in which the mourners believe or feel that someone causes the loss: a doctor gave the wrong injection, a drunk driver caused the fatal accident, and so on. Clinical work with those with complicated mourning (Volkan 1981; Volkan and Zintl, 1993) shows that a mourner cannot accept an apology from another person whom the mourner perceives as the cause of his or her loss until the mourner sufficiently works through his or her mourning process. The mourner who is stuck in the mourning process and is preoccupied with accepting or not accepting the change (the loss) in reality will not be kind to another person who the mourner perceives to have put him or her into this miserable dilemma. In other situations, some people, after severe losses, evolve character traits of a victim. In other words, a sense of victimization becomes part of their identity as years pass by. To accept a perpetrator's apology means to alter once again their "new" identity, which itself will be a new loss. So they do not, in general, accept apologies.

With a few exceptions (Akhtar 2002; Moses and Moses-Hrushovshi, 2002; Volkan 1997), psychoanalysts traditionally have not paid attention to concepts of apology and forgiveness. But they have studied the process of mourning intensively since Sigmund Freud's seminal 1917 work "Mourning and Melancholia" (see, for example, research by Pollock 1989; Volkan 1981; Volkan and Zintl, 1993). In this paper, my focus is on mourning processes seen among large groups (ethnic, national, religious, or ideological groups composed of thousands or millions of individuals). Obviously, a group is not one unique organism; it does not have a "mind." When I speak of large-group processes, I am referring to the *shared* psychological experiences of members of large groups. Of course, in any large group, some members do not share sentiments or activities with others; they may be dissenters. Thus, large-group process refers to general trends that, once initiated, develop their own lives, as we will see in the next section.

3. Large-group Mourning

Large groups mourn after their members share a massive trauma and experience losses (Volkan 2000). Obviously, large-group mourning does not refer to all or many members crying openly and talking about their losses. Large-group mourning manifests itself by different means. One of these is to modify some existing societal processes or initiate new ones. For example, such a mourning process has been studied closely by Williams and Parkes (1975): Following the deaths of 116 children and twenty-eight adults in an avalanche of coal slurry in the Welsh village of Aberfan, there was a significant increase in the birth rate among women in the village who had not themselves lost a child within the five years following the tragedy. The Aberfan tragedy was not caused deliberately by "others" — it was an "act of God." Therefore, there was no humiliation as a result of the tragedy, and the society found a way to balance, so to speak, their losses with gains: more new babies than the statistical average.

Large-group mourning also can exhibit itself in evolving political ideologies. This happens especially when losses are caused deliberately by others. Because the Aberfan tragedy was not caused by others, the society found an adaptive solution to its mourning process. However, when losses are combined with humiliations and helplessness and the inability to turn passive rage into assertion, instead of adaptive, relatively quick solutions, lingering political ideologies develop and express the complications of the mourning process. For example, since the birth of modern Greece in the 1830s, after the Greek struggle for independence and separation from the Ottoman Empire, the Greeks had an ideology called the "Megali Idea," which was a response to the Greeks' experience of many "losses" while they were Ottoman subjects. The Megali Idea refers to regaining all the land that Greeks considered "lost" to others. This ideology was accompanied by a shared sense of "entitlement" to reverse helplessness and humiliation, turn passivity to assertion, and regain "lost" objects. Many authors (see Herzfeld 1986; Koliopoulos 1990; Markides 1977; Volkan and Itzkowitz, 1994) have written about how the Megali Idea played a significant role in the Greek political, social, and especially religious lives because the Greek Orthodox Church was especially active in keeping the Megali Idea alive and active. Since Greece's membership in the European Union, its investment in this ideology has been waning.

There are other large groups, such as Serbians and Armenians, which have assimilated victimhood into their shared identity as a response to their difficulty in large-group mourning (see Emmert 1990, and Marković 1983, about the Serbian sense of victimhood, and see Libaridian 1991, for the Armenians' response to a collective sense of loss). For such groups, the acceptance of an apology then becomes complicated. As I will describe later in this paper, when a group massively traumatized by others cannot do its work of mourning in an adaptive way, cannot reverse feelings of helplessness and humiliation, and cannot turn passivity into adaptive activity, such unfinished tasks become involved in trans-generational transmission (Kestenberg and Brenner, 1996; Kogan 1995; Volkan, Ast, and Greer, 2002) and are passed on to the next generation(s).

Still another way that a large group deals with mourning is to build monuments related to the massive trauma or to their ancestors' massive trauma at the hands of others (Volkan 1988). The scope of this chapter is limited: I will examine some such monuments and illustrate what they tell us about group mourning and the group's possible reactions to acts of apology and forgiveness. I will focus, in particular, on one monument: The *Crying Father* monument in Tskhinvali, South Ossetia. It was built after the bloody conflict between the Georgians and the South Ossetians, which occurred when Georgia regained its independence following the collapse of the Soviet Union. Before describing the *Crying Father* monument, however, I will examine the general psychology of such monuments and the meanings attached to them.

4. Linking Objects and Monuments

Some individuals who are stuck in the work of mourning become perennial mourners (Volkan 1981; Volkan and Zintl, 1993). Psychologically speaking, they do not wish to give up the hope of recovering what has been lost, but at the same time, they wish to complete their mourning, "kill" the lost person or thing, and accept reality. They find a solution in which their conflicting wishes can be expressed but never can be fully gratified; they create "linking objects" (Volkan 1972, 1981).

A linking object is an item chosen by an adult mourner that unconsciously represents a meeting ground for the mental image of the lost person or thing and the corresponding image of the mourners. Not every keepsake is a linking object; the item is a linking object if the mourner makes it "magical" and uses it as a "tool" for postponing the work of mourning. For example: after his father's death, a young man picks up his father's broken watch and hides it in a desk drawer. For the young man, this broken watch becomes "magical." He becomes preoccupied with repairing the watch, but he never gets it repaired. He has to know where this broken watch is, and he has to protect it, but he never opens the drawer to look at the watch, except on the anniversary of his father's death. During his psychoanalytic treatment some years after his father's death, the young man learns that he has been a perennial mourner and that he has used the broken watch as a meeting ground between himself and the image of his father. By keeping the watch locked away, he has locked away his mourning process. His mourning process is no longer an internal process; it is externalized onto his preoccupation with the watch. He has illusions of either bringing his dead father back to life by repairing the watch or "killing" his father by throwing away the watch. He does neither; he remains a perennial mourner.

We see this happen to people living during wars and in war-like conditions. The helplessness and humiliation suffered by these individuals, and their reactions to massive trauma, paralyze many ego functions of the affected individuals. This prevents traumatized individuals from going through a "normal" mourning process. Therefore, after massive violence, we see many individuals become perennial mourners who utilize linking objects. I have observed this among many Cypriot Turks after the hot conflicts in Cyprus in 1963 and 1974 (Volkan 1979). More recently, Croatian psychiatrists Slavica Jurčević and Ivan Urlić (2002) studied the linking objects of Croatians some years after the Croatian–Serb conflict from 1991 to 1995.

If we look at traumatized large groups in their own right, we can say that groups, which have suffered huge losses and experienced helplessness and humiliation, behave like individual perennial mourners. The monuments they build to recall their shared trauma and honor their lost people, lands, and prestige may become shared linking objects. As architect Jeffrey Karl Ochner (1997) states, "We choose to erect grave markers and monuments to commemorate the lives of the dead; we usually do not intend to build linking objects, although objects we do make clearly can serve us in this way" (p. 166).

When a monument evolves into a shared linking object, the functions that are attached to it will vary, depending on the nature of the shared mourning that the group is experiencing. Like an individual perennial mourner's linking object, a monument as a shared linking object is associated with the wish to complete a group's mourning and help its members accept the reality of their losses. On the other hand, it is also associated with the wish to keep the process of mourning active in the hope of recovering what was lost; this latter wish fuels feelings of revenge. Both wishes can coexist: one wish can be dominant in relation to one monument, while the other is dominant in relation to another monument. Sometimes a monument as a linking object absorbs unfinished elements of incomplete mourning and helps the group to adjust to its current situation without reexperiencing the impact of the past trauma and its disturbing emotions.

The *Crying Father* monument was used by the South Ossetians not only to keep the mourning process externalized, but also to fuel feelings of revenge. This monument was built to honor the memory of South Ossetians who were killed during the Georgia–South Ossetia War in the early 1990s. Georgia seceded from the USSR in March 1990 and adopted a declaration of independence in April of the same year. The Republic of Georgia was reborn; it had existed for only a few years (between 1918 and 1921) before it had become part of the Soviet Union. Major ethnic conflict erupted in Georgia in the years following its re-independence as the regions of South Ossetia and Abkhazia declared their independence from the new state (see map 6.1). Some ten years after very bloody conflicts, both regions remain in

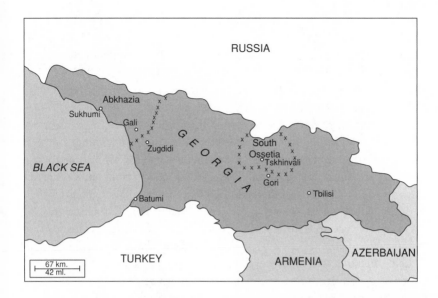

a kind of limbo: though they remain within the internationally recognized territory of the Republic of Georgia, South Ossetia and Abkhazia maintain their own borders and governments.

Along with my colleagues from the University of Virginia's Center for the Study of Mind and Human Interaction (CSMHI), I first traveled to Georgia and South Ossetia in the spring of 1998, and members of our group have returned at least twice each year since that time. Our main purpose is to help the *helpers* of traumatized people; this region, with a population of approximately 5 million, contains more than 300,000 internally displaced people. For the last five years, CSMHI has been facilitating a series of dialogues between Georgian and South Ossetian psychiatrists, psychologists, and other influential people, including those from the media and those from legal professions. This series of dialogues is designed to increase person-to-person interaction between Georgians and South Ossetians.

When Georgian and South Ossetian participants got together, direct and indirect references to "apology" and "forgiveness" came periodically (the accordion is squeezed). For example, during one meeting, some Georgian participants felt that Georgia's own struggle for re-independence had intensified the attitude that "Georgia is for [ethnic] Georgians." These participants, therefore, "blamed" themselves for fighting against South Ossetians and wanted to "acknowledge" their role in "causing" the bloody conflict. Realistically, there were many complicated reasons for the Georgian–South Ossetian conflict, the examination of which are beyond the scope of this brief paper. My focus here is simply to point out that when Georgians and South Ossetians came together and talked with the help of CSMHI facilitators, they sometimes referred to the concepts of "apology" and "forgiveness." The CSMHI facilitators never suggested that the participants consider such concepts; the ideas appeared spontaneously.

However, such ideas were pushed aside when remarks were made to indicate that mourning over the losses of people, land, and prestige on both sides had not yet been completed, or at least not yet worked through to a great extent (the accordion is pulled apart). Participants from one side would not genuinely "hear" the other side's apology and would not genuinely feel a sense of forgiveness as long as they continued to activate their unfinished mourning processes. To feel true forgiveness means to finish the work of mourning: to accept the reality of losses and the changed societal and political situations and not to feel the painful emotions associated with drastic events any longer. But no one can order another person to complete, or to stop, his or her mourning; mourning as a psychological process has to run its own course. During our gatherings, the South Ossetian participants' references to the *Crying Father* monument in Tskhinvali, the capital of South Ossetia, were a clear indication of the intensity of their ongoing mourning process. They would speak about this monument and subsequently change the subject whenever Georgian participants seemed to be ready to acknowledge their own side's role in the bloody conflict.

When I first visited Tskhinvali in 1990, I saw that the infrastructure of the city was basically ruined. Tskhinvali School No. 5 on the city's Lenin Avenue, the future site of the *Crying Father* monument, was no exception. Georgian forces had encircled Tskhinvali for many months during the Georgian–South Ossetian conflict, occupying many areas, including the city cemetery. Thus, when three young South Ossetian combatants died simultaneously during the 1991–1992 siege, they were buried in the yard of School No. 5. The reasoning behind this decision was two-fold: first, the schoolyard was a safe place to bury them, and second, one of the victims had attended the school. In subsequent weeks, more and more dead defenders were buried there, including thirty who apparently were killed on the same day. Except for a few people from a shelter for the elderly, no one who died of natural causes was buried there. Today there are about 100 graves in this schoolyard.

Grieving relatives built a chapel and a statue, which they called the *Crying Father*, near the graves. The monument depicts a man dressed in a sheepskin hat and a burka (a traditional garment with long sleeves) looking at the graves.

In South Ossetian culture, men are not supposed to cry; the paternal tears reflect extreme, ceaseless pain. An iron fence separates the cemetery from the rest of the schoolyard, but as one enters the yard, the statue is visible over the fence. From all three floors of the school, the schoolchildren — who began to attend the school after the hot conflict ended — can look out over the cemetery. Perhaps unsurprisingly, the schoolyard evolved into a sacred site, a symbol of South Ossetians' sense of victimization at the hands of Georgians. The *Crying Father* monument became a concrete symbol of continuing societal mourning.

5. Other Functions of Monuments in Traumatized Societies

There are other monuments that also evolved as shared linking objects, but were associated with functions unlike those of the *Crying Father*. Consider Yad Vashem in Jerusalem. Visiting it definitely induces strong feelings in Israelis, and indeed in all those who allow themselves to feel the impact of the Holocaust. Yad Vashem is a shared linking object that keeps the group's mourning alive. Since the losses incurred during the Holocaust are too huge to be mourned, a monument like Yad Vashem functions as a place where mourning is felt and, in a sense, "stored." Since there have been countless ways to recall and express feelings of mourning regarding the Holocaust — in religious or political ceremonies, in books, in poems, in art, in conferences — Yad Vashem is not associated with keeping the wounds caused by the Holocaust alive in the hope of recovering what has been lost; it is not associated with a deep sense of revenge. However, the task of mourning the Holocaust is passing from generation to generation (for the relevant literature, see Volkan, Ast, and Greer, 2002), and the monument links the descendants to their lost ancestors. It keeps the mourning alive without major or observable consequences.

In the United States, the Vietnam Veterans Memorial also evolved as a shared linking object (K. Volkan 1992; Ochsner 1997) and helped Americans to accept that their losses were real and that life would go on without recovering them. Some may believe that the Vietnam memorial was built by "perpetrators." Although there were many and massive protests against the war in Vietnam, I do not think that, in general, Americans felt themselves as the guilty party. Communism was "bad," and the American war in Vietnam was for the "good" of mankind. This was the "official" view, and the Vietnam War did not make the Americans feel as if they were the "bad" guys. But, certainly, many felt that dying for causes in a far away land was not justified. Thus, it is well known that the Vietnam War divided American society.

When the war came to an end, "the most common response was, in effect, denial" (Ochsner 1997, p. 159). The dead were mourned by family members and friends and were buried quietly. "However, the construction of the Vietnam Veterans Memorial, with the inscribed names of the dead and missing, seemed to change all this" (Ochsner 1997, p. 159). The memorial's young designer, Maya Yin Lin, while planning her design, associated death with "a sharp pain that lessens with time, but can never quite heal over a scar" (Campbell 1983, p. 150). She wanted to take a knife and cut open the earth, and "with time the grass would heal it" (Campbell 1983, p. 150). Kurt Volkan (1992) looked at the Vietnam Veterans Memorial from a psychological angle and showed how this memorial became a shared linking object wherein the images of the dead were linked with the corresponding images of the mourners. "By touching the stone and the etching of the names, the living bonded with the dead — after all, a name is a symbolic term that embodies everything about one's existence" (p. 76). He added: "Thus, this Wall [the monument] can be as personal as a mother crying for her lost son, or as public as a nation weeping for a past history that has yet to be resolved" (p. 76).

The Vietnam Veterans Memorial not only opened a wound, but also helped Americans to develop scars to cover the wound. When a monument becomes a shared linking object that is associated with this type of function by the public, in the long run it may function as a "locked box" (Volkan 1988, p. 171) that contains the group's unresolved shared emotions. This is what has happened to the Vietnam Veterans Memorial. Kurt Volkan (1992) wrote: "The Vietnam War memorial has created a permanent link between the living and the dead. By 'burying' 57,692 of our soldiers in one place, we are instantly connected to the land and the surrounding area, and we are constantly reminded of the past. It is one of the many ways of claiming this land as our own, as a 'linking object' that will tie the living to the dead forever" (p. 77).

There were no diplomatic considerations pertaining to apology or forgiveness between the United States and Vietnam after the war was over. Nevertheless, it can be said that the building of the memorial and the American response to it as a shared linking object, psychologically speaking, was an important step in neutralizing the relationship between the two countries.

6. How the *Crying Father* Monument Complicates Mourning

If, unlike in the previous examples, a victimized group associates a monument with the shared illusion that someday and somehow it will regain what has been lost and reverse its feelings of helplessness and humiliation, the victimizer's apology will not be "heard"—hearing and accepting the apology would rob the victims of the opportunity to fight with the enemy in the future. Thus, there would be no room for assertion and for turning passivity and helplessness into desired revenge and increased self-esteem.

Unlike the Vietnam Veterans Memorial, the *Crying Father* monument was more directly associated with this function of a shared linking object. During the initial years following the 1991–1992 conflict, there were repeated ceremonies at the schoolyard of School No. 5. Authorities would use every possible excuse to hold such ceremonies; they were held for various anniversaries and during religious holidays. The public supported the authorities by participating in such ceremonies en masse. Schoolchildren were encouraged to write and read poetry on victimization, and, more importantly, on revenge. The image of the enemy was reinforced in order to maintain the group's illusion that it may recover its losses from its enemy. Most importantly, during each school day, hundreds of high school students would pass by the "sacred" site and, after the monument was built, would see the "tears" of the *Crying Father*. The youngsters were constantly reminded of South Ossetia's victimization, helplessness, and losses; they were exposed to them to sustain their desire for revenge.

After several years of participation in CSMHI's Georgian–South Ossetian dialogue series, the South Ossetian participants acknowledged that the *Crying Father* monument was poisoning high school students and keeping negative feelings about Georgians alive in the younger generation. They spoke about this to the authorities in Tskhinvali, and later they reported that there were fewer ceremonies held in the yard of School No. 5. Also, the emotions in the poems read by the students were tamed. But the "poisoning" of youngsters passing by the *Crying Father* could not be changed. The South Ossetians participating in the dialogue series began to speak of their dilemma: Either remove the graves to another location or build a new school. The first option was unthinkable, because their religious beliefs forbade them to disturb the dead. Moreover, the South Ossetian authorities, because of their extreme economic difficulties, could not afford to build a new school. When the South Ossetians began to verbalize their dilemma, they appeared more prepared to "hear" the Georgians' apology. When a Georgian said that she was moved by the South Ossetians' dilemma and that she wanted to go to School No. 5 to pay her respects to the dead, the South Ossetians responded to her positively.

7. Trans-generational Transmission

When a traumatized group cannot reverse its feelings of helplessness and humiliation and cannot effectively go through the work of mourning, it transfers these unfinished psychological tasks to future generations. Psychoanalysts and mental health professionals have studied how these trans-generational transmissions occur (for a summary, see Volkan, Ast, and Greer, 2002). In brief, such tasks usually are not transferred openly, but indirectly, through parents' behavior patterns, their physical gestures, and the granting or withholding of affection when a child behaves in certain ways. In other words, such transmissions take place unconsciously within the child–parent (or caretaker) relationship.

Despite the individuality of each child in the "next," or subsequent, generation(s), in a large group whose ancestors have experienced a massive trauma and severe losses, the children of the next generation(s) are given similar tasks: complete the mourning over the losses, reverse the shame and humiliation, and turn helplessness into assertion. Because all the tasks are related to the mental representation of the same massive, traumatic event, this mental representation, as generations continue, connects the members of the group in an invisible way and evolves into a large-group (that is, ethnic) identity marker. I call such shared representation of ancestors' historical wounds "chosen traumas" (Volkan 1997); the historical image of the trauma is "chosen" to represent a particular group. Czechs commemorate the 1620 battle of Bila Hora, which led to their subjugation under the Habsburg Empire for nearly 300 years. In the United States, the Lakota Indians recall the anniversary of their 1890 decimation at Wounded Knee; the image of Wounded Knee is their chosen trauma, a part of their group identity. Once an event becomes a chosen trauma for the next generation(s), its historical truth is no longer important for the group. What is important is that through sharing the chosen trauma, members of the group are linked together.

Large groups may do various things with the tasks transferred to them, depending on the historical circumstances. For example, the next generation(s) may become involved in hostilities with those neighbors who are descended from the victimizers and who symbolically represent the original victimizers. Depending on the circumstances of their "power" (for example, military, political), a group may get involved in war-like situations or become a political thorn in the side of the "enemy." The group's chosen trauma is not the reason for the current wars or war-like conditions, but, when reactivated, it inflames the current conflict. Other groups, who may not have the "power" to turn their passivity into assertiveness, may idealize victimhood and, in turn, will not "hear" an apology offered by the descendents of the perpetrators. In order to accept such an apology and forgive the descendents of their ancestors' enemy, the group would have to remove its shared sense of idealized victimhood, which is now part of its identity.

Indeed, sometimes monuments are erected for the purpose of reactivating a group's chosen trauma. For example, when Slobodan Milošević was stirring nationalist sentiments among Serbians after 1987, he was instrumental in the building of a huge monument on a hill overlooking the Kosovo battlefield. The battle in Kosovo had taken place in 1389 between the Serbians and the Ottomans. Throughout the centuries, the mental representation of this battle — and that of the Serbian leader, Prince Lazar, who fell at the Kosovo battle — had become the prominent Serbian chosen trauma. The building of the monument on the 600th anniversary of the chosen trauma was designed to open Serbians' centuries-old wounds and create enemies; in this case, Muslim Bosniaks stood in for the Ottomans in the Serbian mind.

The Kosovo monument is made of red stone, representing blood (Kaplan 1993). It stands 100 feet over the battlefield; Serbians nicknamed the flowers that grow in the battlefield "grieving flowers." The monument is surrounded by cement pillars shaped like artillery shells and is inscribed with a sword and the dates, 1389–1989. Retrospectively, we can say that the Kosovo monument was built not to complete the Serbians' 600-year-old mourning, but to reopen it; not to allow thoughts of forgiveness, but to stimulate revenge against current enemies (Muslim Bosniaks and, later, Muslim Kosovo Albanians) psychologically representing the original ones (the Muslim Ottomans).

8. Conclusion: Mourning as the Groundwork for Apology and Forgiveness

The contributions to this volume reflect recent thinking on the concepts of apology and forgiveness from various disciplines. I focus more on a related concept — mourning — and on what the monuments that evolve as shared linking objects can tell us about the nature of a group's mourning. A group or its leader asking another group or its leader for forgiveness is a potentially powerful gesture if the groundwork truly has been laid. I suggest, however, that forgiveness is possible only if the group that suffered — or its descendants — has done a significant amount of mourning. Therefore, in dealing with international relations, the focus should not be on the single (seemingly magical) act of apology or asking forgiveness. Rather, it should be on developing strategies for helping the victimized group's work of mourning, which expresses itself in certain societal and political processes and helps to modify such processes for taming feelings of revenge and for peaceful coexistence (Volkan 1999).

There can be powerful reasons for one group to keep its sense of victimhood, especially if it becomes part of its identity or if there are resistances in changing one group's perception of another, usually neighboring, group. By focusing on how a group reacts to some monuments that honor the dead and recall the trauma, I hope to have a look at the complicated psychology that exists between large groups. This may tell us not to make the concepts of "apology" or "forgiveness" magical tools in international relationships without first considering the slow and complicated mourning processes associated with them.

References

Akhtar, S. 2002. "Forgiveness: Origins, Dynamics, Psychopathology, and Technical Relevance." *Psychoanalytic Quarterly* 71: 175–212.

Blos, Peter. 1979. *The Adolescent Passage: Developmental Issues*. New York: International Universities Press.

Campell, R. 1983. "An Emotive Apart." *Art in America* (May): 150–151.

Emmert, T. A. 1990. *Serbian Golgotha: Kosovo, 1389*. New York: Columbia University Press.

Freud, S. 1917. Mourning and Melancholia. *Standard Edition* 14: 237–258.

Herzfeld, M. 1986. *Ours Once More: Folklore, Ideology, and the Making of Modern Greece*. New York: Pella.

Jurčević, S., and I. Urlić. 2002. "Linking Objects in the Process of Mourning for Sons Disappeared in War: Croatia 2001." *Croatian Medical Journal* 43: 234–239.

Kaplan, R. D. 1993. *Balkan Ghosts: A Journey through History*. New York: Vintage Books.

Kestenberg, J., and I. Brenner. 1996. *The Last Witness*. Washington, DC: American Psychiatric Press.

Kogan, I. 1995. *The Cry of Mute Children: A Psychoanalytic Perspective of the Second Generation of the Holocaust*. London: Free Association Books.

Koliopoulos, J. S. 1990. "Brigandage and Irredentism in Nineteenth-Century Greece." In M. Blinkhorn and T. Veremis, eds., *Modern Greece: Nationalism and Nationality*, 67–102. Athens: Sage-Eliamep.

Libaridian, G. J., ed. 1991. *Armenia at the Crossroads: Democracy and Nationhood in the Post-Soviet Era*. Watertown, MA: Blue Cross Books.

Markides, K. C. 1977. *The Rise and Fall of the Cyprus Republic*. New Haven: Yale University Press.

Markovic, M. S. 1983. "The Secret of Kosovo." In V. D. Mihailovich, ed., *Landmarks in Serbian Culture and History*, 111–131. Translated by C. Kramer. Pittsburgh, PA: Serb National Foundation.

Moses, R., and R. Moses-Hrushovski. 2002. "Two Powerful Tools in Human Interactions: To Accept One's Fault and to Ask for Forgiveness." In A. Egrilmez and I. Vahip, eds., *Psikopatoloji ve Psikoanalitik Teknik*. Izmir, Turkey: Meta.

Ochsner, J. K. 1997. "A Space of Loss: The Vietnam Veterans Memorial." *Journal of Architectural Education* 10: 156–171.

Pollock, G. H. 1989. *The Mourning-Liberation Process*, vols. 1 and 2. Madison, CT: International Universities Press.

Tähkä, V. 1984. "Dealing with Object Loss." *Scandinavian Psychoanalytic Review* 7: 13–33.

Volkan, K. 1992. "The Vietnam War Memorial." *Mind and Human Interaction* 3: 73–77.

Volkan, V. D. 1972. "The Linking Objects of Pathological Mourners." *Archives of General Psychiatry* 27: 215–221.

Volkan, V. D. 1979. *Cyprus: War and Adaptation*. Charlottesville, VA: University Press of Virginia.

Volkan, V. D. 1981. *Linking Objects and Linking Phenomena: A Study of the Forms, Symptoms, Metapsychology, and Therapy of Complicated Mourning*. New York: International University Press.

Volkan, V. D. 1987. "Psychological Concepts Useful in the Building of Political Foundations Between Nations (Track II Diplomacy)." *Journal of the American Psychoanalytic Association* 35: 903–935.

Volkan, V. D. 1988. *The Need to Have Enemies and Allies: From Clinical Practice to International Relationships*. Northvale, NJ: Jason Aronson.

Volkan, V. D. 1997. *Bloodlines: From Ethnic Pride to Ethnic Terrorism*. New York: Farrar, Straus and Giroux.

Volkan, V. D. 1999. "The Tree Model: A Comprehensive Psychopolitical Approach to Unofficial Diplomacy and the Reduction of Ethnic Tension." *Mind and Human Interaction* 10: 142–210.

Volkan, V. D. 2000. "Traumatized Societies and Psychological Care: Expanding the Concept of Preventive Medicine." *Mind and Human Interaction* 11: 177–194.

Volkan, V. D., G. Ast, and W. Greer. 2002. *The Third Reich in the Unconscious: Trangenerational Transmission and its Consequences*. New York: Brunner-Routledge.

Volkan, V. D., and N. Itzkowitz. 1994. *Turks and Greeks: Neighbours in Conflict*. Cambridgeshire, England: Eothen Press.

Volkan, V. D., and E. Zintl. 1993. *Life After Loss: The Lessons of Grief*. New York: Charles Scribner's Sons.

Williams, R. M., and C. M. Parkes. 1975. "Psychosocial Effects of Disaster: Birth Rate in Aberfan." *British Medical Journal* 2: 303–304.

CHAPTER 7

Apologies and Reconciliation: Middle Eastern Rituals

GEORGE EMILE IRANI[1]

Fostering peace and thwarting the failure of peace settlements has become one of the fundamental concerns of policy makers and scholars since the collapse of the former Soviet Union.[2] This has been the case in Bosnia-Herzegovina, Rwanda, Somalia, Israel-Palestine, Northern Ireland, and Lebanon. All of these conflicts originate from long years of frustrated victimization evolving into hatred, and finally into uncontrollable violence. The challenge for policy makers and civil society is to find credible and long-lasting methods of conflict management. In the last few years, the debate has centered on the relevance of what the Carnegie Commission on Preventing Deadly Conflict (1997) calls "private sector activity" (p. 50).

I believe that the time has come to rethink how US-based institutions such as NGOs, academic institutions, and governmental bodies export and implement conflict resolution in societies whose culture, history, social structure, and traditions are very different from those of the United States. In order for peace to take hold beyond a small elite in Israel and in the Arab countries, policy makers and outside mediators have to prod Arabs, Israelis, and Palestinians to come to terms with their local histories and grievances, a process that may be facilitated through indigenous rituals and processes of reconciliation. The importance of perceptions and misperceptions, as well as communal psychological "baggage," must be taken into consideration as well.

This essay advances the idea that we ought to look at Arab–Islamic techniques and procedures of conflict management such as the rituals of *sulh* (settlement) and *musalaha* (reconciliation). The process of *sulh* consists of three stages. In the initial stage, respected mediators (*muslihs*) are selected by the families of the victim and the victimizer. The goal is to acknowledge that a crime was committed. The second stage is that of the *musalaha* itself, which is characterized by a pardon and settlement between the parties. The key here is that the parties' honor and dignity have been restored and upheld.

The final stage is a public ritual that brings together the community as the main guarantor of the forgiveness reached between the disputants. Regarding application of these practices to larger scale conflict management, *the intent here is not to adopt the rituals as they are used today in some villages of Lebanon and the Galilee or by the Bedouin in Jordan, but to take their useful and constructive principles (particularly those centering on justice and healing) and apply them in intra- and inter-state peace efforts.*

Over the past ten years, many Middle Eastern scholars and practitioners trained in the United States have returned to their countries of origin, ready to impart what they have learned about Western conflict resolution techniques. In Lebanon, Jordan, Egypt, and other countries of the Middle East, the teaching and practice of conflict resolution is still a novel phenomenon. Conflict resolution is viewed by many in the Middle East as a false Western panacea that is insensitive to indigenous problems, needs, and political processes. Others see it as a US-concocted scheme intended primarily to facilitate and hasten the processes of peace and normalization between Israel and its Arab neighbors.[3] In assessing the applicability of Western-based conflict resolution models in non-Western societies, theoreticians and practitioners alike have begun to realize the importance of being sensitive to indigenous attitudes, feelings, histories, and local rituals for managing and reducing conflicts. Diplomacy does not take place within a vacuum. In addition to empowering non-state actors (civil society) to achieve a more participatory peace process, the cultural values and traditions of Arab–Islamic societies might be incorporated into state-to-state and intra-state diplomatic efforts. This would help to facilitate a legitimate peace through a process that respects cultural realities and previously disempowered non-state actors.

The need for a study of the Arab–Islamic approaches to reconciliation arises from the dearth of available works relating conflict management and resolution processes to indigenous rituals of reconciliation. Since the signing of the Camp David Accords twenty years ago, a plethora of books and studies have assessed the diplomatic process between Israel and Egypt, drawing pertinent lessons for policy makers and potential peacemakers.[4] There is a need to fathom the deep cultural, social, and religious roots of the Arabs' conceptions of and reactions to conflict reduction and reconciliation.[5] This has become more urgent since the end of the regime of Saddam Hussein and the intervention of US troops in Iraq (2003). The current United States Administration, to maintain its status as an "honest broker" in the Middle East, needs to heed the prescriptions advanced in this study.

1. Rituals, Conflict Control, and Conflict Reduction

British sociologist Anthony Giddens (1991) remarks that rituals are crucial to both an individual's emotional well being and communal harmony, and social integration:

> Without ordered ritual and collective involvement, individuals are left without structured ways of coping with tensions and anxieties. [...] Communal rites provide a focus for group solidarity at major transitions as well as allocating definite tasks for those involved. [...] Something profound is lost together with traditional forms of ritual. [...] Traditional ritual [...] connected individual action to moral frameworks and to elemental questions about human existence. The loss of ritual is also the loss of such frameworks (p. 204).

This very important observation brings to the fore the sense of alienation that emerges in some sectors of Western societies where individuals and communities relegate customs and rituals to the trash heap of premodern, nonrational history. In contrast to the family oriented culture of the Middle East, the individual in postindustrial societies must fend for himself or herself through individualistic means. However, this does not denigrate the importance of individual freedoms and responsibilities that is at the core of Western democracies. Of course, in the Middle East, there are many young professional and educated men and women who are struggling to establish secular societies based on individual rights and responsibilities and state accountability.

Related to this, it is very interesting to note that rituals of conflict control and reduction are usually invoked and utilized by the less empowered sectors in a given society. In communally based societies, a blood feud begins with individuals and ends up involving groups. Both the family of the victim and that of the murderer are tied in a process that could either lead to escalation and revenge, or to conflict control and reduction. The whole ritual of *sulh* aims to create a situation of evenness between the two tribes, clans, or families. This is why the role of the mediator is so crucial. The group of elders (both lay and religious leaders) has an important responsibility to restore power by empowering the victim's family and protecting the honor and dignity of the murderer. (For further details, see Hachem El-Husseini 1992). Such rituals readjust individuals and communities to changing aspects of their life-worlds, thereby enabling them to complete difficult and troubling transitions as individuals and as members of a society.

In Lebanon, a country still healing and emerging from sixteen years of civil strife, priorities do not include training for conflict control and reduction. In most Arab societies, Western conflict resolution techniques are learned and adopted by professional groups such as businesspeople, bankers, lawyers, engineers, and so on. For the rest of the population, conflict control and reduction are handled either by state-controlled courts or by traditional ritual means. In this context, one of the basic criticisms launched against Western conflict resolution techniques by Middle Eastern students of conflict resolution is that they are either too mechanistic, or based on individualistic, therapy oriented formulas.

Although Western techniques and skills are relevant and useful, they need to be adapted to indigenous realities. For instance, in Lebanon the majority of social workers are women. They are trained in Lebanon's major academic institutions—the state-controlled Lebanese University and the Jesuit-controlled Université Saint-Joseph. Upon graduating, most of these social workers leave theory behind and confront the conflicts and realities of Lebanese society. During a series of workshops in conflict resolution skills geared to social workers in Islamic NGOs involved in education and family welfare, several common problems quickly emerged. In conflicts involving couples, social workers were usually approached by battered wives; husbands invariably refused to deal with the social worker. The path to resolution thus went through the local religious or political *zaim* (leader), not through the social worker. (As was mentioned above, this is a typical pattern in patriarchal societies.) Another issue facing social workers attempting to mediate family conflicts in Lebanon was child custody. In Middle Eastern societies, fathers have custody of children in the case of divorce. In some instances, mothers try to keep their children. The youngsters become hostages in the two-way conflict that pits their father's family against their mother.[6]

These examples highlight the problem of applying Western modes of conflict control and reduction in communally based societies where patriarchy and religious values are paramount. Arab "citizens" are not citizens in the Western meaning of individuals bound to one another and the state by an agreed-upon interlocking system of rights and duties. Instead, Arabs belong to communities and abide by their rules and rituals. Inhabitants of large Arab cities are more likely than villagers to resort to the official legal system to settle their disputes. The legal system, however, is backlogged, and corruption is pervasive. Moreover, the interpretation of the rule of law in sectarian-based societies or societies based on tribal modes of social interaction has a different meaning than it does in Western states. The law is usually that of the powerful and the wealthy (politicians and clergy), or heads of village clans or Bedouin tribes.[7] The rule of law also has to confront the pervasive and powerful influence of patronage and its strong emphasis on asymmetrical power relationships. For example, an individual who has committed a crime, along with his immediate family, can face both the legal justice system and the tribal mode of conflict control and reduction. Unlike the Western legal system that is based on the rule of *habeas corpus*, in the Arab–Islamic world, legal jurisdiction has three dimensions. The first dimension consists of state laws inherited from colonial times; the second dimension is the Islamic *shari'a* or the confessional laws of various religious communities for non-Muslims; and the third dimension is the customary tradition of private justice.

This situation underlines the importance of closely studying modes of reconciliation and conflict control in an Arab–Islamic environment. The observer interested in conflict control and reduction in non-Western societies also has to look into the rituals that inform individual and community behavior following a crime or any other illegal action.

Let us now introduce a brief Islamic perspective on conflict control and reduction by tracking verses in the *Qur'an* related to group conflict, whether intra-group (as in the case of a dispute between two Muslim groups), or inter-group (as in the case of a dispute between a Muslim group and an outsider group). The general rules mentioned in the *Qur'an* emphasize:

1. Never to begin with aggression (ii.190) (Ali 1989, p. 75).[8]

2. If fighting back is necessary for self-defense, or for reestablishing the rules of the society (as in cases of a Muslim group refusing to pay the Islamic tax, *zakat*), then the use of force is limited by the rule of not to "over-aggress" (ii.191–194) (p. 75–77).

3. If a truce of peace is asked by the other group, all efforts are made to pursue peace (viii.61) (p. 430).

4. Rules of forgiveness and *sabr* (patience) are preferred to retaliation in all cases (xvi.126–128).

5. If intervening as a third party, a "contingency" model (to use Roger Fisher's term) is proposed. Intervening first as a mediator or arbitrator to reconcile differences; siding against the transgressor until the transgression stops; then back to the reconciliatory role once the transgression stops (xlix.9) (p. 1405).[9]

6. And finally, devout Jews, Christians, and Muslims believe that "God is watching us." In all cases of inter-personal disputes, especially those involving marital disputes (including sexual relationships among spouses), the *Qur'an* consistently describes the specific dispute situation, and then follows with a

resolution. The "spirit" in all these instances is that of demanding that parties behave in good faith, with preference given to forgiveness and patience.

The first chapter of the *Qur'an* describes the extent and limits of punishment (*qisas*) and retribution:

> O ye who believe!
> The law of equality
> Is prescribed to you
> In cases of murder:
> The free for the free,
> The slave for the slave,
> The woman for the woman.
> But if any remission
> Is made by the brother
> Of the slain, then grant
> Any reasonable demand,
> And compensate him
> With handsome gratitude.
> This is a concession
> And a Mercy
> From your Lord (Surah 1:178 in Ali 1989).[10]

The *Qur'an* is thus a very important source for those seeking to understand modes of conflict control and reconciliation in Arab–Islamic societies. The holy book of Islam calls for equity in cases of revenge and for forgiveness in cases of apology and "remission."

2. The Rituals of *Sulh* and *Musalaha*

In some Middle Eastern societies, such as Lebanon, Jordan, and Palestine, rituals are used in private modes of conflict control and reduction. Private modes are processes outside state control that utilize traditional steps to restore justice. Sometimes, both private justice and official justice are invoked simultaneously to foster reconciliation. One such step is the process of *sulh* (settlement) and *musalaha* (reconciliation). According to Islamic Law (*Shari'a*), "the purpose of *sulh* is to end conflict and hostility among believers so that they may conduct their relationships in peace and amity. [. . .] In Islamic law, *sulh* is a form of contract (*'akd*), legally binding on both the individual and community levels" (Khadduri 1997, pp. 845–846).[11] Similar to the private *sulh* between two believers, "the purpose of [public] *sulh* is to suspend fighting

137

between [two parties] and establish peace, called *muwada'a* (peace or gentle relationship), for a *specific period of time*" (Khadduri, pp. 845–846, author's emphasis).

In a sense, *sulh* and *musalaha* can be considered as forms of arbitration supported by rituals. They comprise a mediation–arbitration process for communally based societies.[12] The *sulh* ritual, which is an institutionalized form of conflict management and control, has its origins in tribal and village contexts. "The *sulh* ritual stresses the close link between the psychological and political dimensions of communal life through its recognition that injuries between individuals and groups will fester and expand if not acknowledged, repaired, forgiven, and transcended" (King-Irani 2000, p. 131). The judicial system in Lebanon does not include *sulh* as part of the conflict control process. Nonetheless, *sulh* rituals are approved and encouraged in rural areas where state control is not very strong. The ritual of *sulh* is used today in the rural areas of Lebanon (the Bekaa Valley, the Hermel area in eastern Lebanon, and the Akkar region of north Lebanon).[13] In the Hashemite Kingdom of Jordan, the ritual of *sulh* is officially recognized by the Jordanian government as an acceptable tradition of the Bedouin tribes. In Israel, the ritual of *sulh* is still in use among the Palestinian citizens of Israel living in the villages of the Galilee. I will now describe the ritual of *sulh* and *musalaha* and give concrete examples of the ritual process of reconciliation that follows blood feuds, honor crimes, and cases of murder.[14]

As-sulh sayyid al-ahkaam. "*Sulh* is the best of judgments." This is how the Jordanian Bedouin tribes describe the customary process of settlement and reconciliation. According to Jordanian judge Abu-Hassan (1987) there are several types of *sulh*.[15] That is, the term *sulh* can be used both in reference to the parties included in a reconciliation process and in reference to the final outcomes of a peacemaking effort. When *sulh* is used to define a process, there are two subcategories: public *sulh* and private *sulh*. Public *sulh* is similar to a peace treaty between two countries. It usually takes place as a result of conflicts between two or more tribes, which result in death and destruction affecting all the parties involved.

Given the severity of life conditions in the semiarid zones of the Middle East, competing tribes long ago realized that *sulh* was a better alternative to endless cycles of violence and vengeance. In the event of a conflict, each of the tribes initiates a process to take stock of its losses in human and material terms. The tribe with the fewest losses compensates the tribe that suffered most. Oral tradition notes stringent conditions for settling the tribal conflict definitively. The most famous of these conditions is that the parties in conflict pledge to forget everything that happened and initiate new and friendly relations. The consequences and effects of public *sulh* apply whether the guilty party was identified or was unknown at the time of the *sulh* (Abu-Hassan 1987). In contrast, private *sulh* takes place when both the crime and the guilty party are known. The parties may be of the same tribe or from different tribes. The purpose of private *sulh* is to make sure that no one will take vengeance against the family of the perpetrator.

When *sulh* is used in relation to a final outcome, there are two types of settlements: total *sulh*, and partial or conditional *sulh*. The former type ends all kinds of conflict between the parties, who thenceforth decide not to hold any grudges against each other. The latter type ends the conflict between the two parties according to conditions agreed upon during the settlement process (Abu-Hassan 1987).

Here is a brief sketch of how the ritual of settlement and reconciliation is used in the Middle East. Following a murder, the family of the murderer, in order to thwart any attempt at blood revenge, calls on a delegation of mediators comprised of village elders and notables, usually called *muslihs* or *jaha* (those who have gained the esteem of the community). The mediators initiate a process of fact-finding and questioning of the parties involved in the murder. As soon as the family of the guilty party calls for the mediators' intervention, a *hudna* (truce) is declared.[16] The task of the *muslihs* or *jaha* is not to judge, punish, or condemn the offending party, "but rather, to preserve the good names of both the families involved and to reaffirm the necessity of ongoing relationships within the community. The *sulh* ritual is not a zero-sum game" (King-Irani, *ibid.*). To many practitioners of *sulh* and *musalaha*, the toughest cases to settle are those involving blood feuds. Sometimes, a blood price is paid to the family of the victim that usually involves an amount of money, *diya*, set by the mediators. The *diya* (blood money) or an exchange of goods (sometimes the exchange includes animals, food, and so on) substitutes for the exchange of death.

The ritual process of *sulh* usually ends in a public ceremony of *musalaha* (reconciliation) performed in the village square. The families of both the victim and the guilty party line up on both sides of the road and exchange greetings and apologies. The ceremony includes four major stages: (1) the act of reconciliation itself; (2) the two parties shake hands under the supervision of the *muslihs* or *jaha*; (3) the family of the murderer visits the home of the victim to drink a cup of bitter coffee; and 4) the ritual concludes with a meal hosted by the family of the offender. The specific form of the rituals varies from Israel/Palestine to Lebanon and Jordan but the basic philosophy is based on *sulh* (settlement), *musalaha* (reconciliation), *musafaha* (hand-shaking), and *mumalaha* ("partaking of salt and bread," that is, breaking bread together).[17] While *sulh* resembles contemporary Western approaches to mediation and arbitration, a key difference is the relationship of the process to *enduring communal relationships*. *Sulh* does not merely take place between individuals, but between *groups*. Although Western theorists are just beginning to experiment with the reintroduction of non-legalistic community-based approaches to settlement and reconciliation, Arab–Islamic culture has never jettisoned such approaches, which provide a means of negotiating, symbolizing, and achieving a practical transformation of relationships among large numbers of people.

No one can better describe cases of reconciliation than Elias J. Jabbour (1996), who has been deeply involved in cases of *sulh* and *musalaha* in the villages of Galilee:

The following case is unique in my experience. Almost nothing like it has been heard of or remembered in our area for over a century. This truly can be called a unique case of *sulh*. Forty-seven years ago, and immediately before the 1948 establishment of the political state of Israel, a young Bedouin Palestinian from the Hujeirat tribe of Northern Palestine, not far from Shefa-Amer, killed another young man, a 22-year-old Lebanese villager. The Lebanese man, whose family lived in the small village of Bleedah, came to Palestine to the big city of Haifa, to seek work, as the young Bedouin had done. Seeking a place to sleep, both men came upon the identical accommodation, available to only one person. An argument began over who should have the place. Both men were hot-headed with fiery tempers. The quarrel became heated, ending only when the Palestinian Bedouin killed the Lebanese villager. This killing occurred in 1947, near the end of the British Mandate over Palestine. One year later, in 1948 the British pulled out of Palestine, and war broke out between the Arabs and Jews. Ultimately, the political nation of Israel was established and the former British prisons were opened. The Bedouin killer was released to return to his own tribe where he lives to this very day. [...] Forty-seven years later, in 1994, the young Bedouin who killed the Lebanese man, now an old man of eighty, had married and was the head of a large family of his own. His conscience began to disturb him so much that he could no longer sleep well. Being a pious man who had returned to his faith and the worship of God later in life, he began to seek the advice of the sheikhs and religious leaders as to what he should do to find rest. [...] He began to express his deep unrest to his now-grown children, who were married and with children of their own. He complained of his inner conflict to the people of his tribe. As time wore on, the chiefs of this tribe, in an effort to assist him, began to use their influence and connections to locate, in southern Lebanon, the family of the deceased man. By this time, with the Israeli occupation of southern Lebanon, they had ways of contacting some of the family and were able to respond to the request put before them to accept the old man's pleas to make *sulh* and peace. The brothers of the deceased, now living in Beirut, agreed to the demand for making peace, but were prevented from attending in person because of the imposed security at the border. In their place, they asked the *mukhtar* (mayor) of their home village of Bleedah (located now in the buffer zone occupied by Israel) and an older cousin to act on their behalf in *sulh*. Through the mediation of the *jaha*, the peacemaking was arranged to take place in the Bedouin village of Touba, near the town of Kiryat Shemonah on the northern border of Israel. Although Touba's population are descendents of another Bedouin tribe, "El-Heib," they, like the Hujeirat tribe, graciously volunteered to host the proceedings and ceremony in their village, which was closer to the Lebanese border. Normally, it would be the family of the killer who would go to Lebanon to celebrate peace in the village of the murdered man, but this was not allowed under the current political scene. Thus, in a borrowed village, on the 27th of January, 1994, about two hundred men from all over Israel were gathered in Touba, waiting for the "avengers" to arrive from occupied southern Lebanon, so that hands could be clasped, speeches made, terms agreed to, bitter coffee drunk, a meal shared, and an old dispute settled for both sides (pp. 84–88).

3. Implications for Practitioners and Policy Makers: Lessons and Recommendations

Arab–Islamic rituals are an important resource for conflict control and re-duction in the Middle East. They are better adapted to norms, expectations, and the social structure of Middle Eastern societies than most Western ap-proaches. Through adaptation, they could enable peace and reconciliation processes within and between states and communal groups.

1. *Arab–Islamic rituals of reconciliation are a non-Western, indigenous ap-plication of the process of acknowledgment, apology, compensation, forgive-ness, and reconciliation. They constitute a process of arbitration accomplished through rituals and symbols.*

In the Arab–Islamic context, these rituals are by far more effective, com-pelling, and vital than Western modes of mediation and arbitration. Today, in many American suburban and urban areas, conflict control and reduc-tion require the presence of a trained professional mediator and a therapist. This results from society's relegation of the importance of the family to by-gone eras. In Arab–Islamic culture, the family and the community are still strong—perhaps too strong. Through *sulh* and *musalaha*, the ritual of conflict control and reduction take place within a communal, not a one-on-one, framework.

The challenge facing Western approaches to reconciliation is that in Middle Eastern societies, the conceptual category of the individual does not have the same validity and importance as in Western cultures. The individual is enmeshed within his or her own group, sect, tribe, or mileux. Religion continues to play a crucial role in individual and collective lives.[18] It is part and parcel of daily discourse, even in supposedly secularized quarters.

The recent debate in Lebanon over civil marriage is a case in point. In Israel, Lebanon, and other Middle Eastern societies, marriage, like other personal status laws, is dictated by religious authorities. The same applies to divorce, adoption, education, burial, and inheritance.

2. *Arab–Islamic states and societies are neither "traditional" nor "modern," but rather mix the outward forms of the nation-state with a deeply rooted patriarchal social structure and a high concentration of power at the executive level. This complicates efforts at promoting open dialogue in civil society while increasing the importance of integrating tangible benefits and culturally legitimate procedures into conflict resolution efforts.*

A fundamental (yet mysteriously neglected) factor in conflict control and reduction is the role and perception of power. Power in Middle Eastern societies is usually concentrated at the top of the hierarchy, whether in the person of the village *zaim*, or government leaders (presidents, kings, or military autocrats).[19] The state itself is constructed differently from Western nation-states: national "reconciliation" as currently envisioned must occur within entities—nations—that were artificially created after World War II.[20] Moreover, given the absence of participatory democracy and the pervasiveness of autocratic rule, the population at large cannot be convinced of the desirability of reconciliation unless tangible benefits and powerful symbolic gestures ensue. These fundamental realities must be taken into consideration when implementing peace processes in the Middle East.

Notwithstanding the autocratic nature of some Arab regimes, modified rituals of *sulh* and *musalaha* could empower the individual within his/her community, contributing to post-war reconciliation and to the consolidation of civil society. *Sulh* can be utilized not only as an approach to controlling and reducing conflict, but also as a means of building and maintaining that sense of solidarity and participation that is essential to genuine democratic politics. *Sulh* need not be considered a remnant tradition of the past; it could become an integral component of a new communitarian politics in Middle Eastern societies, in which tensions between individualism and communitarianism could be balanced.

3. *While the relevance of sulh and musalaha is obvious at the local village level following a civil war, there are a number of other venues in which these rituals and their underlying principles could play a role. Sulh and musalaha could provide a compelling idiom, symbolic forms, and guiding values for reconciliation efforts at the communal, national, and regional levels.*

The family and the community are the guarantors of the traditional *hodna* (truce) that takes place between two families. The same principle could apply to two or more conflicting communal groups (as in the case of Lebanon) or nation-states (as in the Arab–Israeli conflict).

At the conclusion of the 1994 conference on "Acknowledgment, Forgiveness, and Reconciliation: Alternative Approaches to Conflict Resolution in Lebanon," a suggestion was made by some participants to adapt the ritual of *sulh* in order to facilitate acknowledgment, apology, and forgiveness at the national, not just communal, level in post-war Lebanon. Ghassan Mokheiber, a prominent Lebanese attorney and Member of the Lebanese Parliament who has written about traditional reconciliation rituals in Lebanon, stated that modified processes of *sulh* and *musalaha* could play a similar role to that of truth and reconciliation commissions in Latin America and South Africa. In this context, Mokheiber (1995) pondered the following:

[There is the] question of the transferability of a process from the interpersonal to the national level, from dealing with personal problems between two individuals, to political problems involving a much wider community. This issue is tied up with larger processes which are more or less political in nature, particularly the issue of war crimes tribunals. [...] In the *sulh* ritual, you have to identify the specific parties to the dispute, and even if you manage to do that, you need accepted mediators who will be able to undertake the fact-finding mission of identifying right and wrong, accompanied by the voicing and venting of people's grief and anger, which ultimately leads to acknowledgment and the emotional process of catharsis [...] and the reconciliation of the parties through a mutual exchange of apology and forgiveness. Now, transferring all of this to a national, political level—well, I really can't see it happening except in the context of a war crime tribunal. This, of course is very controversial. [...] It would have to be carried out by civil society, not the Lebanese government. Universally respected and credible members of Lebanese civil society would symbolically "try" the people responsible for the war [in Lebanon], and it should be a trial not only of individuals, but of social, political, and economic causes of the war. Identifying the people and factors that brought about the war, putting them under the scrutiny of respectable people, finding liabilities, validating people's experiences of suffering— all of this should happen. I am a strong advocate of such a process. We cannot go on forever sweeping history under the carpet in Lebanon. Instead of just sanctioning it all in the end, it should lead to a process of forgiveness.

The importance of Arab–Islamic rituals for conflict resolution lies in their communal nature.[21]

4. *The application of the principles of* sulh *to the Arab-Israeli conflict would be challenging but, in the long term, rewarding. Before the ritual of* sulh *can be adapted for Track Two conflict resolution efforts between societies, principles of* sulh *must first be applied at the inter-state level. There is a need for an effective guarantor of the peacemaking and reconciliation process. The guarantor must respect the consensus of the international community, balance power relationships, demonstrate a nuanced appreciation of local histories and cultural values, and engender a context of common security and equity.*

The Arab–Israeli conflict is one of competing claims to justice, marked by competing needs, fears, and insecurities. Many Arab Muslims and Christians feel that their claims have not been heard, or have even been ignored. A recurring question in the Arab body politic today is: "Who will guarantee the implementation of peace?" This is a key question in light of the fact that for the last twenty years only one superpower, the United States of America, has taken upon itself the role of "honest broker" and "mediator." Unfortunately, the overall perception of public opinion in the Arab Middle East is that the United States is not an unbiased and fair broker in the Arab–Israeli–Palestinian conflict. Although Arabs appreciate the ideal of an unbiased, even-handed mediator, their conception of the preferred third party emphasizes the role of the principled guarantor who ensures a settlement based on values of equity and just compensation.

In this regard, it would be helpful for the United States to articulate more clearly the principles underlying its mediation efforts, above and beyond the frequently voiced commitments to preserving the security of Israel and fighting terrorism. Mainstream public opinion in the Arab–Islamic world has accepted that Israel is in the Middle East to stay, and most states and individuals are willing to recognize Israel provided that Israel recognizes and compensates the Palestinians, and provided that mediation between Arabs and Israelis is conducted on the basis of values, which all hold to be legitimate. For the US role to be legitimized in Arab eyes, diplomats must adopt a more neutral stance—a stance that guarantees the fundamental human needs and the essential aspirations *of all parties* for self-determination, security, and development.

The United States has an opportunity to reframe its role in the Middle East. Rather than merely viewing itself as a force for stability, as was the case after World War II, or as a destabilizing force, as has been the case since the United States adopted the principle of preemption in 2002, the United States could instead conceive of its role as active facilitator—helping to empower peoples in the region to develop culturally relevant models of reconciliation, democracy, and development. This would help to ameliorate perceived tensions between modernity and tradition, as well as between secularism and religion.

Notes

1. I am deeply indebted to Nathan Funk, my research assistant at the United States Institute of Peace, for his insight, knowledge, and assistance. I would like to extend my warmest appreciation to Dr. Joseph Klaits, Dr. Sally Onesti Blair, and to Peter Pavilionis for their invaluable editorial help. Special thanks go to my wife, Laurie King-Irani, for her inspiration, patience, and support.

2. See, for instance, Fen Osler Hampson (1996) and David Callahan (1997).

3. See Muhammad Abu-Nimer (1996), who expresses the assumption of many that the teaching of conflict resolution in the Middle East is for "containing" the spread of "Islamic fundamentalism."

4. See, for instance, Raymond Cohen (1997). Cohen explores how cultural factors influence negotiation between diplomats of different ethnic and cultural backgrounds. See also the interesting work by David W. Augsburger (1992).

5. In the late 1960s and 1970s a group of anthropologists (Cathy Witty, Richard Antoun, Laura Nader, Michael Gilsenan, and others) published groundbreaking studies assessing mediation processes and village politics in countries such as Jordan and Lebanon. Since then, other scholars have emphasized the role of culture as a factor in understanding how diplomats interact and how reconciliation is accomplished in various cultural settings. Regarding the impact of culture on negotiation patterns, see Guy Olivier Faure and Jeffrey Z. Rubin, (eds.) (1993) and myself. William Zartman and J. Lewis Rasmussen (eds.) (1997).

6. This is the case in most countries in the Middle East (except for Tunisia). Custody is assigned to the mother, or to her family if she is unfit or dead, until the child reaches a certain age (eleven or thirteen years). Then the child is assigned to the father for custody. The rationale is to support the welfare and well being of the child. It is assumed that the child needs motherly attention at an early age, then the attention of the father as a teenager. Also, in clan-based societies children legally belong to the patriline.

7. For an excellent analysis of the legal system in the Arab world, see Nathan J. Brown (1997).

8. For a recent and excellent analysis of the *Qur'an* in the English language, see also Fathi Osman (1997).

9. I am grateful to my friend and colleague, Dr. Amr Khairy Abdalla, a former Prosecuting Attorney in Egypt (1978–1987), who alerted me to the importance of these verses in the *Qur'an* and their relevance to explain the Islamic worldview.

10. In his commentary on these verses of the *Qur'an* related to retribution and punishment (*qisas*), Abdulla Yussuf Ali (1989) first notes that "this verse and the next make it clear that Islam has much mitigated the horrors of the pre-Islamic custom of retaliation." He then writes: "in order to meet the strict claims of justice, equality is prescribed, with a strong recommendation for mercy and forgiveness. [. . .] Our law of equality only takes account of three conditions in civil society: free for free, slave for slave, woman for woman. Among free men or women, all are equal: you cannot ask that, because a wealthy, or high-born, or influential man is killed, his life is equal to two or three lives among the poor or the lowly. [. . .] A woman is mentioned separately because her position as a mother or an economic worker is different. She does not form a third class, but a division in the other two classes. One life having been lost, do not waste many lives in retaliation. [. . .] But if the aggrieved party consents (and this condition of consent is laid down to prevent worse evils), forgiveness and brotherly love is better, and the door of Mercy is kept open. In Western law, no felony can be compounded. [. . .] The demand [for compensation] should be such as can be met by the party concerned, i.e., within his means, and reasonable according to justice and good conscience. For example, a demand could not be made affecting the honor of a woman or a man" (p. 71).

11. For an in-depth analysis of the legal and religious aspects of *sulh*, see Dr. Yasin Muhammad Yahya (1978). In Islam, the conception of war and peace is guided by the confrontation between the Muslim community of faithful (*dar al-Islam*, the territory of Islam) and the community of nonbelievers (*dar al-harb*, territory of war). There are two distinct terms in Arabic for the word "peace:" *salaam* and *sulh*. According to Dr. Fathi Osman (1998), a prominent Egyptian Islamologist living in the United States, *salaam* is a "permanent state. It is a natural occurrence and has a deeper significance in human relations." *Sulh*, on the other hand, requires the presence of three factors: (a) the presence of a dispute, (b) it is action-oriented (the ritual itself), and (c) can be temporary. According to Osman, "if successful, the process of *sulh* can lead to *salaam*" (Osman 1998). It is very interesting to contemplate the meaning of the word *Shalom* in Hebrew. According to the Jewish commentaries "*Shalom* does not mean merely peace as the cessation of war, of tranquility and good will between fellow humans. Literally, the word *Shalom* means completeness, wholeness. The principle of *Shalom* is not one which seeks to ignore differences and conflict, but rather seeks to integrate differences into a greater whole." I owe this definition to Rabbi Adam Berner.

12. According to the *Qur'an*, God is the ultimate arbitrator/judge ("Who is better than Allah for judgment [*hukm*] to a people who have certainty [in their belief]" [5:50]; the revelation delivered through prophets provides judgment on matters disputed by human beings; revelation becomes a criterion for human judgment ("Who so judgeth [*yahkuma*] not by that which Allah hath revealed: such are disbelievers" [5:44]). According to Lebanese scholar Ahmad Moussalli (in Paul Salem, ed., 1997), to be an arbitrator, one need not have been a chief, but it was important for arbitrators to be considered "men of understanding who had knowledge of traditions and customs. [. . .] Further qualifications included detailed knowledge of genealogies, eloquence, rhetoric, and dialects of the Arabs, as well as skill in communication, because many social cases related to honor and dishonor were presented for arbitration. Arbitration awards, especially in cities like Mecca, were considered civil law and legally binding and were regarded as based on justice and right. . . " (p. 47). With the advent of Islam, many traditional arbitration practices were maintained, provided they did not conflict with Islamic law. Muhammad himself was known as "honest arbitrator" before his prophethood. (Moussalli, p. 50).

13. Nizar Hamzeh, a Lebanese Professor of Political Science (and Chair of the Department of Political Science and Public Administration at the American University of Beirut) provides a thorough overview of the role of the Islamic revivalist group Hizbullah (Party of God) in arbitrating and mediating Lebanese conflicts. While Hizbullah's role as a third party is operative primarily within the Shi'ite communities of South Lebanon, the southern suburbs of Beirut, and the Bekaa Valley, the non-state movement's power and influence have raised its stature to such an extent that representatives of Hizbullah have mediated, arbitrated, and adjudicated cases that involve members of other communities as well. For further details see Nizar Hamzeh (1997).

14. *Sulh* does not apply to cases of theft and fraud. Given the paucity of sources, this essay relies on anthropological studies conducted in Jordan and Lebanon, unpublished dissertations, and books published in Lebanon, Jordan, and Israel, and interviews conducted with attorneys, journalists, and activists in Lebanon and Jordan.

15. For further details on Jordanian Bedouin rituals of reconciliation see Abu-Hassan (1987), pp. 257–259.

16. *Hodna* represents the initial consent by the family of the victim not to retaliate. According to Elias J. Jabbour, a Palestinian citizen of Israel who belongs to a prominent Palestinian family in the Galilee and is himself a mediator, "with this agreement (*hodna*), a limited conditional period of peace begins between the two families, the main condition being that members of the offender's family will at all costs avoid meeting or confronting any male members of the victim's family . . . The *hodna* can be for one month, for six months, or one year. [. . .] Sometimes the *hodna* is made at the cemetery during the burial ceremony." For further details, see E. J. Jabbour (1996), pp. 32–35.

17. Summarizing the basic principles leading to *sulh*, Elias Jabbour (1996) writes: "we must be careful that all the steps of the *sulh* will be taken care of, or else the *sulh* can be violated or broken. So we insist that in every murder case these conditions must be met: (1) forgiveness, (2) shaking of hands, (3) visiting each other in their houses, (4) drinking coffee, and (5) sharing a meal together" (p. 57).

18. In Western societies, from the French Revolution onward, religion was relegated to the "private" sphere in the West. State matters were mostly dictated by economic, military, and other considerations. The citizen's allegiance was primarily to the secular state. In non-Western settings, however, religion is part and parcel of one's identity, worldview, and sense of sociopolitical belonging.

19. In a democracy, peace and reconciliation occur at two levels within two different time frames. For instance, in the case of France and Germany, centuries of hatred and bloodshed were halted because of the will of enlightened leaders such as Germany's Konrad Adenauer and France's Charles de Gaulle. But at the grassroots level, it took much longer to achieve a transformative reconciliation between the citizens of the two countries.

20. This includes the former British and French colonies or countries kept together through the raw power of the bayonet, e.g., the former Yugoslavia.

21. Personal interview, Beirut, August 16, 1995.

References

Abu-Hassan, M. 1987.*Turath al Badu' al-Qada'i* (*Bedouin Customary Law*), 257–259. Amman, Jordan: Manshuraat Da'irat As-Saqafa wa al-Funun.

Abu-Nimer, M. 1996. " Conflict Resolution in an Islamic Context: Some Conceptual Questions." *Peace and Change* 21: 22–40.

Ali, A. Y. 1989. *The Holy Qur'an, Text, Translation, and Commentary*, New Revised Edition. Brentwood, MD: Amana Corporation.

Arana-Ward, M. 1998. "Octavio Paz, Mexico's Great Idea Man." *The Washington Post* April 22, D13.

Augsburger, D. W. 1992. *Conflict Mediation Across Cultures*. Louisville, Kentucky: Westminster/John Knox Press.

Berner, A. 1994. Peshara: "The Law of Compromise and Justice in Jewish Jurisprudence." Unpublished paper.

Berner, A. 1997. "Divorce Mediation: Gentle Alternative to a Bitter Process." In *Jewish Action* 57, 4: 52.

Brown, N. J. 1997. *The Rule of Law in the Arab World*. Cambridge: Cambridge University Press.

Butler, T. "Blood Feuds and Traditional Forms of Peacebuilding in the old Yugoslavia." Unpublished paper.

Callahan, D. 1997. *Unwinnable Wars: American Power and Ethnic Conflict*. New York: Hill and Wang.

Carnegie Commission. 1997. *Preventing Deadly Conflict*. New York: Carnegie Commission on Preventing Deadly Conflict.

Cohen, R. 1997. *Negotiating Across Cultures: International Communication in an Interdependent World*, revised edition. Washington, DC: United States Institute of Peace Press.

Corm, G. 1997. *Le Proche-Orient Eclate-II: Mirages de Paix et Blocages Identitaires 1990–1996*. Paris, France: Editions La Découverte.

Faure, G. O., and J. Z. Rubin, eds. 1993. *Culture and Negotiation*. Newbury Park, CA: Sage Publications.

Giddens, A. 1991. *Modernity and Self-Identity: Self and Society in the Modern Age*. Palo Alto, CA: Stanford University Press.

Hampson, F. O. 1996. *Nurturing Peace: Why Peace Settlements Succeed or Fail*. Washington, DC: United States Institute of Peace Press.

Hamzeh, N. 1997. "The Role of Hizbullah in Conflict Management within Lebanon's Shia Community." In P. Salem, ed.,*Conflict Resolution in the Arab World*, 93–118. Beirut, Lebanon: American University of Beirut.

El-Husseini, H. 1992. *Changement Social dans un Village au Liban*. Unpublished doctoral dissertation presented at the Université de Paris 8.

Jabbour, E. L. 1996. SULHA : *Palestinian Traditional Peacemaking Process*. Shefar'Am, Israel: House of Hope Publications.

Khadduri, M. 1997. "Sulh." In C. E. Bosworth, E. van Donzel, W. P. Heinrichs, and G. Lecomte, eds.,*The Encyclopaedia of Islam*, vol. IX, 845–846. Leiden, Holland: Brill.

King-Irani, L. 2000. "Rituals of Forgiveness and Processes of Empowerment in Lebanon." In .I. William Zartman, ed., *Traditional Cures for Modern Conflicts: African Conflict "Medicine,"* 129–140. Boulder, CO: Lynne Rienner Publishers.

Leach, E. R. (1968). "Ritual." In D. L. Sills, ed., *International Encyclopedia of the Social Sciences*, vols. 3 and 4, 520–526. New York: Macmillan and Free Press.

Mokheiber, G. 1995. Personal interview. Beirut, August 16.

Moussalli, A. 1997. "Constitutional Aspects of Conflict Resolution in Classical Islam." In P. Salem, ed., *Conflict Resolution in the Arab World*, 44–71. Beirut, Lebanon: American University of Beirut.

Nader, L. and H. F. Todd, Jr. 1978. "Introduction: The Disputing Process." In *The Disputing Process—Law in Ten Societies*. New York: Columbia University Press.

Osman, F. 1991. *Concepts of the Qur'an: A Topical Reading*. Los Angeles, CA: MVI Publications.

Osman, F. 1998. Personal interview, April 13.

Papo, E. 1991. *The Essential Pele Yoetz: An Encyclopedia of Ethical Jewish Living*, condensed and translated by M. D. Angel. New York: Sepher-Hermon Press.

Yahya, Y. M. 1978. *'Akd as-Sulh baina as-sharia al-islamiyya wa al kanun al madani: dirasa mukarana, fuqhiyya, qadai'yya, tashri'iyya (The Sulh Agreement Between the Islamic Law and Civil Law: A Comparative Study Based on Judicial, Islamic, and Legislative Sources)*. Cairo, Egypt: Dar al-fiqr al-arabi.

Zartman, I. W. and J. L. Rasmussen, eds. 1997. *Peacemaking in International Conflict: Methods and Techniques*. Washington, DC: United States Institute of Peace Press.

Zartman, I. W. ed. 2000. *Traditional Cures for Modern Conflicts: African Conflict "Medicine."* Boulder, CO: Lynne Rienner Publishers.

PART III

Case Studies: Australia, America, and Europe

CHAPTER 8

The Apology in Australia: Re-covenanting the National Imaginary

DANIELLE CELERMAJER

1. Introduction: The Apology Phenomenon

On October 12, 1997, the expansive green lawn of parliament house was planted thick with several thousand red, yellow, blue, green, black, and white, plastic oversized hands. Fingers reaching up to the sky, each signalled the virtual presence of the Australian woman, child, or man who had sponsored and planted a hand to mark their recognition of violations committed against Indigenous Australians, and specifically the forcible removal of Aboriginal children from their families.[1] Carried by the sea change of reconciliation, this national secular ritual, the *Sea of Hands* washed out from the capital city and the seat of the national Australian Government, north to tropical Darwin, south to rural Victoria, east to Sydney Harbor and Bondi beach, west to Broome's coastal desert and inward to the red center—Uluru (Ayers Rock).

The word "sorry", spoken and written by non-Aboriginal and offered to Aboriginal Australians, has similarly swept across Australia. The apology movement captured the public imagination in a way unseen since the anti-Vietnam protests—far exceeding any public response to other significant domestic human rights concerns previously placed before the Australian public. Moreover, it also sparked a backlash of resistance, provoking some Australians to protest what they saw as an unjust accusation, an imputation of guilt and responsibility for actions they did not *personally* commit.

Underpinning this objection was the familiar liberal demands that individuals be shielded from indiscriminate collective guilt and that modern states craft their institutions of justice in a manner that draws a clear line between those who are responsible for wrongdoing and those who are not. Indeed, since Nuremberg, the international community has been fine-tuning the jurisprudence of individual responsibility for crimes against humanity and developing competent international courts with jurisdiction over individual criminal responsibility with a view to offsetting gross forms of collective attribution.

Even in the face of the liberal objections, however, and even in a liberal democracy like Australia, the popular support for a collective apology persisted. Such persistence, and indeed the emergence at the end of the twentieth century of a range of collective mechanisms for dealing with gross violations suggests that liberalism's jurisprudence of responsibility is insufficient to quell the intuition that systematic identity-based wrongs implicate the collective and demand a response that goes beyond individual perpetrators.[2]

Reading back from the empirical fact of mass apology movements in such liberal democratic contexts, one might infer that collective apologies are not simply throwbacks of primitive collective blame, but can be understood as more sophisticated forms of justice. By extension, one might read in them alternative understandings of the role of the collective in perpetrating and dealing with past wrongs. This chapter contributes to the broader project of this book by interpreting the Australian experience to clarify the distinct place that *apology* holds in the spectrum of mechanisms for 'dealing with the past' that emerged and became prominent during the last two decades of the twentieth century.

To deepen and facilitate this interpretive project, I read the contemporary scene against two background theoretical inquiries. First, I link it with debates about the tension between individual and collective identity and responsibility. By reading back and forth between the theoretical and Australian debates, tracking the nature of the wrong, the circumstances under which it was perpetrated and the different levels of subsequent "righting" that can take place, one can begin to elucidate an emerging and normatively legitimate conceptualization of collective responsibility.

Second, I interrogate what type of act an apology is, or what one is dong by apologizing. The dominant assumption in the literature on political apologies is that the paradigmatic apology is an individual act where the words of apology represent an internal state of regret for wrongdoing and are offered as a form of compensation or way of making up for that wrong. Interpreted against this basic template, collective apologies are, by definition, aberrations, category mistakes that substitute nations for individuals and policy for sentiment. Moreover, when offered in the face of gross violations, they seem to be hopelessly inadequate, if not insulting, forms of compensation.

To challenge this interpretive frame, I draw on the United Nations study that first recommended apology as a form of reparation for gross violations, supplementing this legal study with theories about the link between identity and justice. What emerges is another, quite different trope of apology, closer to promise and reconciliation than to penalty and compensation. Apology in this mode is not intended to make up for the particular wrongs (thus glaringly inadequate in the face of grave volitions) but is rather a means whereby the group recognizes how its collective norms formed the necessary conditions for particular wrongs to occur, and expresses shame for those ethical flaws. This alternative understanding of what an apology does makes a great deal more sense when it comes to interpreting the contemporary practice and explaining its persistence and appeal.

Finally, I allude to the link between the contemporary apology and religious rituals of repentance. I suggest that the admission into the repertoire of modern liberal politics of this apparent interloper may signal liberalism's partnering itself with other modes of political action, supplementing the gaps wrought by its somewhat one-sided individualist principles.

What emerges from this specific analysis of the apology debate are some broader conclusions about the contemporary imperative to rethink justice. The apology movement represents a response to the insufficiency of mechanisms of justice that focus exclusively on the guilt of individual perpetrators in the case of systematic identity-based wrongs, and offers a legitimate, if imperfectly realized attempt to institutionalize a response to collective responsibility. By recognizing that gross systematic wrongdoing can only occur where there is a background legitimation in the political culture for the norms that sanctioned the wrongdoing, one can link members of the broader political community with the wrong, even absent their being part of the causal chain of action. The 'we' of the political community may not have pulled the trigger, so to speak, but that 'we' played, and continues to play a role in upholding and perpetuating these background norms—the necessary conditions for the manifest wrongdoing. Moreover, the *apology* as a specific mode can pick up this dimension of responsibility in so far as one understands it as a form of covenanting, or performative political commitment to fundamental principles of social and political order—alternative norms that would preclude the wrongful acts.

In offering this reading of the apology, I am not arguing that we should see it as an unproblematic act, which now explained should appeal to all good and just citizens. Even if these alternative understandings of responsibility and apology are emerging in contemporary practice, the more habitual understanding of apology as an individual act implicating a guilty actor is bound to retain a hold over our contemporary imagination. In this sense, my analysis speaks also to the ambivalent reception that members of a modern, largely liberal, nation give to any institutional mechanism that seems to contravene dearly held principles of moral individualism. Moreover, the liberal criticisms of the apology carry important warnings about the dangers of collective attribution and highlight the difficulty of articulating a collective response without committing further injustices.

2. Apology for the Removal of Aboriginal Children?

Removal and a Just Response

The apology first appeared on the Australian national stage as one of the recommendations of *Bringing Them Home*, the official report of the Human Rights and Equal Opportunity Commission's *National Inquiry into the Separation of Aboriginal Children from Their Families* (hereafter the *National Inquiry*). Although Aboriginal children had been systematically taken from their families as part of official government policy since 1910 and were still being removed right up until 1970, this report represented the first high-level national and comprehensive study and exposure of this chapter in Australian history. Drawing on official historical documents and extensive first person testimony, it told Australians the compelling and shocking story of the tens of thousands of Aboriginal children who had been forcibly taken from their families and communities, relocated across the country and placed in state- or church-run institutions or in foster or adoptive homes. The report documented the development and legal framework of the policy and provided an official platform where long-silenced Aboriginal people could give voice to their experiences of brutal removal, years of deprivation and abuse, and in the case of families, their frustrated attempts to use the legal system to get their children back.

The National Inquiry opened a debate unprecedented in its breadth and continuity, engaging a huge cross section of Australians and sustaining interest far beyond the normal five minutes of fame which human rights issues are lucky to win. Australians responded emotively and diversely to the findings the report made, to the conclusions it drew about those findings, and to a number of the recommendations it made about how the Australian Government should respond. Many Australians were shocked that this could have been part of what they had believed to be a generally fair and peaceful national history. Others refused to believe it and questioned the report's methodology, impartiality, and accuracy. Some Australians objected to the contentious finding that the practice constituted a form of genocide, and others opposed the recommendations concerning compensation.

Perhaps surprisingly, the most contentious and widely debated issue was none of these apparently more inflammatory or costly findings and recommendations. Rather, it concerned the pair of recommendations that Australian parliaments as well as police forces, churches, and other non-governmental organizations, which played a role in the administration of removal, officially acknowledge the responsibility of their predecessors for the laws, policies, and practices of removal, and extend public apologies to Indigenous individuals, families, and communities.

In the immediate aftermath of the report's release, thousands of individual Australians and a wide range of nongovernment organizations (amongst others schools, churches, and immigrant groups) rushed to offer apologies. Deeply affected by what they had read and heard, they wanted to show that they recognized the wound inflicted on Aboriginal Australians. They also grasped the apology as a readily available gesture acknowledging that as Australians they shared in this national failure and were unavoidably tainted with the legacy of shame. This wave of support was by no means universal, however, and many other Australians vigorously and publicly decried the apology, objecting to what they saw as an unjust penalty that indiscriminately punished them for other people's actions.

This objection was articulated perhaps most pointedly and significantly by John Howard, the conservative Prime Minister and the leading protagonist in the anti-apology movement. "'To say to them that they are personally responsible," he announced, "and that they should feel a sense of shame about those events is to visit upon them an unreasonable penalty and an injustice."[3]

It is worth pausing and examining this statement in some detail, and in particular looking at the assumptions built into it, assumptions which set up the apparently inevitable conclusion. Implicit in his framing are distinct, but by no means necessary or objectively true conceptualizations of key terms in the argument, specifically: the nature of the wrongs to be addressed; responsibility for wrongs; and, what type of act an apology is.

Apology's Injustice and Liberal Jurisprudence

As Howard framed the story of removal, the wrongs that the apology addressed were "the events", by which he intends the specific acts of removal and abuse committed against Aboriginal children. Responsibility, accordingly, is attached to the actions that caused those events. Apology, finally, is interpreted as the penalty that the responsible party ought to bear once found liable. By equating the wrong with the *events*, responsibility with wrongdoing, and apology with the *penalty* attached to liability, Howard's approach tracked the classical liberal jurisprudence of responsibility, a jurisprudence that is structurally hostile to encoding collective responsibility.[4]

The basic formula of this jurisprudence is that guilt can be attributed only to the actor who caused the act (*actus rea*) and did so with intention (*mens rea*). It is possible, still working within this framework, to attribute guilt or responsibility beyond individuals, (most commonly corporations) by recognizing the institution or corporation as a legal subject and finding a binding law that it has violated. Thus, for example, if a government contravened its own laws, or passed laws violating its constitution, or even passed laws violating the provisions of international treaties to which it was party, it could (theoretically) be held liable for the violation. This move to institutional responsibility was not, however, easily achieved in this case, given that the laws sanctioning removal had not contravened Australia's Constitution and the relevant international human rights treaties had not yet come into effect at the time the acts were committed.[5]

One might still be able to argue that the in sanctioning such gross violations the Australian state was liable, even absent positive binding law, because it had contravened binding moral (or customary international) laws. Although legal positivists might object, this line of reasoning remains consistent with liberal jurisprudence. Indeed those who supported the establishment of the Nuremberg Tribunal argued that such universal moral principles provided a sufficient source of law to legitimately prosecute German war criminals in a properly constituted international tribunal, even absent an international treaty outlawing genocide or crimes against humanity.[6]

This appeal to universal morals or customary international legal principles would not work in the Australian case however, as the moral context was more ambiguous. In fact, at the time when Australia was removing Aboriginal children, racial discrimination and nonrecognition of the rights of Indigenous peoples had been the international norm in postcolonial nations. In this sense, Australia, far from being "aberrant," was acting in conformity with the mores of the so-called civilized nations that formed its community of states.[7] Certainly, the whole question of universal moral norms is highly arguable, because at the same time there were strong norms about respect and prevalent antidiscrimination movements. If, however, one looks to the dominant moral framework that informed white Australians at the time, the popular, though perhaps offensive defense offered by many of apology's critics that 'people thought they were doing the right thing' is far from false. Indeed, the problem lies in the fact that they *did* think that they were doing the right thing, but this is not a level of wrong that liberal jurisprudence can speak to.

The legal and conceptual framework that this jurisprudence imports into the arguments does indeed seem to provide the Howard objection with a watertight case. How can one hold Australian citizens of today responsible, and in turn penalize them for actions that other Australians no longer alive and their government *legally* committed in the past? Indeed, by adopting this framework, Howard could (and did), apparently quite rightly, turn the justice of apology on its head. By binding injustice tightly to the direct commission of particular acts, Howard moved the claim of violation away from Aboriginal people and delivered it to white Australians who, in being blamed for something they did not do, could now justifiably count themselves as victims of injustice. Correlatively, it is now those who would falsely accuse, Aboriginal people and their trendy Chardonnay drinking supporters, who are guilty of committing an injustice.

How does one respond to what appeared to be a trumping argument? It is after all perfectly true that contemporary Australians (with very few exceptions) themselves neither made the laws that sanctioned removal nor took the children. How could they justifiably be 'blamed' for those acts? If this is the question, then Howard's answer was right. Individuals cannot be held responsible and penalized for actions that they had no part in bringing about, and there was no way of legitimately arguing this point. The problem, however, was with the way Howard framed the issue, and accordingly, the only way to respond to the objection was to move back to the assumptions he made about what an apology was about. This required reconceptualizing those three terms that drove his argument, the wrong that an apology was crafted to address, the nature of responsibility, and the work that apology does.

3. The Wrong: Apologizing for What?

Starting with the wrongs themselves, one does not have to look very far for an alternative to Howard's narrow definition, because the report itself described the wrong of removal in a very different and far broader way. It did not tell the story of removal in isolation, abstracted from the broader patterns of national practice and culture, but clearly located it as part of the postcolonial national project, laying out the historical, social, legal, and cultural context in which the practice developed and occurred.

It painted the picture of an Australia in which Aboriginality was considered a deficit, an anathema to the progress of civilization, inconsistent with full citizenship, and an impediment to the development of the nation. The removal of Aboriginal children was but a particularly horrendous plank of the more

159

generalized policy of assimilation, designed to expedite the disintegration of Aboriginal communities and the demise of Aboriginality.[8] Assimilation by no means implied a meeting of cultures, but quite vehemently meant becoming white.[9] This was not merely nonrecognition, but institutionalized denigration of all Aboriginal people on the basis of their Aboriginality. Only to the extent that they could be purified of this backward strain (carried in their black blood) would they be able to enter the social and political order of the state. Moreover, providing them with the opportunity to do so represented their only chance to partake in the elevated cultural achievement of European civilization, albeit in its imported form.

The injuries which removal inflicted on Aboriginal people were accordingly portrayed in these broad terms of culture, identity, and citizenship. The report argued that injurious and abusive as the specific violations to body and soul were, the most significant dimension of the injury, as it comes through in the first person testimony of those removed and expert witnesses, was the damage to identity. Aboriginal children were denied all contact with their original family, all knowledge about where they came from, and were forbidden to speak their own languages:

Y'know, I can remember we used to just talk lingo. [In the Home] they used to tell us not to talk that language, that it's devil's language. And they'd wash our mouths with soap. We sorta had to sit down with Bible language all the time. So it sorta wiped out all our language that we knew. (Woman taken from her parents with her three sisters when the family, who worked and resided on a pastoral station, came into town to collect stores; placed at Umewarra Mission).[10]

Not only were Aboriginal people and culture held up by white Australians as objects of condescension, fear, and ridicule, but the Aboriginal children's internalized images of their own Aboriginal identity also became a source of contempt and shame. Most were never told directly that they were of Aboriginal descent or were instructed to conceal their Aboriginality by assuming some more "palatable" ethnic identity (southern European was popular) to explain their darker skin. At the same time, the image of the dirty, inferior black was held over them as an object of fear and threat, ready to drag them out of civilization and into backwardness should they not conform to the behavioral demands of their educators. As one witness put it: "I got told my Aboriginality when I got whipped and they'd say, 'You Abo, you nigger.' That was the only time I got told my Aboriginality."[11]

The full significance of damage to Aboriginal identity goes beyond any inventory of specific losses—language, cultural knowledge and experience, access to land, and now potentially, to native title rights. Damage to identity cannot be reduced to a sum of these components because it is embodied in concrete persons—and so the damage is inflicted at the level of the person's sense of self. From the point of view of the state, Aboriginality was a racial anachronism and impediment to be eradicated; from the point of view of the individuals who were removed, it was their identity—even *them*.[12]

An expert witness psychiatrist, giving evidence to the Royal Commission into Aboriginal Deaths in Custody, pinpointed this identity dimension as the core of the damage to individual indigenous people who had been removed:

The most profound effect of institutionalization, which overrides other well-documented effects of institutionalization generally, was the persistent attempt by authorities to force the boys to identify as European. [...] One was positive reinforcement of the European model, the other was a negative portrayal of Aboriginality combined with a withholding from the boys of any particular knowledge of their immediate family or of Aborigines generally.[13]

Even this portrayal does not fully capture the extent of the abuse or the injury. To achieve this one must widen the frame to take in its pervasiveness as a national policy applied across Aboriginal communities, and focused on the denigration and annihilation of *Aboriginality* per se. The aim was to cleanse the Australian social landscape of a 'type'—but this could only be done through its embodiment in particular individuals. Thus, individual Aboriginal people became the site of specific and general annihilation. They were literally placed in an impossible situation, having to be both that which should be eradicated, and not to be it.

The irony of 'eradication' is of course that colonial, or postcolonial, Australia needed the category of the uncivilized native to affirm its own claim to civil and sovereign legitimacy. Just as the legal fiction of *terra nullius* affirmed in law that Aboriginal people could not and did not own the land, the policy of removal affirmed that Aboriginal people could not and did not have viable societies and civilizations.[14] A nation grounded on illegal occupation and violence required a legitimating narrative—here told in the language of culture and race, and more intimately in terms of who could and could not have a family. Understood within this context, their classification as 'half-castes' was less a biological category than a reflection of colonialism's racism, which needed bodies on which to do its work of racial progress and assert its political legitimacy. In this sense, the very personal story of removal cannot be extracted from the story of the constitution of the Australian nation.

At the same time, it radically contradicted a Constitution and national imaginary that declared Australia the land of the "fair go."

Framed in these broad *political and cultural* terms, the wrong that the report was highlighting through the specific story of removal, and the wrong that apology was addressing, expanded beyond the specific events to encompass the cultural and political constitution of the Australian nation itself. Certainly, one starts with specific incidents—stealing children while their mothers were shopping or sexual abuse in church-run institutions. But this is only the entry point into a more comprehensive context, which one might call the *political culture* of Australia. The pervasive racism against Aboriginal people, the political imperative of delegitimizing Aboriginal people as competent citizens and beyond this the denial of legitimate Aboriginal law and sovereignty were all the conditions of possibility for the specific acts.

Had Aboriginal Australians been recognized as coequal citizens, who had the right to bring up their children or remain with their parents, and the higher order right to legal recourse when deprived of these other rights, then removal could never have become a systematic policy, unnoticed or silently tolerated by non-Aboriginal Australia. Correlatively, one can infer back from these symptoms of racial discrimination to the more comprehensive, albeit invisible, moral grammar of the political community.

Recall above I argued that one of the defenses raised for the practice was that people at the time thought that they were doing the right thing, thus rendering it immoral to condemn the individuals who acted in conformity with this dominant social norm. What this different analysis provides is a way of bringing into view the wrong of this very judgement: that removal was right. It was this higher order fault in the classification of right and wrong that was the wrong, and this was what Australians *now* had to address.

Thus, in answer to Howard's claim that 'the events' were the wrongs to which apology was addressed, the report suggested that the wrongs extended down into this far more pervasive political culture. This then opens the next stage of the inquiry: If Australia's political culture is the wrong to be addressed, then who is responsible for this wrong?

4. Who is Responsible for Political Culture?

Although only implicitly woven into the story of removal, the report itself intimated the answer to this question. If the removal of Aboriginal children was part of the project of whiting Australia—removing the stain of Aboriginality— then in the background was a cultural norm which sanctioned this denigration, and in turn the non-Aboriginal Australia whose purity was at issue. If Aboriginality was the explicit object, then non-Aboriginal Australia was the implicit subject, occupying the position of superiority in a racial hierarchy and claiming the sovereign and legal rights denied to Aboriginal Australians.

But how does one translate this schema into an account of responsibility? The clear line of reasoning that a liberal jurisprudence of responsibility affords is unavailable here, and indeed if one tries to use its template, one quickly runs into serious problems. To say, for example, that individual non-Aboriginal Australians directly cause political culture both incorrectly reifies political culture as a type of object that can be caused, and inappropriately pins causal agency on individuals. This *actus reus, mens rea* model will clearly not work. What we need is an alternative frame for telling the story of responsibility.

Ordinary Australians who defended the apology against the Howard objection did not, of course, describe the problem in these conceptual terms. Nevertheless, the language they used to link themselves with the wrongs of removal, and in particular their substitution of the term *shame* for *guilt* pointed to an alternative, albeit implicit conception of responsibility. Some of the more theoretically sophisticated commentators explicitly recognized that the problem lay in the conceptualization of responsibility and so addressed the Howard objection by redefining both the criteria for responsibility and correlatively the type of responsibility implied by a collective apology.

In doing so, they still had to work within some of the basic normative and pragmatic parameters that had motivated the Howard response, particularly those concerning individual integrity. From a normative point of view, an apology would only be legitimate if it respected the distinction between those who had actively committed the wrong, and others who may be indirectly implicated, but were certainly not directly guilty of wrong*doing*. From a pragmatic point of view, any political campaign that advocated an institution promoting collective, inter-generational blame for the wrong of removal would have had no chance of success in contemporary liberal Australia. Recognizing that no argument could be won if this line was crossed, and the problematic implications of the language of *guilt*, some of the more savvy commentators capitalized on the rhetorical shift to the language of shame.

Robert Manne, one of the leading liberal political philosophers engaged in the debate pinpointed what he saw as a crucial failure among Australians to distinguish between collective guilt and historical shame: "Because guilt for wrongs done is always a matter of individual responsibility the idea of collective guilt genuinely makes no sense. An individual cannot be charged with the crimes of others [. . .] however talk of sharing a legacy of shame is quite another thing."[15] Shame, Manne argued, does not imply the same direct assumption of responsibility for past wrongs, and as such, people can be asked to partake in shame without the sense that they are being blamed. The claim that shame, as distinct from guilt, was a justifiable response in this situation built on certain understandings of the difference in the logical structures of guilt and shame. Specifically, and tracking the liberal jurisprudence, actually committing the particular wrongful act is a necessary condition for guilt, but for shame, a more indirect association with wrongdoing or harm is sufficient. To explain why action is not a necessary condition for shame and to elaborate what is, those arguing in favor of a shift to shame argued that guilt and shame correspond to two distinct dimensions—action in the former case, identity in the latter. Legal theorist Desmond Manderson, for example, argued that whereas "guilt is about taking responsibility for what we did—it stems from our actions...shame is about *who we are*."[16]

This statement is suggestive, but problematic, and certainly requires clarification. What is it about "who we are" that makes "us" a legitimate subject of shame? Or, more precisely, if the responsibility which gives rise to guilt can be assessed through an analysis of the action using the twin criteria of *actus reus* and *mens rea* set out above, what type of responsibility is associated with a political identity which gives rise to shame? This question seemed to lurk in the background of the Australian debate, and the failure to articulate a sufficiently convincing answer was perhaps part of the reason that the same assertions ping-ponged between the opposing sides.

The categories of guilt developed by Karl Jaspers to understand the question of German guilt in the wake of the Nazi atrocities can help to answer this question.[17] Jaspers was alive to the dangers of blaming a nation or a people as an undifferentiated collective and, consistent with the liberal conception of justice and responsibility assumed by Howard, insisted that only individuals could be held directly liable for wrongful acts—the category he called *criminal guilt*. He argued vehemently that generalizing this type of guilt to a collective was not only theoretically specious, but also politically dangerous. Criminal guilt, in turn, constituted the only legitimate basis of punishment.

In contradistinction to Howard's position however, and consistent with the proponents of the apology, Jaspers' rejection of an undifferentiated attribution of "national guilt" did not entail a blanket rejection of collective responsibility. Rather, he agreed that there was something correct in the intuition that responsibility for massive and systematic wrongs went beyond the discrete and directly responsible individual actors. Building on this intuition, but respecting the principles that motivated liberal conceptions of individual justice, he then set about articulating an acceptable conception of guilt beyond the individual perpetrator, and beyond criminal guilt.

As a philosopher well versed in the development of modern liberal theories of justice, Jaspers recognized in this the challenge of developing a more finely tuned system where different shades or dimensions of guilt would allow one to escape the choice between a narrow focus on the direct role of abstracted individuals on the one hand and gross collective blame on the other. For him, as for contemporary proponents of a collective response to wrongs of the past, this entailed avoiding the problematic reification of the collective subject, modelled on the (modern) individual and endowed with all its attributes (intention, the capacity to act), but writ large onto the nation like some type of super-body.

For this guilt adhering to the collective, Jaspers crafted the category of *political guilt*—the state of liability attaching to a political community, but arising from the actions of political leaders and fellow citizens. In Jaspers' words: *Es ist jedes Menschen Mitverantwortung wie er regiert wird.* ("Every person is co-responsible for the way he is governed."). In other words, people other than those who actually committed the wrongful acts are liable by virtue of their relationship to government. He then goes on to elaborate this relationship.

What is so interesting about the way Jaspers does this—even more so because of its uncanny resonance with the Australian debate—is that he does not conceive of the link between the people of the nation and the actions of the state in terms of something they *do*, but in terms of who they *are*, their political identity. As outlined above, liberal jurisprudence links citizens into state action by identifying them as the indirect authors of the law, or the citizen actors who authorize the political representatives who then make the law. Their responsibility is thus still framed in terms of their actions, albeit actions deferred through their representatives.

According to Jaspers' conception, the people's responsibility follows less from their institutional responsibility, and more from their *identity* as the human dimension of the nation. This form of responsibility extends beyond the discrete actor to members of the political community, but not because one can locate them somewhere on the causal chain, which led to that action; for example, "S" voted for the government and the government passed the law which authorized removal. Rather, the people of the nation, taken together, constitute a dimension of the nation, just as the institutions of government constitute a dimension of the nation, and the nation provides the conditions under which the wrongdoing occurred.

Jaspers' shift from an institutional explanation in which citizens play the very limited role as those who authorize the government, to a more personal or societal explanation is also in keeping with the fascinating turn that the Australian case took. Although the Inquiry in fact recommended that parliaments apologize, thus allowing the apology to be conceived in formal institutional terms at a distance from Australian civil society, the proponents of the apology embraced it as a societal apology. They did this both in the sense that a range of civil society groups and individuals apologized *as Australians*, and in their interpretation of a parliamentary apology as *their* apology—and not a formalistic institutional act. Even when the apologies issued from parliaments, the performance was highly personal, with Aboriginal representatives telling their stories, and individual parliamentarians emotionally stepping to the floor to express their sorrow and shame.

The type of responsibility Jaspers is articulating becomes clearer when he explores the intimate relationship between political guilt and moral guilt—a third category defined as the guilt arising from violations of moral principles, irrespective their being violations of positive law. Although Jaspers distinguishes political and moral guilt conceptually, he insists that "the conduct which made us liable rests on the sum of political conditions whose nature is moral," and hence "there can be no radical separation between political and moral guilt."[18]

This combined political and moral guilt arises from the fact that the nation is the political realm in which *ich mein Dasein habe*—I have my being/place of being. *Dasein*, a term that harks back to the Hegelian notion of *Sittlichkeit*, is not simply a physical location, but rather the moral/cultural/political world that is the source of individual and national identity. *Dasein* is the conditions of life, "the whole way of life," and individuals live within them "as links in their chain," even if they oppose particular political actions.

Although Australians did not of course use the term *Dasein*, some of the language they employed to elaborate the notion of shame and identity belongs in the same metaphoric frame. Robert Manne, for example, explained the justification for feeling collective shame with reference to this being the place where we form our identity: "To be an Australian is to be embedded or implicated in this country's history in a way outsiders or visitors cannot be."[19] The word embedded, like the word "dwelling" (used most often in a negative sense of "dwelling in the past") draws on the same notion of a thick space, which members of a political community occupy. This resonance becomes even more pronounced if one extends the play of words through the metaphors of the etymological family—dwelling, habitat, habit, customary, and custom.[20]

This move to identity within a thick cultural space is by no means unproblematic. As soon as one begins to enter this conceptual frame, one is in danger of provoking the classical liberal accusation that one is collapsing the individual into the collective, thus crossing important boundaries of moral individualism. As Weber pointed out in his distinction between *representative* and *solidarity* forms of political association, liberalism's clear institutional lines setting out who is authorized to act for the group were explicitly designed to displace the more primitive (solidarity) forms, where the actions of any member could be the basis for benefits or blame falling on the rest.[21]

Jaspers' description seems to skirt dangerously close to this territory, especially when he claims that all members of the political community bear political guilt, even if they explicitly opposed their government's policies and their society's discriminatory cultural norms. Similarly, one Australian commentator's portrayal of shame could easily be seen as crossing over to crude collectivism: "because shame is about identity, an identity which extends beyond my body to my society, I can and do feel shame for acts which I did not cause or bring about."[22] If this slippage is to be avoided, as it must be, apology's proponents needed a conception of *Dasein*, or being embedded, which linked individual members of a political community with the significant public acts and policies of that community without violating individual integrity.

Neither Jaspers, nor Australian participants in the debate offered a solution to this dilemma—and one could hardly expect them to, given that it has haunted political theory at least since Hegel. But one can find the beginnings of a possible (if always partial) answer in Jaspers' loose discussion of the complex of *political norms* or the *political culture* that provide the context in which formal laws and institutions develop, in which members of the political community form their identity (including their moral values) and in terms of which they evaluate the rightfulness of their acts. Jaspers provides a graphic picture of this interwoven map of morality, daily acts, and specific violations:

Moral failings cause the conditions out of which both crime and political guilt arise. The commission of countless little acts of negligence, of convenient adaptation of cheap vindication, and the imperceptible promotion of wrong; the participation in the creation of a public atmosphere that spreads confusion and thus makes evil possible— all that has consequences that partly condition the political guilt involved in the situation and the events.[23]

This resonates strongly with the Inquiry's finding that the specific violations of removal emerge from the ongoing racially patterned norms regulating who

167

has a right to what and beyond that, with the constitution and ethos of the postcolonial Australian nation. That it was this link between the specific violations and the broad institutional framework of the nation that justified a comprehensive political response explains why the debate rapidly expanded to incorporate grand arguments about Australian history.[24] Those advocating the apology understood that they had to prove that removal was but one plank in Australia's racist political culture; those decrying it similarly understood that their arguments against collective responsibility would be bolstered by evidence that Australia's history was, in general, fair and egalitarian. Or perhaps it was the other way round, and the resistance to apologizing was the tip of the iceberg—the ice underneath being the imperative to retain our image of ourselves as the land of the fair go.

This shift from a causal analysis of acts to a more generalized link between the Australian nation and political culture seems promising, and certainly in keeping with the facts and the tenor of the debate, but still has two obvious weaknesses. First, the notion of a political culture, or background norms, remains vague, and may well strike many critics as an unprovable theoretical construct. Second, even if one is willing to build this notion of political culture into an explanatory framework, this alone does not show how Australians are *responsible*. Justifying responsibility requires a clearer analytic connection between the members of the political community and these ongoing patterns of exclusion or political culture. It is one thing to identify political culture as the conditions of possibility for the wrongdoing and another to show exactly how the populace is implicated in creating, sustaining, or changing those conditions. Only the latter can be considered a conception of human responsibility as distinct from a structural explanation in which members of the political community are simply acting out the cultural script they had been provided.

Some recent reconceptualizations of political culture offer resources for addressing both problems. Traditionally, political culture was conceptualized in either ideal or structural/materialist terms, that is, either as the composite of the ideas in people's heads (people's ideas *cause* political culture and in turn shape political institutions),[25] or as the form of hard institutions (political culture is embodied in objective structures and shapes people's consciousness). This choice between seeing political culture as a free-floating first cause or as an ideological reflection failed to capture the complex interactions between political institutions and the actual people who make judgements and take actions.

Recognizing the theoretical paucity of these approaches, discourse theorists navigate a path between the two poles by reconceptualizing political culture as the pattern of meaning that organizes the full range of institutions, including hard ones like law and soft ones like norms and identity. The grammar of political culture exists and can be read in institutions and at the same time it is patterned as people's beliefs and views about right and wrong.[26] As Sherry Ortner puts it:

All these routines and scenarios are predicated upon and embody within themselves, the fundamental notions of temporal, spatial and social ordering that underlie and organize the system as a whole. In enacting these routines, actors not only continue to be shaped by the underlying organizational principles involved, but *continually re-endorse those principles in the world of public observation and discourse.*[27]

National culture and the nation on this model are not two distinct entities that stand in a causal relationship, which we have to explain, but two dimensions which mutually construct and constrain each other.[28] As Cornelius Castoriadis puts it: "individuals are made by the *instituted society* at the same time as they make it and remake it";[29] or correlatively, "the social-historical object is co-constituted by the activities of individuals, which incarnate or concretely realize the society in which they live."[30]

This remapping allows one to build a role for the people of the nation into the explanation, without falling into the trap of saying that society or people cause culture. Evaluative schemes, actions, systems of belief and assumptions about rightful behavior are sites at which actual people perpetuate or reform political culture. The members of the collective are thus not implicated as they would be were a linear causal model at work, moving from people's ideas or consciousness via their actions to breaches of the law—a model that forms the basis for criminal guilt. Rather, people, along with a range of institutions, are the source *and* the site of the political culture within which it is possible for the wrongful actions to occur. The process is one of interdependence, or, to put it another way, one of multifaceted identity. One of the faces of this web of social norms is society, comprising the ongoing speakers of the social grammar. They cannot be abstracted and blamed; but nor are they automata, merely passive recipients of institutionalized norms. Still, one might ask whether this idea of political culture is sufficiently rigorous to ground a theory of responsibility, and more importantly institutions attributing responsibility.

For critics who insist that only empirically verifiable phenomena suffice for such purposes, political culture as conceptualized here may not be up to the task. However, the various political, legal, and cultural institutions of Australia provide ample empirical support for the usefulness of such a construct.

If one examines Australia's historical, political, and legal institutions regulating land ownership and political rights, the statistics on the distribution of socioeconomic rights and the portrayal of race in literature, the media and scientific theory, one is left with little doubt that there is a common pattern running through them, and that this pattern is organized according to race. It would be methodologically flawed to abstract and reify this pattern and posit it as a cause. But it would be equally flawed to deny that there is a link between the patterning of this broad range of Australian institutions and an apparently discrete aberration of removal.

Again, the Inquiry made this link very clear by showing how the violation of removal was not incidental, but rather one manifestation of a normative structure which deemed Aboriginality and full citizenship incompatible. Moreover, it built the general Australian population into the story by showing that denigration of Aboriginal identity was the logical counterpart to the identity claims of non-Aboriginal people, claims that supported their right to be the sole legitimate bearers of sovereign and citizenship rights. In this sense, the claim that shame arises from *who we are* is in fact very accurate. Australia's very existence as a sovereign, postcolonial nation, constituted on the foundations of British law, rested on the systematic annihilation of Aboriginal rights.

Let us now link this back to the dilemma of how to locate the collective in the production of the conditions for wrongdoing. According to the liberal schema, an individual who directly causes a wrongful action is the subject of criminal guilt. According to this schema, the community is not posited as a causal agent, but rather understood as the subjective dimension of an interdependent set of relations and more precisely the subject of *political* guilt (or shame). Castoriadis' explanation of this web illuminates the distinct conception at work here:

Athenian society is, in a sense, nothing but the Athenians; without them it is only the remnants of a transformed landscape... worn out statues fished out some place in the Mediterranean. But Athenians are Athenians only by means of the *nomos* of the *polis*. In this relationship between instituted society—which infinitely transcends the totality of the individuals that "compose" it, but which actually exist only by being "realized" in the individuals it manufactures—on the one hand—and these individuals, on the other, we witness an original, unprecedented type of relationship which cannot be thought under the categories of the whole and the parts, the set and its elements, the universal and the particular.[31]

The responsibility behind shame does not result from a discrete doing (*actus reus*), but from the people's bearing and perpetuating the cultural and political context that underpinned the doing. Holding this distinction between the two types of explanation is crucial if one is going to avoid the pitfalls so well marked in the well-worn path of theories of collective responsibility.

More positively, this conception of collective responsibility has a number of advantages. First, it does not fall prey to the liberal accusation that the collective is just a sloppy and unethical conglomeration of individuals, but is genuinely and necessarily collective. Political culture, as conceived here is not a sum of potentially separable individual bits. Rather, responsibility for sustaining the social grammar belongs to the community *qua* community. Accordingly, this form of responsibility is fully consistent with—even demands—a collective response.

Second, it provides conceptual tools for beginning to answer questions about who belongs to the shamed society and how far it extends in temporal terms, both of which were major points of contention in this case, where the apology concerned acts committed at a different time and in a society comprising different bodies.[32] If the type of collective one is talking about is an entity (substance), it is difficult to justify transferring it to another different entity (here different people at a different time).[33] If, however, it is conceived of as a political/cultural pattern (form), then it is not, in principle, confined in terms of space and time.

This does not get rid of the problem, and important questions remain about how far, both temporally and spatially, this identity can be thought to extend. I would suggest, very generally, that it extends so far as the patterns in question continue to organize significant aspects of the institutional structure of the political community. This answer allows for a range of interpretations, particularly given that the patterns are by nature mutable. But it does suggest the types of questions that are relevant in working out the legitimacy of shame's reach. For example, so long as the distinction between Aboriginal and non-Aboriginal people continues to organize the distribution of rights, and continues to be a relevant (and negative) marker in the status of Australian citizens, one could argue for continuity and, accordingly, that some transfer of responsibility or shame is legitimate.

This hypothesis is supported by the fact that proponents and opponents of the apology alike saw the importance to the debate of how contemporary Australians were portrayed, and to this end, harnessed competing characterizations of the state of racism today to bolster their respective positions. They too saw that whether or not Australia could now be described as a racist country bore directly on whether contemporary Australians inherited the shame of this past manifestation of racism and the obligation to repair past wrongs.

Were we now truly egalitarian, the charge that we were responsible would have far less traction.

The third advantage of this conception of responsibility is that it provides a basis for showing why a *political* response is required. One requires this type of additional justification because, even if one is convinced that there is a logic to the experience of collective shame, this in itself is not a sufficient reason for the state to craft a public policy response to the experience. The people of the nation may and do experience a myriad of emotions which should not be translated into public policy. If collective shame is a valid basis for public policy, as distinct from the emotional response of gathered individuals, this will only be because it is grounded in the political identity of the nation, linked to some political imperative, and because it serves a political objective, such as doing justice, consolidating the nation, or strengthening or reforming constitutional values. By linking the members of the nation to shame and responsibility via political culture and the production of the conditions for the original political action (removal), one produces a justification for political action (the apology). This shame is not an extra-political response, which we then need to justify bringing into the political sphere. Rather, this shame is itself grounded in the political sphere.

This then opens the third, and final line of inquiry in response to the Howard objection. If the wrong to be addressed is Australia's racially discriminatory political culture and non-Aboriginal Australia collectively bears some type of responsibility for this political culture, then how does a public collective apology pick up on this particular dimension of responsibility?

5. What is Apology?

Like all social practices, apology has no objective, fixed, universal meaning. Rather, actual apologies are bound to give rise to a range of interpretations, derived on the one hand from assumptions people already hold about what it means to apologize and on the other from the particular context in which they occur. This indeterminacy will be particularly pronounced where a social practice traditionally (or habitually) used in certain contexts appears in an unfamiliar and novel context where customarily accepted interpretations have not yet been established. Those interpreting the apology in this new context will inevitably draw on meanings associated with other uses of apology (in personal relationship for example) in making sense of this novel application. The results, as one sees both in the literature and in the political debates, are: first, that some interpreters simply assume that political apology is a category mistake, inappropriately transferred from the individual to the political sphere; and second, that arguments about the practice are distorted because people taking apparently conflicting positions on whether an apology is justified may in fact be arguing on the basis of very different assumptions about the type of practice apology is.

A quick survey of some of the most prominent arguments reveals the range of assumed templates of meaning. In a widely cited article on political apologies, Michel Rolph-Trouillot argues that they fail as political acts because they treat the collective as if it were a (liberal, modern) individual, thereby committing a category mistake unacceptable to modern subjects who are not convinced by the transfer.[34] Implicit in his argument is the assumption that the essential apologizing subject is the liberal individual and, correlatively, that all other apologies are deviations from this prototype. John Howard similarly opposed the political apology on the basis of a preexisting interpretation. His assumed template of apology represents it as an act admitting responsibility for wrongdoing and a form of penalty. Many Aboriginal people opposed the apology because they read it as a substitute for material compensation, and as such judged it to be hopelessly inadequate (cheap) in the face of such serious violations.

That these interpretations have been brought to bear on the contemporary scene makes perfect sense, given their familiarity. Nevertheless, the persistence of the phenomenon in this apparently inappropriate or mistaken context should give us pause before forging ahead with the unexamined assumption that these are the only meanings at work. This theoretical inference, that other meanings may in fact be at work, is supported by the fact that apology's advocates articulated, albeit often implicitly, alternative understandings—understandings that did not give rise to the same objections. The apologies they defended were, variously, expressions of sympathy, forms of acknowledgement of the other's suffering and recognition of their experience, and declarations about race, equality, and reconciliation in Australia.

In this final section, my intention is not to establish a full inventory of the significances of apology, nor to evaluate these different interpretations against each other. Rather, in much the same way as I fleshed out alternative conceptions of responsibility that would make better sense of the intuition that a collective could be responsible, here I mine some alternative contexts and understandings of apology to make sense of an apology in this collective, public, and inter-temporal context.

First, and most obviously, one might look to *The National Inquiry* itself, which was the official source of the apology recommendation. What one finds here is that apology is represented as a form of *satisfaction*, where satisfaction is one dimension of reparation for human rights violations. That said, the National Inquiry does not explain what dimension of reparation satisfaction affects. Indeed, the category of satisfaction is something of an anomaly within the reparative, let alone retributive, justice approaches and all but ignored in the plethora of recent literature on restorative justice.[35] To work out what it is that is being repaired or restored and how apology does this, one has to extrapolate from the Inquiry, drawing once again on its picture of removal and supplementing this with a richer understanding of the relationship between justice and identity.

At a very general level, the Inquiry adopted a restorative or reparatory, as distinct from a retributive justice approach, thus constructing its specific recommendations in line with the overall goal of restoring the *status quo ante* or repairing the damage done by the wrongful acts.[36] To work out what this should look like, the Commission drew guidance from the "Van Boven principles," which had been generated from a 1989 United Nations study on the right to restitution, compensation, and rehabilitation for victims of gross violations of human rights and fundamental freedoms.[37]

The van Boven principles break the broader restorative goal down into four components: (1) restitution; (2) compensation; (3) rehabilitation; and (4) satisfaction and guarantees against non-repetition—each of which is to be effected through concrete interventions. Apology, including public acknowledgment of the facts and acceptance of responsibility, appeared in the fourth category. It should be noted here that the apology recommendation was presented as part of a broader reparatory strategy. Thus, apology was certainly not seen as a sufficient response, but it was a necessary one. From this alone, one can deduce that satisfaction affects a distinct type of reparation and cannot be reduced to one of the other, more familiar, dimensions. However as neither the Inquiry nor the van Boven report elaborate the category, we still have to work out what characterizes satisfaction.

To do this, one might first try to abstract the common, distinguishing feature from the various interventions that fall under this category: apology, verification of the facts and full public disclosure of the truth, official declaration or judicial decision restoring the dignity, reputation and rights of the victim, judicial or administrative sanctions against persons responsible for the violations, commemorations and paying tribute to victims, and inclusion in human rights training and history text-books of an accurate account of the violations. At first glance, this seems like little more than a disparate collection, but on reflection, one notices that they all operate within the *symbolic* or *discursive* dimension of harm. What distinguishes this dimension of reparative justice is that it does not seek to make up for some material, physical, or emotional loss, but rather to address the damage to the identity of the victim and more broadly the social and political messages about history, identity, and right. All members of this category respond by publicly retelling the story of the past in a manner that establishes and validates the judgement that significant wrongs occurred.

Once again, recognizing the inseparability of the identity of the victim group and the broader political culture is central to understanding the interventions. The identity at issue here is not a private, monological characteristic of the person or group, or even an idea that other people carry in their minds. Rather, it is a social construct that is embedded in a broader network of political norms about rights and race, carried by and patterning a range of political and social institutions. Accordingly, repairing identity entails altering the patterns of meaning that reside in and are perpetuated by concrete social practices, including the institutions that organize the distribution of rights and generate the language used to characterize groups of people. The interventions designed to effect satisfaction are thus all communicative or discursive strategies, practical interventions in official narratives about the nation, history, identity, and rights. Concretely, they work by rewriting the texts that inform these categories—the history books that teach the nation's children, the laws that declare who has a right to what, and official public declarations about the character of the nation. Moreover, they are not only concerned with the substantive content of the identity in question (Aboriginality), but also with the dynamics of identity, the relationships between identity groups. As such, they shift problematic patterns of inclusion and exclusion by recognizing the legitimacy of voices, subject positions, and recollections that had previously been written out of the "official story."

If this is the work that apology does in the political sphere, its inclusion in the repertoire of mechanisms addressing removal makes a great deal of sense. In fact, as a relational act, apology represents a very unique and powerful way of shifting entrenched patterns in public identities and relationships between them. Moreover, apologizing does more than simply name a shift in the relationship or identities; the act itself brings a different type of relationship into being. Apology's particular magic lies, in this sense, in its structural contradiction: in one move, the apology acknowledges that the apologizing party is responsible and has denigrated and excluded the other party; in a simultaneous move, it enacts respect and recognition. This *performative* quality makes apology a very appropriate political intervention.[38]

Apology in this mode is certainly quite different to the one assumed in the Howard objection. Whereas Howard saw the apology as essentially backward-looking and compensatory, the Inquiry's apology is far more concerned with reconstructing social meanings in the present and the future. Whereas Howard's apology was punitive, this apology is reconciliatory.

Austin's speech act theory, in particular his distinctions between the different things one can do *in* saying something and *by* saying something, illuminate this distinction. Howard's apology is what Austin called a *behabitive*: it expresses a response, or an attitude to, or feeling about the events of the past. Apology understood as a form of satisfaction, by contrast, conforms more closely to what Austin calls a *commissive*: speech that commits the speaker (or the collective on behalf of which the speech act is made) to a certain course of action or way of being. It is closer to a promise than it is to a penalty.

Again, my point here is not to argue that this is the *true* meaning of apology, but rather to offer an interpretation that makes sense of the empirical fact that an apparently private, emotional act emerged in the public sphere of politics, and continued to attract popular support even in the face of strong and 'reasonable' normative objections. This conception explains not only why apology is relevant to *this* issue and how it makes sense in a political context, but also how it can operate as a form of political action without raising the normative objections elicited by the punitive, compensatory apology. If, in apologizing, the subject is taking responsibility for committing a wrongful act, expressing regret and being penalized, then 'contemporary Australia' hardly constitutes a legitimate apologizing subject. If, however, the apologizing subject is making certain declarations about its normative position and making normative commitments for the future, this is exactly the type of thing that collective political entities like nations do, as is evident in the preambles of national constitutions.

This apology provides a means for Australia to explicitly shift its political culture. Using the authoritative voice of state representatives, the apology officially delegitimizes a political cultural norm that says that treating Aboriginal people as less than full citizens and human beings is acceptable in this country. At the same time, it legitimizes Aboriginal people's experience of suffering and being wronged, thereby according them a full subject position, as against the history of marginalizing and silencing them.

However, the question remains as to whether this conception *was* in fact at work in the Australian debate. It is one thing to theoretically derive an ideal conception that *would* or *should* make sense in this context; it is quite another to see if it does. Turning back to that debate, what one finds is that this conception fits the tenor adopted by many of the apology's advocates, who recognized its potential to reconfigure Australia's political position on race and rights and thus located it within the broader reconciliation project. This orientation to the present and the future came through explicitly in the words of Michael Dodson, the Aboriginal man who headed the National Inquiry:

And it's also not just about our national honor, it's about the legacy we want to leave our children and our grandchildren. Will we be the generation of Australians who go down in history as denying the truth that's been placed in our hands? Are we going to be the generation that will go down in history as being unable to face and amend the wrongs of our past? Are we going to be the generation that's recognised as being complicit in the ongoing dispossession of indigenous Australians? Or will we be the generation that insists that we move forward into the next century of our nation with honesty, with an acceptance of shame at the parts of our history that fill us with shame? And with courage—are we going to go forward with courage, with pride, and maturity, and above all with honour?[39]

Picking up on another dimension of the *commissive* apology, the Governor General, and former High Court Justice, Sir William Deane underlined the dimensions of commitment and declaration:

It should, I think, be apparent to all well-meaning people that true reconciliation between the Australian nation and its Indigenous peoples is not achievable in the absence of acknowledgment by the nation of the wrongfulness of the past dispossession, oppression and degradation of the Aboriginal peoples. That is not to say that individual Australians who had no part in what was done in the past should feel or acknowledge personal guilt. It is simply to assert our identity as a nation and the basic fact that national shame, as well as national pride, can and should exist in relation to past acts and omissions, at least when done or made in the name of the community or with the authority of government. Where there is no room for national pride or national shame about the past, there can be no national soul.[40]

The Governor General's final reference to the "national soul" may seem out of place in the political sphere, but translated into more secular language, it expresses the same idea that has underpinned my analysis of the essential wrong to which the Inquiry and the apology spoke. What Deane was pointing to was apology's capacity to express and reform a dimension of the nation that cannot be reduced to particular institutions, acts or individuals, but provides them all with the grammatical rules, the categories they assume, and their normative assumptions.

In modern secular politics (and political theory), we struggle to find a term to describe this pervasive, underlying ethos that religious communities may have called the collective soul. Correlatively, we struggle to find institutions to respond to faults in this ethos. Perhaps that is why the Governor General reached back to a religious framework, where the idea of a general collective ethos is quite natural and institutions to address it are highly developed. Indeed, when Jaspers came to discuss the appropriate institutions for responding to these different levels of responsibility, he suggested that whereas punishment is the appropriate response to criminal guilt, *penance and renewal* are required for moral/political guilt. In the closing pages of his text, passionately addressed to his contemporaries, he writes that it was now incumbent on "we Germans" to attend to this work of moral/political renewal, to meet the call of "a common inspiring task—of not being Germans as we happen to be, but becoming Germans as we are not yet but ought to be, and as we hear in the call of our ancestors rather than in the history of our national idols."[41]

To the modernist, staunch secularist ear, these religious overtones are likely to ring alarm bells. Perhaps, however, the emergence of a collective penitential ritual in the sphere of secular politics is a gesture toward finding a contemporary institution that can fill this gap in our political repertoire. That this new institutional form has a family resemblance to the institutions once prominent in the religious sphere should not in itself lead us to exclude it from the repertoire of contemporary liberal democratic politics. On the contrary, political forms, including liberalism, are at their best and most promising when they can partner themselves with other complementary modalities.

The conception of apology I have derived here thus seems to meet the demands I set out. It explains not only why the apology made sense in this apparently inappropriate context, but also how it speaks to the particular wrongs that the Inquiry addressed and how it avoids some of the serious normative objections that one would have expected to stop the movement in its tracks. At the same time, this interpretation does not get rid of the more standard understanding of apology as personal remorse or compensation. To the contemporary modern mind, the alternative trope or understanding will inevitably face fierce competition from the more familiar meanings. Indeed, this definitional ambivalence was precisely what one saw in the Australian debate, where emerging conceptions of a political apology came face to face with the more traditional interpretations brought across from non-political contexts. Given liberalism's extreme wariness about collective attribution, any collective apology will almost inevitably raise the suspicion that it is a throwback from a primitive, premodern conception of collective guilt from which we have thankfully freed ourselves. Perhaps, though, from a normative point of view, this may not have been a bad thing, in so far as the liberal critique keeps alive the critical importance of distinguishing responsibility. A richer liberalism, however, would be sufficiently capacious to encode responsibility in its various dimensions.

6. Conclusion: Apology and the Two Poles of Injustice

This analysis of the tropes of apology as they played out in the Australian context provides rich insights not only for our understanding of political apologies, but also more generally for questions about effecting justice in the face of past political wrongs, questions pressing in a world of countries seeking to deal with pasts they might once have hoped to continue or forget.

The opponents and proponents of the collective political apology can be seen as advocates of two conceptions of justice—both of which press on our political conscience, sometimes in opposing directions. Each camp identified with the cause of justice, or with the avoidance of injustice—each tailoring its response to a particular type of injustice. On one side is the injustice of attributing responsibility where it does not lie, or developing institutional responses inappropriate to the particular type of responsibility that the parties can be rightfully said to bear. The emphasis which liberal institutions place on individual responsibility and direct causality has in large part been motivated by concerns about this form of injustice, and it is against this injustice of inflicting penalties where they are *not due* that opponents of the collective apology are steeling the system. On the other side is the injustice of failing to attribute responsibility where it *does* lie, including those subtler, less direct forms of responsibility omitted in the picture of criminal guilt. The impulse toward the apology marks an appeal against the omissions of this second form of injustice.

Locating the apology within the context of contemporary political responses to the wrongs of the past, I would thus suggest that the apology movement is a gesture toward finding rituals or institutions which can pick up that aspect of responsibility for systematic political violations that the collective does, and can, bear. On one side, one can see the strength of the cry against misattribution of responsibility and the careful development of human rights law targeting criminal responsibility for crimes against humanity as the fruit of the twin liberal principles of individual integrity and individual responsibility.

On the other, one can read the apology movement as an attempt to balance out the excesses wrought by these principles.

As a gesture in this direction, the political apology remains a somewhat clumsy institution, walking an unsteady path between the two poles of injustice. Its persistence should nevertheless train our eyes on the pressing demand for institutions to respond not only to the injustice of the acts which violate, but also to the degeneration in the fabric of our social and political cultures. Sin, with its narrow connotations of sexual aberration and repentance, imagined as the self-flagellating individual, may well have fallen out of social favor—and with good reason. Yet, echoes back to the idea of fidelity to principles, which make social and political life both possible and good, seem to have found a resonance in very real and pressing contemporary political needs.

Notes

1. There are in fact two indigenous peoples in Australia, Aboriginal and Torres Strait Islander peoples. Both were effected by removed policies. Throughout I refer to Aboriginal people only, but both should be understood.

2. The apology movement in Australia is itself part of a broader international trend of political apologies which, as this volume documents, emerged in approximately the last fifteen years of the twentieth century. This movement can in turn be located within the more general proliferation of institutional mechanisms designed to deal with wrongs of the past—truth commissions, domestic and international trials, reparation schemes, lustration, and memorials.

3. House of Representatives *Hansard*, the Hon. John Howard MP, August 26,1999, pp. 9206–9207.

4. A number of liberal theorists have sought to articulate a richer conception of collective responsibility, notably Joel Feinberg in, *Doing and Deserving: Essays in the Theory of Responsibility* (Princeton: Princeton University Press, 1970) and more recently David Miller, "Holding Nations Responsible," *Ethics* 114 (January 2004): pp. 240–268. Miller is, however, concerned with what he calls "outcome responsibility" as distinct from moral responsibility, where the former concerns responsibility for bearing the costs of an action or state of affairs, irrespective of moral blame. He actually raises the question of political apologies and suggests that, while they appear to imply moral responsibility, they may in fact imply only outcome responsibility, an argument with which I disagree.

5. Note, Australia does not have a Bill of Rights, and the Constitution does not proscribe racial or other forms of discrimination. The *International Covenant on Civil and Political Rights* and the *Convention on the Elimination of All Forms of Racial Discrimination*, both of which would be relevant here, were not ratified by Australia until 1980 and 1975 respectively, and were not explicitly encoded into domestic law

until 1986and1975 . Australia has been party to the *Genocide Convention* since 1949; however, this did not provide jurisdiction with respect to genocidal acts in Australia.

6. The question of whether morality was sufficient to prosecute Germans in the absence of positive law was debated in a pair of unparallel articles by the legal positivist L. H. A. Hart and the natural law theorist Lon Fuller in L. H. A. Hart, "Positivism and the Separation of Law and Morals," *Harvard Law Review* 71, 4: February 1958, and Lon Fuller, "Positivism and Fidelity To Law—A Reply to Professor Hart," *Harvard Law Review 71*, 4: February 1958.

7. This is certainly not to say that there was no dissent either internally or externally, but rather that the dominant normative standard against which Australia would have judged its own norms did not recognize this dissent. In fact, this marginalization and the need to encode dissent into the mainstream political culture is part of what is at issue here.

8. The first Commonwealth and State Native Welfare Conference in 1937 noted: "Anybody who knows anything about these groups cannot deny that their members are socially and culturally deprived. What has to be recognized is that the integration of these groups differs in no way from that of the highly integrated groups of economically depressed Europeans found in the slums of any city and in certain rural areas of New South Wales. In other words, these groups are just like groups of poor whites. The policy for them must be one of welfare. Improve their lot so that they can take their place economically and socially in the general community and not merely around the periphery. Once this is done, the break-up of such groups will be rapid.", quoted in Bell, James, H., 1964, "Assimilation in NSW", in Marie Reay, ed., *New Perspectives in the Study of Aboriginal Communities*, p. 68. London: Angus and Robertson.

9. As per Paul Hasluck, federal Minister for Territories from 1951 and architect of assimilation policy: "Assimilation means, in practical terms, that, in the course of time, it is expected that all persons of aboriginal blood or mixed blood in Australia will live like other white Australians do." Paul Hasluck, 1953, *Native Welfare in Australia*, p. 16, Perth: Paterson, Brokenshaw.

10. Confidential evidence 170, South Australia., *Bringing Them Home, op. cit.* p. 154.

11. Confidential evidence 139, Victoria: removed 1967. *ibid.* p.157. "'Your family don't care about you anymore, they wouldn't have given you away. They don't love you. All they are, are just dirty, drunken blacks.' You heard this daily... When I come out of the home and come to Redfern here looking for the girls, you see a Koori bloke coming towards you, you cross the street, you run for your life, you're terrified." Confidential evidence 8, New South Wales: woman removed to Cootamundra Girls' Home in the 1940s, ibid. p. 156.

12. I do not mean here that Aboriginality *is* the primary identity, in an essential sense. On the contrary, it was the fact that race (Aboriginality) was such a central term in the grammar of identity construction in Australian society and law that it was central in their experience and sense of self.

13. Commissioner Elliott Johnston, QC, *Royal Commission into Aboriginal Deaths in Custody*, Canberra: AGPS, 1991. National Report vol.2, p. 76.

14. Until the High Court overturned it in its famous *Mabo* decision in 1992, the doctrine of *terra nullius* or empty land was law in Australia, meaning that there was no legal recognition that Aboriginal people had owned the land when white colonizers arrived and declared British sovereignty and claimed title to the entire continent.

15. Robert Manne, "Forget the Guilt, Remember the Shame", *The Australian*, July 8, 1996.

16. Desmond Manderson, "Shame is part of healing process", *Sydney Morning Herald*, January 28, 1997.

17. Karl Jaspers, 1947, *The Question of German Guilt*, trans. E. B. Ashton, New York: Dial Press.

18. *Ibid.*, pp. 76–77.

19. Robert Manne, "Forget the Guilt, Remember the Shame", *The Australian*, July 8, 1996. The constant use of the word "dwelling" with reference to the past is also interesting here. When objecting to the apology, many critics spoke about not dwelling in the past, thus invoking the conception of the past as a home, and environment, a *Dasein*.

20. The Greek word *ethos* means habit, customs, and character. The word moral originates from the Latin expression *mor, moris*, which means dwelling.

21. The critique developed of organic forms of social organization is discussed in Hanna Fenichel Pitkin, 1967, *The Concept of Representation*, Berkeley: University of California Press. p. 40ff.

22. Robert Manne, *op. cit.*

23. Jaspers, *op. cit.* p. 34.

24. The so-called "history wars" that ensued involved historians lining up behind political positions with their evidentiary documentation of diametrically opposed histories. Cf. "History Wars: the TLS debate", *Times Literary Supplement*, August 29, September 26, 2003. For further links to coverage of this debate see *The Sydney Line* at http://www.sydneyline.com/Fabrication.htm.

25. "Meaning is not an effect, a result, a product or a static quality, or something that can be coded out." See Norman, K. Denzin, "Reading Cultural Texts: Comment on Griswold,"*American Journal of Sociology*, 1990, 95, 6: May, pp. 1577–1580, 1579.

26. "A practice approach has no need to break the system into artificial chunks like base and superstructure (and to argue which one determines which), since the analytic effort is not to explain one chunk of the system referring to another chunk, but rather to refer to the system as an integral whole." Sherry Ortner, "Theory in Anthropology since the Sixties", *Comparative Studies in Society and History*, 26, 1: January 1984, 126–166, at p. 148.

27. Ortner, *op. cit.* p. 154.

28. This approach has generated a great deal of controversy, as Berezin puts it: "the fissures lie between scholars who privilege the possibility of explanation . . . and

those who privilege exegesis or interpretation." Berezin, Mabel, "Fissured terrain: Methodological Approaches and Research Styles in Culture and Politics", in Crane, Diana, ed., *The Sociology of Culture: Emerging Theoretical Perspectives*, Oxford, UK; Cambridge, Mass.: Blackwell Publishers, 1994, 91–116, p. 94.

29. Cornelius Castoriadis, 1991, "Power, Politics and Autonomy" in David Ames Curtis, ed., *Philosophy, Politics, Autonomy*; p. 145. Oxford: Oxford University Press.

30. Castoriadis, "Individual, Society, Rationality, History" in *Philosophy, Politics Autonomy*, op. cit. p. 60.

31. Cornelius Castoriadis, "Power, Politics and Autonomy" in *Philosophy, Politics, Autonomy*; op. cit. p. 145.

32. This point led to a very interesting exchange, where Howard at one point argued against the apology on the grounds that 40 percent of Australians were immigrants, and so could not rightly be held accountable. In response, the representative body of ethnic communities released a statement saying that when they took on Australian citizenship, they also accepted the inheritance of responsibility for Australia's shameful past acts.

33. The simple answer would be that it extends just as the state extends, that is, where there is institutional continuity. In this case, however, because the apology implies more than formal institutional responsibility, embracing also what I have called political culture and society, so this definition will not be sufficient.

34. Michel Rolph-Trouillot, "Abortive Rituals; Historical Apologies in the Global Era," *Interventions*, vol. 2,2: pp. 171–186.

35. One article specifically on this question treats satisfaction as a subjective state, in the sense of the various parties being "satisfied," but also attempts to operationalize it. This does not get at what satisfaction means in this context. Cf. Daniel W. Van Ness and Mara F. Schiff, 2001, "Satisfaction Guaranteed? The Meaning of Satisfaction in Restorative justice", in Gordon Bazemore and Mara Schiff, eds., *Restorative Community Justice: Repairing Harm and Transforming Communities*, pp.47–62 (Cincinnati, OH: Anderson Publishing Co).

36. This arose in part from the nature of the jurisdiction of the Commission and antidiscrimination and human rights law in Australia, which is not part of the criminal law, but rather emphasizes reparations achieved through conciliation, or if necessary a hearing before an administrative tribunal.

37. van Boven, T, 1996: Revised set of basic principles and guidelines on the right to reparation for victims of gross violations of human rights and humanitarian law prepared by Theo van Boven pursuant to Sub-Commission decision 1995/117, UN Doc. E/CN.4/Sub.2/1996/17, May 24, 1996 (hereafter the van Boven Principles).

38. At work here is Austin's distinction between constatives, speech that conveys information or names or states that something is so—and *performatives*—speech acts that themselves bring a state of affairs into being. Cf. J. L. Austin, 1962, *How to Do Things With Words*, Cambridge, Mass.: Harvard University Press.

39. Michael Dodson, Speech at Southern Highlands Community Center, May 1997, available at http://www.hinet.net.au/~sally/cultures/reconc4.htm.

40. Sir William Deane, 1996, *Some Signposts from Daguragu: The Inaugural Lingari Lecture*, Kingston, ACT: The Council for Aboriginal Reconciliation.

41. Jaspers, *op cit.* p. 81.

CHAPTER 9

The BIA's Apology to Native Americans: An Essay on Collective Memory and Collective Conscience

REBECCA TSOSIE [1]

1. Introduction

The year 2000 marked a new millennium for the global populace, and thus, a particularly important occasion for collective reflection on where we—as distinct nations and peoples—had been, and where we were headed. An important part of this process, of course, was to acknowledge who "we" are: what is the collective identity of the United States of America as a nation? Who are "Americans" as a people? Moments like these are rare, and the process of self-reflection comes at a significant cost. Because, of course, to understand who "we" are, we must acknowledge where "we" come from.

The creation of the United States has its own mythology, reflected in notions of "pilgrim pride," the brash forging of a new "democracy" free of European hierarchies and monarchies, and the scrappy and entrepreneurial "pioneers" who "settled" the "Wild West." The reality of the United States, however, reflects a seamier and more unsavory side based on the plantation labor of enslaved Africans and the massive dispossession of Native peoples from their lands, cultures, and lives. We all know that equality never was an organizing principle of this Nation. And today, hundreds of thousands of Americans, including the survivors of these past horrors, continue to experience the often profound social, political, cultural, and economic inequalities that permeate our society.

It was against this fabric of emerging social conscience and consciousness that Kevin Gover, the Assistant Secretary for Indian Affairs during the Clinton administration, apologized to Indian nations and to Indian people, for the past harms wrought by the Federal Indian policy, as implemented by the Bureau of Indian Affairs. The occasion was the 175th anniversary of the establishment of the Bureau of Indian Affairs. In Assistant Secretary Gover's speech, delivered on September 8, 2000, he commented on the appropriateness of self-reflection:

> We have come together today to mark the first 175 years of the institution now known as the Bureau of Indian Affairs.
>
> [...]
>
> It is appropriate that we do so in the first year of a new century and a new millennium, a time when our leaders are reflecting on what lies ahead and preparing for those challenges. Before looking ahead, though, this institution must first look back and reflect on what it has wrought and, by doing so, come to know that this is no occasion for celebration; rather it is a time for reflection and contemplation, a time for sorrowful truths to be spoken, a time for contrition.[2]

Specifically, Assistant Secretary Gover extended "a formal apology to Indian people for the historical conduct of this agency."[3] The apology speech inspired sorrow, relief, resentment, skepticism, anger, and a host of other strong emotions from Native Americans across the country. Perplexed reporters were unable to glean whether "Native Americans" perceived the apology as "good" (for example, sincere, helpful) or "bad" (for example, an insincere political ploy). Subsequent critics have pondered whether "words alone" are ever sufficient, and why Native people should believe a government that continues to appropriate their lands, resources, and basic rights to sovereignty, culture, and self-determination. Hoopa leader, Lyle Marshall, for example, who spoke at the conference that inspired this volume of essays, found the apology "inadequate" because "it came from the wrong person" and "offensive" because "it was not followed by any action to right the offenses it mentioned."[4] Marshall firmly concluded: "Until the government and Congress are bound to action, no apology will be sufficient. Indian survival depends on the American conscience."[5]

This essay analyzes the BIA's apology to Native Nations and peoples, and Native peoples' reactions to it, within the intercultural context that frames the use of apology by public entities to acknowledge historic wrongs. The essay evaluates the context of the apology, its function, and its significance to broader notions of "reparation" or "reconciliation" for Native peoples. The essay concludes that the "success" of this apology cannot be measured by its significance as an "event." Rather, in accordance with Trudy Govier's notion that apology is "a process, not an event," I argue that the significance of this apology was to probe the collective memory of Americans on the historical events it related, and to inspire a dialogue to inform the "collective conscience" of contemporary Americans, which, as Lyle Marshall observed, is essential to the future of US/Native relations in this country.[6]

2. The Context of the BIA Apology

To understand the significance of this apology, several preliminary questions are in order. First, was the speech actually an "apology?" If so, who was the apology from? What was the apology for? Who was the apology directed to? At each level, one could ask whether the apology was adequate or inadequate: for example, did it come from the right entity? Did it identify the relevant harms? Was it made to the appropriate parties? To engage these questions, I will use a particular framework and structure that I have found helpful in my thinking about the questions. I would like to acknowledge at the outset that the scholarly discourse on apology illustrates considerable disagreement on whether this is the appropriate structure, and I do not engage that debate. I merely employ the structure as a means to critique this apology and reserve the larger scholarly debate for another day.

The Structure of Apology

The word "apology" has been used to cover a variety of acts. As Trudy Govier and Wilhelm Verwoerd observe, there are at least three basic senses of apology: "the apology as a defense (as in Socrates' Apology), the apology as excuse or account ("Sorry I was late, but I was interrupted just as I was leaving"), and the moral apology, which is an expression of sorrow for moral wrongdoing."[7] Assistant Secretary Gover's remarks in no way offered a defense for past actions, nor any excuse for these actions. The role of the speech as an apology was purely an expression of sorrow for moral wrongdoing and an attempt to accept "the moral responsibility of putting things right."[8]

In that sense, the moral functions of apology represent "a cluster of interrelated beliefs, attitudes, emotions, and intentions."[9] In the context of interpersonal apology, Kathleen Gill distills this complex universe into five specific elements:

1. An acknowledgment that the incident in question did in fact occur.
2. An acknowledgment that the incident was inappropriate in some way.
3. An acknowledgment of responsibility for the act.
4. The expression of an attitude of regret and a feeling of remorse.
5. The expression of an intention to refrain from similar acts in the future.[10]

Gill observes that not every element will be present in every apology; however, she claims that there are certain necessary conditions for apologizing, which must be present in order for the apology to be sincere. For example, "at least one of the parties involved" must believe "that the incident actually occurred" and at least one of the parties must believe "that the act was inappropriate."[11] Moreover, the party making the apology must either take responsibility for the act, or be in the type of relationship with the responsible party that makes it justifiable for her to offer an apology.[12] The apologizer must also express an attitude of regret and remorse, and the person to whom the apology is made must be justified in believing that the offender will refrain from similar offenses in the future.[13]

Examining the BIA apology in this context raises several important issues. First, what was the significance of the historical events outlined in the apology speech, given the fact that the collective memory of Native peoples is likely to differ from that of non-Native peoples? In other words, would all Americans agree that the enumerated events happened? If so, would they all agree that the events were morally reprehensible and therefore, a "wrong" had been committed?

Secondly, was Assistant Secretary Gover making the apology on behalf of a government—the United States? On behalf of an institution—the Bureau of Indian Affairs? Was he making the apology in his capacity as a Pawnee Tribal member whose family had personally suffered the wrongs he described? Was he making the apology as a government official who was in a relationship with the culpable party?

Finally, and perhaps most problematic, in the context of the relationship between the US government and Native nations, is there a sense in which the US can be viewed as having "regret" or "remorse" for the actions it took in past centuries? What if these events are directly responsible for its contemporary status as a global superpower? Would it not be disingenuous for a superpower to express "regret" for the very actions that enabled such status? How should contemporary Native people evaluate the sincerity of the United States government? By its current actions? By its commitment to "do better" in the future?

The BIA Apology

Assistant Secretary Gover started the apology by reciting several historical harms that BIA policy and actions perpetrated upon Native peoples. Most importantly, he acknowledged that the original mission of the Office of Indian Affairs, which started out in the Department of War and then was moved to the Interior Department after most of the Indian Wars had been concluded, was to pave the way for the United States to appropriate lands from tribal ownership for the benefit of US citizens.[14] This, in turn, was accomplished by "ethnic cleansing," intentional physical harm "on a scale so ghastly that it cannot be dismissed as merely the inevitable consequence of the clash of competing ways of life"—"the deliberate spread of disease, the decimation of the mighty bison herds, the use of poison alcohol to destroy mind and body, and the cowardly killing of women and children" in massacres such as those at "Sand Creek, the banks of the Washita River, and Wounded Knee."[15] Assistant Secretary Gover then listed the BIA's subsequent efforts to "annihilate Indian cultures," and destroy Indian economies by inculcating a forced dependency upon the United States and the Bureau of Indian Affairs. Gover concluded: "poverty, ignorance, and disease have been the product of this agency's work."[16]

Under Gill's matrix, the acknowledgement of historical harm by a representative of the culpable party (the United States) appears central to the integrity of the apology. It is not unusual to hear tribal leaders relate this litany of harms and others similar to these. However, until this speech, it was unheard of for a US government official to talk about the United States' Indian policy as "ethnic cleansing."[17] The American public easily dismisses the comments of tribal leaders about historical harms as a "gripe" by a "special interest group" looking for increased government benefits. After all, the "official version" of the US dispossession of Native Nations generally hinges upon the justification that because of the "savage" character of the tribes, they were unable to "hold property rights" on the same level as civilized people, and thus were "necessarily" conquered by a more civilized nation. As the US Supreme Court found in *Tee-Hit-Ton Indians v. United States*: "Every American schoolboy knows that the savage tribes of this continent were deprived of their ancestral ranges by force and that, even when the Indians ceded millions of acres by treaty in return for blankets, food and trinkets, it was not a sale but the conqueror's will that deprived them of their land."[18] It is not so easy, however, to dismiss the comments of an appointed public official speaking on behalf of an agency of the US government.

That brings us to the next inquiry. Who made this apology and to whom was it made? Lyle Marshall emphasized that Assistant Secretary Gover's apology was inadequate "because it came from the wrong person: It was not Gover's place to apologize."[19] Similarly, the popular response to the apology included the following query in a Letter to the Editor: "One has to wonder why it was not a senior ranking official selected to offer the apology? Surely an apology should not have to come from a member of the very group that has been treated so abysmally. [...] What significance does that have and what message does it send? Would the government ever dare ask an African-American official to apologize for slavery?"[20]

This response indicates a perception that the United States may have been motivated by the contemporary need to gain popular support for the BIA so it "sent" an Indian to deliver an "apology" for past misdeeds, which put the Indian in a very uncomfortable position because it looked like a "victim" was being sent to apologize to "other victims" for the perpetrator's bad acts. How could that be a credible apology? In fact, however, Assistant Secretary Gover is the one who generated the apology on behalf of a federal agency that he was appointed to lead. Assistant Secretary Gover clearly emphasized that he did not intend to speak "for the United States." That, he says, is the "province of the nation's elected leaders." He acknowledges, however, that he is "empowered to speak on behalf of this agency, the Bureau of Indian Affairs," and that his words "reflect the hearts of its 10,000 employees."[21] Assistant Secretary Gover is clearly an enrolled citizen of the Pawnee Nation, and yet he was making the apology not in his role as a Pawnee tribal member, but in his role as an US official and the leader of the BIA. He made the apology on behalf of the Agency to all Native peoples who have been harmed by the bad acts of the BIA, which, in a very real sense, includes himself as a Native person, his family, and his Nation. In that respect, one should query whether the personal identity of the speaker is in fact the true marker of the credibility of the statement. In his official capacity, Assistant Secretary Gover could well have focused on the better moments of the Agency in "celebration" of the 175th Anniversary of the BIA. He could have trumpeted the fact that the BIA today supports a variety of tribal services and programs that are invaluable to Native communities, or that employment within the BIA is today predominantly Native, making the BIA the single largest employer of Native people. After popping some balloons and cutting the cake, everyone could go home happy. Right? Wrong. Assistant Secretary Gover specifies that the anniversary is *not* an occasion for celebration. It is, rather, a "time for reflection and contemplation [. . .] a time for contrition."[22] Why does he say this? Simply because he perceives the Agency's mission as not merely to deliver social services. Rather, by accepting the historical legacy of the Institution as one of "racism and inhumanity," the Agency must also accept "the moral responsibility of putting things right."[23] And Assistant Secretary Gover, as the leader of that Agency, has a pivotal role in accepting that moral responsibility.

On the first and second levels of Gill's matrix, the BIA apology is clearly an attempt to acknowledge moral responsibility for past wrongs by an institution, the Bureau of Indian Affairs, which is in privity with the historical wrongdoers. There is also an unbroken chain of identity in the group that is the subject of the apology. Assistant Secretary Gover acknowledges the intergenerational consequences of these harms for all Native peoples in the United States. However, the final inquiry is quite perplexing. What measure should we use to assess whether this apology embodies sincere regret and remorse? Should contemporary Native people be justified in believing such a statement of remorse? Is there a potential for future bad acts? If so, this would indicate that, as Lyle Marshall opined, these words were "hollow" and do not "jibe with actions taken by the Feds" in contemporary federal policy.[24] In order to evaluate the sincerity of the apology, it is necessary to look at its function. What was the apology intended to do? What was it NOT intended to do? Did the apology succeed or fail in its intended purpose?

3. The Function of the BIA Apology

To understand the function of the BIA apology, we must first understand what the apology was NOT intended to do. It was *not* meant to be an official apology from the US government for its brutal and still troubled history with Native Nations. That would be a complex political undertaking for the United States, and the United States has, to date, been unwilling to acknowledge broad and general responsibility for past bad acts toward either African Americans or Native Americans.[25] So, although a White House spokesperson acknowledged that Gover had sent the President a copy of his speech, and that "the White House didn't object to it" that was hardly a ringing endorsement of the sentiments expressed by the BIA apology.[26] No, the BIA apology is purely an apology by one federal agency, which is charged with implementing Indian policy. Nor is the apology intended to ask forgiveness from Native Americans for the BIA's misdeeds. Assistant Secretary Gover clearly states that it would be inappropriate to ask forgiveness while "the burdens of this agency's history weigh so heavily on tribal communities."[27] So, if this is not an apology from the United States and it is not a mechanism to ask forgiveness, what, if any, utility does the apology have? In this respect, it is necessary to evaluate the functions of the apology according to its intended purpose.

First, the apology is intended to issue a corrective history to evaluate past conduct. American history books and law books are replete with the justificatory approach to past bad acts toward Native Americans. In the words of the *Tee-Hit-Ton* Court, it is no wonder that "every American schoolboy" knows that "conquest" of a savage people is responsible for the birth of a "civilized" nation.[28] After all, most history textbooks used to teach American students are written by the descendants of the "conquerors."[29] This understanding, in turn, is used by Supreme Court justices and policy makers in issuing current policies. In *Tee-Hit-Ton*, the "savage" nature of the Tee-Hit-Ton Indians, as a group of itinerant "hunter-gatherers" excuses the United States from any contemporary Constitutional obligation to pay "just compensation" for the taking of their traditional lands. In a different context, Chief Justice Rehnquist's dissent in *United States v. Sioux Nation* relies on the same rationale to excuse the obligation to pay the Lakota for the taking of treaty guaranteed lands. Relying on the "Oxford History of the American People," Rehnquist alludes to the "savage" nature of the Lakota people, who "lived only for the day, recognized no rights of property, robbed or killed anyone if they thought they could get away with it, inflicted cruelty without a qualm, and endured torture without flinching."[30] Rehnquist's conclusion is telling:

That there was tragedy, deception, barbarity, and virtually every vice known to man in the 300-year history of the expansion of the original 13 Colonies into a Nation which now encompasses more than three million square miles and 50 states cannot be denied. But in a court opinion, as a historical and not a legal matter, both settler and Indian are entitled to the benefit of the Biblical adjuration: 'Judge not, that ye be not judged.'"[31]

In other words, the longstanding approach within American history and law has been to neatly sanitize the litany of harms to Native peoples into a broad and glorious justification based on the triumph of civilization over savagery. This "evolutionary approach" relies on commonly shared understandings about the "way the world works," which excuses Americans from any deep contemplation about their history. The impact of this history and popular understanding upon Native peoples, however, is profound. Not only does the United States fail to acknowledge the vast and complex nature of the harm that it has wrought upon Native peoples, but it also appears to place the blame for this harm squarely upon the Native people themselves. The American version of history blames Native people for their "savage" nature, for their failure to adhere to the "civilized norms" of property ownership and individual rights that Christian peoples hold, and for their "brutality" in defending themselves against the onslaught of non-Indian settlers. The message to Native people is simple: "If only you had been more like us, things might have been different for you."[32]

   A classic example of this sentiment is reflected in Chief Justice John Marshall's famous 19th Century case, *Johnson v. McIntosh*, which holds that the Doctrine of Conquest, within the Law of Nations, which protects conquered citizens of European nations from complete divestiture of property and civil rights upon a change in government, cannot extend to Indian people because of their savage nature. These protective rules, Marshall says, could not extend to "the tribes of Indians inhabiting this country," because they were "fierce savages, whose occupation was war and whose subsistence was drawn chiefly from the forest. To leave them in possession of their country, was to leave the country a wilderness; to govern them as a distinct people, was impossible, because they were as brave and as high spirited as they were fierce, and were ready to repel by arms every attempt on their independence."[33] Instead, the applicable rule that defines Native rights is the Discovery Doctrine, which was designed to determine the ownership interests of European nations to "vacant" or "uninhabited" land. Because the Indian nations are characterized as "uncivilized" and "non-Christian" peoples, their occupancy of land is legally irrelevant.[34] Marshall notes, however, that the "potentates of the old world" saw no injustice in applying this rule. Rather, they considered themselves to have made "ample compensation to the inhabitants of the new [world], by bestowing on them civilization and Christianity" in exchange for taking "title" to their lands.[35]

One of the most valuable aspects of Assistant Secretary Gover's apology, then, is to change this perception of history. For once, a US official acknowledges the version of history that Native people know to be true. Gover specifically acknowledges that the United States, through its agents and instrumentalities, intentionally destroyed the buffalo, introduced alcohol into Native communities, massacred helpless women and children, outlawed the speaking of Native languages and the practice of Native religions, outlawed traditional governments, suppressed traditional economies, and created a culture of "shame, fear, and anger" among American Indian peoples. It is not Native people who are to blame for this history, Gover's words instruct. It is the United States, who intentionally committed these acts to assure its status as a superpower among world nations.

Secondly, and building upon this historical foundation, Assistant Secretary Gover's apology locates responsibility where it belongs: on the original wrongdoers and those in privity with them. Gover acknowledges that "the BIA employees of today did not commit these wrongs," but they must "acknowledge that the institution [they] serve did."[36] All employees of the BIA "accept this inheritance, this legacy of racism and inhumanity. And by accepting this legacy, we accept also the responsibility of putting things right." In this sense, Assistant Secretary Gover's approach builds upon what Peter

French and others call "collective responsibility."[37] Some scholars locate collective responsibility for past wrongs under a "benefits theory."[38] Peter French, however, makes a compelling case for collective responsibility among contemporary governments, groups, and institutions for past wrongs based upon the idea of collective ownership of "public memory."[39] "Public memory casts the past into our present," French argues, "and well it should because it is our past or what we are jointly committed as a group to being our past. We, as a collective, are the continuation of the projects of our collective's past."[40] Public memory is the repository of our collective identity, and to the extent that it is managed by public officials, governments, and institutions, it represents our commitment to a collective past for our contemporary group. Thus, Assistant Secretary Gover's remarks are particularly important because they recast the collective memory of the United States and American citizens as a way to acknowledge collective responsibility for past wrongs.

In that respect, the third important function of Assistant Secretary Gover's apology is to differentiate the impacts of the harms and show the continuing nature of the historical wrongdoing. So, Gover's apology speaks not only to the historical physical harm (for example, "ethnic cleansing") perpetrated upon Native peoples, but also the economic harm (destruction of traditional food sources and economies, forced dependency), and the cultural harm (prohibiting Native language and religion). All of these harms resulted from tangible and overt laws and policies of the United States.[41] However, the result of these harms is far more complex: a constellation of emotional and spiritual trauma that extends from generation to generation within Native communities. The primary instrumentalities for this broad and intangible harm were the BIA boarding schools, which forcibly seized Native children, sent them to distant locales to be "civilized," banned them from speaking their Native languages or practicing Native customs, and often forbade them from visiting family members.[42] Assistant Secretary Gover comments: "the Bureau of Indian Affairs committed these acts against the children entrusted to its boarding schools, brutalizing them emotionally, psychologically, physically, and spiritually."[43] The intergenerational harm of these misdeeds continues to haunt Native people:

The trauma of shame, fear, and anger has passed from one generation to the next, and manifests itself in the rampant alcoholism, drug abuse, and domestic violence that plague Indian country. Many of our people live lives of unrelenting tragedy as Indian families suffer the ruin of lives by alcoholism, suicides made of shame and despair, and violent death at the hands of one another.[44]

Assistant Secretary Gover affirmatively states that "[t]hese wrongs must be acknowledged if the healing is to begin."[45] And in that sense, the single most important purpose of the apology was to set the process for healing in motion. What does it mean to "heal" Native communities? What is the moral responsibility of the BIA in this process? Assistant Secretary Gover's apology is intended to do several things to facilitate the process of healing. First, it is intended to set a moral boundary against which to measure future behavior:

Never again will this agency stand silent when hate and violence are committed against Indians. Never again will we allow policy to proceed from the assumption that Indians possess less human genius than other races. Never again will we be complicit in the theft of Indian property. Never again will we appoint false leaders who serve purposes other than those of the tribes. Never again will we allow unflattering and stereotypical images of Indian people to deface the halls of government or lead the American people to shallow and ignorant beliefs about Indians. Never again will we attack your religions, your languages, your rituals, or any of your tribal ways. Never again will we seize your children, nor teach them to be ashamed of who they are. Never again.[46]

Secondly, the apology is intended to inspire a policy template to deal with legal and political redress for past wrongs, which are often reflected by the current needs of Native communities. It is clear from Gover's remarks that the harms are much too complex and serious for a "quick fix." Perhaps Native economies can be bolstered by gaming policies. Perhaps Native governments can be supported by the self-determination and self-governance acts and policies. But the process of healing for Native communities will require a much more nuanced version of federal policy dedicated to a moral, as well as legal, commitment to the notion of self-determination. Moreover, the "moral debt" clearly requires a substantial commitment of material resources. What does it mean to facilitate "tribal self-determination" if tribal governments are still controlled by the federal government and its larger agenda to American citizens? How can tribes become "autonomous" if the majority of their populations lack the educational or material resources to be fully autonomous citizens of either their own government or the United States? If a significant number of Native adults are incarcerated and in poverty, if a significant percentage of Native families are torn apart by substance abuse and domestic violence, how can a "tribal community" be a vibrant repository for self-determination? These are the paradoxes of contemporary Indian policy that Gover acknowledges, and this is what the process of healing must engage.

Finally, Assistant Secretary Gover's apology is intended, on a spiritual level, to set in motion the process of redirecting blame, healing spiritual trauma, and promoting a larger sense of collective responsibility on the part of the US government and its citizens. Importantly, the apology alone *cannot actually do* any of those things. Rather, it is intended to start that process in motion and begin a dialogue about what must be done to heal the past. As Gover says, "we desperately wish that we could change this history, but of course we cannot." The most that can be done is to "accept the moral responsibility for putting things right."[47] The next section of this essay looks at the intercultural context of apology and its spiritual and emotional, as well as social and political, contours.

4. Coming to Terms with the Past: The Role of Apology in Achieving Intercultural Justice

In their introduction to this volume, Elazar Barkan and Alexander Karn suggest that apology "can perform two different, though not necessarily contradictory, tasks: it can function as the right thing to do (because it is viewed as a step toward justice and the settling of accounts), and it can function to rebuild damaged relationships (because reconciliation is sometimes viewed as primary to justice).[48] Is Assistant Secretary Gover's apology a step toward social, political, or legal "justice" for Native Americans? Is it a step toward "reconciliation" between Indians and non-Indians, or between Indian governments and the US government?

It would be difficult to argue that the history of US/Indian relations is not replete with moral and legal wrongs, or that the injustice that Native people face in their involuntary incorporation into the United States is merely a historical phenomenon. Injustice continues today in every federal law and federal court decision denying the political and cultural rights of Native peoples.[49] It continues today in the overwhelming poverty rate among Native Americans, their disproportionate rates of incarceration, alcoholism, infant mortality, and suicide. The question is: what can we, as a society, do to overcome the legacy of the past?

Assistant Secretary Gover's apology makes two important suggestions in the context of relations between the BIA and Native peoples. First, the BIA as an institution must acknowledge its own role and complicity in the historic wrongs committed by the United States against Native peoples, as well as the contemporary impact and consequences of those wrongs on Native peoples. Second, the BIA, as the government agency that continues to have the most significant duties to Native peoples, must assume a responsibility to work *with* Native governments and communities to begin a "healing" process.

In the first sense, Gover's apology corresponds to Nicholas Tavuchis' notion that apology requires "not detachment but acknowledgment and painful embracement of our deeds, coupled with a declaration of regret."[50] Similarly, Martha Minow argues that apologies must "acknowledge the fact of harms, accept some degree of responsibility, avow sincere regret, and promise not to repeat the offense."[51] Gover's apology clearly acknowledges the painful history and contemporary injustices that Native people suffer, as well as the BIA's role in these injustices. In the second sense, Gover's speech suggests that apology is a fundamental part of healing historic trauma and its contemporary manifestations because it acknowledges the reality of the past and places the blame for the wrongdoing, not on the victim, but on the responsible party. Importantly, this transfer of blame occurs through the *acceptance* of responsibility by the wrongdoer and not through the accusations of the victim. This is important, because the US government's general approach has been to blame the victim (for example for being "uncivilized" or "violent") and to dismiss the victim's accusations as instances of "politically correct revisionist history." If we do not acknowledge the past, Gover suggests, we cannot heal the future.

Assistant Secretary Gover's apology, however, raises some interesting connections and distinctions between the conceptions of "justice," "reconciliation," and "healing." First, although the concepts are importantly distinct, there is a tangible connection between the concepts of "justice" and "reconciliation." As Professor Jeffrie Murphy argues in his analysis of the South African Truth and Reconciliation Commission, "reconciliation" is a "process" that allows groups with a history of conflict to work together toward a "democratic and just future."[52] Professor Murphy is careful to note that, in the South African case, the perpetrators were required to make a full confession and accept responsibility, but they were not required to "repent, show remorse, or even apologize."[53] Consequently, the victims had no obligation (nor any motivation) to grant "forgiveness" or even try to achieve a "change of heart." It was enough that each group committed to "a viable transition from apartheid to democratic government." Thus, under this analysis, "reconciliation" entails a mutual commitment to achieve "justice," but does not necessarily require groups to go beyond this and engage in demonstrations of remorse, regret, forgiveness, or any of the other emotions that we might believe are necessary to emotionally or spiritually resolve historic trauma.[54]

Assistant Secretary Gover's remarks, however, concentrate on the role of apology as a way to commence healing. His remarks focus on the harms of historic trauma that continue to manifest in Native communities, and his apology indicates that healing is a dynamic and necessary process between groups that suffer a damaged relationship caused both by historical trauma and by contemporary inequality. The link between "healing" and "reparative justice" has been made in several scholarly accounts on how to rebuild damaged relationships between nations, peoples, and groups. Some of these accounts focus on the dynamic of apology, some on the idea of reparation, and some on the notion of reconciliation. The common element, however, as Eric Yamamoto observes, is that some notion of intergroup "justice" is necessary in order to establish a foundation for the process of healing to begin.[55] In the context of American race relations, Yamamoto suggests that justice involves four components of "combined inquiry and action": (1) recognition of group harms and grievances; (2) accepting group responsibility for healing the wounds; (3) reconstructing intergroup relations through particular acts (for example, apology, forgiveness); and (4) reparations, which involves making material changes (social, economic, and political) to rebuild the structure of the relationship in a tangible way (not "just talk").[56]

To the extent that Native peoples seek to renegotiate their relationship with the dominant society upon a more principled and just basis, it becomes important to examine this process of reconstructing group relations. Building on Professor Yamamoto's account, it appears that there are at least two critical aspects to the process. First, the groups must reconstruct their relationship through acts that indicate acknowledgment of wrongdoing and a commitment to "make things right." Secondly, the process depends upon a material commitment of resources, rights, political/cultural/social recognition, or whatever else might be needed to facilitate the economic, social, and political changes necessary to overcome past and present injustice.

Using this framework, it is clear that Assistant Secretary Gover's apology was purely intended to function at the first level. By acknowledging wrongdoing and a commitment to "make things right," the apology was intended to *start* the healing process. There was no intent to offer reparations, or to suggest that "mere words" could substitute for tangible resources in a process of reparation. In fact, Assistant Secretary Gover limits his remarks to the BIA's side of the intergroup dynamic and disclaims any intent to ask Native people for forgiveness. Because of these limitations, some Native respondents were cynical about the sincerity or merit of the apology. Lyle Marshall, for example, finds it offensive that the BIA attempted to "apologize" when it was not prepared to take substantive action to remedy injustice.

The problems of insincerity are endemic in the contemporary apology literature, and thus, it is both appropriate and important to inquire whether the apology is "sincere" or whether it is "hollow." For purposes of this article, I will assume that this apology was sincere in the BIA's acknowledgment of the harm, acceptance of responsibility for causing the harm, and commitment to work with Native people on a process of healing. I would also like to suggest that acknowledging *responsibility* for causing the harm is a necessary prerequisite to accepting liability to *make appropriate amends* for the harm. Those are two separate acts and, although both are necessary to effect reparative justice, they should not be conflated. Finally, I would like to suggest that the process of healing from historic trauma has intangible and tangible components. The emotional and spiritual (intangible) components of healing must be experienced for the healing to be complete. In that sense, even material (tangible) reparations made to a group without the necessary spiritual and emotional components would be insufficient to heal the wounds. Assistant Secretary Gover's apology could not accomplish all of these ends, nor could it bind the United States as a Nation. However, the apology is historically significant because it establishes a precedent for the United States and suggests a model to commence healing.

5. Healing from Historic Trauma: Notions of Reconciliation and Intercultural Justice

The process of healing from historic trauma caused by intercultural conflict is both a *cultural* and an *intercultural* process. In order for any people to heal from historic trauma, there must be a cultural process that comes from within the group or community, as well as an external, dynamic process that engages both parties to the original wrongdoing. The latter process may be linked with reconciliation efforts (although it is clearly not coextensive with such efforts). There are important cultural, emotional, and spiritual qualities to the healing process, which will be reflected in the internal process. I would like to suggest, however, that those qualities must at least be *acknowledged* by the external, intergroup process for that process to have any credibility or impact. Let me offer an example.

Native Hawaiian peoples have a long tradition of resolving interpersonal conflicts through a process called "Ho'oponopono," which means "to make things right."[57] Within this tradition, the healing process is considered to be both emotional and spiritual, and is premised upon the idea that the perpetrator and the person wronged are bound together in a relationship of negative entanglement called "hihia." The healing process must "untangle" these negative emotions to facilitate a mutual understanding of the "emotional truth" of what happened, a sincere appreciation of the effects of the bad behavior, a confession of the wrongdoing and seeking of forgiveness by the perpetrator, the act of granting forgiveness, and the ultimate "release" of negative emotions. The final phase of "kala," which means to "release, untie, and free each other completely"—follows the phase of forgiveness. Thus, the idea of "kala" is importantly distinct from that of forgiveness. The actual phrase, "Ke kala aku nei 'au ia 'oe a pela noho 'i 'au e kala ia mai ai" means "I unbind you from the fault, and thus may I also be unbound by it." As Manu Meyer observes, "kala seeks to strip the incident of its pain-causing attributes."[58]

Interestingly enough, the only other official apology to Native Americans was contained in P.L. 103–150, the 1993 Native Hawaiian Apology Resolution, which acknowledged the complicity of the US government in the illegal overthrow of the Hawaiian monarchy in 1893, and expressed regret for the resultant hardships that occurred for Native Hawaiians. Congress issued the apology resolution to begin the process of "reconciliation" between the United States and the Native Hawaiian people.[59] The Apology Resolution expressly responds to an earlier public apology by representatives from the United States Church of Christ to Native Hawaiians for that institution's historical complicity in the overthrow.

Senator Daniel Akaka from Hawaii linked the reconciliation process with the Hawaiian cultural concept of "ho'oponopono." He said:

The process of reconciliation is a process of healing, which should not be viewed as one particular issue or a narrowly defined process. It should be viewed as a multitude of positive steps between Native Hawaiians and the federal government to improve the understanding between each party, to improve the social and economic conditions of Native Hawaiians, and to resolve long standing matters of political status and land claims.[60]

Culturally, the process of reconciliation with Native Hawaiian people would lack any credibility without some overt acknowledgment of an egregious historical wrong—the overthrow of the Hawaiian kingdom—by the US government, its agents, and instrumentalities, and without a commitment to "heal" the wounds caused by that painful past. The values of the "internal" process must be present, to some extent, in the "external" process.

Most Native cultures share this emphasis on "restoring balance" and "right relations" after conflict and trauma. The sincerity of the wrongdoer is of utmost importance in healing the damaged relationship. Thus, regardless of whether or not Indian Nations ever "forgive" the United States or whether the United States is willing to make appropriate material reparations, the process of reconciliation—of healing—could not even *begin* without an acknowledgement of responsibility for the historical wrongs and their continuing effect. This was the primary purpose of the BIA apology: to start the process of healing, which is required to overcome the insidious harms that continue to affect Native peoples in the United States.

Thus, the two most important aspects of the BIA apology as a precedent for future acts of the US government are its effort to acknowledge the truth of the history and accept responsibility for that history and its commitment to a dynamic, intergroup process of healing. I will situate those two aspects of the apology in my discussion of the intercultural value of apology.

Collective Memory and Collective Conscience

Is the United States responsible for the harm suffered by Native Americans in the process of its efforts to "conquer" Native peoples and colonize them? Much of the philosophical literature on governmental apologies for historic wrongs focuses on the problems of imposing a moral responsibility on contemporary nations for the wrongs committed by other actors in a past generation. If the current government of the United States is not responsible for those bad acts, then why should it apologize for them? Assistant Secretary Gover's apology indicates that the current representatives of an institution are in privity with their predecessors, and thus, they share in the moral responsibility for past wrongs.

To build on Peter French's notion of the collective responsibility of modern governments for past wrongs, the "collective memory" invoked by Gover's apology is central to a notion of a "collective responsibility" for the US government's past wrongs toward Native nations. Professor French argues that our "public memory 'historicizes the present for us.' It makes the distant past of our society and culture (as well as the recent past) present 'by situating it in our midst.'" "Collective memory" is morally important because "it links us to shared collective responsibilities."[61] Professor French claims that public institutions are often the "stewards" of such collective memory. They manage this history and promote it as the collective "heritage" of the Nation. Members of the Nation have access to that shared history as their own heritage and identity. Consequently,

You as an American, we as Americans, should be ashamed that we permitted slavery on our soil and that we massacred native peoples at Sand Creek and Wounded Knee though you never owned slaves, couldn't own slaves, and had no control with respect to the massacres of native peoples, and [...] regardless of any benefits you do or do not now enjoy because of slavery or the massacres of native peoples in our past."[62]

In sum, the "shared ownership" of this history and memory permits, and indeed, may require, the contemporary citizens of a collective to assume responsibility for past wrongs.

Up until Assistant Secretary Gover's apology, none of the institutions, agencies, and entities that represent the US government and embody the "public memory" of its citizens had ever publicly acknowledged the nature and severity of the wrongs committed against Native Americans. This apology set a precedent for the US government to assume moral responsibility for its past bad acts, and for the continuing legacy of those acts in Native communities.

In addition, the apology works to build a shared cultural understanding of the past. In the context of intergroup historic trauma, collective memory differs dramatically from group to group. Assistant Secretary Gover evoked the collective memory of Native people when he named the wrongful acts deliberately perpetrated against Native people: the spread of disease, the decimation of the buffalo herds that sustained many Native Nations, the use of alcohol to destroy Native minds and bodies, the massacre of helpless women and children. He dismantled the justificatory approach of American "public memory" when he described those acts as deliberate and not "accidental"—a "tragedy on a scale so ghastly that it cannot be dismissed as merely the inevitable consequence of the clash of competing ways of life."[63] But most of all, he confirmed what Native people know to be true: "We will never push aside the memory of unnecessary and violent death at places such as Sand Creek, the banks of the Washita River, and Wounded Knee."[64] "Great nations of patriot warriors fell" during the US/Indian Wars, but the descendants of those Nations survive today, and the collective memory they share continues to inspire an active resistance to US laws and policies that have sought to further dismantle tribal governmental and cultural autonomy.

A shared understanding of the past is necessary if contemporary non-Indian citizens are to have any sense of "conscience" toward Native peoples. Lyle Marshall's claim that "Indian survival depends upon the American conscience" is correct in a very real sense.[65] The contemporary legal status of Native peoples depends upon an accurate understanding of their sovereign nature and the duty of the United States government to protect tribal sovereignty and rights to culture, land, and resources. Both features are a product of the historic, often treaty-based, interactions between the United States and the Native nations. Why should Congress continue to respect its historic bargain with Native peoples if the citizens of the United States begin to doubt the existence or validity of those agreements? Current controversies between non-Indians and tribes over water rights, hunting and fishing rights, language rights, gaming rights, and land rights are often beset with accusations that Indians are somehow not entitled to these "special" rights and that they should be content to be "equal citizens" and not separate governments. These arguments largely rest on the "justificatory approach" of American history. Thus, quite apart from any argument for "reparations," it is vital to the continued legal rights and status of Native Nations that Americans have an *accurate* understanding of how the past informs the political and legal requirements of the present and the future. Assistant Secretary Gover's apology is intended to emphasize that historical understanding.

The Process of Healing from Historic Trauma

I feel like I have been carrying a weight around that I've inherited. I have this theory that grief is passed on genetically because it's there and I never knew where it came from. I feel a sense of responsibility to undo the pain of the past, the history and the trauma. It has been paralyzing to us as a group.
　　　　—A Lakota/Dakota woman (Brave Heart & DeBruyn, 1998)[66]

"Collective memory" also has a very negative legacy for contemporary Native communities. Assistant Secretary Gover acknowledged that legacy as the "trauma of shame, fear, and anger" that has passed from one generation to the next, and "manifests itself in the rampant alcoholism, drug abuse, and domestic violence that plague Indian country."[67] This legacy has been described under the rubric of "historical trauma"—the "cumulative emotional and psychological wounding, over the lifespan and across generations, emanating from massive group trauma experiences."[68] Therapists and physicians, in turn, have documented a range of individual reactions to this trauma, which may include substance abuse and "other types of self-destructive behavior, suicidal thoughts and gestures, depression, anxiety, low self-esteem, anger, and difficulty in recognizing and expressing emotions."[69] At the heart of this phenomenon is "historical unresolved grief," which reflects strong emotional responses to trauma that are "impaired, delayed, fixated, and/or disenfranchised." Resolution of historic trauma and its manifestation in Native communities and individuals will entail many different strategies, and a great deal of both individual and community work. An "apology" is obviously insufficient to effect complete resolution of such deep-rooted trauma. However, the importance of Assistant Secretary Gover's apology is to acknowledge this phenomenon as a *reality* for Native peoples and to suggest that government agencies and institutions have a role to play in the healing process. Thus, "historic trauma" is not just a reflection of "Indian problems," like poverty, alcoholism, or social dysfunction. It is a reflection of past and current social policy and the US government's consistent efforts to victimize Indian people (for example, by inculcating group dependency and stripping individuals of a secure cultural context) and then to *blame them* for the victimization.[70]

The "Indian Wars" of the 19th century clearly had a tremendous physical cost for Native peoples, which can only be described as "genocide." The estimates of population loss among Native people in the United States during the process of colonization—from disease, forcible removal, and warfare—are staggering.[71] In California alone, scholars estimate that there were approximately 300,000 Indians at the time of contact with Europeans. "By 1850, when the miners were pouring in, there were 100,000 left. By 1870, there were some 30,000; by 1880, 20,000; and by 1910, 16,000."[72] These deaths resulted from a lethal combination of forces (disease, warfare, alcohol, and murder) officially ordered and condoned by the US government and its agents in some cases, and tolerated surreptitiously by the government in other cases. The corruption and graft of the Bureau of Indian Affairs during Westward settlement is legendary. Many of the Indian "uprisings" that the American public feared so much were the direct result of the exploitive practices of BIA agents who pilfered and sold at a profit rations that were treaty-guaranteed to Indians who consented to go onto reservations.[73] The spoiled, maggot-infested remains went to the starving Indian families, who were in most cases barred from hunting or trapping in their traditional areas.[74]

It is ridiculous to assume that Indian people can or should "forget" the horrific events of this very recent "past." Indeed, the response of the descendants of the survivors to Gover's apology is telling. One White Mountain Apache student said:

It should have been my great-grandmother who was witness to this. [...] While I was listening to [Assistant Secretary Gover] say those things about what we, as Native Americans, have gone through [...] I felt sad because I knew that all of those statements were in fact true. [. . .] We have gone through much in just 100 years. We have been waiting for so long for that apology, too long. Yet, at the same time, I felt anger. [. . .] It angered me because I feel that I should not have been witness to this event. It should have been my great-grandmother who was witness to this, an apology to what her mother and even what she has gone through."[75]

Sue Masten, Chairwoman of the Yurok Nation and then-President of the National Congress of American Indians, also acknowledged the sadness of the historic memories revived by the apology. However, she stated that Gover's apology marked "a very heroic and historic moment. "For us, there was a lot of emotion in that apology. It's important for us to begin to heal from what has been done since non-Indian contact."[76]

Masten's comments evoke the emotional and spiritual consequences of these traumatic historic events. The psychological cost of the Indian Wars, both for survivors and for their descendants, is tremendous: a pervasive sense of guilt, impotence, and loss characterizes the response of the survivors. Black Elk, a Lakota survivor of the Wounded Knee Massacre, told his story about witnessing the carnage left by the soldiers who fired their Hotchkiss guns on helpless men, women, and children that cold December day in 1890: "When I saw this, I wished that I had died too, but I was not sorry for the women and children. It was better for them to be happy in the other world, and I wanted to be there too."[77] Looking back, Black Elk says that the deaths that day went beyond that of the individuals who were murdered. "Something else died there in the bloody mud, and was buried in the blizzard. A people's dream died there. It was a beautiful dream."[78] Black Elk's comments refer to the Ghost Dance, a messianic movement among many of the Plains tribes during the late 1800s, which promised a vision of rebirth and strength for Native people at a critical point in their struggle for survival. Big Foot, the leader of the Lakota people massacred at Wounded Knee, was a compassionate and spiritual man who encouraged his band to follow these teachings and pray for a better time to return. The US military justified its conduct at Wounded Knee by claiming that the Indian Agent "feared" that the Ghost Dancers would "become violent" and would "disrupt" the "peaceful" Indians who had surrendered to the Agency. The murders at Wounded Knee were intended to strip the Lakota people of their "dream" that they would rise again as a powerful and independent Nation.

Of course, the tragic qualities of historic memory for the Lakota people are replicated for countless other Native Nations, tribes, and bands: the descendants of the California tribes, the descendants of the Cherokee and other

Southeastern tribes that were removed from their treaty-guaranteed home-lands on the "Trail of Tears," the descendants of the Cheyenne people who lost their lives in the massacre at Sand Creek, the descendants of the Apache people who were shipped to Florida and then to Fort Sill, Oklahoma, after the US Army routed the "hostile" Apaches from their homes in Arizona and New Mexico. Thus, to borrow the phrase from "ho'oponopono," the "negative entanglements" caused by historic bad acts and contemporary inequalities continue to cause a great deal of trauma and pain for Native peoples.

The BIA apology, of course, does not prescribe the manner in which healing should occur. Rather, it is up to the Native Nations to define the terms of the healing according to their own understandings of what "justice" entails and what steps are necessary for "healing" to occur. Thus, although the process of healing is set in motion by these words, the template for healing is still a work in progress.

Some might be tempted to employ a "common" understanding of healing from intergroup trauma as assuming responsibility, expressing regret, and asking for forgiveness and reconciliation. Assistant Secretary Gover, however, did not suggest that such a process would be a possible or appropriate outcome for his apology. In fact, he specifically says that it would not be appropriate to ask for forgiveness while the "burdens of this agency's history weigh so heavily on tribal communities."[79] Native nations will have to reach their own understandings of what the healing process must entail, at both the internal and external levels.

As Professor Jeffrie Murphy acknowledges, "forgiveness" is not an essential element of "reconciliation."[80] The nature of the past harms to Native peoples may embody an evil that cannot and should not be forgiven. In fact, Professor Murphy suggests that victims often demonstrate their essential commitment to "self-respect" by refusing to forgive those who have wronged them and by sustaining attitudes of moral resentment for past wrongs.[81] However, as the tradition of ho'oponopono demonstrates, "forgiveness" may be a cultur-ally necessary condition of "healing" for groups who believe that forgiveness possesses a unique and spiritual agency in the healing process.

A great deal of the contemporary philosophical literature defines and ana-lyzes the "spiritual" qualities of "forgiveness" within a Christian framework.[82] Thus, the words of Jesus and interpretations of Biblical text by theologians define the essential moral nature of human beings and their duties to other human beings. In the process of healing intercultural historic trauma, it will be necessary to evaluate other cultural conceptions of the spiritual quality of healing. Christianity, for example, is not the cultural benchmark for Native peoples' views on "forgiveness" or "reconciliation." Those notions will be evaluated within Native communities using their own cultural understandings.

Native cultures are often founded upon a spiritual understanding of the Universe, which ties their own existence to the other aspects of Creation. Although philosophers often dismiss the notion of "spirituality" as a "New Age" concept, and resort to the canons of Judeo-Christian religious traditions to assess the "spiritual" content of human existence, this is a mistake within the context of reparative justice for intercultural harms.

The concept of "healing" within Native traditions is a powerful one, shaped by cultural notions of spirituality and the appropriate relationship of thought, emotion, and belief to one's physical well being.[83] Native spiritual leaders from various tribes have expressed differing views on the appropriate ways to think about historical trauma, including their understanding of "forgiveness." There is no simple way to "unify" these views or suggest a "solution" to the often staggering problems that confront Native communities. I merely suggest in this essay that the process of reconciliation should include an intercultural dialogue on healing and a commitment to mutual respect for the need of particular cultures and groups to have their fundamental values respected in this process. In sum, "reconciliation" is not a "one-size fits all" proposition.

6. Conclusion

Assistant Secretary Gover's apology opened the door to an intercultural dialogue on reconciliation, and thus, started the process of healing. It is now incumbent upon the Indian Nations and the United States to continue the process, even if that means confronting facts about the past and the present that are tragic and uncomfortable. The statistics on Native poverty and rates of substance abuse, suicide, incarceration, and domestic violence provide empirical proof that the past is not behind us. However, if we do not acknowledge the past, we will not heal the future.

Assistant Secretary Gover's apology acknowledges that Native governments have endured and will endure into the future, despite the challenges and harms that they have suffered. Consequently, the United States will always have the obligation to respect and work cooperatively with these governments and peoples. Given this reality, engaging the process of healing is not even an "option." It is a requirement to achieve intercultural justice in the future.

Now, skeptics may still insist that the United States is not likely to accept this perspective. After all, why should the "dominant" society care about a numerically small and impoverished group like Native Americans? To the skeptics, I would argue that no nation can defend its position of "dominance" purely by force. As Justice Black commented in his dissent in *Federal Power Comm'n v. Tuscarora Nation*, just because the United States has the power to divest Indian nations of their lands in violation of its treaties and agreements with them, does not mean that it should do so. Rather: "Great nations, like great men, should keep their word."[84] There is a moral quality to leadership that is important to its ability to sustain itself over time. This is true of individuals, and it is also true of nations. By accepting responsibility for past wrongs, the United States can help heal the wounds that could dismantle this society. If it does not, the United States' greatest strength—the diversity of cultures and peoples that comprise "America"—could also prove to be its greatest liability.

Notes

1. I am indebted to my colleague, Professor Kevin Gover, for offering me his views on the context and function of this apology. I am also very appreciative to my colleagues, Dr. Jeffrie Murphy, Regent's Professor of Law and Philosophy, and Dr. Peter French, Professor of Philosophy and Director of the Lincoln Center for Applied Ethics, for generously sharing with me their work and their thoughts on many of the themes that frame this essay. I also acknowledge the hard work and contributions of my administrative associate, Sunny Larson Reedy, my research assistant, Christopher Love, and my librarian, Alison Ewing.

2. *Congressional Record.* 106th Cong. 2d. sess., 2000, vol. 146, pt. E 1453–03. (Hereafter referred to as Gover, Apology Speech). Remarks of Kevin Gover, Department of the Interior Assistant Secretary of Indian Affairs, at the Ceremony Acknowledging the 175th Anniversary of the Establishment of the Bureau of Indian Affairs, September 8, 2000.

3. Id.

4. Record of conference proceedings prepared by Alexander Karn.

5. Id.

6. See Trudy Govier and Wilhelm Verwoerd, "Taking Wrongs Seriously: A Qualified Defence of Public Apologies," *Saskatchewan Law Review* 65 (2002): pp. 139, 143. Govier and Verwoerd argue: "Commitments to reform and practical amends are forward thinking aspects of apology. These aspects suggest that apology should be construed as a process and not simply as an event."

7. Trudy Govier and Wilhelm Verwoerd, "The Promise and Pitfalls of Apology," *Journal of Social Philosophy* 33,1 (Spring 2002): pp. 67–82.

8. Gover, Apology Speech.

9. Kathleen Gill, "The Moral Functions of an Apology," *The Philosophical Forum* 31,1 (Spring 2000): pp. 11–27.

10. Id. at p. 12.

11. Id. at p. 13.

12. Id.

13. Id.

14. Gover, Apology Speech.

15. Id.

16. Id.

17. Id.

18. *Tee-Hit-Ton Indians v. United States*, 348 US 272 (1955).

19. See supra note 3.

20. Barbara L. Taverna, "Letters to the Editor: Apology to Indians Hollow Without Action," *Rochester Democrat and Chronicle*, September 22, 2000, p. 11A.

21. Gover, Apology Speech.

22. Id.

23. Id.

24. See supra note 3.

25. There have been several attempts over the past few years to introduce legislation into Congress to apologize to African Americans and to Native Americans for the various historic wrongs committed against these groups, and to study the need for reparations to these groups. See, e.g., H.R. 40, 108th Congress, 1st Session (2003), Commission to Study Reparations Proposals for African Americans Act; S.J. Res. 37, 108th Congress, 2nd Session (May 6, 2004), Joint Resolution to "acknowledge a long history of official depredations and ill-conceived policies by the United States Government regarding Indian tribes and offer an apology to all Native People on behalf of the United States." To date, none of these proposals has achieved the necessary political support to be enacted into law.

26. "Indians Receive Apology from BIA," *Seattle Post-Intelligencer*, September 9, 2000, sec. News, p. A1. (quoting Lynn Cutler, President Clinton's "chief advisor on Indian affairs").

27. Gover, Apology Speech.

28. *Tee-Hit-Ton*, 348 US at p. 289.

29. It should be noted that this situation is changing, as school districts, textbook authors, and teaching professionals seek to incorporate more critical views of American history into the required curriculum. It should also be noted that in many regions of the country, conservative educators have challenged these critical approaches as "revisionist" history. In American college and university settings, the critical approach has achieved a great deal of success. See, e.g., McKay, *History of World Societies*, 6th ed. (A world history textbook for college students, which refers to the "Native-American Holocaust" and presents the story of "westernization" in a critical light).

30. *United States v. Sioux Nation of Indians*, 448 US 371, 437 (1980). The majority of the Court held that the treaty-guaranteed nature of these lands did require the US to pay just compensation to the Lakota for the taking of these lands.

31. Id.

32. See e.g. Johnson v. McIntosh, 21 US (8 Wheat.) 543 (1823).

33. Id. at p. 590.

34. Id. at p. 573.

35. Id.

36. Gover, Apology Speech.

37. Id.

38. See, e.g., Howard McGary, "Morality and Collective Liability," *Journal of Value Inquiry* 20 (1986).

39. Peter French, "You Must Remember This/We'll Always Have Paris" (mss., 2003); Peter French, "Memories are Made of This" (mss., 2004). Both manuscripts address the issue of public memory and collective responsibility, and are hereafter referred to as "French manuscripts, 2003, 2004."

40. Id.

41. See, for example, the Code of Federal Regulations, which in the 19th century, expressly criminalized the practice of Native religions and customs.

42. Allison Dussias, "Let No Native Child Be Left Behind: Re-Envisioning Native American Education for the Twenty-First Century," *Arizona Law Review* 49 (Winter 2001): p. 819.

43. Gover, Apology Speech.

44. Id.

45. Id.

46. Id.

47. Gover, Apology Speech.

48. Elazar Barkan and Alexander Karn in their introduction to this volume, "Group Apology as an Ethical Imperative."

49. See, for example, *Oliphant v. Suquamish Tribe*, 435 US 191 (1978) (holding that tribes may not prosecute non-Indians for misdemeanor crimes committed against the tribe and its members on the reservation); *Montana v. US*, 450 US 544 (1981) (holding that Crow tribe could not exercise hunting and fishing jurisdiction on non-Indian owned fee lands within the reservation); *Lyng v. Northwest Indian Cemetery Protective Ass'n* 485 US 439 (1988) (holding that free exercise clause did not protect Native peoples from federal road projects that would desecrate sacred lands and preclude practice of religion); *Employment Div., Dept. of Human Resources of Oregon v. Smith*, 494 US 878 (1990) (holding that free exercise clause did not protect right of Native American Church members to use peyote in Church sacraments).

50. Nicholas Tavuchis, 1991, *Mea Culpa: A Sociology of Apology and Reconciliation*, p. 19 (Stanford: Stanford University Press).

51. Martha Minow, 1998, *Between Vengeance and Forgiveness*, p. 112 (Boston: Beacon Press).

52. Jeffrie Murphy, 2003, *Getting Even: Forgiveness and Its Limits*, p. 15 (New York: Oxford University Press).

53. Id.

54. Id.

55. Eric Yamamoto, 1999, *Interracial Justice: Conflict and Reconciliation in Post-Civil Rights America* (New York: New York University Press).

56. Id.

57. See Manu Meyer, "To Set Right–Ho'oponopono: A Native Hawaiian Way of Peacemaking," *The Compleat Lawyer* 30 (Fall 1995).

58. Id.

59. As previously noted, *S.J. Res.* 37, which was introduced into the Senate on May 6, 2004 and has been referred to the Committee on Indian Affairs, would, if passed, constitute an official "apology to all Native Peoples on behalf of the United States." It remains to be seen whether this Resolution can garner the broad political support needed to pass through Congress. The Resolution, as currently drafted, recognizes the "special legal and political relationship" between the Indian tribes and the United States, acknowledges the "official depredations, ill-conceived policies, and breaking of covenants by the United States," "apologizes on behalf of the people of the United States to all Native Peoples for the many instances of violence, maltreatment, and neglect inflicted on Native Peoples by the citizens of the United States" and calls for healing and reconciliation between the people of the United States, the US government, and the Indian tribes. *S.J. Res.* 37, 108th Cong., 2nd Session (May 6, 2004).

60. See "Reconciliation at a Crossroads: the Implications of the Apology Resolution and *Rice v. Cayetano* for Federal and State Programs Benefiting Native Hawaiians: Summary Report of the August 1998 and September 2000 Community Forums in Honolulu, Hawaii," Hawaiian Advisory Committee to the US Commission on Civil Rights (June 2001) at p. 19 (quoting Senator Akaka's statement at a community forum held in Honolulu, Hawaii, on September 29, 2000).

61. French manuscripts, 2003, 2004.

62. Id.

63. Gover, Apology Speech.

64. Id.

65. See supra note 5.

66. As cited in Maria Yellow Horse Brave Heart, "The Historical Trauma Response Among Natives and its Relationship with Substance Abuse: A Lakota Illustration," *Journal of Psychoactive Drugs* 35 (January–March 2003): p. 1.

67. Gover, Apology Speech.

68. Yellow Horse Brave Heart, "The Historical Trauma."

69. Id.

70. James P. Sterba, "Understanding Evil: American Slavery, the Holocaust, and the Conquest of the American Indians," 106 *Ethics* 424 (January 1996).

71. Id.

72. Robert Burnette and John Koster, 1974, *The Road to Wounded Knee*, p. 3 (New York: Bantam Books).

73. See Id. at p. 1 (quoting an interview with Captain Fred Benteen after the Battle of the Little Bighorn in which Captain Benteen alleged that the "Indian outbreaks," which plagued the frontier, were the result of the "enormous pilfering and stealing" of the agents of the Indian Bureau: "No agent can save $13,000 or $15,000 annually legitimately out of a salary of $1,500, and yet numbers of them do it. [...] It is this constant robbery which goads [the Indians] to outbreaks.").

74. See testimony recorded in Roxanne Dunbar Ortiz, 1977, *The Great Sioux Nation: Sitting in Judgment on America Based on and Containing Testimony Heard at the Sioux Treaty Hearing Held December, 1974, in Federal District Court, Lincoln, Nebraska* (San Francisco: American Indian Treaty Council Information Center, Moon Books).

75. Brenda Norrell, "American Indians Respond to the Bureau of Indian Affairs 'Reign of Terror,'" *Indian Country Today*, September 15, 2000 (quoting Cricket Johnson, a student at St. Mary's High School in Phoenix).

76. Brian Stockes, "Bureau of Indian Affairs Official Apologizes for Atrocities of the Past," *Indian Country Today*, September 15, 2000.

77. John G. Neihardt, 1961, *Black Elk Speaks* p. 221 (Lincoln: University of Nebraska Press).

78. Id. at p. 230.

79. Gover, Apology Speech.

80. Murphy, *Getting Even*, p. 13.

81. Minow, p. 10, citing Murphy.

82. See, for example, Murphy, *Getting Even*, pp. 87–93.

83. See, for example, Bear Heart and Molly Larkin, 1996, *The Wind is My Mother: The Life and Teachings of a Native American*, Shaman (New York : Clarkson Potter/Publishers) (reflections of a Muscogee Creek spiritual leader); Pete Catches, Sr., 1999, *Sacred Fireplace (Oceti Wakan): The Life and Teachings of a Lakota Medicine Man* (Santa Fe: Clear Light Books).

84. *Fed. Power Comm'n v. Tuscarora Nation*, 362 US 99, 141 (1960).

CHAPTER 10

The New Patriotism and Apology for Slavery

ROY L. BROOKS

1. Introduction

In the wake of the terrorists' attacks on the World Trade Center and the Pentagon on September 11, 2001, Americans on both sides of the color line have become self-consciously patriotic in ways we have not seen since the days of World War II. Some fly the American flag from their porches. Others display it proudly in their car windows. Both children and adults recite the pledge of allegiance with deep conviction, if not reverence. The country's national anthem plays everyday at noon on many radio stations, and even high-priced professional athletes, perhaps the most egotistical of all Americans, seem less distracted during the singing of the nation's hymn at the beginning of professional sporting events.

This, then, would not seem to be the proper time for African Americans to point an accusatory finger at our government, let alone raise the issue of apology for slavery. What could be more unpatriotic than to raise the ugly specter of slavery at a time when Americans should be pulling together, closing ranks behind our President to fight a protracted war on terrorism? What could be more socially divisive than to resurrect a national embarrassment that ended some 140 years ago? In the wake of September 11, in short, patriotism and apology for slavery would seem to be as incompatible as George Washington and Osama bin Laden.

In this essay, I should like to offer a dissenting view that at first glance may seem somewhat curious. I shall develop two lines of thought that attempt to demonstrate how and why an official government apology for slavery might materialize in the aftermath of September 11. The first line of thought has historical and political elements and goes as follows. Given the fact that, historically, the most significant advancements in racial progress have come during times of major wars, the war on terrorism, should it escalate into a major conflict, might precipitate racial progress that could include the federal government's tender of apology for slavery. Having made this historically correct observation, I am quick to add that I do not favor this form of apology—"political apology"—because it lacks moral pedigree. Apology in response to an atrocity as great as slavery should not carry the look or smell of a political machination, nor should it arise out of the normal ebb and flow of civil rights reforms. Apology in the aftermath of an atrocity is not civil rights as usual—it is special; it must be genuine rather than politically motivated

For those reasons, I favor a second kind of apology—"moral apology"—which, like political apology, finds fertile ground in post-September 11 American culture. If, as some conservatives claim, one lesson to be taken from September 11 is the realization that the Islamic world believes the United States is a morally bankrupt nation, apologizing for slavery can help to demonstrate our government's virtue or morality and, in the process, give content to a new patriotism. This new patriotism is far more robust than the old patriotism, as it encourages us to love our country not simply because it is our country, but because it is lovely—that is, virtuous. Thus, my argument is that the government's apology for slavery, if morally rather than politically grounded, can help Americans embrace a richer form of patriotism, which can help the United States win the war on terrorism.

There are, then, two types of apology for slavery that might arise in the aftermath of September 11. Political apology can emerge within the normal flow of civil rights advancements that have the peculiar habit of appearing primarily during times of large-scale wars. Moral apology, in contrast, can arise as the government's expression of deep remorse for the commission of a gross violations of human rights, called an atrocity. Qualitatively, moral apology is, in my view, the better form of apology for slavery.

Before proceeding with my argument, it might be useful to suggest a different way of conceptualizing apology for slavery, and to explain why I do not pursue that path. Hannah Arendt distinguishes between "political responsibility" (and, hence, political apology) and "moral responsibility" (and, hence, moral apology). The former is defined as guilt "for the sins of our fathers or our people or of mankind, in short, for deeds we have *not* done." It is a kind of original sin, or as Hamlet said: "The time is out of joint; O cursed spite; That ever I was born to set it right!" In contrast, moral responsibility or apology arises from guilt for having done something "specific." "Morally speaking," Arendt writes, "it is as wrong to feel guilty without having done anything specific as it is to feel free of all guilt if one actually is guilty of something." When people apologize for something of which they are personally innocent, "the result of this spontaneous admission of collective guilt" is not only "moral confusion" but also an "unintended whitewash" of those who had in fact committed the deed: "where all are guilty, no one is."[1]

Arendt's distinction between political and moral apology differs from the distinction drawn in this essay in several ways, and for good reason. First, her concept of political apology sweeps more broadly than mine. Arendt's concept makes governments (and, indeed, all humans) politically responsible "for the deeds and misdeeds of its predecessor and every nation for the deeds and misdeeds of the past." I, on the other hand, attach political responsibility only to governments and, then, only for the misdeeds they themselves have committed. In the context of political discourse, one gets little traction in holding a government (or a people) guilty for transgressions beyond its control. To turn Arendt's admonition against her: "where all are guilty, no one is." Second, Arendt seems to draw no distinction between extraordinary misdeeds (for example, slavery or genocide) and ordinary misdeeds (for example, occasional or systemic acts of employment discrimination). In contrast, I do make such a distinction, saving political apology for the latter and moral apology for the former. The failure to distinguish between the two has the unintended effect of trivializing, or "whitewashing," atrocities. Again: "where all are guilty, no one is."[2]

In short, I do not believe Arendt's interesting concept of "political responsibility" is particularly useful in discussing apologies for past atrocities. Her concept fails to recognize logical connections between perpetrators (whether governments or individuals) and atrocities. It also fails to observe logical differences between extraordinary wrongs and quotidian wrongs. On the other hand, Arendt's concept of "moral responsibility" is useful because it operates in personam (as do my concepts of moral apology and political apology), but it ultimately fails because it does not observe any distinction between types of wrongs—atrocities versus quotidian wrongs. We need sharper conceptual tools to dissect apology for slavery.

2. Political Apology for Slavery

Civil rights leaders and scholars have long noted a curious historical fact in America's long and erratic march toward racial equality. It is simply this: the greatest movement toward racial progress has come primarily during times of war. The Revolutionary War brought forth a rhetoric of individual liberty and equal rights. Although "black slavery had long since become an accepted part of life in all of the thirteen colonies,"[3] the colonists' struggle for independence was also in effect the beginning of a political struggle for black rights. Many signers of the Declaration of Independence certainly discerned this relationship. The Pennsylvania delegate Benjamin Rush, for example, urged his colleagues, "ye advocates for American liberty," to "work for the liberty of blacks as well."[4] The Revolutionary War's contribution to racial progress was not simply ideological, as important as that was. Many blacks were freed from slavery as a result of the War's rhetoric. Rush had himself freed his slaves, as did John Hancock, Benjamin Franklin, and many other northerners.[5]

The War of Independence set in motion forces that would lead to another war, an internal war over the issue of southern slavery. What can be viewed as a war of independence for blacks fought not entirely by proxy—blacks did fight for the union army—the Civil War created tremendous racial progress. Not only were 4.4 million blacks freed from human bondage, a significant development by itself, but they also made significant gains during Reconstruction, the period immediately following the war. For example, "Between 1869 and 1901, two Negroes served in the Senate and twenty in the House of Representatives."[6] Blacks were educated in unprecedented numbers and made significant economic gains, and, for the first time, enjoyed a wide range of legal rights "which the white man was bound to respect."[7]

This unlikely relationship between war and racial progress—a kind of "Mother Courage" phenomenon of racial progress[8]—continued into the twentieth century. World War I brought well-paying jobs to blacks in northern industrial centers. This, in turn, created the first great northern migration of blacks in the twentieth century. Northern migration was important because it not only resulted in better jobs for blacks, but it also gave them better social conditions and educational opportunities. It improved their quality of life significantly. World War II brought more jobs and another wave of northern migration. Mass production of the mechanical cotton picker in the 1940s, which took away thousands of unskilled jobs on which blacks had relied since Reconstruction, helped to drive "the great black migration" to "the promised land" that would eventually end in the late 1960s at five million strong.[9]

More significantly, World War II and its aftermath, particularly the Cold War, helped to pave the way for the two most significant civil rights laws since Reconstruction. The first was the Supreme Court's 1954 school desegregation decision in *Brown v. Board of Education*. Indeed, the government's amicus curiae brief in *Brown* referred to Secretary of State Dean Acheson's report stating that "racial discrimination in the United States remains a source of constant embarrassment to this Government in the day-to-day conduct of its foreign relations; and it jeopardizes the effective maintenance of our moral leadership of the free and democratic nations of the world."[10] Fighting the cold war also precipitated passage of the most important civil rights legislation since Reconstruction, the Civil Rights Act of 1964. Ugly racial confrontations reported daily not only on the evening news in American homes, but also around the world made it difficult for the United States to refute the communist claim to Third World nations (largely a world populated by people of color) that America's brand of democracy amounted to little more than second-class status for them. If the United States was going to win the cold war, especially the hearts and minds of the developing nations, it behooved Congress to enact laws banning racial discrimination in public accommodations, education, employment, voting, and other areas of American life.[11]

The "Mother Courage" phenomenon sketched above has been well-documented and comprehensively explained in several excellent books. In one of the most important of these books, *The Unsteady March: The Rise and Decline of Racial Equality in America*,[12] the authors, Philip A. Klinkner and Rogers M. Smith, argue that without war there would be little meaningful racial progress in American society. Significant racial progress comes from the convergence of three war-related forces, according to Klinker and Smith. The first is the government's preoccupation with waging a big war. A large-scaled conflict requires the mobilization of enormous amounts of military supplies and personnel. Social unrest can easily distract the government's attention and, hence, disrupt the flow of goods and people. Another requirement is the presence of a demonic enemy of democracy, a nefarious character. This must be someone who can inspire American political leaders to preach "the American Creed"—the ideals of freedom and democracy rooted in the Declaration of Independence—with greater vigor than is usually done. Isolating a person on whom to focus—a Hitler or "evil doer," to borrow from President George W. Bush—also provides a means of personalizing the war, putting a face on an amorphous enemy. The third condition is black leadership. Those in the vanguard of the movement for racial equality must be astute enough to exploit opportunities presented by the first two conditions. These leaders, such as an A. Philip Randolph or a Martin Luther King, must pressure now-vulnerable political leaders to follow through on their passionate progressive rhetoric. Such pressure is usually applied through the use of civil rights marches, boycotts, and other public demonstrations.

Daniel Kryder makes a similar "mother courage" argument in his excellent book, *Divided Arsenal: Race and the American State During World War II*.[13] Unlike Klinker and Smith, however, whose approach is more longitudinal, Kryder focuses primarily on a single war, World War II. Kryder also stresses the political dimension of war-induced racial progress, especially the desire of President Franklin D. Roosevelt's Democratic Party to remain in office. Any major disruption in the movement of military supplies and people would be politically fatal to the party in power during times of war. Thus, like President Abraham Lincoln's Republican Party during the Civil War, which also sought to retain political power, President Roosevelt's Administration was compelled to respond to black demands.

Clearly, then, A. Philip Randolph, the most powerful black union leader of the day, knew precisely what he was doing when he called on black workers to stage a March on Washington in protest of racial discrimination in the defense industry, while at the same time exhorting President Roosevelt "to emulate the courage of Abraham Lincoln who, faced with a grave wartime emergency, preserved American democracy by proclaiming the slaves free."[14] On June 25, 1941, six days before the March was scheduled to take place, President Roosevelt signed Executive Order 8802, which not only banned racial discrimination in the defense industry, but also established a new federal agency, the Fair Employment Practices Committee, to investigate reports of discrimination. Furthermore, between 1946 and 1951, President Harry S. Truman convened several commissions to study the race problem, each of which issued reports calling for the end of legalized racial discrimination. Accordingly, on July 26, 1948, President Truman issued two executive orders: Executive Order 9980, which prohibited racial discrimination within the federal government's civilian departments, and Executive Order 9981, which did the same for the armed forces.[15]

Divided Arsenal and *The Unsteady March* debunk a theory about racial progress that traces back to at least Gunnar Myrdal's 1944 classic book, *An American Dilemma*.[16] This seminal statement on American race relations asserts that racial progress takes place in our society through white self-awareness; in other words, when white Americans come to understand the obvious incongruity between racial inequality and the American Creed. The inability of whites to reconcile their racism with the American Creed creates what Myrdal called the "American Dilemma." *Divided Arsenal* and *The Unsteady March* clearly demonstrate that significant racial progress occurs *in spite of*, not because of, white enlightenment on racial matters. White political leaders pursue racial justice primarily out of a well-honed sense of self-interest.

But can it still be said that racial progress during times of war is in large part the result of a moral rather than a political calculation? Do wars simply "inflate moral claims and expose moral contradictions" regarding the plight of black Americans? It is, of course, quite possible that some political leaders might in fact be morally myopic when it comes to racial matters, and that it takes an event as earth-shattering as war to awaken their moral sensibilities. Possible, but highly unlikely for most politicians.

One simply does not attain high political office in this country by being politically obtuse or otherwise unfamiliar with the large issues of the day, and race has been one of these since the founding of this Republic under the Constitution in 1787. If supporting progressive racial policies were politically unsound, most politicians would not support them. Conversely, if supporting such policies were politically popular, most politicians would do so simply to get elected.

A case in point is President Lyndon B. Johnson (LBJ). Though he opposed President Truman's civil rights initiatives during the 1940s, including the attempt to transform and expand the antidiscrimination executive orders into civil rights legislation, he had a change of heart by the time he ran for the Senate in 1948, telling his aide, Horace Busby, "The Negro fought in the war, and now that he's back here with his family he's not gonna keep taking the shit we're dishing out. We're in a race with time. If we don't act, we're gonna have blood in the streets." As LBJ began to think about running for the presidency in the late 1950s, he also began to take a more public stance against segregation, including pushing the Civil Rights Act of 1957 through Congress. LBJ simply wanted "to mak[e] himself attractive to a national constituency." This one-time segregationist did not wish to repeat the mistakes of "great Southern politicians" whom he believed "had thrown away their chance to be national figures because of segregation."[7]

Thus, while it is true that civil rights would eventually become a moral issue for LBJ, perhaps even something of a moral crusade by the time he had reached the pinnacle of his political career in the 1960s, it is also true that he did not start out that way. As with most politicians, there was no moral awakening in LBJ due to war. His wartime conversion was no more genuine than a Supreme Court's justice's confirmation conversion. It was only *after* a war-induced political maneuver and a subsequent presidential calculation that LBJ grew into a deeper concern for racial progress.

This is not to say that morality plays no role in the racial politics. Again, some politicians, and certainly some of their constituents, do proceed from high moral ground, sometimes at great political risk. In fact,

I am hoping for a wider moral awakening within the ranks of our federal government in response to the moral argument in favor of apology, which I shall make in a moment. But as a matter of *routine* political behavior on racial matters, the moral element seems to me to be insufficiently robust to override the political exigencies of the moment. In this regard, there is a remarkable congruence between the astute observations made in *Divided Arsenal* and *The Unsteady March* and public choice scholarship, which essentially holds that "the primary motivation of the legislator is to be re-elected."[18]

Dick Morris, perhaps the most skillful political analyst in the last dozen years, adds an important addendum to this understanding about political behavior. In *Power Plays: Win or Lose—How History's Great Political Leaders Play the Game*,[19] Morris argues that politicians succeed in pushing their ideas when they are able to appeal to the common good. Political leaders, in other words, must restate personal interests in the language of universal values. They must repackage individual desire into something that looks like the public interest. President Lincoln was successful in mobilizing the North to fight a civil war, Morris argues, because he was able to translate his personal abolitionist goals into the universal value of unionism. Morris argues that, in contrast, President Woodrow Wilson failed to launch the League of Nations because he was unable to repackage his personal goals into values most Americans deemed important at the time. The lesson Morris takes from such experiences is this: the political leader who best serves the people serves himself/herself.[20]

I do not believe the war on terrorism has reached the above-mentioned historical and political conditions necessary for significant racial progress; conditions that could prompt the government to issue an official apology for slavery. Except for the identification of a demonic enemy of democracy—Osama bin Laden or al-Qaeda—none of the conditions for racial progress are in place today. The war would have to expand to the point of requiring massive movements of military equipment and personnel. Equally importantly, African Americans would have to become more passionate about the issue of apology to stage civil rights protests, civil rights marches, and other forms of public demonstrations. African American leaders would then have to use this power of demonstration to exert pressure on our political leaders to take political risks.

Should these conditions emerge in the future, as the movement for slave redress continues to gain momentum among African Americans, and should the government decide to issue an apology for slavery in response to these conditions, the apology would, in my view, be the wrong kind. A politically induced apology for slavery, even when the reparations designed to make the apology believable are substantial, strikes the wrong chord within the perpetrator. True, the ensuing reparations might still be useful to African Americans, but so would welfare. Political apology, then, is too inelegant to redress slavery. As part of a political deal, political apology carries the look or smell of a political machination. It is not genuine but, instead, is forced and, therefore, tainted. Apology that arises out of the normal ebb and flow of civil rights reforms cannot, in short, do the heavy lifting that is required in the response to slavery. Political apology provides, at best, a feeble demonstration of "new moral aspirations."

Seeking an apology to help redress slavery should, in my view, be about honor, not alms. It should be about black pride and dignity, and, more than that, it should be about honoring and memorializing the slaves who were denied freedom so that all Americans today might live in the freest and most prosperous nation mankind has ever known. Slavery was not the garden-variety type of discrimination for which our civil rights laws were designed. Human bondage was an exceptional act of human suffering—an atrocity—that lasted two-and-one-quarter centuries. Only moral apology— apology that embraces a post-Holocaust spirit of heightened moral- ity, identity, egalitarianism, and restorative justice—can properly redress slavery.

3. Moral Apology for Slavery: Toward A New Patriotism

Let me begin with what I take to be self-evident: Loving one's country is a weaker form of patriotism than loving one's country because it is virtuous. Even conservatives like Dinesh D'Souza would agree with this observation. Indeed, D'Souza, an opponent of reparations, makes the point quite elegantly in *What's Great About America.*[21] Patriotism in its highest form, D'Souza argues, is more than just enthusiastic flag waving in the days and months following September 11. It is more than joining the armed services to fight bin Laden or al-Qaeda. Patriotism is rallying to our country because its citizens and institutions—its culture—function on high moral ground. America tries to do the right thing, and that is why we love America. D'Souza quotes Edmund Burke's lovely words, "To make us love our country, our country ought to be lovely."[22]

In fact, D'Souza argues, Americans cannot effectively respond to the most intelligent Islamic critique of American culture without basing that response on virtue. It is not enough to say our culture is better than the Islamic culture because we are more prosperous than Islamic societies. Nor is it sufficient to say we are better because we exercise more freedoms—especially political and religious freedoms—or because we are more tolerant of others—particularly of women and foreigners—than Islamic regimes. In short, American Exceptionalism is not a good defense of America these days.

The best Islamic critics do not deny American Exceptionalism. But, as D'Souza correctly observes, they demur to it, dismissing our prosperity and freedoms as "worthless triviality." The best and the brightest of Islamic scholars argue that the things that make us exceptional are not the most important values of a society—virtue is. Virtue is the highest value of the good society. Virtue is the will of God, and it is the will of God that the Islamic world is trying to implement. That is what makes the Islamic culture morally superior to America and to Western culture in general. Even though we may have fallen short of our goal, the Islamic argument continues, at least we are trying. Yes, "the United States and the West may be materially advanced, but they are morally decadent..., especially in the sexual domain."[23] Jerry Springer; Howard Stern; Dennis Rodman; Madonna; the Artist Formerly Known as Prince. "Hey! American man! You are a godless homosexual rapist of your grandmother's pet goat."[24] D'Souza believes America must respond to the Islamic critique of the West by acknowledging the fundamental truth of the Islamic premise—in other words, virtue is the highest goal of the good society—but then follows that admission with a brilliant observation: the Islamic societies can never be truly virtuous because they lack what the West has in abundant supply—namely, liberty. Freedom is a necessary (although not sufficient) condition of a virtuous society. The Islamic woman who is *required* to wear a veil is not modest, D'Souza argues, because she is being forced to wear it. A coerced virtue is no virtue at all:

The fundamental difference between the society that the Islamic fundamentalists want and the society that Americans have is that the Islamic activists seek a country where the life of the citizens is *directed by others*, while Americans live in a nation where the life of the citizens is largely *self-directed*... The Islamic fundamentalists presume the moral superiority of the externally directed life on the grounds that it is aimed at virtue. The self-directed life, however, also seeks virtue—virtue realized not through external command but, as it were, 'from within.'[25]

Liberty is what makes the West more likely to achieve virtue than the Islamic world, although decadence is an inescapable possibility of a free society.

4. The Anatomy of Moral Apology

With this type of thinking, D'Souza should be an unabashed supporter of apology for slavery; but he is not. Like most conservatives, D'Souza does not believe "that racism today [is] potent enough and widespread enough that it could prevent [any person of color, including blacks] from achieving their basic aspirations."[26] These aspirations, according D'Souza are "to be in the entering class at Berkeley and Yale," to have "more seats in the board-room at Microsoft and General Electric," and "greater representation in the Congress."[27]

While I certainly do not agree with D'Souza's argument that race has become a trivial matter for blacks in our society,[28] which argument is quite beside the point here, because apology is about virtue. Apology is the virtuous act of honoring the lives of the millions of dead slaves who contributed to the economic development of this country without so much as receiving a paycheck or a "thank you." If it is virtuous for the federal government to construct a memorial in remembrance of the 3,016 innocent people who perished in the World Trade Center and the Pentagon at the hands of the terrorists, as well as for the federal government to pay $3 billion to the victims' families, then it is surely virtuous for the federal government to make a similar gesture toward the millions of blacks whom *it* enslaved and who died in service to *this* country.

Apology is virtuous in another way as well. It restores honor to the per-petrator of an atrocity. In the case of slavery, apology enables the United States government to recover a measure of moral capital lost as a result of the commission of a human injustice. Apology is not a punishment for guilt, but rather an acknowledgement of guilt; it reestablishes moral character. It is a way in which a government may learn of its guilt and repent. The govern-ment that apologizes *and means it* regards the misdeed as substantial (that is, an atrocity) rather than as trivial. When a government apologies *and means it*, it does four things: confesses the deed; admits the deed was an injustice; repents; and asks for forgiveness. All four conditions are essential ingredients of a moral apology—as opposed to a political or some other form of apology.

Some might add as a fifth condition to the requirement of moral apology that the perpetrator must change its behavior toward the victim. The purpose of this requirement is to ensure, as much as possible, that the atrocity will never be repeated. This, of course, assumes that the behavior giving rise to the atrocity has ended. It makes no sense to consider a tender of apology a true apology while the atrocity is still raging on.

I think it makes more sense to treat the behavioral element not as an ingredient of apology (which is essentially rhetoric, albeit essential rhetoric), but as an element of a meaningful reparation. Reparations serve many purposes, one of the most important of which is to make apologies believable or meaningful. When apology is thus solidified, it gives a measure of assurance that the perpetrator will not repeat the atrocity. Reparations concretize apologies; which is to say, they turn the rhetoric of apology into a meaningful, material reality.[29]

More to the point: *When a perpetrator responds to an atrocity with an asymmetrical measure, what is it if not a reparation?* Reparation is by nature asymmetrical. Only victims of the atrocity are eligible to receive a reparation. A scholarship program for African Americans as a form of redress for slavery is a reparation. A scholarship program for "minority and women students," even when presented as a form of redress for slavery, is no more a reparation than Holocaust payments to American gentiles. Asymmetrical civil rights policies—reparations—are not, however, intended to displace ongoing civil rights enforcement or other social reforms. These symmetrical human rights measures are equally accessible to all victims of discrimination or persons in need of other forms of government assistance. Employment discrimination laws, for example, are open to blacks, other persons of color, women, and whites. Though there may be some duplication, symmetrical and asymmetrical human rights measures are not mutually exclusive. Japanese Americans who have received reparations from the federal government were not precluded from participating in other social programs and continued to receive the protection of our civil rights laws, while they were receiving reparations. That is how it should be. Symmetrical and asymmetrical human rights measures serve different purposes. Thus, I would think that the only type of behavior we can *legitimately* ask a perpetrator to change in response to an atrocity is behavior that is essentially reparative; otherwise we are asking the perpetrator to perform some other task, which perhaps it ought to be doing anyway.

Treating the doing of a deed as part of the reparation makes additional sense in situations where, as in the case of American slavery and the Holocaust, all or most of the direct victims have died by the time the apology is tendered. Many victims of an atrocity do not survive the atrocity. Hence, as to dead victims, it makes no sense to require the perpetrator to change its behavior toward the victim other than by providing a meaningful reparation. Such a reparation could be the construction of a memorial honoring the lives of the dead victims.

The matter of dead victims raises the difficult question of how far back does the duty of apology go? Does the perpetrator have anything to apologize for if all the victims are dead? The easy answer is that the question of apology is moot if there are no living victims. Viewed in this way, the living-victims requirement acts as a kind of statute of limitations on redressing past atrocities. The easy answer is not always the best answer, however. I believe the victim's death is irrelevant to the question of how far back the duty to apology extends. The atrocity and the victims, though obviously connected, are distinct considerations. Polish President Aleksandr Kwasniewski took this position when he declared in remarks given in 2001 at a ceremony honoring 1,600 Jews murdered by Polish civilians on the eve of World War II: "For this crime, we should beg *the souls of the dead* and their families for forgiveness. Today, as a man, citizen, and president of the Polish republic, I ask pardon in my own name and in the name of those Polish people whose consciences are shocked by this crime."[30]

This is not to say, however, that timing is irrelevant. Arguably, the closer apology is to the atrocity the more virtuous it is, because the perpetrator is in a position to provide a timely response to the atrocity. The atrocity's effects do not linger intergenerationally. Also, it is perhaps easier for the public to accept the idea of a government apology when the latter's responsibility is clear and present. On the other hand, one could argue that a tender of apology when memories of the atrocity have long faded is more virtuous, because the perpetrator is under no external pressure to issue it given the fact that the atrocity did not occur on its watch. The tender of apology, then, serves no self-interest other than retiring the perpetrators' moral duty to atone. The one exception, of course, is the situation in which the atrocity has lingering effects. In this instance, the perpetrator's redress, which presumably is directed toward the needs of the victim's descendants, helps to create a healthy social environment, and this ultimately serves the perpetrator's political interest.

Notwithstanding the timing issue, my fundamental point still holds. The imposition of a statute of limitations on the moral duty to apologize is improperly legalistic. Because we are dealing with a matter of morality rather than legality, the duty to apologize does not perish with the victims. The perpetrator still has something for which it should apologize. It is only the tender of apology (followed by reparation) that retires the moral duty to apologize, which removes the moral stain.

Two other considerations—one favoring the victim and the other favoring the perpetrator—add further support to my argument that the unfulfilled duty to apologize survives the death of the victims. First, it would be a cruel irony if the perpetrator could absolve himself/herself of the moral duty to apologize by simply wiping out all his victims. Second, the perpetrator should not be denied the opportunity for redemption if, for example, living victims decided not to come forward and make their presence known, as was the case with many of the "comfort women" during the early stages of their redress movement in Japan (though the Japanese Diet still refuses to issue an apology).[31] This argument speaks to an essential feature of apology, often overlooked in the literature on apology as well as in the black redress movement. I shall take a moment to elaborate on this important point.

When the government makes a tender of apology, it is attempting to reclaim its humanity, its moral character, and its place in the community of civilized nations in the aftermath of the commission of an unspeakable human injustice. While I would not go so far as to say that apology is for the perpetrator and reparation is for the victim, I would say that, in a real sense, apology is as much for the perpetrator as it is for the victim. What this means, of course, is that apology—moral apology—must of necessity be voluntary. It cannot be coerced, such as by court order, judicial settlement, or political deal making. Though the needs of the victim or political considerations might broach the idea of apology, a true apology is freely bestowed. It comes from the heart, and cleanses the perpetrator's character after the commission of an atrocity.

In sum, the presence of the victim is not necessary for the tender of apology, or for that matter, reparations, to take effect. If there are no living victims that simply means there may be no one to accept the tender of apology and its implementing reparations—in other words, no one to forgive the perpetrator—save perhaps the whole of civilized society. If the victims have living descendants, then they are qualified to forgive as the next-best class. The living descendants may themselves be victims of the lingering effects of the atrocity, in which case they would also be qualified to forgive on behalf of themselves as indirect victims. But if no qualified person were available to accept a tender of apology and implementing reparations, the *redemptive* effect of the apology should still stand. It would be better, of course, if the victims were able to witness this special occasion, but their absence should not invalidate the redemption—the perpetrator's ability to redress its self-inflicted moral wound.

If an unaccepted apology still has redemptive effect, why should the perpetrator be required to seek forgiveness? At an earlier stage in my thinking about apology, I did not include forgiveness among its elements precisely because I did not (and still do not) believe that the victims' presence was a necessary precondition for the perpetrator's redemption to take effect. But upon further reflection, I have decided that apology, in the Judaic tradition, must impose an affirmative duty on the perpetrator "to seek forgiveness from the person harmed."[32] I found Elie Wiesel's rabbinical reflections on the matter to be most persuasive. On one recent occasion, the dedication of a Holocaust Remembrance site at the Brandenburg Gate in Germany, *The New York Times* reported Wiesel's remarks on the subject as follows:

Mr. Weisel concluded by urging Parliament to pass a resolution formally requesting, in the name of Germany, the forgiveness of the Jewish people for the crimes of Hitler. 'Do it publicly,' he said. 'Ask the Jewish people to forgive Germany for what the Third Reich had done in Germany's name. Do it, and the significance of this day will acquire a higher level. Do it, for we desperately want to have hope for this new century.'[33]

Seeking forgiveness enriches the moral quality of apology. It makes apology more believable and, hence, the prospect that the atrocity will recur more unlikely.

What role does justice play in moral apology? Mark Gibney and Erik Roxstrum argue in their excellent analysis of state apologies that retributive justice should be viewed as an essential feature of apology, or at least in assessing the adequacy of apology. Individuals who carried out the wrongs must be held accountable if they are still living.[34] This argument is generally correct except for special occasions when other moral precepts must override justice. A case in point is South Africa. While conceding that the South African Truth and Reconciliation Commission's decision to grant amnesty to perpetrators of atrocities presents an intense conflict between retributive justice and other moral precepts, such as "truth, reconciliation, peace, [and] the common good," Wilhelm Verwoerd, a South African philosophy professor, correctly observes: "in the context of a fragile transition to stable democracy," amnesty combined with "public shaming" and institutional restructuring is the right, morally correct thing to do.[35] Without amnesty, there would be no prospect for peace and harmony in South Africa. Another reason justice should not be included among the essential ingredients of apology is because it may be more appropriate to view the perpetrator as the government entity itself—focusing on the government's corporateness—rather than as individual members of the government. John J. McCoy was alive when Congress was considering reparations for Japanese Americans. Of what benefit would it have been to place him in jail as one of the chief architects of the World

War II internment camps? Retribution may yield a measure of justice, but it is not necessarily the moral thing to do.

5. Conclusion

Although the terrorist attacks against America on September 11, 2001 were unspeakable acts of violence, they may have provided hidden opportunities for racial progress in our society. Should the protracted war on terrorism escalate into a large-scale war on the order of previous American wars—the Revolutionary War, World Wars I and II, and the Cold War—then we might see significant racial progress. Historically, this has been the "unsteady march" of racial progress since the Revolutionary War. The government's apology for slavery could likely emerge from within this cycle of racial progress.

But a state apology formulated within the normal cycle of racial progress—within the politics of racial progress—would not, in my judgment, be appropriate for the extraordinary event that slavery was. Political apology is primarily a matter of whose ox shall be gored. It is not remorseful and, consequently, it has little redemptive value. The slate is not wiped clean; the moral stain remains on the perpetrator.

Moral apology, on the other hand, is different. It provides the requisite remorse to redress the moral enormity of slavery. Moral apology, unlike political apology, is non-calculating. It is neither half-hearted nor expedient, but rather it speaks directly from the heart to the heart. Moral apology for slavery is too special to be considered as a mere aspect of routine, ongoing civil rights reforms. Political apology is for everyday civil rights. Moral apology is for slavery.

To ensure that moral apology does not slip imperceptibly into political apology, the perpetrator government must provide meaningful reparations. Apology standing alone does not demonstrate sufficient remorse. As an example, many Native Hawaiians correctly rejected President Clinton's expression of apology made on behalf of the federal government for the United States' overthrow of the Hawaiian sovereign nation in the late nineteenth century. President Clinton's apology, like many state apologies in this "age of apology,"[36] was empty; it was not backed up with anything tangible. Saying "I'm sorry" isn't enough when a government has committed an atrocity. In the face of such an egregious wrong, a tepid apology can be worse than no apology because, without accompanying reparations, a government apology seems so insecure, so politically expedient, so self-serving, and so cheap.

Reparations, then, are necessary (though not sufficient, as I shall explain in a moment) for the expression of a moral apology. They turn the rhetoric of apology into a meaningful moral message. I have argued on other occasions for a National Museum of Slavery honoring the slaves and an Atonement Trust Fund providing educational funds and venture capital for the descendants of slaves as meaningful demonstrations of remorse for slavery.[37] These reparations are substantial enough to add moral weight to an apology that would otherwise be an empty political gesture. *Moral apology means apology plus reparations.*

More than that, moral apology speaks to the moral enormity of slavery in a way that political apology simply cannot. Moral apology treats the matter of apology as something special, as a sacred event that takes place outside the traditional realm of civil rights legislation. To understand this point, one must first understand that civil rights legislation has, historically, been *symmetrical* in its application. That is, civil rights policies typically apply to all groups. The Fourteenth Amendment, for example, provides that "No State shall . . . deprive *any person* life, liberty, or property, without due process of law; nor deny to *any person* within its jurisdiction the equal protection of the laws."[38] Title VII of the Civil Rights Act of 1964 makes it unlawful for employers to discrimination against "*any individual* . . . because of such individual's race, color, religion, sex, or national origin."[39] The Voting Rights Act of 1965 guarantees the right to vote to "*All citizens* of the United States who are otherwise qualified by law to vote at any election [under state or local law] . . . without distinction of race, color, or previous condition of servitude."[40] And racial preference law (affirmative action) applies to racial minorities, women, and even veterans.[41] Thus, many groups have access to our antidiscrimination laws. Civil rights legislation does not apply only to blacks.

In contrast, reparations for slavery, like reparations for other atrocities, are necessarily *asymmetrical*—they apply only to the victims of the atrocity in question. Focusing on the moral enormity of slavery provides not only a rational, but also a moral basis for singling out blacks for special treatment. It is the only way other protected classes (such as, Latinos, Asians, Native Americans, and women), who are accustomed to being treated pari passu with blacks, can properly understand and hopefully accept this departure from standard civil rights treatment. Here the government is not demonstrating racial neutrality. Blacks are receiving something of value from the government that is not equally available to other traditionally subordinated groups. This large asymmetrical undertaking can only be justified within our liberal democratic state as a one-time response to a one-time event of extraordinary proportions. To explain slave redress as simply a matter of politics as usual will not suffice when other groups can also lay claim to social disadvantage.

Treating slave redress as politics as usual also trivializes slavery and our memory of the slaves. The federal government needs to say to blacks and, indeed, the entire world, "We are apologizing and offering reparations not because it is politically expedient to do so, but because both acts are the right things to do." The government needs to say this to establish a heightened sense of morality, to affirm the common humanity between victim and perpetrator, and to bring a measure of restorative justice to the matter. Moral apology, in sum, is an active rather than a passive apology (it entails reparations); is presented as an extraordinary, not-to-be-repeated exception to the traditional way in which civil rights policy is politically formulated in our society (this is not racial politics as usual); and raises the moral threshold of society (presents a vision of heightened morality, identity, and restorative justice).

Although certainly not a precondition for the tendering of moral apology, the war against terrorism may, nonetheless, give a boost to this moral endeavor. The events of September 11 have changed American culture. They have precipitated unabashed expressions of patriotism and a concomitant need to rethink the concept of patriotism. *What does it mean to be a patriotic American given the shift from a polycentric world to American hegemony?* The answer I offer in this essay is rather straightforward: to be patriotic is to love one's country because it is a virtuous country—a country that tries to do the right thing rather than exert power for the sake of power. This richer form of patriotism is good for the collective soul of our nation and may prove to be an effective weapon against terrorism. Virtue, rather than America's prosperity, freedoms, or military capabilities, may, in fact, be the only way to secure a lasting victory in this protracted war.

This is not to suggest that the Islamic critique regarding the conditions constitutive of the good society is entirely correct. Virtue is the highest value, but not the only value. Virtue needs liberty to sustain itself. Without liberty, virtue cannot exist. Virtue must be chosen; it cannot be coerced. It must, in other words, be the result of free will.

Apologizing for slavery is an important demonstration of American virtue. Simply put, no government can commit an atrocity as large as American slavery and simply walk away from it without so much as offering an apology and expect to have credibility in the community of moral nations. Apologizing for slavery is something our government, with the support of the American people, should choose to do because it is the morally correct (rather than the politically expedient) thing to do. Moral apology, in the end, gives shape and substance to flag waving. It says to the world that America has not only grown stronger over the years, but it has also grown up, too.

Notes

1. Hannah Arendt, 2003, *Responsibility and Judgement*, Jerome Kohn, ed., pp. 27–28 (New York: Schocken Books).

2. Ibid.

3. David McCullough, 2001, *John Adams*, p. 131 (New York: Simon & Schuster).

4. Ibid., p. 133.

5. W.E.B. DuBois frames the "American dilemma" when he observes, "From the day of its birth, the anomaly of slavery plagued a nation which asserted the equality of all men, and sought to derive powers of government from the consent of the governed." W.E.B. DuBois, 1969, *Black Reconstruction in America: 1860–1880*, p. 3 (New York: Atheneum, originally published 1935).

6. John Hope Franklin and Alfred A. Moss, Jr., 1988, *From Slavery to Freedom: A History of Negro Americans* 6th edition, p. 220 (New York: Knoft).

7. This reference is to the Supreme Court's antebellum ruling in *Dred Scott v. Sanford*, 60 US 393 (1856), wherein the Court ruled that blacks "had no rights which the white man was bound to respect." The Reconstruction Amendments, 13th, 14th, and 15th, effectively overruled *Dred Scott*.

8. "Mother Courage" is Anna Fierling, the protagonist in Bertolt Brecht's play, "Mother Courage and her Children." Following the war around Europe, selling loaves of bread to the army and ammunition to the opposing army, Anna reveals many contradictions in her character, one being her attempt to exploit the war by profiting from it. She, in fact, is in the business of profiting from the war. See, e.g., Bertolt Brecht, *Mother Courage and her Children*, translated by Eric Bentley, 1966 (New York: Grove Press). The self-serving, pseudo-heroism exhibited by Mother Courage comes at tremendous cost: all three of her children are killed by the war. With the death of each child, Mother Courage learns nothing.

9. See, e.g., Nicholas Lemann, 1991, *The Promised Land: The Great Black Migration and How it Changed America* (New York: Alfred A. Knopf, Inc.); Roy L. Brooks, 1990, *Rethinking the American Race Problem*, pp. 27–28 (Berkeley: University of California Press).

10. Derrick Bell, "Brown v. Board of Education: Forty Years After the Fact," *Ohio Northern University Law Review* 26 (2000): pp. 171, 179–180 (citing Brief for the United States as Amicus Curiae in *Brown*). See Roy L. Brooks, 2002, *Structures of Judicial Decision-Making from Legal Formalism to Critical Theory*, p. 284 (Durham: Carolina Academic Press). Though the United States won the Cold War, it has managed to lose the hearts and minds of many in the Third World. Perhaps this shows that

although it may be possible for a government to achieve a degree of success in the international arena (at least for a while) without following moral rhetoric with moral policies, eventually the hypocrisy will take its toll. While I certainly do not view the September 11 attacks as the latest chapter in the saga of the "ugly American," I do argue that if anti-Americanism in some part springs from a reaction to immoral policies (whether domestic or international) or to dishonesty that results from the disconnect between rhetoric and reality, it behooves our government to change its policies if it can do so without endangering national security.

11. The voting rights provisions of the 1964 Civil Rights Act were actually quite weak. It was not until one year later that Congress passed a stronger voting rights bill, the Voting Rights Act of 1965. The 1964 Civil Rights Act also lacked a strong housing provision. This defect was remedied with the passage of the Fair Housing Act of 1968.

12. Philip A. Klinkner and Rogers M. Smith, 1999, *The Unsteady March: The Rise and Decline of Racial Equality in America* (Chicago: University of Chicago Press).

13. Daniel Kryder, 2000, *Divided Arsenal: Race and the American State during World War II* (Cambridge, UK: Cambridge University Press).

14. Ibid., p. 4.

15. See, e.g., Brooks, *Rethinking the American Race Problem*, pp. 27–28; *African Americans: Voices of Triumph—Leadership*, pp. 84–85, Roberta Conlan, ed., 1993 (New York: Time-Life Books).

16. Gunnar Myrdal, 1944, *An American Dilemma: The Negro Problem and Modern Democracy* (New York: Harper & Brothers).

17. The quotations in the paragraph are taken from Lehmann, *The Promised Land*, pp. 136–137.

18. See, e.g., Roy L. Brooks, 2002, *Structures of Judicial Decision-Making from Legal Formalism to Critical Theory*, pp. 150–151 (sources cited therein) (Durham: Carolina Academic Press).

19. Dick Morris, 2002, *Power Plays: Win or Lose—How History's Great Political Leaders Play the Game* (New York: HarperCollins).

20. See Ibid.

21. Dinesh D'Souza, 2002, *What's Great About America* (Washington, D.C.: Regnery Publishing, Inc.).

22. Ibid., p. 28.

23. Ibid at p. 133.

24. Ibid, quoting Salman Rushdie.

25. Ibid at pp. 189–190.

26. Ibid at pp. 101–102.

27. Ibid at p. 172.

28. For much of the last dozen years, I have attempted to document and argue that race matters. See, e.g., Brooks, *Rethinking the American Race Problem*; Roy L. Brooks, 1996, *Integration or Separation? A Strategy for Racial Equality* (Cambridge: Harvard

University Press). Roy L. Brooks, Gilbert Paul Carrasco, Michael Selmi, 2000, *Civil Rights Litigation: Cases and Perspectives* 2d edition (Durham: Carolina Academic Press).

29. See Roy L. Brooks, 1999, "The Age of Apology," in *When Sorry Isn't Enough: The Controversy over Apologies and Reparations for Human Injustice*, pp. 8–11, Roy L. Brooks, ed. (New York: New York University Press).

30. Ian Fisher, "At Site of Massacre, Polish Leader Asks Jews for Forgiveness," *New York Times*, July 11, 2001, p. A1 (emphasis added).

31. See, e.g., George Hicks, "The Comfort Women Redress Movement," in Brooks, 1999, *op. cit.*, p. 113.

32. Louis E. Newman, "The Quality of Mercy: On the Duty to Forgive in the Judaic Tradition," *Journal of Religious Ethics* 15 (Fall 1987): pp. 155, 155.

33. Roger Cohen, "Wiesel Urges Germany to Ask Forgiveness," *New York Times*, January 28, 2001, p. A3.

34. See Mark Gibney and Erik Roxstrom, "The Status of State Apologies," *Human Rights Quarterly* 23 (2001): pp. 911, 931.

35. Wihelm Verwoed, "Justice After Apartheid? Reflections on the South African TRC,"in Brooks, 1999, *op. cit.*, pp. 479, 480–482.

36. See Brooks, "The Age of Apology," in *When Sorry Isn't Enough*, pp. 3, 511–513.

37. These forms of redress have been developed in several speeches and academic papers given since 2000, and are part of the "atonement model" of slave redress that will be more fully developed in a forthcoming book, tentatively titled "Atonement and Forgiveness."

38. US Constitution, Adt. 14, Sec. 1.

39. 42 USC 2000–2(a)(1).

40. 42 USC 1971(a)(1).

41. See generally, Brooks, et al., *Civil Rights Litigation*, ch. 10.

CHAPTER 11

The Tulsa Race Riot Commission, Apology, and Reparation: Understanding the Functions and Limitations of a Historical Truth Commission

ALFRED L. BROPHY[1]

In 1997 the Oklahoma legislature established a Commission to investigate the 1921 Tulsa Race Riot. The Commission was charged with preparing a fuller, more accurate history than had previously been available, collecting names and stories of survivors, and making recommendations regarding reparations.[2] The sponsors of the Commission in the legislature wanted to move the riot to the center of Oklahoma's history and also to arrive at some sort of justice, and perhaps even reconciliation, for a tragedy that was long-forgotten.[3] Moreover, the victims of the riot hoped that the Commission would not only tell their story, but many hoped that it would also help the request for reparations.[4] The Commission's experiences provide an important window into how a truth commission negotiates the conflicting politics surrounding race, apologies, and reparations. It shows what truth commissions can be expected to accomplish, as well as their limitations.

The Tulsa Race Riot Commission, which had eleven members drawn from leaders in the Oklahoma legislature, as well as local historians, educators, and a businessman and a survivor of the riot, hired a team of distinguished historians. The Commission's historians were John Hope Franklin, son of riot survivor B. C. Franklin and author of the leading work in African American history *From Slavery to Freedom*, and Scott Ellsworth, author of the leading book on the riot, *Death in a Promised Land*. The historians, assisted by members of the Commission, began investigating many of the stories that had grown up around the riot, such as the use of airplanes to bomb the black section of the city, where the riot was concentrated; the story that the *Tulsa Tribune* had run an editorial encouraging a lynching; and the story that many people who died had been buried in unmarked graves. Throughout 1998 and 1999, the Commission's work attracted progressively more media attention, as Tulsans rediscovered the riot, talked about it and its origins in the conflicts between blacks and whites, and the nature of the riot as an effort to run blacks out of town.[5]

The Commission and its historians began wading through decades of myths and stories about the riot. It found very different memories of the event among those in the black and white communities. In the black community, there was widespread talk that the riot was the result of a preplanned conspiracy to burn out the black community, known as Greenwood, and take the land it was on to expand the nearby railroad yards and industrial area. In the white community the talk was most commonly of the role of aggressive black veterans in starting the riot and in the way that a small segment of the white community then attacked, looted, and burned the black community. Certainly, the "black" and "white" interpretations were not monolithic. Some in the black community laid blame on a small group of agitators who started the riot. And some white Tulsans, particularly in the days immediately following the riot, focused on the tragedy that a white mob had destroyed the black community. Others recognized the tragedy, but said the community should not dwell on something that occurred so long ago. The Commission had to negotiate those competing interpretations and reactions. It was established with the optimistic—and perhaps unrealistic—goal of arriving at a true and complete story of the riot. In that way, the Commission sought to act as a third party mediator. Given the entrenched opinions of Commission members, which spanned the spectrum from a conservative Oklahoma state senator to several African American studies scholars, it was predictable that the Commission could not agree on their interpretation of the riot. The Commission ended up, then, with histories that took account of each competing perspective.

1. Early Interpretations of the Riot

There have been several dominant accounts of the riot, which the Riot Commission had to evaluate and reconcile. The most comprehensive contemporary account by whites appeared in the Oklahoma Supreme Court's decision in a lawsuit filed by a Native American, William Redfearn, to recover on his fire insurance policy. Redfearn lost the case because there was a "riot exclusion clause" in his policy, which exempted the company from liability if the loss was caused by riot. The Oklahoma Supreme Court's account, based on the testimony in the case was:

[O]n the 31st day of May, 1921, it was rumored in and around the city of Tulsa that a negro then confined in jail would be lynched that night. The negroes residing in the northeast part of [...] Tulsa, [...] became excited over the rumored lynching, and a great many of them armed themselves for the declared purpose of preventing the lynching. By nine or ten o'clock in the evening, the streets about the courthouse in Tulsa were congested with white people, men, women, and children. A number of armed negroes in automobiles drove around the courthouse two or three times and drove away. They returned, parked their cars, and marched single file down west of the courthouse. As they neared the courthouse a shot was fired, following which there were a great many shots fired and one white man was killed. [. . .] A large number of white men then broke into a hardware store, a pawnshop, and another place, where arms were kept, and armed themselves with guns, revolvers, and ammunition, and in a short while after the firing occurred at the courthouse the streets were full of armed white people. Two or three hundred armed men assembled around the police station and were sent out to different parts of the town ostensibly to guard the town. From that time until about 9 or 10 o'clock the following day there was a great deal of shooting, [. . .] and a number of men were killed.

[. . .]

About daylight on the morning of June 1st, at the sound of a whistle, shooting became rather general. [. . .] Armed white men, [. . .] traveling in groups of from a dozen to twenty, rounded up the negroes [. . .], and took or sent them to the convention hall where they appear to have been detained. A number of witnesses testified that these groups of white men, many of them wearing police badges and badges indicating that they were deputy sheriffs, after removing the negroes from buildings, went inside the buildings and, after they left, fires broke out inside the buildings.[6]

The Redfearn opinion is important for its relatively evenhanded inter-pretation of the concern in Greenwood for the threat of lynching, as well as for its acknowledgment that many of the people doing the burning were wearing badges. Now, let us move from that self-consciously balanced (and dryly factual) interpretation to two others, which make more judgments about the riot's origins: that of the all-white grand jury and that of the Greenwood residents.

A headline in the *Tulsa World* summarizes the grand jury's account: *"Grand jury blames negroes for inciting race riot; whites clearly exonerated."*[7] The grand jury found the riot was "the direct result of an effort on the part of a certain group of colored men who appeared at the courthouse on the night of May 31, 1921, for the purpose of protecting one Dick Rowland [. . .] in the custody of the sheriff [. . .] for an alleged assault upon a young white woman."[8] The jury thought there was no fear of lynching: "There was no mob spirit among the whites, no talk of lynching and no arms. The assembly was quiet until the arrival of armed negroes, which precipitated and was the direct cause of the entire affair." Yet there were other, more remote causes of the riot: the breakdown of law, not in white Tulsa, but in Greenwood, and the "agitation among the negroes of social equality." That talk of social equality was widespread in Greenwood:

We find that certain propaganda and more or less agitation had been going on among the colored population for some time. This agitation resulted in the accumulation of firearms among the people and the storage of quantities of ammunition, all of which was accumulative in the minds of the negro which led them as a people to believe in equal rights, social equality and their ability to demand the same.[9]

The *Oklahoma City Black Dispatch* grimly concluded about the grand jury report that "there is a white wash brush and a big one in operation in Tulsa."[10]

At the same time the grand jury was formulating its version of the riot, Greenwood residents also told their own version, which centered around culpability of the city and state in fueling the destruction, and to the breakdown of law in protecting Greenwood residents. Greenwood residents were talking about the need to be vigilant against lynchings well before the evening of May 31, 1921. They feared that Tulsa officials would not protect them against lynching and they spoke of the need to arm themselves for protection.

Those fears were well founded. On the last weekend in August 1920, there were two lynchings in Oklahoma: one of a white man in Tulsa, one of a black man in Oklahoma City. The attorney general's investigation later disclosed that there was official involvement in both lynchings. The Tulsa sheriff did virtually nothing to protect his prisoner; white police officers (and maybe a black one, too!) were present at the lynching. In Oklahoma City it was even worse: a sheriff planned the lynching. The *Tulsa Star*, the weekly newspaper of the Greenwood community, editorialized: "While the boy was in jail and while there was danger of mob violence any set of citizens had a legal right—it was their duty—to arm themselves and march in a body to the jail and apprize the sheriff or jailer of the purpose of their visit and to take life if need be to uphold the law and protect the prisoner."[11]

There were two other lynchings in December 1920; then in March, some black men in nearby Muskogee freed a prisoner they feared was being led to a lynching by police officers. Leaders of the Greenwood renaissance talked about the need to get the word out about this action—we know about it because a white man was eavesdropping on their conversation at a theater in Greenwood. The refrain was often heard in the vaudeville shows there, "don't let the white man run it over you, but fight."[12]

So when the *Tulsa Tribune* published a story alluding to Dick Rowland's attempted rape of Sarah Page in its afternoon paper on May 31, 1921, there was immediate fear in Greenwood that Rowland would be lynched. Leaders of the Greenwood renaissance, including World War I veterans, met at the *Tulsa Star*, plotting their next moves. Those veterans had fought in France; they had traveled the world and seen other ways of living, which did not include the same patterns of deference that white Tulsans expected of Greenwood residents. So when they saw a threat of lynching, they resolved to take action. About seven o'clock some veterans showed up at the courthouse and offered their services at protecting Rowland. The sheriff convinced veterans to go home, but he failed to disperse the whites. So at ten o'clock, there was another visit from Greenwood veterans. The leader was identified later as a person named Mann "who had come back from the war in France with exaggerated notions of social equality and thinking he can whip the world."[13] At that point, a police officer tried to disarm him; he refused to give up his weapon. A shot went off, and "all hell broke lose." The veterans retreated across the railroad tracks separating Greenwood and white Tulsa.

In white Tulsa, the police department commissioned several hundred white men and issued them weapons. Some testified later that they were instructed "to get a n—." Those deputies, under the supervision of the police, drove along the perimeter of Greenwood. As one newspaper stated, they formed "a circle of steel around Little Africa"—which is what the newspapers called Greenwood.[14] Throughout the night, there is fighting across the railroad tracks; in the early morning of June 1, the local units of the National Guard, in conjunction with the police department, planned to arrest every Greenwood resident they could find, bring them to what the newspapers referred to as "concentration camps" around the city.[15]

At dawn on June 1, the police and their deputies, in conjunction with the local units of the National Guard swept through Greenwood, disarming most people and taking them into custody. Most gave up their guns willingly; some would not. About fifty men were scattered in a skirmish line and they "fought like tigers." At that point, some were killed. Then, after the Greenwood residents were disarmed and their property left vacant, the deputies—and at least some uniformed police officers—came along, looted, and set fire to the buildings. There are stories—preserved in a poem by *Tulsa Star* editor A.J. Smitherman distributed at Christmas time in 1921—that the looters pulled out phonographs and played them in the street:

> Bent on murder, out for plunder,
> Hoodlums on their mission gay,
> Pausing just inside the parlor,
> Set the phonograph to play.

Thus they stood there, heartsick, speechless,
Hearing plainly every sound,
Heard the fiends cry out "All ready"
Saw the coal oil trickle down,

Then they heard the roaring blazes
When the torch had been applied,
Soon they heard the falling timber,
"Oh—we're lost!" the mother cried.[16]

Greenwood residents were victimized again—by the city council, which passed a zoning ordinance a few weeks after the riot that prohibited rebuilding unless fireproof materials were used. That essentially made it too expensive for residents to rebuild. Mayor Evans praised the ordinance as getting further distance between the races. At last there was a court decision overturning the ordinance.[17] But the Tulsa courts continued to treat Greenwood residents as people who (in Ralph Ellison's phrase) were counted but not heard.[18] None of the more than 100 Greenwood residents who sued the city and their insurance companies ever recovered for riot damage. So, once again, the losers were—as Ralph Ellison said of race more generally in America—left to "grapple with the issues that are left unresolved."[19]

2. Current Understanding of the Riot's History and What to Do About It

The Commission was left to struggle with those competing narratives of the riot. It had to try to make sense of how the riot began, which involved complex issues of apportioning responsibility for the riot's origins, to interpret the culpability of the city and state government, and to gauge how Greenwood residents were treated after the riot. Competing narratives are central to understanding the conflict in Tulsa today and the Commission's role at the center of that conflict. Some in the black community, including several on the Riot Commission and advisors to the Riot Commission, wanted a version of history that emphasized the oppression of the black community by the white community, particularly that the riot was a preplanned conspiracy.[20] It was, one might think, a case of remaking history. Some blacks feared—and were quite probably right—that the legislature would not grant reparations, so the history would be the only form of reparations.[21] That history, which made the white government and businesses into especially heinous villains and blacks into martyrs, was their reparation. But it is less clear whether that form of history would transform intergroup relations. It is more likely that such history would perpetuate a division within black and white Tulsa. For whites would be uninterested in the findings (and unlikely to accept them) and blacks would see the findings as confirmation that the white community wanted to destroy their community. Histories of victimization provide a certain comfort to the victims by confirming their identity as victims and linking them together against the outside, oppressor community. They also add to the community's sense that their version of history has been heard.[22] Those who held out hope for reparations might have also seen a history that portrayed a conspiracy as the best way to make out a case for reparations. The more that whites—and especially government officials—were implicated, the more likely reparations would be.[23] There actually was something to that belief, because Oklahoma Governor Frank Keating told the *Washington Post* that he would support reparations if there were government culpability *and* there were still living survivors.[24]

Representative Don Ross, the leader of the Tulsa riot reparations movement—and the legislator who is responsible for establishing the Commission—had a more moderate approach. Some of his relatives are riot survivors and he grew up in the Greenwood community. He has a long-standing interest in the riot and the preservation of the memory of it, as well as reparations to victims. Ross—the consummate politician—asked the Commission to focus less on issues like a preplanned conspiracy and sensational issues like use of airplanes in bombing and hidden graves. Instead, he asked the Commission and journalists covering the Commission's work to focus on less sensational issues, like governmental culpability and the failure of the city to help rebuild Greenwood afterwards.

The Riot Commission's lead historian, Scott Ellsworth, labored to establish his own, independent version of the riot. He took the lead in writing the bulk of scholars' report and he had to negotiate two competing versions of history: the black story—with its emphasis on preplanned conspiracies to burn out Greenwood residents, then buy their land, sensational stories about Dick Rowland's affair with Sara Page, and heroic defenders of Greenwood—and the "Tulsa booster" story, which alleged that Dick Rowland was safe from lynching, which saw Greenwood veterans as lawless instigators of riot who had no business showing up at the courthouse, and which argued that the efforts of the police and National Guard to take Greenwood residents into "protective custody" was both appropriate and saved many lives. Moreover, the "Tulsa boosters" said, the burning was done by a very small group; and that sensational stories about bombs dropped from airplanes were untrue.

Ellsworth worked hard to document the competing claims, although he was obviously more sympathetic to the Greenwood perspective. As a leading proponent of oral history, Ellsworth drew frequently on survivors' testimony, which led him to give perhaps more credence than is due to stories of bombs dropped from airplanes.

In the white community, there were similarly mixed reactions. Some enjoyed talking about the riot, in part because it gave them a chance to vindicate the role of Tulsa's white community. They blamed the black community for stirring up trouble, when Dick Rowland was so obviously safe in the jail; and after the riot began, they thought that authorities did what was proper under the circumstances: they gathered the blacks together in a way that would protect them and cause a minimum of loss of life. It was a struggle to preserve the memory of Tulsa's founding generation. Other members of the white community, particularly those associated with Tulsa churches, saw the Commission as an opportunity for reconciliation. They sponsored their own discussions and even collected money to pay token reparations, of a few hundred dollars, to survivors.[25]

For more whites, however, the Riot Commission was an ugly reminder of a period they would increasingly prefer to forget. They also saw the talk of the riot as further special pleading by blacks, who dwelled on an unfortunate period in now long-past history. That attitude was captured in several ways. There was a fairly constant refrain that talk of the riot stirred up racial hatred, when people should instead have been attending to current problems;[26] that paying reparations was someone else's responsibility because most of Tulsa's current taxpayers were not alive in 1921, and few of their ancestors were Tulsa residents;[27] and, finally, paying reparations would be insufficient to remedy the past tragedy.[28] Some Oklahoma newspapers tired of talk of the riot as well, headlining editorials "Enough is Enough" and—in a perverse turn of phrase on a Cinemax documentary on the riot "The Tulsa Lynching"—"Tulsa Lynched."[29] The later editorial complained that Tulsa was being portrayed unfairly in national media coverage of the riot. Instead of leading to healing, the Commission and the media attention it generated seemed to be polarizing Tulsa.

The moral theory behind the reluctance to pay reparations was not developed well in the Oklahoma newspapers. There are, of course, critical issues in decisions whether it is proper to impose liability on subsequent generations for the acts of previous generations, or for making one group pay for harms to another group.[30] In Oklahoma, reparations opponents seem to have started from the position that it is improper to ask succeeding generations to pay for past harm or that anyone other than the people who committed the harm might have a responsibility to pay, even if well-established principles of corporate liability and the tradition that communities help repair damage to individuals who suffer extraordinary hardship suggest otherwise.[31]

The reasons listed for stopping talk about the riot often reduced down to the theme that blacks should "get over" the riot. It was related to the rhetoric that blacks are best served if they strive to make the best of their current situation, without asking for reparations for past injustices.[32] At bottom it is an argument to accept the present distribution of wealth (or lack of it), even though that distribution is closely related to past racial crimes. There is something to be said for such an argument. One should not allow oneself to be disabled by past injustice. However, the calls to stop talking about the riot represent a pessimistic view that racial understanding is impossible—and perhaps a view that it is not wanted anyway. For if talk is only seen as stirring up old antagonisms, it cannot be seen as a solution. And the reason it cannot be a solution, is that there are issues that are irresolvable. It is also the argument that powerful parties make to justify inaction regarding the distribution of power. Given the different narratives and reactions of the black and white communities, the Riot Commission struggled to reach a consensus. One Republican state senator, for instance, appeared unwilling to agree to reparations of any sort, and the first chair, Bob Blackburn, appeared unwilling to advocate publicly funded reparations.

There was, in fact, strong opposition to paying reparations no matter what evidence the historians' report produced. A poll of Oklahomans in January 2000 indicated that 57 percent opposed any form of reparations payments, whether tax money was used or not. Only 12 percent said reparations should be paid with tax money.[33] That political fact made reparations unlikely, no matter what the Commission's findings might be. Or, as a leading black member of the Riot Commission lamented, "[W]hen it involves black Americans, they don't want to give us anything."[34] But there the competing visions of history sweeping through Tulsa affected the Riot Commission as well. By February 2000, the African American members of the Commission were annoyed that Ellsworth did not support more vigorously their ideas—based on long-standing stories in the community—that the riot was a preplanned conspiracy by the KKK and business interests to take Greenwood residents' land. Meanwhile, other, more conservative (and perhaps pragmatic) members of the Commission feared that Ellsworth and his scholars would produce a report that leaned too heavily in the direction of Greenwood. As a result, the Commission hired another historian, Professor Danny Goble of the

University of Oklahoma, to provide a summary of the scholars' findings. Goble's background as a historian of Oklahoma and as a professor at the state's leading university, gave him credibility with more conservative elements. It also meant, perhaps, that he could not be—or would not feel FREE TO BE—as critical of Tulsa as the facts bore out. Still, Goble's report emphasized the government's culpability, as well as the issues that were left unresolved by the Commission. This emphasis on governmental culpability demonstrated that he was independent;[35] nevertheless, his emphasis on the issues left unresolved provided support to those who wanted to avoid action, because they could then turn to Goble's discussion and say that so much was still unknown.[36] Some did focus on the issues unresolved, like the number of deaths. But why should it matter whether the official death count of about forty, or the more sensational numbers like 300, was accurate?[37]

The Commission, nevertheless, went ahead with plans for reconciliation and reparations. Even before the final report was completed, the Riot Commission voted to recommend some form of reparations.[38] Their nearly unanimous vote in February 2000 was to recommend reparations, but not to identify the entity that would pay reparations. As with the Riot Commission report, which left many critical details—like the number of people killed—unsettled, the Commission's recommendations were so general that they could gain wide acceptance. They were also so general that they provided insufficient guidance to the legislature.[39] The one dissenter was a state senator, who expressed reservations about paying reparations for any long-past event.[40] Another state senator, who was not on the Riot Commission, appeared on Pacifica radio to complain about the focus on the riot. "It just makes black people hate white people and vice versa," he said.[41]

3. The Legislative Interpretation of the Riot

The Oklahoma legislature was, indeed, reluctant to pay reparations. A year later, in February 2001, the Commission's historians delivered a report that emphasized the pervasive racial conflict of Oklahoma at the time. Danny Goble's summary was placed at the beginning of the scholars' report and then delivered to the legislature. The historians' report, written by Professor John Hope Franklin of Duke University and Dr. Scott Ellsworth, located the riot in the context of pervasive violence and racial legislation, and so made the threat of lynching real. It portrayed sympathetically the black veterans who went to the courthouse to try to stop the lynching, although it acknowledged that their presence contributed to the outbreak of violence. Then it assigned blame to the city for the failure to protect Greenwood—and even for deputizing members of the mob.[42]

The Riot Commission told a story about the riot, which historians found persuasive, but their audience stretched beyond other professional historians. They were preparing a report for the legislature and the media, which then made their findings available to the public through newspaper and radio stories. The historians' message about culpability and racial violence was blurred because it was impossible to arrive at definitive answers on many events. For example, it was impossible to determine the number of people killed and whether airplanes were used to bomb Greenwood or merely for surveillance. The lack of evidence on critical issues left historians in a particularly precarious position. They had to extrapolate based on limited data points. Much critical evidence had been destroyed; for example, the grand jury testimony and testimony in one important civil trial was no longer available. Historians could reasonably draw inferences about critical questions, such as the motives of the police department's mass arrests of Greenwood residents. However, while many in the historical profession might accept those inferences, within the contested realm of Oklahoma politics, many of the powerful decision makers—Oklahoma legislators—would not accept such conclusions. The standard of proof became extraordinarily high.[43] Moreover, on many questions of interpretation of the riot—such as whether it was appropriate for the veterans to go to the courthouse to protect Dick Rowland—the facts about the riot cannot provide those answers.[44]

Following the completion of the Riot Commission report in February 2001, the debate shifted to the legislature for discussion of what to do next. Members of the Oklahoma legislature ran from the issue as if it were radioactive. It would, quite simply, be political suicide for a legislator to support reparations.[45] After limited debate—and without hearing from a single riot survivor or conducting any kind of hearing—the legislature settled on a compromise: a strong condemnation of the Tulsa riot, the establishment of a corporation to provide scholarships to descendants of riot survivors (no public money went into the scholarships), and the establishment of a riot memorial commission, which received seven-hundred fifty thousand dollars of state money. The Oklahoma legislature also approved of the use of the state seal on medals, to be minted with private funds, and awarded to riot survivors.[46] Those medals, which turned the riot victims into a form of achievement, seem particularly perverse. They were a form of acknowledgement and, strangely, avoidance of the issue of doing something more meaningful. The legislature seemed willing to take any action, so long as it did not spend money on survivors.

The legislature also passed the "1921 Tulsa Race Riot Reconciliation Act," which presented a brief history of the riot. The act found that some local government officials "failed to take actions to calm or contain the situation once violence erupted, and in some cases, became participants in the subsequent violence [. . .] and even deputized and armed many whites who were part of a mob that killed, looted, and burned down the Greenwood area."[47] It also pointed to the city's attempt to prevent Greenwood residents from rebuilding after the riot, as well as the city's "conspiracy of silence" in the years after the riot. Perhaps most important, however, was the final paragraph, which acknowledged Oklahomans' moral culpability: "there were moral responsibilities at the time of the riot which were ignored and ha[ve] been ignored ever since rather than confront the realities of an Oklahoma history of race relations that allowed one race to 'put down' another race."[48] Thus ended the legislature's official action on the Tulsa Race Riot.

So the Oklahoma legislature left the scene, having granted an apology, but little else. How satisfying was that? Did the acknowledgement lead to healing or only aggravate the sense in the African American community that it was victimized as much as (or perhaps more than) it validated their stories? Within the African American community, there were certainly elements that felt abandoned—again—by the Oklahoma government. Some survivors seemed pleased by the acknowledgement. And within the white community, some expressed the sentiment that now that there has been an acknowledgement, it was time to move on, seemingly without an understanding that the acknowledgement and apology had much meaning. For that element had wanted to move on long before there had even been an apology.

4. The Functions and Limitations of the Tulsa Riot Commission

Tulsa presents an important sight for viewing the ways that truth commissions can function—and their limits in bringing about reconciliation. The Tulsa Riot Commission first allowed the community to debate their interpretations of the riot presented, then presented a nuanced picture of the riot. It left some questions, such as the number of people killed, unresolved. The Commission left issues of interpretation for individuals to resolve, such as whether it was appropriate for the Greenwood veterans to go to the courthouse to protect Dick Rowland. Those issues of interpretation of facts were left to individuals, who often opposed reparations because they viewed the city as lacking culpability. Moreover, there was opposition to—or lack of interest in—reconciliation in large segments of the white community and within certain segments of the black community as well.

The Riot Commission scored some important triumphs. It is remarkable that it was even established in the first place; that alone is testimony to Oklahomans' courage and interest in reexamining their past. The Commission started a national dialogue. There swirled around the Commission a host of stories about the riot—a Cinemax documentary, three books, a lengthy article in the *New York Times Magazine*, a cover story in *The Nation*, and multiple stories in the *New York Times, Washington Post, Los Angeles Times,* and *Chicago Tribune*. Those stories had impact far beyond Tulsa and contributed to a national debate on race and reparations.

The Commission and the work it inspired gave us a fuller understanding of the riot, which has utility in both the black and white communities, if anyone cares to pay attention. Over the nearly four years that the Commission was in operation, it brought significant attention to the riot in the national as well as local media. That discussion allowed Oklahomans to learn about the riot and—again, if they chose to—learn about the history of government-sponsored discrimination and violence in their history. So the task of remembering the riot became a voluntary project. Those who cared could read the report; everyone could ignore it. The problem of memory is compounded by the fact that several years after the Riot Commission finished its work there is still no memorial.[49]

The Commission demonstrates to the black community that Oklahoma has some interest in and concern for the community and recognizes the legitimate claims of the black community. It is a validation of the grievances of members of the black community. It stirred some unpleasant feelings and probably left some people feeling more alienated and bitter than they had been before. However, on balance it seems to have been an important vehicle for the black and white communities to recover their shared past even if the communities placed different emphasis on that past. The acknowledgment of the harm done to the black community validates, at the very least, the concerns of members of the black community. It has repaired some of the damage done to the truth, restored a history, and rewritten the record to reflect more accurately the obstacles that the community faced and overcame. It helps break down a segregation of memory of the riot in the black and white communities.[50] Still, there is concern that the apology is insufficient—and that the Oklahoma legislature's failure to pay reparations indicates a lack of interest in really addressing the riot. As the *Pittsburgh Post-Gazette* grimly concluded, "After the last elderly witness to the atrocity at Greenwood has died, perhaps the monument will bear an inscription that honestly reflects the sentiment of the Oklahoma Legislature: 'A piece of rock is cheaper than justice.'"[51]

The Riot Commission contributed to the community's understanding of its history, and the Commission also brought an apology from the legislature.[52] Many said that the Commission makes it less likely that a similar tragedy will recur, or at least commemorates the fact that a riot will not recur.[53] But another riot is not likely—this is about how we view history. It may help to build something positive for the future, because there is both a memorial in the planning and some serious talk of privately funded reparations. And perhaps it may even lead to some reconciliation. It has, after all, started a lot of people talking, even if they are also sometimes mad.[54] The history will make it harder for anyone to say now that there is a level playing field for blacks; it makes every fair-minded observer more sensitive to issues of race; and sensitizes others to the problems that the Tulsa black community faced not so long ago.[55] In refocusing on the past, there is, of course, a danger that the past will become a distraction. The effects cannot be measured right now, because the Riot Commission has the promise of continuing to influence for years the education of future Oklahomans.

The Riot Commission also raised the hopes of riot victims that they would receive more than an apology and a richer history of the riot. They hoped for money. Those hopes are unlikely to be fulfilled by either the city or state government.[56] Amid many successes, then, the Riot Commission also had limitations. It failed to deliver government-sponsored payments to survivors, because it did not convince Oklahomans of the moral case for them—perhaps because that was not possible to do so. That might very well have been an impossible task from the beginning, for Oklahomans are reluctant to accept responsibility for the acts of others, even their predecessors.[57] Such failure to bring about reorientation of racial attitudes points to the limits of truth commissions to bring about justice. They cannot perform magic; they cannot transform all entrenched ideas. What they can do is fill the gaps between competing conceptions of justice—no amount of money paid will be enough in the minds of some; any will be too much in the minds of others. The riot commission is a place where we can still seek the elusive goal of truth and the promises for better understanding that it holds out. That may be the most amount of justice that is obtainable.[58]

Still, the Commission must be examined in the context of racial politics in Oklahoma.[59] So while many survivors—and other people interested in the riot—were disappointed by the lack of reparations, one must look at how far the Commission was able to move public knowledge of the tragedy—and how much it moved public debate about reparations. The Tulsa Riot Commission could not bring about the justice that is purchased through reparations to survivors. But even the request for reparations pointed up a conflict: the mere suggestion of reparations engendered animosity against the Greenwood community. There is a tension between reparations and continued harmony. In order to obtain government-sponsored reparations (or even to talk about them), Greenwood residents would have to be willing to accept a great deal of animosity.

The failure to obtain reparations is the most notable, but not the only limitation of the Riot Commission. The Commission also failed as a point of reconciliation for some. Of course, for some reconciliation is impossible. There are entrenched beliefs or a lack of desire for reconciliation, in part because some whites think the riot is someone else's fault and blacks think it is another example of mistreatment. As with reparations, however, one must look at how far the Riot Commission spurred public discussion—and one hopes, understanding.

Perhaps, as was said of the South African Truth and Reconciliation Commission, truth was emphasized by the Riot Commission at the expense of reconciliation (or justice).[60] But we have the amount of reconciliation and justice that our institutions permitted us. The Riot Commission emphasized truth—the quality that is most achievable. It brought, one suspects, some reconciliation and left justice for a later time. There were many reactions to the Riot Commission—some people who did not want reconciliation or even discussion.[61] But for others—and one hopes that this group is growing—the Riot Commission facilitated a discussion they wanted.

Still the victims of Tulsa await justice in the form of reparations, amid some waning hope there may be privately funded reparations. About 120 of the surviving riot victims filed a lawsuit in February 2003, alleging that the city and state participated in the riot.[62] Amidst claims that the lawsuit was doing even more of what the Riot Commission had done—stirring up racial animosity—Judge James O. Ellison, the federal judge hearing the case, immediately focused around the statute of limitations.[63] (Under usual circumstances, lawsuits alleging that government officials in Oklahoma violated plaintiffs' constitutional rights must be filed within three years of the government officials' actions. In this case, the statute of limitations, absent some kind of special circumstances, would have expired in 1924.) Judge Ellison granted the plaintiffs "limited discovery" rights to collect information through the summer of 2003 to establish the reasons why the plaintiffs had failed to file sooner. The plaintiffs developed evidence that the plaintiffs were effectively closed off from using the courts for relief in the 1920s. For instance, the Tulsa Courts were dominated by the Ku Klux Klan in the years immediately after the riot. They effectively had no shot at justice in the Oklahoma courts at the time.[64] Unavailability of relief is a classic basis for stopping the running of the statute of limitations. Hence, the plaintiffs hoped to use the unavailability of the courts as a basis for extending the statute of limitations; they then hoped to argue that the Riot Commission's report restarted the running of the statute of limitations in 2001.

In March 2004, Judge Ellison dismissed the case. He acknowledged that the Oklahoma courts were unavailable at the time of the riot and potentially for decades later. That acknowledgment was a welcome and important conclusion, for it added the power of the federal judiciary to the riot victims' narrative: that they could not effectively obtain justice at the time or perhaps for decades later. However, Judge Ellison concluded that at some unspecified later time, the courts became available and that the lawsuit was filed outside of the statute of limitations. Once again, the Tulsa riot victims were told by the government that they had been wronged, but could now not obtain relief.[65]

The unsurprising dismissal, which was affirmed by the United States Court of Appeals in September 2004,[66] is the final chapter in the legal system's abandonment of Tulsa riot victims. Few would expect relief decades later, of course. The decisions of the district court and court of appeals stand as grim testimony that thousands of riot victims could not obtain relief at the time. At some unspecified later time, the court of appeals believes that the courts were available and the statute of limitations began to run.[67] That conclusion bars a suit now.

Perhaps saddest of all was that even as the United States Court of Appeals affirmed the dismissal, it recounted a misleading version of the riot. For, despite the extensive work by the Commission and the acknowledgement by the state legislature that the riot's destruction was the work of special deputies, the court spoke about a "white mob" that "ravaged Greenwood."[68] Although the opinion acknowledges that the mob included newly deputized men, the Court of Appeals' opinion leaves the misimpression that the riot's destruction was not the fault of official, government actors. In essence, the opinion continues an incomplete history of the riot. While it is unlikely that had the Court of Appeals correctly understood the nature of the riot that it would have reached a different result—for the court affirmed the dismissal of the lawsuit based on subsequent availability of relief, not what happened in the 1920s—that incomplete history points up a limitation of truth commissions. The court of appeals' opinion also suggest THE casual attitude that has been shown toward the truth since the grand jury report in 1921.

The dismissal was to be expected, of course; for had the riot victims won, the theory that supported it (that the statute of limitations should be tolled for Jim Crow-era racial crimes when the courts were unavailable) might have been applied in other suits.[69] Yet, the City's failure to make good the damage reminds us, as the *New York Times* observed shortly after the lawsuit was filed that: "in the moral sense at least, Tulsa and Oklahoma have already lost. They did so by failing to accept responsibility for one of the most blood-curdling events in American history."[70]

We should expect some very specific results from truth commissions. They should provide a solid, accurate, and complete history of historical tragedies. Yet, we should not expect too much of truth commissions. Their power to undo or to remake the world is limited; they have only the power to revisit and correct the story we tell about that past. Then, through much long effort, almost imperceptibly, those new understandings may remake how the entire community thinks and behaves. Truth commissions can expand our historical knowledge; the rest of the discussion and action is up to us.[71]

Notes

1. I would like to thank Elazar Barkan, Xan Karn, and Sara Patterson for their guidance in writing this essay.

2. The Commission began as a joint resolution in 1997. See Oklahoma Statutes 74 § 8201 (amending House Joint Resolution No. 1035, at p. 2834, Oklahoma State Laws 1997, as amended by section 24, chapter 410, Oklahoma State Laws 1997 (74 O.S. Supp. 1997, section 8201). The Act provided that:

The Commission shall undertake a study to develop a historical record of the 1921 Tulsa Race Riot including the identification of persons who:

1. Can provide adequate proof to the Commission that the person was an actual resident of the Greenwood area or community of the City of Tulsa on or about May 31, 1921, or June 1, 1921; or

2. Can demonstrate to the satisfaction of the members of the Commission that the person sustained an identifiable loss to their person, personal relations, real property, personal property or other loss as a result of tortuous or criminal conduct, whether or not the conduct was ever adjudicated, occurring during the period beginning on or about May 31, 1921, and ending not later than June 30, 1921, resulting from the activity commonly described as the 1921 Tulsa Race Riot. [. . .]

The Commission shall produce a written report of its findings and recommendations. [...]
The report may contain specific recommendations regarding whether or not reparations can
or should be made and the appropriate methods to achieve the recommendations made in the
final report.

3. Brent Staples, "Unearthing a Riot," *New York Times Magazine* (December 19,
1999) (discussing motives of Representative Don Ross of the Oklahoma House of
Representatives).

4. Adrian Brune, "Tulsa's Shame: Race Riot Victims Still Wait for Promised
Reparations,"
The Nation (March 18, 2002); Duncan Campbell, "80 Years On, Hope of Repara-
tion for Race Riot Victims," *The Guardian* (March 2, 2001).

5. Brent Staples, "Searching for Graves—And Justice—In Tulsa," *New York Times*
(March 19, 1999) ("After eight decades of silence, Tulsans are talking about June
1921 and are nowhere near ready to stop."). Now many of them seem ready to stop
talking.

6. See Redfearn v. American Central Ins. Co., 243 p. 929 (Oklahoma 1926). See
also Alfred L, Brophy, "The Tulsa Race Riot in the Oklahoma Supreme Court,"
Oklahoma Law Review 54 (2001): pp. 67, 119.

7. *Tulsa World* 1, 8 (June 26, 1921).

8. Id.

9. Id.

10. See "In Name Only," *Black Dispatch* 4 (July 8, 1921) ("We observe that the only
really definite statement made in the whole [grand jury] report is that THE NEGRO IS
TO BLAME, a conclusion they seemed to have arrived at through evidence unsupported
by any facts which they present.").

11. "The Facts Remain the Same," *Tulsa Star* 8 (September 18, 1920). The Okla-
homa lynchings received relatively little attention from prosecutors. However, there
were some attempts to investigate the August 1920 lynchings. See Attorney General's
Investigation of Lynching of Roy Belton, Oklahoma Attorney General case file 1017,
Oklahoma State Archives; Investigation of Lynching of Claude Chandler, Oklahoma
Attorney General case file 1018, Oklahoma State Archives.

12. Henry Sowders testimony in Stradford v. American Central Ins. Co., Superior
Court of Cook County, Case No. 370, 274 at p. 126 (1921).

13. "Negro Tells How Others Mobilized," *Tulsa Tribune* 1 (June 4, 1921).

14. "New Battle Now in Progress," *Tulsa World* 1 (June 1, 1921) (2nd edition).

15. John W. McCuen, "Duty Performed by Company 3d Inf. Okla. National Guard
at Negro Uprising May 31st 1921" (undated) at p. 2, Oklahoma State Archives; see
also "First Detailed Story of How Riot Started," *St. Louis Post-Dispatch* 21 (June
3, 1921) ("Last night 1000 or more negroes were being cared for in concentration
camps.").

16. The Tulsa Massacre, available in A. J. Smitherman file, NAACP Papers, Library
of Congress.

17. The zoning ordinance was attached as an interference with the rights of Greenwood property owners—many of whom were white. Property owners argued that the ordinance, by preventing them from replacing what they had, deprived them of their property. The Tulsa district court struck down the ordinance in early September 1921, just in time to allow Greenwood residents to build permanent structures for the winter.

18. Ralph Ellison, *Juneteenth* 4 (1999) ("We're from down where we've among the counted but not among the heard.").

19. Ralph Ellison, 1995, "Going to the Territory," in John F. Callahan ed., *The Collected Essays of Ralph Ellison*, pp. 591, 595.

20. See also Randy Krehbiel, "Opposing Theories Offered on Race Riot," *Tulsa World* (March 5, 2000) ("The riot wasn't a riot at all, it was a planned plot to rid the Negroes of their land.") (Quoting Robert Littlejohn a local black historian). Historian Eddie Faye Gates, author of several books on African American history and a member of the Riot Commission, often focused on the stories of oppression and seemed willing to accept every story of atrocity during the riot, as well as accept uncritically accounts of high death toll.

21. As Riot Commission member Pete Churchwell said in 1997, when the Commission was just beginning its work, there "may be other things more important— more appropriate—things" than payment of money, "like public statements, public proclamations, publicly hearing from people who survived the devastation." Michael Overall, "Mending Fences: Panel to Eye '21 Race Riot Reparations," *Tulsa World* A19 (August 17, 1997).

22. Cf. Roy Brooks, "Rehabilitative Reparations for the Judicial Process," *N.Y.U. Annual Survey of Am. Law* 58 (2003): p. 475 (discussing need for recognition of black views of justice).

23. "Tragedy Trade-off: Bombing, Riot Comparisons Off Target," *Daily Oklahoman* (December 7, 2000) ("The more Ross and others can claim victimhood, the greater their chances for persuading lawmakers to grant reparations."). See also "The Unethical Eye: CBS Airs Tulsa Riot Myth as Fact," *Daily Oklahoman* (July 19, 2001) ("What is known about the riot is very little. This is why claims that have no basis in fact are best left to fear mongers. They have no place in a news story. By driving up the death toll, the race baiters hope to gain support for riot victims or their supporters.").

24. Lois Romano, "Tulsa Airs a Race Riot's Legacy; State Historical Panel's Call for Restitution Spurs a Debate," *Washington Post* (January 19, 2000) ("But it has to be shown that there was real harm to existing, living individuals and that direct action by the city and the state caused the harm. [. . .] It's going to be a very slippery slope to climb [to support] using current taxpayers' money to compensate for the acts of past taxpayers.") (Quoting Governor Keating).

25. "TMM Fund Distributes $12,000 More," *Tulsa World* (August 9, 2002) (reporting that Tulsa Metropolitan Ministries distributed a total of approximately $36,000 to riot survivors).

26. "Tragedy Trade-off: Bombing, Riot Comparisons Off Target," *Daily Okla-homan* (December 7, 2000) ("The 1921 tragedy has now been thoroughly examined. The commission needs to wrap up its work and move on. Pursing the reparations strategy is divisive and futile"); "Bad Precedent: Riot Payments Won't Bring Closure," *Daily Oklahoman* (March 2, 2001) ("Cash payments to surviving riot victims... will divide the state and bring about more racial rancor instead of healing the commission seeks to bring about."); "Enough is Enough," *Daily Oklahoma* (May 24, 2001) ("The Legislature and the state government have spent enough time debating how the state should recognize the causes and effects of the riot. It's time to move on and allow the good citizens of Tulsa to control the destiny of further plans to commemorate or atone for the riot.").

27. See also "Tragedy Trade-off: Bombing, Riot Comparisons Off Target," *Daily Oklahoman* (December 7, 2000) ("While local law enforcement may have partici-pated in the riot, the state dispatched forces to quell the violence and protect black citizens. This means that any reparations should be paid by Tulsa, not the state.").

28. "Tragedy Trade-off: Bombing, Riot Comparisons Off Target," *Daily Okla-homan* (December 7, 2000) ("no amount would be enough in the eyes of reparations advocates"); "Bad Precedent: Riot Payments Won't Bring Closure," *Daily Oklahoman* (March 2, 2001) ("No one has yet assigned a value to the payments, but it's cer-tain that no matter the amount it will eventually be deemed insufficient."). That argument is related to the Supreme Court's requirement that race-based set asides have a definite ending point. See, e.g., Croson v. City of Richmond, 488 US 469 (1989).

29. "Tulsa 'Lynched': Cinemax Special Feeds the Myth," *Tulsa World* (May 22, 2000) ("Tulsans should get braced for still another unfair and inaccurate depiction of the infamous race riot of 1921.").

30. See, e.g., Elazar Barkan, 2000, *The Guilt of Nations: Restitution and Negoti-ating Historical Injustice*, pp. 336–342 (New York: Norton).

31. For further discussion of the theories supporting reparations for Tulsa victims, see Alfred. L. Brophy, *Reconstructing the Dreamland: The Tulsa Riot of 1921 — Race, Reparations, Reconciliation*, pp. 103–119 (Oxford University Press, 2002).

32. See "The Unethical Eye: CBS Airs Tulsa Riot Myths as Fact," *Daily Okla-homan* (July 19, 2001) ("Dredging up old myths and half-truths may be good for the race baiters, but it does nothing for the people of Tulsa today who must work to get along and improve the city's racial climate. For a news organization to climb in bed with the race baiters while continuing to claim objectivity is a descent into an unethical abyss.").

33. Rob Martindale, "Oklahomans Opposed to Paying Riot Reparations," *Tulsa World* (January 10, 2000).

34. Hugh Aynesworth, "Report on '21 Riots Divides Tulsa Again," *Washing-ton Times* A2 (February 4, 2001) (Quoting Riot Commission Member Eddie Faye Gates).

35. Goble found, for instance, that "At the eruption of violence, civil officials selected many men, all of them white and some of them participants in that violence, and made those men their agents as deputies. In that capacity, deputies did not stir the violence but added to it, often through overt acts themselves illegal." Danny Goble, "Final Report," in *Oklahoma Commission to Study the Tulsa Race Riot of 1921*, Tulsa Race Riot 1, 11 (2001).

36. Thus, Goble asked many questions about the Klan's involvement in the riot, the first detailed evidence of the Klan's presence in Tulsa, then he switched to questions about meaning: "Does this mean the Klan helped plan the riot? Does it mean that the Klan helped execute it? [...] Or does it mean that any time thousands of whites assembled—especially if they assembled to assault blacks—that odds were there would be quite a few Klansmen in the mix?" Id.

For Goble, such questions seemed particularly perplexing—and he seemed incapable of providing even an educated guess. He stated that not everyone agrees on an interpretation. "Nor will they ever. Both the conspiracy and the Klan questions remain what they always have been. [...] Both are examples of nearly every problem inherent to historical evidence. How reliable is this oral tradition? What conclusions does the evidence permit? Are these inferences reasonable? How many ways can this be interpreted." Id. at p. 11. Goble's doubts allowed others to conclude that there was no accurate story of the riot. He retreated from his duty to draw conclusions—or at least provide some assessment of the relative validity of accounts.

Professor Goble's summary began with hand-wringing about how difficult it was to prepare a history in the tough political climate. By emphasizing the questions left unanswered, Goble legitimized those who wanted to do nothing because of unanswered—and unanswerable—questions. It also legitimized those who wanted to claim that each side had its own, valuable, and non-disprovable interpretation.

37. See "The Unethical Eye: CBS Airs Tulsa Riot Myths as Fact," *Daily Oklahoma* (July 19, 2001) ("Let's examine the myths. No one knows how many were killed in the riot or even if more blacks than whites were killed. A state–funded commission investigated the riot and failed to document that vast numbers of blacks were killed. As we've said before, that even one person died is tragic enough, but the facts don't justify the hysterical claims of race baiters who seek a higher body court only in order to fuel emotions.").

38. Or, as Don Ross once said to me in a revealing moment, "I do not need a memorial; my anger is my memorial. I want money for the survivors."

39. Randy Krehbiel, "Riot Panel Votes for Reparations: Legislators on Commission Say Proposal Doomed to Rejection," *Tulsa World* (February 5, 2000). The Commission ranked five goals: payments to living survivors; payments to descendants of those who lost property; a scholarship fund; business tax incentives for Greenwood; and a memorial.

40. Lois Romano, "Tulsa Airs a Race Riot's Legacy; State Historical Panel's Call for Restitution Spurs a Debate," *Washington Post* A3 (January 19, 2000) ("What about

the other situations where people had losses because of actions by prejudiced people? The chances of it passing the legislature are very slim. This was a long time ago.") (Quoting state senator Robert Milacek).

41. The program is available at: http://www.webactive.com/pacifica/demnow.html (February 8, 2000.

42. The Riot Commission report is available at: http://www.ok-history.mus.ok. us/trrc/freport.htm. The core of the Riot Commission report is the historians' report; in front of that report are introductions by Representative Don Ross and a summary of the historians' report by Professor Danny Goble. Dr. Goble's summary emphasized the culpability of governmental officials.

43. Despite a virtual consensus among the historians who have looked at the riot regarding state government's culpability, Governor Frank Keating denied that the state had any liability. See Randy Krehbiel, "Keating Riot Pay From State Not Likely," *Tulsa World* (August 10, 2001) ("Speaking during a Racial Reconciliation Forum at Oklahoma State University—Tulsa, Keating said he doesn't believe that the state was shown to be a fault in the 1921 melee. [. . .]").

44. Randy Krehbiel, "Answers the Facts Cannot Provide: Riot Recalled; Good Will, Action Urged," *Tulsa World* (June 5, 2000) (Quoting historian John Hope Franklin).

45. Lois Romano, "No Vow to Make Amends for Tulsa; Legislators' Sidestepping Disappoints Survivors of 1921 Race Riot," *Washington Post* (March 1, 2001).

46. See *Tulsa Race Riot—Legislative Findings and Intent,* sec. 74–8000.1 Oklahoma Statutes (2001); Tulsa Race Riot of 1921 Survivors—Authorizing Oklahoma Medal of Distinction, 2001, *Okla. Sess. Law Serv. House Conc. Res.* 1014; Appropriations—historical Preservation, 2001, *Okla. Sess. Law Serv.* ch. 342 (S.B. 203) (appropriating $750,000 for riot memorial).

47. Tulsa Race Riot—Legislative Findings and Intent, sec. 74–8000.1.

48. Id.

49. See, e.g., Randy Krehbiel, "Land Ok'd for Race Riot Memorial," *Tulsa World* A1 (February 22, 2003).

50. Tony Norman, "Righting a Wrong—Reluctantly," *Pittsburgh Post Gazette* (March 6, 2001) ("Even foot draggers in the state legislature couldn't muffle the sounds of 80 years of ignorance collapsing.").

51. Id.

52. Tulsa's Mayor, Susan Savage, was more guarded in her apology, which was limited to the "lack of action by public officials to head off the riot." See Randy Krehbiel, "Answers the Facts Cannot Provide: Riot Recalled; Good Will, Action Urged," *Tulsa World* (June 5, 2000). Earlier, Savage said: "the whole community regretted the event." See Rik Espinosa, "Apology Alone Just 'Hot Air'," *Tulsa World* (June 22, 1997).

53. See, e.g., "Riot-Reparation Report Wraps Up," *Tulsa World* (March 1, 2001) ("Today in Oklahoma we would not tolerate the actions that took place during the

riot.") (Quoting Riot Commission Chair Pete Churchwell); Arnold Hamilton, "Commission Urges Reparations for Survivors of Tulsa Race Riot," *Dallas Morning News* (March 1, 2001) ("Now is the time for our state and our city to send a clear message to the world that we reject racism, violence, terror and death and that we support acceptance, forgiveness, reconciliation and justice for all citizens.") (Quoting Churchwell). Cf. Randy Krehbiel, "Speaker Leading Push for Slave Reparations," *Tulsa World* (September 26, 2002) ("The Tulsa case is a page in history we all want to forget, yet it tells us that regardless of how much headway we make, it can be taken away at a moment's notice.") (Quoting Harvard Law School Professor Charles Ogletree).

54. The conflicting interpretations of the riot among whites and blacks may make reconciliation difficult. Brent Staples' article on the riot, for instance, catalogs the cooling of the friendship between Representative Don Ross and Ed Wheeler, author of an important study of the riot and a former general in the Oklahoma National Guard, as the riot became a more important part of their lives. See Staples, "Unearthing a Riot," *New York Times Magazine* 64, 69 (December 19, 1999) ("Between the two of them, Don Ross and Ed Wheeler cracked the walls of silence and made it possible to speak openly about the riot for the first time in fifty years. But Ross and Wheeler take opposite sides of the reparations issue, chilling what was once a warm relationship. Wheeler is opposed to reparations and believes that modern-day Tulsans are not responsible for the sins of their fathers. Ross, of course, believes that reparation is the one and only issue and will think so until the day he dies.").

55. If, as many say, that reparations talk is more about truth than money, then the Commission has been very successful. See, e.g., Ronald Roach, "Moving Towards Reparations," *Black Issues in Higher Education* (November 8, 2001) ("[T]he demand for reparations is fundamentally not about the money. The money is secondary. The primary reason is for the truth to be told.") (Quoting Professor Manning Marable). The student newspaper at the University of Oklahoma, for instance, editorialized that there should be reparations payments to survivors, but not to descendants. See "Tulsa Riot Reparations Should be Made Cautiously," *Oklahoma Daily* (March 2, 2001).

56. As the Daily Oklahoman said in an editorial, "Although the state-funded Tulsa Race Riot Commission recommended reparations, it's not going to happen—at least not with state dollars." "Enough is Enough," *Daily Oklahoman* (May 24, 2001).

57. Rick Montgomery, "Panel Wraps Up Inquiry into Tulsa Race Riot," *Kansas City Star* (February 26, 2001) ("Our people are saying, 'If this is leading to money. . .the answer is no.' We had nothing to do with it. We're not paying any reparations.") (Quoting Tulsa radio talk-show host); Arnold Hamilton, "Medals to Honor Riot Survivors," *Dallas Morning News* (April 2, 2001) ("I know they won't give us anything here in Oklahoma," said riot survivor George Monroe, 84. "If we were in New York, Baltimore or Boston, you might get reparations, but not here in Tulsa, Oklahoma. We didn't expect anything since 1921.").

58. Cf. Joseph Singer, *Entitlement: The Paradoxes of Property* (2000), pp. 195–196. ("We are left with hopeless demands of justice. They are impossible to fulfill. We

cannot undo what was done or even adequately acknowledge what has happened, much less compensate for it. [...] The impossibility of doing justice does not leave us free to escape responsibility.").

59. Adrian Brune, "Tulsa's Shame: Race Riot Victims Still Wait for Promised Reparations," *The Nation* (March 18, 2002) ("Those were the concepts that were politically possible.") (Quoting Representative Don Ross on the race riot memorial committee and the scholarship and community development funds—which, para-doxically, did not receive any state funds).

60. See Alex Boraine, *A Country Unmasked* (2000), p. 217 (discussing reactions to South African Truth and Reconciliation Commission); cf. Martha Minow, *Between Vengeance and Forgiveness: Facing History After Genocide and Mass Violence* (1998), pp. 52–90.

61. See Richard A. Wilson, *The Politics of Truth and Reconciliation in South Africa: Legitimating the Post-Apartheid State* (2001) (discussing the many interests that opposed the goals of the Truth and Reconciliation Commission).

62. Randy Krehbiel, "Leader Promises Action on Riot Issue," *Tulsa World* (April 27, 2001) (exploring the possibility of reparations paid by the Tulsa Chamber of Commerce); "Double Jeopardy Suit Cites Statute of Limitations," *Daily Oklahoman* (February 28, 2003); Adrian Brune, "A Long Wait for Justice," *Village Voice* (April 30, 2004).

63. See, e.g., Arnold Hamilton, " '21 Tulsa Riot Case Polarizes Some See Suit Emerging As Bellwether For Black Reparations Movement," *Dallas Morning News* (June 23, 2003).

64. See, e.g., Scott Gold, "Reparations Sought Decades After Race Riot; A Lawsuit for Damages from Oklahoma and Tulsa May Set the Tone for a National Campaign," *Los Angeles Times* (February 13, 2004) (discussing legal theory of tolling the statute of limitations); Alfred L. Brophy, "Norms, Law, and Reparations: The Case of the Ku Klux Klan in 1920s Oklahoma," *Harvard Black Letter L. J.* 20 (2004): pp. 17–48 (summarizing evidence presented in the riot victims' federal lawsuit regarding the Klan's domination of the Oklahoma courts and local government in the 1920s). The plaintiffs' lawyers, led by Harvard Law Professor Charles Ogletree, also theorized that the Tulsa Riot Commission Report reawakened the statute of limitations, by notifying the plaintiffs that they had been harmed. For the lawyers argued that once the courts were unavailable, the statute of limitations would not start until there was affirmative governmental action telling the plaintiffs that they had been harmed.

65. The plaintiffs also argued that there was a conspiracy of silence, which prevented them from having the information necessary to file a lawsuit. The complete case for tolling the statute of limitations rests on the unavailability of the courts in the decades following the riot. Even once the courts became generally available, the riot victims themselves could not obtain relief, because they had been threatened and told for so long that they had no right to relief and that the courts continued to be unavailable to them. It was not until the release of the Tulsa Riot Commission

Report in 2001 —or maybe until the passage of the Tulsa Riot Reconciliation Act in June—that the plaintiffs had the information necessary and the ability to file suit.

66. See Alexander v. Oklahoma, 328 F.3d 1206, rehearing denied 391 F.3d 1155 (10th Cir. 2004).

67. Id. ("Fundamentally, however, the issue is whether, based on the allegations in the complaint and the record, those circumstances existed through the issuance of the Report in 2001. In making this determination, we need not pinpoint an exact date when the exceptional circumstances ended. Rather, the judgment must stand if, based on the undisputed facts available, those circumstances ended sometime prior to February 2001.").

68. Id. In fairness to the court of appeals, it must be observed that the court's opinion mentions that special deputies joined the mob. Id.

69. See, e.g., Alfred L. Brophy, "Reparations Talk: The Tort Law Analogy and Reparations for Slavery," *Boston College Third World L.J.* 23 (2004): p. 128 (discussing the possibilities of lawsuits for Jim Crow crimes); DeWayne Wickham, "Tulsa Case Is Key Reparations Test," *USA Today* (March 25, 2003) (portraying the Tulsa case as a key test of reparations lawsuits).

70. Brent Staples, "Coming to Grips With the Unthinkable in Tulsa," *New York Times* sec. 4, at p. 12 (March 16, 2003).

71. Compare Ralph Ellison, "The Perspective of Literature," in John Callahan ed., 1995, *The Collected Works of Ralph Ellison*, p. 781 ("The law ensures the conditions, the stage upon which we act; the rest of it is up to the individual.").

CHAPTER 12

The Apology Moment: Vichy Memories in 1990s France

JULIE FETTE

In societies coming to terms with past injustices, public apology has emerged as a powerful force. This is particularly true of France in the 1990s, where the state has served as a catalyst for a multifaceted apology trend within civil society for the persecution of Jews in France during the Second World War. Following President Jacques Chirac's official apology in 1995 for the Vichy regime's anti-Semitic policies, various civil groups stepped forward to address their specific pasts, contributing to what one French political scientist called "the time of repentance."[1]

Scholars have suggested several reasons for the emergence of apology on a global scale at the end of the twentieth century: a new international focus on morality;[2] a revised understanding of universal human rights, state sovereignty and international law;[3] a willingness of state actors to show feelings of caring and regret and to view apology not as a weakness but a manifestation of strength;[4] the globalization of memory in the post-Cold War era;[5] as well as increased demand for recognition by past victims.[6] In addition to these transnational factors, particular developments in France prepared the ground for the emergence of public apologies in the 1990s. The expansive historiography of the Vichy era and media-saturated trials of Vichy bureaucrats have established the responsibilities of the state and certain segments of French society for the passage of racial laws and the deportation of Jews.

The extent of Vichy collaboration in the Final Solution has been fully documented for several decades. The consensus today is to view the Vichy regime as fully immersed in the legal, social, and eventually physical separation of Jews from the French national community. Renée Poznanski, among many others, offered a vivid description of the gradual identification, exclusion, spoliation, internment, and deportation of Jews in wartime French society.[7] Although three-quarters of the Jewish population in France survived the war experience, 76,000 were deported, of which 2,500 returned. But before this history became known in the 1970s, several myths dominated French

thinking: the Gaullist "resistancialist" myth that France was a nation of re-
sisters; the "parenthesis theory" alluding to the exceptionality of the Vichy
regime in French history; and the argument that French anti-Semitic policies
and actions were imposed by the Nazi occupants.[8] These myths were broken
down and a new era of memory work began in France in the 1970s, which
historian Henry Rousso designated a period of "obsession" with French guilt,
and which has endured to the end of the century.[9] As a years-long series of
fiftieth anniversary commemorations of World War II events ran its course in
the early 1990s, multiple questions about the past continued to be raised by
filmmakers, television producers, novelists, historians, journalists, and mem-
oirists. Amidst this surge, the remembrance of Jewish deportation took center
stage in public debate.[10]

The late-century emergence of Vichy memory in France arose in the
shadow of several high-profile court cases trying wartime actors accused of
crimes against humanity. This legal context weighed heavily upon the apology
trend. After the German Klaus Barbie was tried in France in 1987 and the
efforts to bring Jean Leguay and René Bousquet to justice were aborted by
their deaths, two Frenchmen were brought to trial and found guilty for crimes
against humanity: Paul Touvier, former chief of intelligence of the *milice* in
Lyon, and Maurice Papon, secretary general of the Gironde prefecture during
the war. Papon's trial in 1997–1998 for his role in the deportation of 1,690 Jews
from Bordeaux was significant in that the accused was not a zealous *milicien*
but a public servant. As a result, his trial became not that of an individual, but
of the French state as a whole and its administrative role in the Holocaust.

In addition to the growing memorialization of Vichy and the legal context
of the 1990s, scandals about the legacy of Vichy emerged constantly, followed
by public demands for reckoning. Pierre Péan's 1994 biography of President
François Mitterrand revealed to much public sensation information about
the socialist's flirtation with an extreme right league when he was a law student in the 1930s, his decoration from Vichy authorities in 1943, his post-war
friendship with Vichy police chief and accused war criminal, René Bousquet,
and his insistence on posing a flower on the tomb of Marshal Pétain in the
1990s.[11] Revelations that the city of Paris still possessed Jewish property that
had been "aryanized" during the occupation[12] and that French national museums still held thousands of works of art that had been stolen from Jews in
France during the war[13] led state authorities to review their records and make
reparations. In addition, a "Jewish card file" created by the Paris police during
the war was found in the archives: such a discovery of French fingerprints

on anti-Semitic policies shocked public opinion and led to the creation of a historical commission and to facilitated access to wartime records.

All of these developments paved the way for apology to become a tool in a national healing process. An interconnected triptych of apology, court trials, and reparations to address the Vichy past transpired in 1990s France. This chapter focuses specifically on the dynamics of apology, marked by the descent of the practice of atonement into the public sphere. Indeed, one of the unique elements of the French case is the transfer of apology from the official level into civil society. Triggered by President Chirac, apologies, recognitions, and acknowledgments were offered by professional groups, the Catholic church, and state institutions for their particular roles in wartime anti-Semitism. The apology trend in France in the 1990s responded to a social demand: rather than an obsession or a narrow communitarian movement, apology satisfied a widespread desire of French society to face the past.

1. State Apology: A Radical Departure from the Past

When Jacques Chirac was elected to the Presidency in May 1995, succeeding François Mitterrand's fourteen-year mandate, he marked his arrival to power and his distinction from the departed socialist with several brash moves.[14] In addition to relaunching nuclear test blasts in Mururoa and slashing the budget to qualify for the euro, Chirac became the first French president to acknowledge French responsibility in the Holocaust. On July 16, 1995, the 53rd anniversary of the "Vélodrome d'Hiver" tragedy, whereby French authorities rounded up 13,000 Jews in this former bicycle stadium in Paris, interned them in concentration camps, and supervised their deportation, President Chirac officially recognized the French state's role in the Final Solution.

By all accounts, Chirac's statement of recognition radically departed from prevailing official attitudes toward the Vichy past. Chirac admitted French guilt and took responsibility for its "collective fault:" "France, land of the Enlightenment and of Human Rights, land of hospitality and asylum, France, on that day, committed the irreparable." Chirac alluded to a sentiment of debt to Jewish victims, without specifying whether it was moral or material: "We have an immutable debt toward those left unprotected by France." He finished with a warning against future injustice and a hope for an open, tolerant France: "Let us know how to learn the lessons of history. Let us refuse to be passive observers or accomplices of the unacceptable."[15] Although

Chirac did not offer any reparation to Jews, his proclamation that France was accountable for the crimes of Vichy allowed for that eventuality.[16]

Having thus officially and unambiguously taken responsibility for Vichy crimes, Chirac was nonetheless careful in his declaration to remind that the French deviation from human rights ethics was influenced by the context of defeat and occupation: "Yes, the criminal folly of the occupant was seconded by the French, by the French State." Further, Chirac specifically distinguished another France, a France that "had never been at Vichy [. . . but was] alive and thriving in London," a France that "saved three-quarters of the Jewish population." Several observers noted that such emphases in fact diluted the impact of Chirac's declaration and perpetuated the ambivalent distancing between Vichy and the Republic in a pernicious manner.[17] Henry Rousso, on the other hand, congratulated Chirac's careful rendering of the historical complexities of the period.[18]

Generational change partially explains the shift in paradigm that allowed for a Fifth Republic president to apologize for the crimes of the Vichy regime. Mitterrand's compromised personal history in Vichy events prevented him from leading the nation to come to terms with the past. In the last few years of his presidency, he refused to apologize for Vichy despite mounting pressure from intellectual circles and Jewish groups.[19] Mitterrand conceded in 1993 to make July 16 a national day of commemoration for racist and anti-Semitic persecutions, but he reaffirmed in 1994, "I will not apologize in the name of France. The Republic has nothing to do with that. I believe that France is not responsible."[20] Paradoxically, it took a direct inheritor of Gaullism to finally shatter the myth of Vichy's historical parenthesis. Chirac was seven years old at the beginning of the Second World War: his lack of direct involvement in wartime events enabled him to apologize without risking his personal career. As historian Raoul Girardet has asserted more generally, Chirac could only benefit from taking a moral stand against others' failings.[21] Nonetheless, juxtaposed against Mitterrand's refusals and reactive half-gestures, Chirac's precise inventory of French responsibilities, full apology, and call to avoid injustice in the future satisfied the majority of the French public.[22] A public opinion poll conducted a few days after the ceremony at the Vélodrome d'Hiver revealed that 72 percent of the French people approved of Chirac's declaration,[23] indicating that the reception of apology went well beyond the vindication of Jewish claims.

Chirac's clear "acknowledgment of the human dignity and moral worth of victims"[24] engendered an unsurprisingly positive response from French Jews. All the major Jewish leaders including Joseph Sitruk, the chief rabbi of

France, Henri Hajdenberg, president of the Representative Council of Jewish Institutions in France, Serge Klarsfeld, president of the Association of Daughters and Sons of Deportees, and Robert Badinter, former Minister of Justice under Mitterrand, saluted Chirac's declaration.[25] Among Jewish intellectuals, Alain Finkielkraut and Blandine Kriegel supported the initiative,[26] but Claude Lanzmann raised questions about the artificiality of apology. For the author of *Shoah*, official recognition has devoided remembrance of its true content. Before July 16 was designated a national holiday, he reminisced, "the ceremonies at Vél' d'Hiv' had warmth: people who gathered there fervently shared a very strong memory, like a shared secret. Now there are dignitaries sitting on government-issue chairs reading ministerial speeches. It is what Flaubert in *Madame Bovary* called 'the mechanical genuflection of hurried parishioners.'"[27]

Political reaction to Chirac's declaration revealed that a consensual vision of the Vichy past had not yet been achieved. Rather, the Manichean divide between True France and Vichy France was forcefully reiterated in the political arena. Old guards of Gaullists and Mitterrandists shared a concern about the wording over exactly who or what was guilty. Some of Chirac's fellow party members heavily coated with the Gaullist heritage rejected his apology outright. Philippe Séguin refused to link the Vichy state with the French nation and rejected an admission of collective guilt; Pierre Mazeaud argued that the French republic had continued to exist in exile in London under General de Gaulle; and Jacques Baumel, one of the last "historic Gaullists," complained that Chirac's apology diminished the legacy of the resistance.[28] In the Mitterrandist camp, socialists Jack Lang, Claude Bartolone, and Louis Mexandeau similarly insisted that the only guilty party was the Vichy regime and not the French republic.[29] However, Lionel Jospin, leader of the socialists in the post-Mitterrand era, strongly seconded Chirac's apology,[30] as did other socialists such as Jacques Attali, Robert Badinter, and Michel Rocard,[31] and head of the French Communist Party Robert Hue.[32] On the extreme right, National Front leader Jean-Marie Le Pen vehemently refused any French collective responsibility and claimed that Chirac's declaration dirtied the honor of the nation.[33] Le Pen further accused Chirac of using the apology to pay an electoral debt to the French Jewish community.[34] Political responses to Chirac's declaration, convincingly argued Nathan Bracher, attested to "stubborn ideological contentiousness and [...] persistent efforts to make the memory of the past subservient to present political agendas."[35] The divisiveness of the political arena, therefore, contrasted with the overwhelmingly positive reception of Chirac's apology in public opinion.

Despite the polarization of political reactions, Chirac's state apology and the Papon trial together symbolized a climate of change. The causal link between apology and judicial reckoning was stressed in many instances. *Le Monde* viewed the court ruling that allowed the Papon trial to finally occur after decades of legal wrangling as a radical shift: "France no longer has the same regard for its history since Jacques Chirac publicly recognized its immutable debt towards Jewish deportees from France. The long parenthesis of the Gaullist mythology, which overestimated resistance France to better hide collaborationist France, is over. Officially."[36] Yet on the other hand, Chirac's apology reduced the stakes of the Papon case. The trial was no longer the exclusive means of coming to terms with the Vichy past, because apology and reparation constituted new forms of redress.[37] Papon's lawyer was quick to utilize this evolution for the benefit of his client by arguing that apology should substitute for judicial process and Papon should not have to stand trial.[38] These debates posited two views: on the one hand, the official state apology was a finality and an ultimate resolution of the past. On the other hand, Chirac's apology was just a beginning, a point of departure from state recognition of official complicity in the Holocaust to the particular examinations of responsibility of civil groups in French society.

2. Apology's Civil Turn: Professional Recognition of Responsibility

In April 1997, former Minister of Justice Robert Badinter published a book documenting the French legal profession's role in the Holocaust. It told the story of how the French law bars carried out Vichy's exclusionary legislation establishing a 2 percent quota on Jewish lawyers. French lawyers evaluated the personal, professional, and military credentials of their Jewish colleagues and decided whom to ban from law practice. Badinter summarized the complacency of the legal community toward Jews: "Throughout it all, in the countryside as well as in Paris, not at any moment [. . .] was a single protest made against the exclusion of Jews from the Bar [. . .], not a single declaration of principles formulated, not a single gesture of solidarity offered to fellow colleagues who would be thus eliminated."[39] Dozens of Jewish lawyers were caught in round-ups and imprisoned in the Drancy camp outside of Paris, including some of the most well-respected bar members of interwar Paris. Lawyers' precipitous, active response to Vichy's exclusionary legislation can be explained by the widespread belief of professional overcrowding that permeated the law profession in the twenty years prior to the war. Among other factors, the anti-Semitic quota was seen by many lawyers as a felicitous chance to reduce competition.[40]

A mere few weeks after Badinter's publication, the Paris law bar issued a resolution recognizing the injustices committed toward Jewish and foreign lawyers during the war. Mentioning the historical evidence presented in Badinter's book, the law bar Council admitted that contrary to its mission, its members did not refuse to apply the so-called laws of 1940 and 1941 excluding Jews and foreigners from practice. The recognition concluded, "Conscious of its responsibilities to the history of the bar, the Council bows its head to those who had been victims." At the same time, the Paris bar signaled to the press that it would open its archives.[41] Although the apology was not representative of the entire French legal profession—there is no national centralized leadership among law bars in France—the Paris bar is by far the most prestigious and dominant bar in France, whose actions had affected the greatest number of Jews during the war.[42]

The facts in Badinter's book were not entirely new; scholars had begun to examine the wartime moral collapse of the French legal profession a few years earlier.[43] But lawyers paid attention to this publication because of Badinter's reputation and public role. A prominent member of the Paris bar and former president of the elite Constitutional Council, he had earned his fame for abolishing the death penalty in France in 1981 as Minister of Justice under Mitterrand. In addition to Badinter's singular influence, other reasons explain why the law profession was the first civil group to face its past and take responsibility for its predecessors' actions. Looming on the legal horizon was the trial of Maurice Papon, which would raise new questions about the links between justice and history. Because institutions often apologize "in order to restore an institutional reputation [. . .] or to defuse a volatile situation,"[44] the lawyers' initiative was likely motivated in part by a desire to face the past on their own terms before being dragged into it by the media covering the Papon trial. But pragmatism did not alone prompt the legal profession to become the first civil group to recognize its specific responsibility in Vichy anti-Semitism. Lawyers' recognition of past faltering in their very mission to serve the rights of man and to protect the oppressed was matched by a more activist role in moral legal issues in contemporary France. In early 1997, for example, the council of the Paris law bar intervened several times in parliamentary debates over immigration to call for the removal of measures that would harm the dignity of foreigners and their individual freedoms guaranteed by the Constitution.[45] The law bar declaration of 1997 can therefore be viewed as "an act of discourse that modifies a situation."[46] It signified a broad evolution of the law bar away from its conservative past toward an identity more steeped in post-1989 human rights culture.

3. Catholic Repentance for Passivity

Bishops representing the French Catholic church offered an apology to the Jewish community in a solemn commemoration at the site of the former Drancy camp outside Paris on September 30, 1997, a week before the opening of the Papon trial. A "declaration of repentance" was pronounced by the bishop of the Saint-Denis diocese where the Drancy camp had existed, and was signed by all bishops whose diocese had housed an internment camp controlled by Vichy. With no media pomp, words held center stage at the ceremony, which was followed by separate religious observations by bishops and rabbis.[47]

For what did the Catholic church repent? Whereas the French state and the law bar apologized for their active participation in the Holocaust, the French episcopate apologized for not having raised its voice against persecution, for its silence and passivity. No official protest was ever made by the Catholic church at the promulgation of the Statute of the Jews. Silence was the French church's response to discriminatory legislation and mounting social exclusions. Only after the very public roundups in the southern zone in the late summer of 1942 did any church official publicly denounce the treatment of Jews. Although a handful of bishop-resistants emerged in the late years of the war, only six of the seventy-six bishops ever spoke out against Vichy's anti-Semitism.[48] Numerous factors prompted the Catholic church's embrace of Vichy's "National Revolution," broadly, the return to conservative religious values and the restoration of the church's prestige (concretized by the restitution of religious teaching in public schools and of church property appropriated in 1905).[49] The bishops' apology in 1997 directly criticized their church's loyalty to the Vichy regime: "In their majority, the spiritual authorities, entangled in a loyalism and docility going well beyond traditional obedience to established powers, remained stuck in an attitude of conformism, prudence, and abstention."[50]

It is useful to consider in detail the bishops' speech act, because it set the benchmark, well beyond Chirac's declaration, for a candid apology. It specifically acknowledged the church's silence in the face of anti-Semitism: "In February 1941, 40,000 Jews were interned in French camps, while [...] the church hierarchy was concerned about protecting its own faithful and maintaining its institutions. [...] Facing the breadth of the drama and the extraordinary character of the crime, too many pastors of the church, by their silence, offended the church itself and its mission." An explicit connection was made between past and present clergy members: "It is our church, and we must recognize that ecclesiastical interests interpreted in an excessively restrictive manner came before the commandments of the conscience and we must ask ourselves why." Furthermore, the bishops linked the church's failure during Vichy with centuries of Catholic anti-Judaism: "On this soil flourished the venomous plant of hatred for the Jews." The declaration concluded: "This failing of the church of France and its responsibility toward the Jewish people are part of our history. We confess this sin. We beg forgiveness of God and ask the Jewish people to hear these words of repentance."

Not unexpectedly, the bishops' declaration was heavily imbued with religious language. In particular, the words "repentance" and "sin" (*faute*) are semantically significant in two ways. First, one writer pointed out the stiff, literary, and almost medieval evocation of the word "repentance" and suggested that the church had chosen it carefully in order to distance the wartime acts from the present church.[51] Second, the bishops' apology used "sin" and "repentance" as concepts that apply to both individuals and institutions. As such, the significance of the declaration resides in its denunciation of the church as an institution and of its leaders as a group, creating the conditions for a thorough "examination of its collective conscience."[52]

The French Catholic church's apology is best understood in the context of three distinct evolutions. First, the church repentance reflected the new contours of memories of Vichy in French society. Second, it can be viewed in the perspective of transnational Catholic calls for repentance. The French declaration was a response to the Vatican's signal for national churches to reconcile with communities that had suffered from Catholic intolerance. The Polish and German episcopates had already set such an example for the French church, and Swiss bishops followed in 2000.[53] Third, the apology testified to a transition toward greater social activism on the part of the French church in the 1990s. Like the legal profession, the church had begun to criticize harsh policies toward immigrants, and drew up a document about immigration for Catholic parishioners entitled "A Call to Live Together."[54] This progressive stance was reflected in the French church's commitment to apply the lessons of Vichy to contemporary human rights abuses. One framer of the church apology noted the precedent set by public repentance: "If we repent for what happened under Vichy, it is also in order to think, for example, about what is currently happening in Algeria, in East Africa, about everything that, in the West, can lead to denials of the conscience. The church must speak out. No matter what the situation."[55]

The church apology was symbolically validated by the formal acceptance of the French Jewish community. Henri Hajdenberg, for instance, responded to the bishops at the Drancy ceremony, "Your request for forgiveness [...] cannot but be heard by victim survivors and their children."[56] Jean Kahn, president of the Central Consistory of France, welcomed the apology despite its tardiness and its limited number of signatories.[57] For his part, former chief rabbi of France René-Samuel Sirat found it theologically impossible to grant forgiveness on behalf of the victims: "Pardon cannot be given by those who were not offended. [...] The request for forgiveness is pronounced, but there is no response. We are simply witnesses of this act."[58]

General public opinion was also favorable to the bishops' repentance. In a poll taken a few days afterward, 45 percent of French approved of the declaration, while 41 percent declared themselves indifferent, and 9 percent disapproved.[59] With one year's distance from the event, 68 percent of French polled said the bishops were right to apologize; 24 percent disapproved.[60] Such high approval ratings demonstrate that apology was not just an affair between victims and perpetrators, but impacted on the whole of French society, although attitudes among practicing Catholics indicate a more divided reaction.[61] Whereas the Catholic press was unanimously supportive of the repentance,[62] parishioners expressed hostility in their correspondence with the clergy.[63] Common criticisms postulated that the church's apology overshadowed Catholics' rescue efforts during the occupation,[64] and that the church would be weakened by focusing on its mistakes.[65] On the contrary, a writer for *La Croix* insisted, "The image of the church will emerge from this event reinforced."[66]

Against the view that institutions apologizing for wartime wrongs had purposefully waited for protagonists to die off so as to distance themselves from their past,[67] church historian Etienne Fouilloux observed, "Even though the church could have spoken out fifty years ago, it is not so late either: the university, the magistrature, the medical order ... also have something to say along the lines of what the church pronounces today. The state did so, recently and with difficulty. The church's gesture is part of a movement of general recognition that I esteem important for Jewish communities and that I hope will take on even greater scope."[68] Fouilloux was not the only one to call for other civil groups to follow the church's lead.[69] Henri Hajdenberg publicly hoped that similar engagements would be taken by professionals and by state organs such as the police, the Councilors of State (who put into technical application the Statute of the Jews), magistrates (who interpreted the Statute), and professors (who taught the Statute in their law courses).[70] Novelist and member of the Académie Française Bertrand Poirot-Delpech also called on state organs, in particular the university (which had implemented the Vichy dictate of a 3 percent quota on Jewish students), to imitate the church's apology.[71]

4. Police Embrace the Ritual of Apology

Immediately following the French Catholic church's declaration of repentance, an important organization of police officers stepped forward to apologize for the active collaboration of the French police in the rounding up and deporting of Jews during the war. The ritual of public apology in France was by now well established. First, the National Union of Uniformed Police (SNPT) issued a press release recognizing the guilt of its predecessors and expressing its "eternal regret." Second, an apology was offered in an organized ceremony with representatives of the Jewish community at the memorial of the Unknown Jewish Martyr in Paris. Third, the speech act contained specific acknowledgment that 4,500 Parisian policemen participated in the Vélodrome d'Hiver roundup and that throughout the war the French police served as a zealous assistant to state policies of internment and deportation. Finally, the police union requested pardon from the French Jewish community for the actions of their predecessors "in the name of the republican policemen that we represent, so that never again will men let themselves commit such acts of barbarity."[72]

The apology was limited, however, by strong dissent within the police corps. Another police union, the SGP-CUP (*Syndicat général de la police-Centrale unitaire de la police*), whose membership counted the majority of Parisian uniformed police officers, characterized the SNPT gesture as "incoherent:" "It is stupid and borderline dangerous to equate collaborators with resistants and traitors with patriots by assuming a collective responsibility of the 'police institution.'"[73] Nevertheless, the apology was significant for two reasons. First, as the SNPT noted, the role of police personnel in the persecution of the Jews in Vichy France was particularly direct and physical, in contrast to Maurice Papon's bureaucratic paper-pushing. The police apology thus constituted a straightforward look at strong-arm actions most commonly associated with the Holocaust in the public mind. Second, as a branch of the state government, the police were theoretically "covered" by the official state apology offered by Chirac, yet nonetheless embraced the ritual therapy of apology.

5. Turning the Unread Page in Medicine

The descent of apology into civil society also reached the French medical profession. At an annual meeting on October 11, 1997, the Order of Doctors issued a declaration of regret for discrimination against Jewish doctors during the Vichy period. Protectionist and xenophobic sentiment had culminated during the war in a hasty adoption of anti-Semitic and anti-foreigner regulations. Like lawyers, it was doctors themselves, through their professional Order, who put into practice the 2 percent quota on their Jewish colleagues. In a "symbolic request for forgiveness in the name of the medical community" extended to Jewish doctors, the president of the Order, Bernard Glorion, admitted, "Colleagues became guilty, voluntarily or not [. . . and] had to participate in this sad and shameful operation of discrimination and exclusion. [. . .] We can only regret and repudiate with gravity and humility." The Order's pronouncement concluded, "It is up to us today in the name of the medical community to remind all those who succeed us that our duty, their duty, will be to never yield to the temptation of exclusion and to never accept, even by our silence, any discrimination or rejection of any group."[74] The apology was complemented by an effort at transparency: the Order agreed to open its archives to the public; something historians and doctors had requested for years.[75] At stake was the release of internal records that would elucidate denunciation and exclusion practices within the medical corps. It was reputed that sacks filled with thousands of letters from French doctors denouncing colleagues as Jews, foreigners, and charlatans were found after the war and subsequently burned in an effort to rebuild the nation. The surviving records of the Order had never before been made public.

The Order's apology contained several weaknesses. Ambivalent references to doctors who "voluntarily or not," "had to participate" in anti-Semitic actions constituted a significant recoil from responsibility. The "duty to remember" invoked by the Order only called for remembrance of the "admirable and anonymous behavior of doctors who, risking their lives, obeyed their duty and assisted the sick and often their fellow colleagues" and not of excluded Jewish doctors. The apology was further undermined by an artificial distancing between past and present: the declaration asserted that the Order of Doctors was refounded after the Liberation and was therefore a completely distinct institution from the wartime Order. The tainted origins of the Order—created by the Vichy regime after decades of medical lobbying (partly so as to exclude unwanted categories from the profession)—had been a source of illegitimacy for the post-war medical profession. Many of the same doctors who had participated in discriminatory policies and collaborative activities during the war persisted in Order leadership roles after the war. Only with institutional cleansing performed through memory work, apology, and mourning, Bernard Kouchner provocatively argued, could the Order reclaim its dignity.[76]

The most serious problem with the apology was that the Order as a whole did not support it. The representatives of the medical institution did not debate, approve, or publicize the initiative of their president.[77] The Order's monthly journal made no mention of the apology in the months surrounding it,[78] and no sign of it appears on the institution's web site.[79] Nor were Order leaders cooperative in the national directive to open archives.[80] Vice-president of the Gironde departmental Order council proclaimed, "It's very late, too late. We should have opened the drawers in the 1950s. To do so today is to attack the memory of those who had taken on responsibilities and whom we are incapable of judging outside of the context of the period." For the president of the Northern departmental Order council, there was nothing of interest in the archives.[81] Because of insufficient representation, the Order's apology can be categorized as one "undercut by subsequent denials from others within it."[82] Indeed, physicians' letters to the editors of medical journals provided evidence of acerbic dissent. One doctor, for instance, had "had enough of these mediatized-epileptic tremors over the Second World War. I was not there. I did not do anything. So leave me alone. [...] Collective responsibility does not exist."[83] The claim that some doctors assisted Jews figured prominently among the reactions to the apology:[84] "What would all the big names in French medicine who fought against the invader and who constantly risked their lives to save Jewish lives think of this 'repentance?'"[85]

Nonetheless, positive reaction to the apology was to be found within the French medical profession. Despite disappointment about the ambivalence of the declaration's language, Jewish doctors expressed overall satisfaction.[86] Several medical journals followed up on the apology by investigating the history of the profession under Vichy.[87] A grim view of the Order's past emerged from these inquiries: "Zealous and obedient creature of Pétain . . . the Order was subservient to the regime. The departmental medical council leaders were the perfect implementers of the exclusionary laws."[88] For some, the apology came as a long-awaited reckoning: "Fifty-seven years! We had to wait fifty-seven years for the Order to beg forgiveness."[89] Furthermore, doctors sought to link the apology to contemporary French debates about immigration and public memory. The Committee of Foreign-Diploma Doctors drew a comparison between wartime exclusion and current discrimination against foreign doctors.[90] Others expressed hope that a similar process of acknowledgment would be undertaken for acts of torture committed during the Algerian War.[91]

Since its Vichy origins, the Order of Doctors has had a conservative reputation both for its role in sociopolitical affairs (for example, its fight against the legalization of abortion) and for its internal governance (namely, its favoring of colleagues over patients in medical disputes). But it has nonetheless evolved in recent years toward more open and democratic ways, especially during the presidency of Glorion.[92] His recognition of medical anti-Semitism during Vichy can be viewed as part of this evolution. Ultimately, however, the declaration was an abortive apology. Although it stimulated discussion of the Order's past after it was issued, the declaration was ambivalent, unrepresentative, and it gave the impression that it was reluctantly given. Conflicts were buried anew with no final sense of reconciliation.[93] One doctor's frustration summed it up: "This individual and timid 'repentance' is not enough. [...] The Order wants us to 'turn the page' that no one has read yet."[94]

6. Short of Apology, State Institutions Acknowledge their Pasts

The wave of recognition for Vichy injustices took one of the most prestigious state institutions in its wake. The Council of State is the highest administrative court in France. It is consulted for interpretation of legislative texts and is responsible for elaborating laws into applicable decrees. At issue during this apology moment was the role played by the French legal positivist tradition in the legitimization of wartime exclusionary laws. In a seminal article, legal scholar Danièle Lochak has argued that the French judiciary system during Vichy interpreted anti-Semitic law under the guise of neutralism. Accordingly, French jurists' resolute commitment to objectivity blinded them to the ethical and human consequences of the discriminatory legislation. Their elaboration of legal doctrine and jurisprudence also served to normalize anti-Semitic law as a legitimate discipline with its own set of legal experts.[95]

This critical view of the French judiciary during the war made its way into the leadership of the Council of State in 1997. In a colloquium, the Council of State recognized its legal conformism and admitted that its members interpreted anti-Semitic and xenophobic laws in a rigidly Cartesian manner. Occasionally, they also demonstrated an unmistakably discriminatory bent in their opinions. Indeed, a French legal scholar has documented that most Council of State members during Vichy never tried to impede or stall the application of anti-Semitic law, and, in fact, widely approved its content.[96] In its defense, however, the Council of State argued in 1997 that its jurisprudence tended to be more liberal after 1942 and that its margin of maneuver under Vichy authorities was particularly narrow.

Similar to other institutions, internal reactions were split over the Council of State's acknowledgment of its Vichy record. Some members deemed it courageous and honest, and suggested that the institution could in fact have done better to counter anti-Semitism, whereas others expressed outright anger.[97] Had the declaration been approved by the members of the Council of State and issued by its president (it was delivered by the president of the finance section, Jean Massot), it would have constituted a more representative and authoritative recognition of responsibility. The declaration was not quite an apology. Different in nature from the more repentant tone of other civil groups' declarations, this gesture nonetheless represented a breakthrough for the French judicial system in general. Because the Council of State is one of the *grand corps* of the French state, it was in theory sheltered (like the police) by the official apology for Vichy offered by Chirac in 1995. Though rather than considering the Council of State exempt from historical reckoning, the issuer of the acknowledgment stressed the influence of Chirac's apology on the institution's desire to come to terms with its past.

Concretely, the Council of State's revisiting of its history was perceptible in its involvement in the Papon trial. Following Papon's condemnation for crimes against humanity, the Council of State determined that the French state was obliged to pay half of Papon's legal fees owed to victims because the "acts and actions of the French government, which did not directly result from the constraints of the occupier, allowed for and facilitated, independently of the personal actions of Maurice Papon, operations that constituted the prelude to deportation."[98] This ruling put legal teeth behind Chirac's symbolic recognition that Vichy was not a parenthesis in French history.

The Council of State was the last state institution to engage in declarative recognition of its Vichy past, a pattern common to public apologies in France in the 1990s. However, performative apology was not the only avenue for state organs to address their history. At the end of the decade, the creation of historical commissions researching institutional activities during Vichy coincided with the apology trend. For instance, the Ministry of Youth and Sports established a historical commission in 1997 to examine its role in propaganda and collaboration.[99] Similarly, and in response to lawsuits alleging complicity in crimes against humanity, the French national railroad company (SNCF) initiated a research colloquium in 2000 to examine its involvement in the deportation process.[100] For its part, the magistrature had already organized an investigative colloquium in 1993 entitled "To Judge under Vichy."[101] Like trials, professional historical commissions brought historians and apologizers into a close relationship criticized by proponents of scholarly distance from current events. The rise of the "historian-expert" in the 1990s dismayed many members of the historical profession who resented the transformation of scholarship into narrow expertise put to use in trials and commissions.[102] Despite this controversy over the historians' role, apology elicited and benefited from new scholarly inquiry.

7. The Apology Model Applied to New Historical Objects

The French wave of apology for World War II injustices ended with the acknowledgment of the Council of State. Public satiation served to brake the phenomenon. While several of the apologies had received minimal press coverage, those offered by Chirac and the Catholic Church attracted saturation-level coverage. One observer bemoaned, "I repent, we repent... It is currently the most common verb in the French language. The churches, the doctors, and the police parade and contrive. We are now waiting for the postmen, the train conductors, and the truck drivers to join the great self-flagellating movement [...] Me, too, I ask for forgiveness. Forgiveness for not wanting to repent."[103] After the first few mediatized acknowledgments of responsibility, apologies became perceived as empty words and routinized display. As a French political scientist put it, "Repentance is not a miracle remedy. It is also fundamentally 'impure,' inseparable from power struggles, weighted with ulterior motives and calculations. [...] In the end, everything gets old; what was originally a grave gesture becomes mechanical with time."[104]

Consequently, several arguments against public apologies had become commonplace by the end of 1997: one cannot apologize for the actions of predecessors; institutions cannot be guilty; individuals cannot apologize for a collectivity.[105] The argument that "apologies have their place, but they cannot be substitutes for action,"[106] was expressed scathingly by a philosophy professor who labeled repentance a gratuitous "rip off" serving as a screen against truth and reparations, especially in the case of colonialism.[107] Others denounced the inconsistency of the apology trend: why were apologies only being offered for certain injustices? Such criticism led to a phenomenon of "victim competition" and to the politicization of apology as an ideological gesture.[108] This occurred notably when, in reaction to the publication of *The Black Book of Communism*,[109] the political right countered the focus on Vichy with a competing narrative of communist criminality. The far-right National Front went so far as to demand from French communists an apology for Stalin's crimes.[110] The overwhelming focus on Vichy alone bothered several intellectuals. Raoul Girardet warned against "selective repentance,"[111] whereas François Maspéro urged the French to also pay attention to current events for which they might have to apologize in 2040.[112]

The social demand for apology did in fact reach beyond the Vichy question into other episodes of the French past. At the centenary of Emile Zola's "J'accuse" in January 1998, the Catholic journal *La Croix* apologized for the treatment of Jews in its pages during the Dreyfus Affair.[113] The 150th anniversary of the abolition of slavery in France that same month also prompted calls for a state apology, although a plan for reparations did not achieve unanimity.[114] In February 1998, the treatment of indigenous populations came to the forefront of the apology agenda when New Caledonia demanded repentance for French brutality during the conquest of the island in 1853.[115] Although these requests mostly remained unmet, their widespread occurrence indicated the rooting of apology in French public discourse.

The main influence of the Vichy apology trend was in its shift to the Algerian question as the next historical object of reckoning. Apologizing for Vichy had paved the way, linguistically and legally, for a French engagement with its colonial past. It is revealing, for instance, that the Papon trial not only served as a nexus of Holocaust memories, but also rekindled French debates over the Algerian war.[116] The parallel between the memory of Vichy and Algeria has elicited scholarly interest.[117] It also has had tangible repercussions in public opinion. In the last few years, many signs testify to a demand for transparency in regard to the practice of torture in Algeria. Following the provocative memoirs of retired French general Paul Aussaresses justifying the use of torture and summary executions by French troops in Algeria during the war,[118] 56 percent of French surveyed were in favor of an official apology.[119] Although Chirac has so far demurred on calls for an official declaration of state repentance, archives have been opened to facilitate historical inquiry.[120] An apology does not seem to be far off, in part because of the normalization of apology and its perceived benefits as a means of mourning the past and ameliorating the future. A consensus has grown that an apology would improve Franco-Algerian relations and enhance the integration of Maghrebi immigrants in contemporary French society.[121] An apology would thus help to reshape the identities of weak and vulnerable population groups by publicly recognizing that "the culture of the victim group is not now, and never was, morally inferior to that of the offender group."[122] France facing its Algerian past, albeit slowly and with difficulty, signifies a new and huge market for apology in a postcolonial world.

8. Did Apology Mourn the Past and Ameliorate the Future?

Apology is in vogue, noted an American journalist in Paris in the late 1990s, "But nowhere, perhaps, is the process more fraught or obsessive than in France's contemplation of its treatment of the Jews during World War II."[123] Whether obsessive or not, the apology trend reversed the terms of French public memory. Less than a year before Chirac's declaration, few could imagine the possibility of a radical departure from post-war myths. Tony Judt, for instance, argued in 1994 that the "absurd sophism" of denying the Republic's responsibility for the acts of Vichy would prevent France from ever coming to terms with its past.[124] For Judt, reincorporating Vichy into the mainstream course of French history seemed like a daunting prospect precisely because in France, "modern identity is indissolvably linked to the idea of the universal Republic." Yet, triggered by Chirac's formal statement, apologies for Vichy ultimately served to stimulate a public reexamination of a buried past. Moreover, apology in France has affirmed a historical continuity and a symbolic generational link between "them" (the actors of 1940–1945) and "us" (French society today).

Apology has also fostered the integration of Jewish memory into the French national historical narrative. The Shoah is no longer external to the classic dichotomy between resistance and collaboration, but rather part and parcel of the French wartime history. The focus of apologies on the theretofore-neglected Jewish experience has not only been seized upon by political circles such as the National Front, but also became a point of scholarly criticism. Students of French memory Conan and Rousso have warned against the "temptation of 'Judeocentrism,' which seeks to reread the entire history of the Occupation through the prism of anti-Semitism."[125] Against this view, political scientist Pierre Birnbaum maintained that the only way to overcome the obsession was "to leave the book of The History of France open to this page just a bit longer."[126] Similarly, historian Olivier Wieviorka resisted the notion of a debilitating obsession: rather, demands for apology only showed that "many French people want to know more."[127] Public opinion did not seem to perceive the forceful emergence of Jewish memories as problematic. When polled in October 1998, 58 percent of French people (and a higher percentage among 18–24 year-olds) claimed that discussion of the extermination of Jews during World War II "was not excessive."[128]

The French case provides a unique way to understand the impact of apology on a society struggling with its history. If strictly used as a process of *judgment*, public apology can appear as a limited, mechanistic condemnation of the past without any far-reaching pedagogical dimension. In fact, many in France objected to this perfunctory "devoir de mémoire" (memory duty) performed through public atonement. A well-known historian of the post-war period found only formalism in repentance: "Making apologies does not connect history to our lives and hardly returns the French community to a place of self-confidence. Memorial piety and judicial interpellations seem to be neither consoling nor prophylactic. [...] If it is accepted that the more we confess, the better we will become, it is because we lack the force to reformulate an identity enlightened by experience."[129] This may be a valid critique of the ritualism and political correctness of the apology trend. Yet this criticism focuses solely on apology as condemnation and contrition and remains blind to the important hermeneutical potential embedded in this practice: a process of *critical inquiry*, which can "raise the moral threshold of a society," as Roy Brooks claimed.[130] Despite its limits, the descent of apology into civil society can ultimately be seen as introspective and demystifying, allowing French society to "move on" in a cleansed way. Compared to only ten or fifteen years earlier, court trials, historical commissions, monetary and symbolic reparations, the inauguration of commemorative days, and the revision of textbooks in the 1990s all testify that the apology trend coincided with a manifold reexamination of the past in France. As such, apologies for Vichy were most effective when they combined both critical inquiry and judgment, thereby engendering a healthier relationship between past and present, between the duty of memory and the necessary travail of forgetting.

Notes

1. Philippe Moreau Defarges, 1999, *Repentance et réconciliation* (Paris: Presses de Sciences Po), p. 9. (All translations are by the author.)

2. Elazar Barkan, 2000, *The Guilt of Nations, Restituting and Negotiating Historical Injustices* (New York: Norton).

3. Mark Gibney and Erik Roxstrom, "The Status of State Apologies," *Human Rights Quarterly* 23 (2001), pp. 923–926; Mireille Delmas-Marty cited in Dominique Dhombres, "De la difficulté de vivre ensemble," *Le Monde* (December 12, 1998).

4. Nicolaus Mills, "The New Culture of Apology," *Dissent* 48.4 (Fall 2001), pp. 113–116.

5. Claire Andrieu cited in Philippe Bernard, "Réparer les crimes du passé," *Le Monde* (April 10, 2002).

6. Michael Cunningham, "Saying sorry: The Politics of Apology," *The Political Quarterly* 70.3 (July–September 1999), p. 292.

7. Renée Poznanski, 1994, *Etre juif en France pendant la Seconde Guerre mondiale* (Paris: Hachette).

8. Henry Rousso, 1987, *Le Syndrome de Vichy: de 1944 à nos jours* (Paris: Seuil).

9. Eric Conan and Henry Rousso, 1998, *Vichy: An Ever-Present Past* (Hanover: UP of New England).

10. Olivier Lalieu, "L'Invention du 'devoir de mémoire,'" *Vingtième siècle* 69 (January–March 2001), pp. 83–94.

11. Pierre Péan, 1994, *Une jeunesse française: François Mitterrand, 1934–1947* (Paris: Fayard).

12. See Brigitte Vital-Durand, 1996, *Domaine privé* (Paris: First).

13. See Hector Feliciano, 1997, *The Lost Museum* (New York: Basic Books).

14. Sylvie Kauffmann, "Le bulldozer Chirac étonne les Américains," *Le Monde* (August 11, 1995).

15. "Pour la première fois, un président français reconnaît la responsabilité de la France dans la déportation et l'extermination de juifs pendant la seconde guerre mondiale," *Agence France Presse* (July 16, 1995). Database online. Available from Lexis-Nexis.

16. Félix Chiocca, "Une juste réparation morale," *Témoignage Chrétien* (July 21, 1995).

17. Peter Carrier, "'National Reconciliation?' Mitterrand, Chirac and the Commemorations of Vichy 1992–95," *National Identities* 2.2 (2000), pp. 135–136, 139–140; Alain-Gérard Slama, "Le nostra culpa du Président," *Le Point* (July 22, 1995).

18. Henry Rousso, "Sortir du dilemme: Pétain, est-ce la France?" *Le Débat* 89 (March–April 1996), pp. 198–204.

19. For a full account, see chapter 1 in Conan and Rousso, *Vichy: An Ever-Present Past*.

20. Quoted in Jean Baptiste de Montvalon, "M. Chirac reconnaît la faute collective commise envers les juifs," *Le Monde* (July 18, 1995).

21. Raoul Girardet, "Repentances sélectives," *Le Figaro* (October 29, 1997).

22. "Le président du CRIF salue le discours que l'on n'attendait plus," *Le Monde* (July 18, 1995).

23. Maurice Szafran, "Vichy et les juifs: Chirac a raison," *L'Evénement du jeudi* (July 27, 1995); "M. Badinter approuve la prise de position de M. Chirac sur Vichy," *Le Monde* (July 28, 1995).

24. Trudy Govier and Wilhelm Verwoerd, "The Promise and Pitfalls of Apology," *Journal of Social Philosophy* 33.1 (Spring 2002), p. 69.

25. Félix Chiocca, "Une juste réparation morale," *Témoignage Chrétien* (July 21, 1995).

26. Blandine Kriegel, "Pardon et crime d'état," *L'Histoire* 193 (November 1995).

27. Claude Lanzmann, "Parler pour les morts," *Le Monde des débats* (May 2000).

28. Patrick Jarreau, "Vichy: Lionel Jospin en juge de paix," *Le Monde* (October 23, 1997).

29. Jean-Baptiste de Montvalon, "La controverse provoquée par François Mitterrand s'estompe dans les rangs du Parti socialiste," *Le Monde* (October 8, 1997); Pascal Virot, "Déportation: les propos de Chirac sèment la discorde au sein du PS," *Libération* (July 20, 1995); "Les propos de M. Chirac sur Vichy divisent le Parti socialiste," *Le Monde* (July 19, 1995).

30. "Vichy; Jospin approuve Chirac," *Les Echos* (July 26, 1995); "M. Jospin approuve la position de M. Chirac sur Vichy," *Le Monde* (July 26, 1995); *Le Monde* (October 8, 1997).

31. "Jacques Attali crédite Jacques Chirac d'une image de dynamisme et d'action," *Le Monde* (August 18, 1995); Michel Rocard, "Les mots justes de Jacques Chirac," *Le Monde* (July 19, 1995); Robert Badinter, "L'Etat criminel," *Le Nouvel observateur* (August 2, 1995).

32. *L'Humanité* (July 24, 1995); "Etat Français: Robert Hue se déclare sans hésitation d'accord avec l'essentiel des propos tenus par Jacques Chirac," *Le Monde* (July 26, 1995).

33. Christiane Chombeau, "M. Le Pen accuse M. Chirac de salir la nation," *Le Monde* (July 20, 1995).

34. "Polémique," *Les Echos* (July 18, 1995).

35. Nathan Bracher, "La Mémoire vive et convulsive: The Papon Trial and France's Passion for History," *The French Review* 73.2 (December 1999), p. 323.

36. Laurent Greilsamer, "Un arrêt historique," *Le Monde* (September 20, 1996). See also Dominique Vernier, "Papon, un accusé combatif et plein d'assurance," *Le Monde* (April 1, 1998).

37. Chirac's apology has led to reparations. The Matteoli Mission documented hundreds of thousands of instances of Jewish spoliation in France during the war, offered compensation of 1 billion francs to orphans of Jewish deportees, and created a memory foundation with 1.4 billion francs to provide assistance to Holocaust victims and heirs in need. French insurance companies and financial institutions restituted an additional $22.5 million as part of an agreement signed between France and the United States, one of the legal bases for which was Chirac's 1995 declaration of responsibility. See *Embassy of France in the US—Matteoli Commission*, http://www.info-france-usa.org/news/statmnts/2000/jewish.asp (February 14, 2003).

38. "L'Etat de santé de Maurice Papon pèsera sur la suite du procès," *Le Monde* (October 11, 1997).

39. Robert Badinter, 1997, *Un antisémitisme ordinaire, Vichy et les avocats juifs (1940–1944)* (Paris: Fayard), p. 190. See also Josyane Savigneau, "La douleur de Robert Badinter; soumission ou complaisance?" *Le Monde des Livres* (April 25, 1997).

40. Julie Fette, 2001, "Xenophobia and Exclusion in the Professions in Interwar France." Ph.D. dissertation, New York University.

41. "France-justice-juifs," *Agence France Presse* (May 13, 1997) Database online. Available from LexisNexis; "Occupation: le barreau de Paris bat sa coulpe," *Les Echos* (May 14, 1997); "Antisémitisme: le conseil de l'ordre du barreau de Paris . . ." *Le Monde* (May 15, 1997).

42. A few months later in the midst of the Papon trial, a former president of the Bordeaux law bar asked for forgiveness for the five wartime victims of his bar and urged his colleagues to do the same. Dominique Simonnot, "'Moi si je vole, je vais au gnouf tout de suite,'" *Libération* (October 14, 1997). While the 1997 apology may have thus had resonance beyond Paris, no other bar seconded the gesture.

43. See, for example, Richard Weisberg, 1996, *Vichy Law and the Holocaust in France* (New York: NYU Press); *Juger sous Vichy*, 1994, (Paris: Seuil, Le Genre humain); *Le Droit antisémite de Vichy*, 1996, (Paris: Seuil, Le Genre humain).

44. Robert R. Weyeneth, "The Power of Apology and the Process of Historical Reconciliation," *The Public Historian* 23.3 (Summer 2001), p. 22.

45. "Avocats," *Les Annonces de la Seine* 19 (March 10, 1997).

46. Olivier Abel, "Le pardon ou comment revenir au monde ordinaire," *Esprit* (August–September 2000), p. 76.

47. Marie-Françoise Masson and Bernard Gorce, "Maintenant, nous pouvons nous embrasser," *La Croix* (October 2, 1997).

48. Patrick Henry, "The French Catholic Church's Apology," *The French Review* 72.6 (May 1999), p. 1102.

49. Robert O. Paxton, 1972, *Vichy France: Old Guard and New Order, 1940–1944* (New York: Columbia UP), pp. 148–153. See also Etienne Fouilloux, 1997, *Les chrétiens français entre crise et libération, 1937–1947* (Paris: Seuil).

50. The integral text was reprinted in *La Croix* (October 2, 1997) and *Témoignage chrétien* (October 3, 1997). *Le Monde* had published a draft of the text on October 1, which differed significantly from the final version. Jean Duchesne, "Letter from Paris," *First Things* 80 (February 1998), pp. 12–14.

51. Pierre Georges, "Repentance,"*Le Monde* (October 1, 1997).

52. Henri Tincq, "L'épiscopat français va demander pardon à la communauté juive," *Le Monde* (September 22, 1997).

53. Ironically, the Vatican's own acknowledgment, filled with ambiguity and euphemism, was a disappointment to Jews and many others when it was finally issued in March 1998. Zeev Sternhell, "Une occasion manquée," *Le Monde* (March 21, 1998). See also Henri Tincq, "Le silence persistant du Vatican sur la Shoah," *Le Monde* (October 2, 1997); François Bédarida, "Des controverses à la repentance," *Le Monde* (September 30, 1997).

54. Henri Tincq, "L'épiscopat souhaite un changement d'orientation de la politique d'immigration," *Le Monde* (November 11, 1997).

55. Mgr. de Berranger quoted in Jean-Paul Monferran, "Déportation des juifs sous Vichy: l'épiscopat français se repent," *L'Humanité* (September 30, 1997).

56. "Votre déclaration marquera son temps," *La Croix* (October 2, 1997); and quoted in Anne-Emmanuelle Kervella, "Une aussi longue attente," *Réforme* (October 16, 1997).

57. "Déclaration de repentance des évêques; un acte 'positif' mais 'tardif'," *Agence France Presse* (September 29, 1997). Database online. Available from Lexis-Nexis.

58. Quoted in Claude-François Jullien, "Nous nous retrouverons tous à Jérusalem," *Le Nouvel observateur* (October 2, 1997).

59. "Le repentir de l'Eglise catholique laisse de nombreux Français indifférents," *Agence France Presse* (October 8, 1997). Database online. Available from Lexis-Nexis.

60. Henri Tincq, "L'acte de 'repentance' des évêques largement approuvé," *Le Monde* (November 27, 1998).

61. Jean Duchesne, "Letter from Paris," *First Things* 80 (February 1998), pp. 12–14.

62. Henri Tincq, "La presse confessionnelle unanime après la repentance de Drancy," *Le Monde* (October 4, 1997).

63. Elie Maréchal, "Mgr. de Berranger: 'L'Eglise doit se purifier,'" *Le Figaro* (November 6, 1997); "La déclaration de repentance de l'Eglise suscite des incompréhensions," *Le Monde* (November 6, 1997).

64. Albert Chambon, "Le 'silence de l'Eglise,'" *Le Figaro* (October 16, 1997); Henri Tincq, "Pour Henri Hajdenberg, la repentance de l'Eglise est un acte capital," *Le Monde* (October 1, 1997); "Les évêques de France se moquent du monde!" *Minute* (October 1, 1997); Henri Tincq, "La presse confessionnelle unanime après la repentance de Drancy," *Le Monde* (October 4, 1997).

65. Abbé René Laurentin, "L'autoaccusation de l'Eglise," *Le Figaro* (October 3, 1997); Claude-François Jullien, "Une très discrète 'repentance,'" *Le Nouvel observateur* (October 23, 1997).

66. Michel Kubler, "Entre repentance et espérance," *La Croix* (November 4, 1997).

67. Annie Delorme, "Demandes de pardon," *Réforme* (October 30, 1997); Christian Terras, "L'Eglise et les juifs, le repentir ambigu," *L'Evénement du jeudi* (October 2, 1997).

68. Quoted in Jean-Paul Monferran, "Déportation des juifs sous Vichy: l'épiscopat français se repent," *L'Humanité* (September 30, 1997).

69. Gobry, Pascal, "Le devoir de responsabilité des fonctionnaires," *Le Monde* (October 14, 1997); Daniel Psenny, "Les pages noires du patronat," *Le Monde* (October 27, 1997).

70. "Réaction d'Henri Hajdenberg à l'annonce d'une déclaration de repentance sur les silences de l'Eglise pendant la période de Vichy," *Le Monde* (July 12, 1997); Henri Tincq, "Pour Henri Hajdenberg, la repentance de l'Eglise est un acte capital," *Le Monde* (October 1, 1997).

71. Bertrand Poirot-Delpech, "Mea culpa," *Le Monde* (October 1, 1997).

72. Philippe Bernard, "Un important syndicat policier demande pardon au 'peuple juif'," *Le Monde* (October 8, 1997).

73. "Vichy," *Le Monde* (October 9, 1997).

74. Bruno Keller, "Le Pr Glorion: 'Un sentiment de regret, un souci de vérité, un devoir de mémoire,'" *Le Quotidien du médecin* (October 14, 1997).

75. Philippe Roy, "Vichy: après la repentance, l'ouverture des archives," *Le Quotidien du médecin* (October 15, 1997).

76. Cited in Annette Lévy-Willard, "L'examen de conscience de l'ordre des médecins," *Libération* (October 11, 1997).

77. Jean-Yves Nau, "Le président de l'ordre des médecins fait acte de 'repentance'," *Le Monde* (October 12, 1997); H.R., "Le mea culpa de l'Ordre," *Impact médecin hebdo* (October 17, 1997).

78. Search undertaken for the *Bulletin de l'Ordre des médecins* from September 1997 to January 1998.

79. See *Conseil National de l'Ordre des Médecins*, http://www.conseil-national.medecin.fr (February 14, 2003).

80. Philippe Roy, "Vichy: l'Ordre des médecins entre en repentance," *Le Quotidien du médecin* (October 10, 1997).

81. Roy, "Vichy: après la repentance, l'ouverture des archives."

82. Trudy Govier and Wilhelm Verwoerd, "The Promise and Pitfalls of Apology," *Journal of Social Philosophy* 33.1 (Spring 2002), p. 76.

83. "Le Quotidien des lecteurs," *Le Quotidien du médecin* (October 20, 1997).

84. Roy, "Vichy: après la repentance, l'ouverture des archives."

85. "Le Quotidien des lecteurs," *Le Quotidien du médecin* (October 23, 1997).

86. Philippe Roy, "L'Ordre sous Vichy: le Pr Kahn critique les conseils départementaux," *Le Quotidien du médecin* (October 13, 1997).

87. For example, see the dossier "Les médecins de Vichy," *Impact médecin hebdo* (October 10, 1997).

88. "Pétain impose ses lois," *Impact médecin hebdo* (October 10, 1997).

89. Roy, "Vichy: l'Ordre des médecins entre en repentance."

90. Keller, "Le Pr Glorion: 'Un sentiment de regret, un souci de vérité, un devoir de mémoire.'"

91. "Le Quotidien des lecteurs," *Le Quotidien du médecin* (October 20, 1997).

92. Paul Benkimoun, "L'homme qui a fait bouger l'ordre des médecins," *Le Monde* (July 11, 2001).

93. See Mark Gibney and Erik Roxstrom, "The Status of State Apologies," *Human Rights Quarterly* 23 (2001), pp. 929–934.

94. "Le Quotidien des lecteurs," *Le Quotidien du médecin* (October 20, 1997).

95. Danièle Lochak, "La doctrine sous Vichy ou les mésaventures du positivisme," in CURAPP, *Les usages sociaux du droit* (Paris: PUF, 1989), pp. 252–285; Danièle Lochak, "Ecrire, se taire... Réflexions sur l'attitude de la doctrine française," in

Le Droit antisémite de Vichy, pp. 433–462. Against Lochak, Michel Troper argued that, on the contrary, it was because the French judiciary lost touch with its positivist heritage during Vichy that it supported legal exclusion. See M. Troper, "La doctrine et le positivisme (à propos d'un article de Danièle Lochak)," In *Les usages sociaux du droit*, pp. 286–292.

96. Jean Marcou, "Le Conseil d'Etat: juge administratif sous Vichy," *Juger sous Vichy*, p. 92.

97. Patrice-Henry Desaubliaux, "1940–1944: les accommodements du Conseil d'Etat," *Le Figaro* (November 17, 1997); Rafaële Rivais, "Le Conseil d'Etat reconnaît ne pas avoir lutté contre Vichy," *Le Monde* (November 16–17, 1997).

98. "L'Etat français responsable des déportations sous l'Occupation," *Libération* (July 9, 2002); J.-M. Dy, "Le Conseil d'Etat oblige l'Etat à payer la moitié du montant des condamnations civiles prononcées contre Maurice Papon," *Le Monde* (April 13, 2002).

99. Benoît Hopquin, "Le sport français s'interroge sur son attitude sous Vichy," *Le Monde* (December 11, 1998).

100. Clara Dupont-Monod, "La SNCF rattrapée par les fantômes d'Auschwitz," *Marianne* (August 23–29, 1999), pp. 26–29; Philippe Boggio, "La juste distance," *Marianne* (August 23–29, 1999), p. 28; "La SNCF poursuivie pour complicité dans l'Holocauste," *Le Monde* (June 15, 2001); Emmanuelle Réju, "La SNCF fait son devoir de mémoire," *La Croix* (June 21, 2000).

101. *Juger sous Vichy*, 1994, (Paris: Seuil, Le Genre humain).

102. See among others, Gérard Noiriel, 1996, *Sur la "crise" de l'histoire* (Paris: Belin).

103. Luc Beyer de Ryke, "Refus de repentance," *Réforme* (November 13, 1997).

104. Philippe Moreau Defarges, "Repentance, la rédemption et le calcul," *Débat* 112 (2000), pp. 133–134.

105. See for example, François Maspéro, "Tous coupables?" *Le Monde* (December 11, 1997); Pierre Bourget, "Au guichet de la repentance," *Le Monde* (October 23, 1997).

106. Robert R. Weyeneth, "The Power of Apology and the Process of Historical Reconciliation," *The Public Historian* 23.3 (Summer 2001), pp. 25–29.

107. Jean-Jacques Delfour, "L'Arnaque des repentances," *Raison présente* 133 (2000), pp. 63–68.

108. See Jean-Michel Chaumont, 1997, *La concurrence des victimes: génocide, identité, reconnaissance* (Paris: Découverte).

109. Stéphane Courtois et al., 1997, *Le Livre noir du communisme: crimes, terreur et répression* (Paris: Robert Laffont).

110. Christiane Chombeau, "Un meeting catholique traditionaliste dénonce les crimes du communisme," *Le Monde* (November 11, 1997); Lucien Kieffer, "Les mêmes instincts," *Le Monde* (December 15, 1997); Pascal Virot, "Ouverture du XXXe congrès du PCF," *Libération* (March 23, 2000).

111. Raoul Girardet, "Repentances sélectives," *Le Figaro* (October 29, 1997).

112. François Maspéro, "Tous coupables?" *Le Monde* (December 11, 1997). See also Max Milner, "De quoi oublierons-nous de nous souvenir?" *Le Monde* (November 22, 1997).

113. "La République célèbre le 'J'accuse'," *La Tribune* (January 12, 1998); Alain Salles, "La repentance de *La Croix* et l'affaire Dreyfus," *Le Monde* (January 13, 1998); Pierre Georges, "Ici et maintenant," *Le Monde* (January 16, 1998); Daniel Schneidermann, "Au revoir, M. Zola," *Le Monde* (January 19, 1998).

114. Philippe-Jean Catinchi, "Penser l'abolition; Réponse à la mondialisation," *Le Monde* (April 24, 1998); "La dette de l'esclavage," *Le Monde* (April 27, 1998); Jean-Louis Saux, "Une proposition de loi qualifie l'esclavage de crime contre l'humanité," *Le Monde* (February 19, 1999); Louis Sala-Molins, "Esclavage: une mémoire à peu de frais," *Le Monde* (February 23, 1999); Amadou Lamine Sall, "Pardonner sans jamais oublier," *Courrier international* (March 18, 1999).

115. Jean-Louis Saux, "Le document confidentiel sur le contentieux colonial," *Le Monde* (February 25, 1998).

116. As police prefect in Paris, Papon was responsible for the killing of Algerian demonstrators on September 17, 1961.

117. See for example, Henry Rousso, "La guerre d'Algérie et la culture de la mémoire," *Le Monde* (April 4, 2002); Rousso, "La guerre d'Algérie, la mémoire et Vichy," *L'Histoire* 266 (June 2002), pp. 28–29; William B. Cohen, "The Algerian War and French Memory," *Contemporary European History* 9.3 (2000), pp. 489–500.

118. Paul Aussaresses, 2001, *Services spéciaux Algérie, 1955–1957* (Paris: Editions Perrin).

119. "Plus de la moitié des Français pour la repentance," *Agence France Presse* (May 9, 2001). Database online. Available from Lexis-Nexis.

120. "Guerre d'Algérie: Lionel Jospin se dit hostile à une repentance générale," *Les Echos* (May 17, 2001); Sylvia Zappi, "M. Chirac exprime 'la reconnaissance de la nation' aux combattants harkis," *Le Monde* (September 26, 2001).

121. Alain Joxe, "Repentons-nous sur l'Algérie et parlons vrai," *Le Monde* (November 11, 1997); Jean Baptiste de Montvalon, "Alain Madelin célèbre la France pluriculturelle et plurielle et appelle à la repentance," *Le Monde* (November 11, 2000); Mohamed Haddouche and André Wormser, "Justice pour les harkis, en Algérie et en France!" *Le Monde* (June 17, 2000); "Plus de la moitié des Français pour la repentance," *Agence France Presse* (May 9, 2001) Database online. Available from Lexis-Nexis; Nacira Guenif-Souilamas, "En finir avec l'impensé colonial," *Libération* (January 24, 2002).

122. Kathleen Gill, "The Moral Functions of an Apology," *Philosophical Forum* XXXI (Spring 2000), p. 23. On the power differential between perpetrator and victim groups, see also J. Harvey, "The Emerging Practice of Institutional Apologies," *The International Journal of Applied Philosophy* 9.2 (1995), pp. 57–65.

123. Roger Cohen, "France Confronts Its Jews, And Itself," *New York Times* (October 19, 1997).

124. Tony Judt, "Entre le tabou et l'obsession," *Le Monde* (September 21, 1994).

125. *Vichy: An Ever-Present Past*, p. 198.

126. Pierre Birnbaum, "Sur un lapsus présidentiel," *Le Monde* (October 21, 1994).

127. Quoted in H.R., "Procès Papon; 'Une fonction pédagogique'," *Impact médecin hebdo* (October 10, 1997).

128. Nicolas Weill, "Les Français face à la mémoire de Vichy et de la Shoah," *Le Monde* (November 27, 1998). This nonetheless represented a decrease from 79 percent who expressed the same opinion in July 1995. Maurice Szafran, "Vichy et les juifs: Chirac a raison," *L'Evénement du jeudi* (July 27, 1995).

129. Jean-Pierre Rioux, "Devoir de mémoire, devoir d'intelligence," *Vingtième siècle* 73 (January–March 2002), p. 161.

130. Roy L. Brooks, "The Age of Apology," In Brooks, ed., 1999, *When Sorry Isn't Enough*, p. 3 (New York: NYU Press).

CHAPTER 13

Justice, Apology, Reconciliation, and the German Foundation: "Remembrance, Responsibility, and the Future"

J . D .   B I N D E N A G E L

The growing shortage of labour also led to a shift in the function of the SS-run concentration camps... Whereas prior to 1942 they had been run primarily as institutions of 'destruction through work', with the work performed there having no real economic function, they were thereafter used as sources of additional labour for direct and indirect deployment in armaments production.

—Neil Gregor, 1998, in *Daimler-Benz in the Third Reich*, p. 194, Yale University Press

On orders from my department, I too drove a gas van from Berlin to Minsk. These vans had been constructed with a lockable cargo compartment, like a moving van... I was detailed with the gas van to about twelve convoys of arriving Jews. It was 1942. There were about a thousand Jews in each convoy. With each arrival I made five or six trips with my van. Some of the Jews were shot. I myself never shot a single Jew. I only gassed them...

—Erich Gnewuch's personal testimony in E. Kogon, H. Langbein, and A Rueckerl, eds., 1993, *Nazi Murder: Documentary History of the Use of Poison Gas*, pp. 57–59, Yale University Press

It is now therefore even more important that all survivors receive, as soon as possible, the humanitarian payment agreed today. I know that for many it is not really the money that matters. What they want is for their suffering to be recognized as suffering and for the injustice done to them to be named injustice. I pay tribute to all those who were subjected to slave and forced labor under German rule, and, in the name of the German people, beg forgiveness. We will not forget their suffering.

—German President Johannes Rau, Statement before Holocaust survivors at Schloss Bellevue in Berlin, December 19, 1999

1. Introduction: The Holocaust, Forced Labor, and Reconciliation

Sixty years after millions perished in the horrific events of the Holocaust, the Holocaust continues to serve as an ever-present reminder of what can happen when individuals allow racial, ethnic, and religious differences to divide a local, regional, and even international community. The images of malnourished men, women, and children being worked to death in concentration camps in support of the Nazi war effort, being gassed in chambers and burned like rags, continue to haunt and remind us of the importance of tolerance and the need to fight xenophobic nationalism. Fortunately, the end of World War II brought an end to National Socialism and the enslavement of more than ten million people who served as forced laborers in nearly every economic sector—manufacturing, service industry, agriculture, social services. The US occupation authorities launched the first German restitution and compensation programs in 1947 and sowed the seeds for hopes of reconciliation among those nations whose surviving victims' lives had been shattered. Unfortunately, a few short years after the end of the Second World War and after West Germany created its restitution and compensation laws that included payments to Holocaust survivors and support for the State of Israel, new compensation programs that could reach the majority of forced labor survivors—Poles, Ukrainians, and Russians—were no longer initiated. Reconciliation between perpetrator and victim, particularly victims who were behind the Iron Curtain, was set aside with the onset of the Cold War.

The 1948 Berlin Blockade ended the Second World War Great Powers Alliance and began the division of Germany and Europe into competing ideological camps across the Cold War divide. On August 12–13, 1961, the Berlin Wall was erected to serve as a physical barrier dividing Berlin. East Germans viewed the wall as an encroachment on their freedom and fled the country in secret compartments of cars, inside surfboards, in balloons, and in makeshift planes. Originally erected with barbed wire and cinder blocks, this symbol of divided Europe was later transformed into a massive structure made of concrete walls, topped with barbed wire and guarded with watchtowers, gun emplacements, and mines. From the time it was erected until its collapse, the wall had at least three major purposes: as a deterrent to the East German "brain drain," as an "antifascist protection barrier" for the East German government, and as an obstacle to restitution efforts in Eastern Europe for surviving Holocaust and forced labor victims. With the fall of the Berlin Wall in 1989 and the collapse of the Soviet Union in 1991, hopes of reconciliation were rekindled.

Beginning in 1947 with the US Occupation Law 59 and continuing through West German claims processes such as the BEG and Brueg restitution programs as well as Adenauer's Luxembourg Agreement through 1970, the US and German governments set about to make compensation and restitution in the West. In addition, the Conference on Jewish Material Claims against Germany was established in 1951 and has continued through unification to administer programs for Holocaust victims. As the heir to heirless Jewish property, it sells the property to make compensation or other payments in memory of the Holocaust.

Continuity in German compensation programs was assured by the Baker-Genscher exchange of letters in 1990 at the time of unification. In these letters, which came as the Cold War ended, the German Government assured the US Government with the 1990 agreement on Germany's unification, the Final Treaty on Germany (also known as the 2+4 Treaty) that it would continue its compensation after unification; and Germany did launch a $700 million humanitarian effort in the 1990s for victims in Eastern Europe. After the fall of the Berlin Wall and dissolution of the Communist East German regime, the US Government has continued to work with the German Government to engineer significant and successful efforts to bring justice to victims of the Holocaust and forced labor survivors. In 1998, the United States, France, and the United Kingdom established the International Nazi Persecutee Relief Fund (NPRF) for humanitarian relief. Developed in the midst of legal battles and with contributions from countries that had participated in the Nazi-looted gold Tri-Partite Gold Commission, the NPRF, a $60 million fund, assisted victims of the Nazi regime who had received little or no compensation in the past and were in need of financial assistance. The United States and likeminded leaders in Germany, Austria, France, and others in Europe have worked together to restore victims' property and provide humanitarian payments—not reparations payments—to victims of the Nationalist Socialist regime, although acceptance of responsibility and apology have not always followed.

In addition to compensation programs, the international community has also taken steps in the late 1990s to address the attitudes that foster intolerance, prejudice, and ethnic hatred. Through the work of the Task Force for International Cooperation on Holocaust Education, Remembrance, and Research, individuals are becoming educated about the past in order to prevent future occurrences of violence and genocide. More than fifteen national governments are cooperating to support the work of educators in developing curriculum and relevant materials to teach the enduring lessons of the Holocaust. As a result of these actions taken by the international community, the process of reconciliation has accelerated.

Individuals often consider reconciliation and apology to be synonymous terms. However, defining and achieving reconciliation requires that words be accompanied by action. The United States government, along with the international community, collaborated to create a systematic approach to reconciliation for victims of Holocaust injustices: apology, monetary compensation, and preservation of memory. While none of the three alone can adequately address the needs of victims or further reconciliation efforts, together they are capable of facilitating tremendous results. Although this process has been successful in reconciliation for the injustices of the Holocaust, its applicability to other victims of injustices will test its longevity. This is really the challenge facing the politics of reconciliation. This is where this systematic approach to reconciliation for victims of Holocaust injustices—apology, monetary compensation, and preservation of memory—will be tested. The critical element is whether payments can reach survivors in their lifetimes, and if not, whether the preservation of memory can be the basis for reconciliation.

Over the past few years, leaders in the United States, Germany, Poland, the Czech Republic as well as other Central and Eastern European countries and the State of Israel engineered a significant and successful effort to bring an additional measure of justice to Holocaust and forced labor survivors since the early 1950s. Through eighteen months of negotiation culminating in the signing of a US-German Executive Agreement, legislative action in the Bundestag and dismissal of lawsuits against German firms in the United States by US courts, a German Foundation, "Remembrance, Responsibility, and the Future," was created to deliver dignified payments to survivors.

An official apology from the President of Germany recognized the victims' suffering and asked forgiveness, paving the way for reconciliation among perpetrators and victims of the twentieth century's most horrible crime. The Foundation must distribute the money in the survivors' lifetimes and also establish a program in the Future Fund to preserve the memory of those who died. The Foundation also has helped create legal peace for German companies in the United States for crimes arising from the National Socialist era and World War II.

2. The Task of Remembrance

Apology cannot come without understanding. Understanding history comes from knowing historical facts. Without the truth, history will remain an obstacle to the future. Former German President Richard von Weizsäcker recognized that the unspeakable truth of the Holocaust was, and will remain, part of German history. Nevertheless, in a speech on May 8, 1985, the fortieth anniversary of the end of the Second World War in Europe, he said: "There is no such thing as the guilt or innocence of an entire people. Guilt, like innocence, is not collective but individual."

Weizsäcker stressed, however, the importance of memory when he said: "All of us, whether guilty or not, whether old or young, must accept the past. We are all affected by its consequences and held responsible for it. Young and old must and can help one another to understand why it is vitally important to keep the memory alive." Weizsäcker noted that for the victims of the Holocaust the desire to forget prolongs their exile, whereas memory is the secret of redemption.

The dimensions of the Holocaust and World War II forced labor require careful examination and recognition that historical identity is not fixed. Neither is historical interpretation of a country's past immutable. History is written as much to shed light on the present as on the past. Our understanding of the past reflects our perceptions and evaluation of the present.

In our search both for justice for survivors and reconciliation between perpetrators and victims, the parties in this process faced daunting twin problems of remembrance and responsibility. Recognition of the horrible suffering of those forced laborers who survived led the United States to two goals: justice for survivors in the form of payments, and making those payments in their lifetimes. The wrongs committed by the Nazis were so horrible in fact, so pervasive in impact, and so injurious to human dignity as to challenge the concept of obtaining justice. The very idea of achieving justice for so many, for such suffering, and over such a prolonged period of time was discouraging. Money alone could not compensate the victims for their suffering. It is too crass a commodity of exchange, and, in any event, there is not enough of it. Money could not be the last word on the Holocaust. Survivors insisted that they were not interested in payments alone; there must also be efforts to protect the memory of the Holocaust and the crime of forced and slave labor.

3. Developing US Policy: Remembrance and Justice

Remembrance of the Holocaust was not a concern only for Germans. Leading American political figures at the end of the twentieth century also recognized that, symbolically, the international community needed to reaffirm its commitment to human dignity and resolve twentieth century issues before a new century began. The United States could not rely on earlier programs, which did not reach a majority of the surviving victims.

As the international community revisited the history of World War II and its aftermath, a consensus for action was shaped in stages from ignorance to awareness, denial to recognition, evasion to acceptance of responsibility, apology to reconciliation, and sometimes forgiveness. At the beginning of this long process, ignorance—willful or not—of a conflict and accompanying wrongs needed to be replaced by facts and truth, with all parties, including victims, perpetrators, and bystanders participating in the process. Truth is not easy to come by, even in the best of circumstances.

War and its aftermath obscure, misplace, and destroy information. Witnesses, victims, and malfeasants are killed or disappear. They grow old and senile. For example, of the two dozen or so senior officials who participated in the January 1942 Berlin Wannsee Conference, in which the participants reached a consensus to destroy the Jews of Europe, only a few principal perpetrators survived the War, Adolf Eichmann, the being most notable.

Nevertheless, research on the unfinished business of restitution and compensation was made possible after the close of the Cold War when newly available archives opened hope that understanding the facts would lead to historical truth. The issues of delayed justice and reconciliation were stirred by a growing awareness that began slowly, in an unexpected way. Suddenly, the end of the Cold War made possible commemorations of the Fiftieth Anniversaries of World War II. Although the Fiftieth Anniversary of the September 1, 1939 invasion of Poland preceded the fall of the Berlin Wall, major battles from Stalingrad to D-Day were commemorated. By 1995, after the last Russian troops had departed Berlin and VE-Day was celebrated, attention turned to the unfinished business of understanding the full extent of the history of the Second World War.

Archives opened. Scholarly books began to examine restitution. Lynn Nicholas published *The Rape of Europa* (1994) and revealed that the Nazis had stolen more than 600,000 works of art during World War II. She noted that while the bulk of looted art had been returned after the war, some artworks found their way into museum collections and private hands instead of being returned to the true owners. Other authors wrote of expropriated or unpaid dormant bank accounts and of unpaid insurance claims of Holocaust victims.

Americans also have recognized the need to understand our own treatment of American citizens by the US Government in the Second World War and to consider action to redress historical injustice. The 1990s were a time of apology. In America, we had already examined events in our own history and offered an apology—and sought the victims' acceptance and reconciliation—as well as their offer of forgiveness. In seeking reconciliation with American citizens, Congress in 1988 had passed a law (Public Law No., 100–383) that apologized on behalf of the people of the United States for the evacuation, relocation, and internment of US citizens or permanent residents of Japanese ancestry during World War II. This apology was accompanied by a payment of $20,000 to each victim. However, good intentions to reach the truth, as Bishop Desmond Tutu observed, are not easy. He said that the truth by itself could sometimes just make people even angrier. With these examples in mind, the US negotiators knew from the outset of the negotiations to create the German Foundation that revisiting the history of the Holocaust would prove to be a painful experience, especially for survivors who would relive some of their horrible experiences.

Openness toward historical truth was a first step toward understanding and reconciliation. The 1998 Washington Conference on Holocaust-Era Assets began a new international effort to open archives and research the past, although openness is never as simple and obvious as it sounds. At the Washington Conference, an international consensus was reached on opening archives. During the Washington Conference delegates of the "Task Force for International Cooperation on Holocaust Education, Remembrance, and Research" issued a declaration about the opening of archives pertaining to the Holocaust. The Conference participants endorsed the concept of full archival openness on the Holocaust. The delegates from around the world were determined that the Holocaust is neither to be forgotten nor distorted, and that healing is a solemn duty of all who cherish freedom and human dignity. US negotiators sought to continue the international debate to help guard against biased research that could promote ahistorical local mythologies, ideologies, or politics. A notable example of the success of this approach was the Polish government's acceptance of Polish responsibility of a massacre of Polish Jews by Poles at Jedwabne, as reported by Jan Tomasz Gross in his book *Neighbors* and by the Public Prosecutor Radoslaw J. Ignatiew, of the Polish Commission for the Prosecution of Crimes against the Polish Nation. Acknowledgment of responsibility helps set the standard for truthfulness, acceptance of responsibility, and teaching history. Polish President Aleksander Kwasniewski, speaking on July 10, 2001, the Sixtieth Anniversary of the Jedwabne massacre said: "For this crime we should beg the souls of the dead and their families for forgiveness. This is why today, as the President of the Republic of Poland, I beg pardon. I beg pardon in my own name and in the name of those Poles whose conscience is shattered by that crime."

Historical research was underway throughout the world when the international community gathered in Washington in the fall of 1998. The Vatican offered to open its archives for historical research of the Holocaust in a step toward fulfilling the concept of full archival openness on the Holocaust endorsed at the Washington Conference. The Vatican established a joint research commission, the Jewish-Christian Reconciliation Commission of the

Holy See, which was expressly charged to research the Vatican archives for the role of the Catholic Church during World War II. In addition, the Vatican issued a 1998 statement, "We Remember: A Reflection on the Shoah," in which it acknowledged the role of individuals in the Holocaust and took responsibility for the centuries-long persecution of Jews. However, the statement was not fully accepted as an apology. The Jewish-Christian Reconciliation Commission was fraught with contention and demonstrated the difficulty and emotion involved in the search for reconciliation between the perpetrators and the victims. Nevertheless, despite the Vatican's commitment to continued research on this period, which is not in doubt, much more historical research from more open archives is necessary to understand the role of the Church in this critical period and to find reconciliation with victims.

More than twenty countries had established historical commissions to review their own countries' behavior during the Holocaust. The United States' commitment to historical research is manifest in the creation of a Presidential Advisory Commission on Holocaust Assets in the United States, which issued its report early in 2001.

A year after the Washington Conference, the Swedish government hosted the Stockholm International Forum on the Holocaust in January 2000, inviting the heads of government from European countries, Israel, Argentina, and the United States to attend. They declared their commitment to plant the seeds of a better future from the soil of a bitter past. Their commitment was to remember victims who perished, respect the survivors still with us, and reaffirm humanity's common aspiration for mutual understanding and justice.

4. Waiting for an Apology

Why did many Nazi victims and their families have to wait a half-century to receive the kind of recognition and tangible demonstration of remorse—the apology—that they so deserved? Why was so much left undone in the compensation programs at the end of the Second World War? Did the compensation programs of the post-war period not close that chapter of history?

One fundamental reason that these issues were reopened in Europe in the 1990s was that the Cold War that had divided Europe finally ended. Millions of Nazi victims who were beyond the reach of international compensation or assistance, so-called "double victims" who suffered under both National Socialism and Communism, could now be reached. In Western Europe, compensation programs initiated by the United States government during the occupation of Germany in 1947—and continued with strong US government encouragement and as a precondition for Germany to reintegrate into the community of nations—were very different; they reached individuals. Survivors of the Nazi terror benefited from serious efforts to return property, as well as special payment and pension plans. West German government compensation programs were quite extensive, and the Germans continue to pay for these programs today. Over 100 billion German marks, some 70 billion dollars, have been paid out directly to victims.

Memory also played an important role in postwar efforts for reconciliation. The horrible suffering of these people was recognized as such, and through education programs and memorials, successive German governments have pledged themselves to bring meaning to the words, "never again." However, although many programs were implemented in Western Europe, survivors in Eastern Europe where most of the survivors lived, were not reached as the Cold War division of Europe cut them off from compensation programs. Despite the fact that much effort had gone into compensation between 1947 and 1956, when the Cold War was at its most dangerous, new compensation initiatives for material losses ended when the programs were completed in 1970. Nevertheless, Americans and Germans take pride in the knowledge that the early US-led compensation effort from the 1940s continued in West Germany throughout the 1960s and was largely successful, if primarily only in the West.

However, after the Korean War broke out, political priorities changed and multinational initiatives to return stolen property to Holocaust victims largely ended. Although the San Francisco Treaty was signed with Japan, ending compensation and reparations claims against them, Germany remained divided and questions of reparations and other claims remained open. However, the US role in occupied Germany diminished with the end of the High Commissioner on Germany. With West Germany joining us as an ally, we turned our attention from the aftermath of the terrible and destructive Second World War to deter and, if necessary, to defend ourselves in a third world war.

The situation of the double victims in Eastern Europe finally began to change fundamentally with the emergence of the Solidarity movement in Poland in 1980, the flight of young East Germans through Hungary to Austria and to freedom in the West, and with the 1989 Democratic Revolution, which brought the fall of the Berlin Wall—the symbol of divided Europe. The 1989 Democratic Revolution in Europe led to the unification of Germany and to the end of the Soviet Union. Those events made it possible for the international community to return to the unfinished business left behind in the 1950s and to reach out to the "double victims" of the National Socialists who were trapped behind the Iron Curtain. Only after the fall of the Berlin Wall and the end of the Cold War could those victims become the center of international attention. Only then could the forgotten victims be recognized by an international community looking for ways to address their suffering.

In the mid-1990s, the international public became outraged that so many victims had remained uncompensated for so long after the Second World War. The Swiss case was illustrative. They had developed and believed in the myth that as neutrals they carried no responsibilities for the victims' fate. When asked about possible dormant accounts they responded with an accounting, but denied political or moral responsibility. Consequently, the Swiss banks became the center of an effort to assign responsibility for compensation to Holocaust victims that began to indict other countries. Austria's belief in its own victimhood as the first victim of Nazi aggression came to an end with Chancellor Vranitsky's 1993 declaration that Austria, too, had some responsibilities that it had not met. The floodgates opened with new historical analysis and new lawsuits in the United States against European banks and companies for crimes arising out of World War II.

5. Assessing and Protecting US Interests

The source for the German Foundation lay in negotiations that began in May 1999. While the political fallout of the Swiss obstructionism was clear to all, the German industry moved to accept responsibility and won the support of the new German government to propose the Foundation Initiative of German Enterprises in February 1999.

A key element in the US Government's decision to negotiate a new compensation program came after leading German industrialists raised the possibility of negotiations with the newly elected German Chancellor Gerhard Schröder. Schröder, who led the Social Democratic Party, which was persecuted by the National Socialists, was very willing to help resolve the forced labor issue with the United States in the fall of 1998. The US Government chose to join the German industry's initiative.

The United States actively intervened to advance broad US policy objectives of pursuing justice through a number of measures, which included:

• First, renewing US sponsorship of justice for victims of National Socialism through a broadly based effort to return stolen property, obtain recognition of suffering, and establish education and social programs in the memory of the victims.

- Second, reminding the international community that the evil forces then tearing at Yugoslavia had relatively recent antecedents and must not be ignored.
- Third, engaging Eastern European countries to reach out constructively to their individual citizens, and also demonstrate in tangible ways what Western democracies — the standard to which the newly independent states of Eastern Europe aspire — have, at their core, fundamental precepts, most especially the sanctity of human dignity.
- Fourth, demonstrating that the international community will hold accountable those who do wrong.
- Fifth, creating international solidarity to address issues, which go beyond a single nation's responsibility, and touch each country, including our own, which failed in some way or other to do its utmost to bring justice to the victims of Nazi terror.
- And sixth, encouraging the developing relationship between Germany and the newly free and democratic nations of Eastern Europe at a time when old wounds were complicating their political relations.

Other forces were at work as well. Plaintiffs' attorneys filed lawsuits in American courts against European businesses operating in the United States. Some cases were against Swiss banks; other lawsuits alleged that Holocaust victims or surviving forced and slave laborers had not been compensated. More lawsuits were filed against German and Austrian companies in forced labor cases, banking issues, and for unpaid insurance claims.

Public opinion in the United States began to be aroused and brought intervention from US state banking and insurance regulators, as well as state treasurers, who questioned the way foreign companies, doing business in their states, had managed banking and insurance accounts during the Holocaust period.

The growing interest in justice for Nazi victims through lawsuits and statements by the World Jewish Congress posed a serious threat to US national interests and brought the plight of victims into government action once again. Our relations with our most important partner in Europe, Germany, could have been at risk if no action were taken. For example, court judgments, regulatory sanctions, and public boycotts against German companies were distinct possibilities. The German and American economies are too closely linked, too mutually dependent, to ignore any potential disruption. German investment in the United States is responsible for more than 600,000 jobs in America. German industrial investments are the key businesses in several regions of the United States. The operations of more than 1,800 American companies in Germany make vitally important contributions to their economy and ours.

This litany of potentially dangerous economic consequences does not even address the effect sanctions, boycotts, and court judgments would have on US political and security interests. We also faced the distinct possibility that public or private actions against Germany or its companies likely would result in retaliation against American firms by the European Union. The US Government began to recognize that in reinvigorating its effort to right old wrongs, the United States could advance both important foreign policy objectives, and also ward off a serious threat to US interests.

It was in this context that in response to German industry and the German government that the United States decided to help untangle the historical injustice of forced labor from the conduct of business in the United States by German firms.

6. Responsibility for Historical Injustice

It did not take long to understand that facts and information alone, essential as they are, are not sufficient to resolve the conflicts that continued to fester among the victims because of historical injustice. The next, equally important, step was recognition and acceptance of responsibility for historical injustice. Individuals, groups, and governments need to confront the past honestly, without excuses or evasion. German industry voluntarily accepted the historical responsibility of German business during the Third Reich. This German industry acceptance triggered a painful, complex, and anguishing negotiation.

The willingness of German industry, under the leadership of Dr. Manfred Gentz of DaimlerChrysler, Dr. Rolf Breuer of Deutsche Bank, and Dr. Henning Schulte-Noelle of Allianz, was quite remarkable. In the fall of 1998 when German businessmen first approached the United States and expressed willingness to accept responsibility for German industry in World War II, even when the individual companies established after the Second World War had no legal predecessors to companies that were complicit in the National Socialist crimes, German industry offered to create a new German foundation to make payments to victims. German industry's February 1999 announcement of the "Foundation Initiative of German Enterprises" to address forced labor and other claims arising out of the National Socialist period launched negotiations among survivors, industry, and governments to find a mutually acceptable solution.

7. Negotiations for a German Foundation and Legal Peace for Germans

The negotiations that led to a US-German Executive Agreement and a Joint Statement of the negotiating parties were not about money and legal peace alone; the United States also sought reconciliation among survivors and the Europeans for injustices arising out of World War II. Holocaust survivors and Eastern European forced laborers, especially Polish, Russian, and Ukrainian forced labor survivors who were denied compensation in the Cold War, were joined together in this effort from the start by US efforts to include forced laborers in the negotiations along with Holocaust survivors.

Reconciliation between the perpetrators and victims; that is, between the Germans and the Poles and the Holocaust survivors was a key aspect of the negotiation and it required creative American diplomacy. In the middle of the negotiations President Clinton wrote to German Chancellor Schröder on December 13, 1999 and argued that German-American relations are based on our common commitment to human dignity coming from a shared history of democracy for over fifty years. Clinton praised this unique German initiative to reach out to the victims of this century's most horrible tragedy, and he argued that it would convey dramatically to the entire world Germany's commitment to justice and human rights. Clinton stated that the German initiative would allow the United States and Germany to enter the new millennium together, determined to protect the inviolability of human dignity. Germany embodied its commitment to human dignity in the first article of the constitution for the Federal Republic of Germany founded in 1949. Chancellor Schröder, when he replied to President Clinton on December 14, 1999, said that "[m]ore than anything else, the understanding reached on the Federal Foundation is a significant humane gesture of our responsibility toward Nazi victims at the close of this century."

The negotiations opened new avenues for communication and mutual understanding among the many involved governments, businesses, and interest groups. The United States took on a facilitation role that followed an American tradition of mediation of disputes between governments. This role is as old as Theodore Roosevelt's success in ending the Russo-Japanese War in

1905 (when the Russian Foreign Minister was Vladimir Lambsdorff, a distant relative of the German negotiator Graf Lambsdorff). However, US involvement in private lawsuits, such as those brought by former forced and slave laborers against Nazi industry, was unprecedented and required a unique formulation.

While the negotiations to establish the German Foundation focused on legal issues for the companies and monetary compensation for victims, the preservation of Germany and America's commitment to the inviolability of human dignity remained the political underpinning of the talks; reconciliation was an important goal.

8. Eighteen Months of Negotiations

Dr. Otto Graf Lambsdorff, Special Representative of the Chancellor, and Stuart E. Eizenstat, US Deputy Treasury Secretary, ably led the negotiations. Both sides sought dignified payments for survivors and negotiated US help to achieve the dismissal of the lawsuits against German business. Victims' groups were well represented by US plaintiffs' attorneys, their governments, and by foundations and NGOs. For example, the Conference on Material Claims against Germany, the World Jewish Restitution Organization, the American Gathering of Holocaust Survivors, and the Israeli Survivors Organization represented Jewish victims with the representatives of the State of Israel. Reconciliation efforts on behalf of the perpetrators fell to German President Rau, who recognized the suffering of forced laborers, which was necessary for reconciliation.

In the negotiation itself the US negotiators, which was a part of, faced competing agendas from the participating parties. The large number of players made traditional diplomatic negotiations between governments unworkable. In addition to the government of Germany, there were other players in the forced and slave labor negotiations: the numerous companies that employed Nazi victims; international Jewish agencies that had never stopped seeking justice; the governments of countries where most of the unrecognized Nazi victims resided (Eastern Europe and Israel); five non-governmental organizations from Eastern Europe dedicated to assisting victims; and scores of plaintiffs' lawyers. There also was the need to consult closely with our own state and local governments; they sought to impose sanctions on German companies or seek divestment by State treasurers of funds invested in Germany. We wanted their actions to advance, not retard, our efforts to reach agreement.

For the forced labor negotiations—the centerpiece of our efforts—we assembled an unusual interagency US Government team of diplomats and lawyers from the Departments of State, Treasury, and Justice capable of negotiating, simultaneously, with representatives of several foreign governments, hundreds of European companies, a score of American class action lawyers, Central and Eastern European reconciliation foundations, a United Nations organization, and forced and slave labor survivor groups. We opened and maintained a regular dialogue with Congress and with state-level agencies, such as treasurers, comptroller's offices, and pension funds that had a stake in the result. This was a unique organizational and procedural approach to an extremely complex international negotiation.

United States negotiators were clear on the criticality of the issues that they faced. They had identified the US national interests at stake and chose a role, however, as a facilitator of negotiations among victims' groups, companies' representatives, lawyers and government officials. Because standard diplomatic practices alone, such as government-to-government talks, would not work, we invented new ones to include businesses, lawyers, NGOs, State government officials, and foreign foundations. In addition to governments, we worked closely with survivors in Poland and East Europe as well as the Jewish Claims Conference and Holocaust survivor organizations from the United States and the State of Israel. The creative process included a new role for plaintiffs' attorneys and state regulators in diplomacy. It was the state regulators, for example, who formed the International Commission on Holocaust Era Insurance Claims and in New York created the Holocaust Claims Processing Office.

Agreement was reached in December 1999 on the ten billion German marks to capitalize the new German Foundation, and reconciliation was strengthened by President Johannes Rau's eloquent apology to survivors. In March 2000 agreement was reached on the allocation of the money to the partner organizations, property issues, and the Future Fund. However, before we could sign the US-German Executive Agreement in July 2000, issues of legal peace needed to be decided.

9. The Challenge of Legal Peace

The challenge we faced was how to convert existing class action lawsuits by former slave and forced laborers—which covered only a few thousand plaintiffs and would have dragged on until most of those eligible for benefits had passed away—into elements of a statement of interest in the US-German international negotiation that potentially could benefit over a million surviving victims, and furthermore, how to complete the negotiations within the lifetimes of the survivors. The tension between the class-action lawyers representing the victims and the company representatives seeking legal peace often overshadowed their common goal of reaching out to the victims.

Nevertheless, all sides knew that the key to success and payments for the victims was the resolution of the issue of "legal peace"—dismissal of the lawsuits against companies. European—Swiss, German, Austrian, and French—companies wanted assurances that all litigation and other legal action against them would cease and that they would never be sued again. The US Government could not make such absolute guarantees for two reasons. Our legal system does not work that way. And the US Government would not bar Holocaust survivors who were US citizens from having their cases heard in their own courts. However, we were successful in negotiating an agreement that created a new ten billion German mark (five billion dollar) German Foundation to make payments to victims, while committing the United States, in statements of interest in US courts, to recommend dismissal of all lawsuits arising out of the National Socialist era and World War II against German firms that were pending in US courts as well as any new suits as being in our foreign policy interest.

Here, again, these negotiations called for not just new techniques and formats for managing a complex negotiation, but new approaches to the substance of the negotiation as well. It was the request that the United States file "statements of interest" recommending the dismissal of pending and future cases that required a unique solution never before used. The United States agreed to submit, in each case, a "Statement of Interest," complete with an affidavit by the Secretary of State, citing the important foreign policy considerations that led us to the conclusion that the German Foundation should be the exclusive remedy for these wrongs and urging the courts to agree. After the agreement was signed, the US Government filed statements of interest in numerous cases and based these filings on US foreign policy interests. After long deliberation, the Europeans concluded such statements gave them sufficient confidence the cases would be dismissed for them to agree to our proposed settlement. The courts have dismissed all cases.

The eventual agreement was based on a number of disparate, but key elements:

• The class-action lawsuits brought by American plaintiffs' attorneys on behalf of victims using the 1789 Alien Torts Claims Act as a basis for suing;

- The "Foundation Initiative of German Enterprises," which accepted historical responsibility and in February 1999 proposed establishing a German Foundation to make dignified payments to surviving forced laborers;
- Threats of financial boycotts if the companies did not pay victims were leveled by the World Jewish Congress and the US State Treasurers as well as in public media campaigns against German and Austrian companies;
- US Government agreement to assist in achieving legal peace for German companies in the United States for crimes arising out of National Socialism and the Second World War;
- German Chancellor Gerhard Schröder who, in the midst of a severe budget cutting exercise, pledged full German government financial support for the agreement; and
- German President Johannes Rau, whose poignant words of apology to the victims in the presence of Holocaust survivors, were so healing and so necessary.

10. Examining the Apology

In the presence of Holocaust survivors, President Rau said:

It is now therefore even more important that all survivors receive, as soon as possible, the humanitarian payment agreed today. I know that for many it is not really the money that matters. What they want is for their suffering to be recognized as suffering and for the injustice done to them to be named injustice.
[...]
I pay tribute to all those who were subjected to slave and forced labor under German rule, and, in the name of the German people, beg forgiveness. We will not forget their suffering.

The perpetrator can and should admit his wrongs and ask forgiveness, but only the victim can complete the process. Only the victim can say, "I accept your apology. I forgive you." Obviously, this is the most difficult act of all. On behalf of the victims, Roman Kent spoke after President Rau to explain the pain still suffered by the victims and called for the continued respect for the memory of those who died. Only then, when the victims can accept the apology, is the process complete.

11. Achievements Reached

After the US-German Executive Agreement and the Joint Statement were signed on July 17, 2000, and in order to release the ten billion German marks (five billion dollars) to surviving forced and slave laborers, the US Government engaged in intensive efforts to help secure legal peace for German companies in the United States. This included successful dismissal of some sixty-five lawsuits against German companies by three US Courts. During the months-long process two courts dismissed the slave and forced labor lawsuits and the cases against the insurance companies in the fall of 2000; however the banking cases' dismissal was delayed as an unusual step was taken to seek a writ of mandamus to relieve a federal judge of her decision-making authority. The Second Circuit Court of Appeals considered the writ of mandamus request and ordered the dismissal of the suits against German banks in May 2001.

The dismissal of these final cases ended the delay and reaffirmed the power of the executive branch to set foreign policy goals in international agreements, such as in this case to reach Holocaust survivors and surviving forced laborers. Following that court decision, the United States worked closely with Dr. Otto Graf Lambsdorff to ensure that the Bundestag would vote that "adequate legal peace had been achieved" for German companies in the United States. On May 30, 2001, the Bundestag passed that resolution. German companies then transferred their contributions to the German Foundation, which then began to make payments to survivors.

In its first year of operation, the Foundation Directors reported that nearly 800,000 survivors had received a total of nearly three billion German marks. Such a significant amount of money reaching individuals in such a short time is a tribute to the close cooperation among the partner organizations, notably the Foundation for Polish-German Reconciliation and the Conference on Jewish Material Claims Against Germany.

These positive results reflect the real work of the German Foundation, although there was continued criticism of opponents who would note the outstanding issues of possible additional interest earned during the fund-raising, the ongoing, unsettled negotiations on additional insurance claims process procedures, and money management issues such as the dispute over Zloty exchange rate loss for the Polish allocation. The German Foundation Directors have reported interest earnings that will ensure all commitments to survivors are met. Negotiations have been held between the Foundation and the International Commission for Holocaust Era Insurance Claims (ICHEIC) to resolve the remaining insurance claims handling procedures, including publication of policyholders' lists, audits, and administrative costs. The DM 550 million insurance allocation from the Foundation has been made available for claims and humanitarian payments.

12. Related Agreements Reached in Europe

The United States, the Federal Republic of Germany, Poland, as well as other Eastern European countries, and in other cases Austria, France, and Switzerland, have worked in close partnership to establish institutions through international agreements that hold great promise, not only to do justice for past wrongs, but also to advance the cause of justice in public policy into the future. These institutions include the German Foundation "Remembrance, Responsibility, and the Future," the Austrian Reconciliation Fund, the Austrian General Settlement Fund, and the French Banks supplemental fund. Their establishment of these institutions is tangible evidence of the internationalization of these issues and the promise that the work of justice and remembrance will continue.

In addition, these new institutions will serve to support democracy and freedom in the Central and Eastern European countries as well as to provide benefits to nearly one million of their citizens. One of our most important achievements has been to provide a measure of justice not only to Jewish victims of the Nazi era, but also belated recognition and payments to the hundreds of thousands of "double victims" of two of the twentieth century's worst evils: Nazism and Communism. Moreover, by bringing together Germany, Poland, Austria, France, the State of Israel, and others in the creation of these institutions, we created a new dimension in international cooperation.

These new institutions represent a fulfillment of the United States' postwar effort to address the concerns of victims and the consequences of the Nazi era. They will contribute substantially to US-European efforts to create a stable and humane international community based on democracy, rule of law, and respect for human rights. This kind of international cooperation among the world's strongest allies is crucial to the foreign policies of our countries and to the promotion of peace and stability in Europe. The very complexity of the negotiations—the number of issues and the number of players—became one of its strengths.

The forced labor US-German Executive Agreement is widely accepted as fair, in large part because so many had a real hand in its resolution. Through efforts by US state government officials, plaintiffs' attorneys, authors, publicists, and distinguished political leaders, as well as by leaders of German enterprises and of the governments of Germany, Poland, Austria, France, and others, long-delayed justice has been brought to surviving forced and slave laborers, property is being returned, and insurance policies are being paid.

13. Implications for Future Negotiations

The slave and forced labor agreements reached in 2000–2001 sought to address injustices borne of hatred, racism, anti-Semitism, xenophobic nationalism, and other grievances that led to World War II. Through diplomacy and political negotiations new legal tools were created and played a larger role in diplomacy. Some of our novel solutions have subsequently sparked controversy. Writing in *Foreign Affairs* magazine, Anne-Marie Slaughter and David Bosco assert, "US courts have become a venue of choice for such [Holocaust survivor] suits because they offer plaintiffs the benefits of procedural mechanisms . . . not to mention the prospect of unparalleled media coverage and US Government involvement." The authors go on to name this "Plaintiffs' Diplomacy." Indeed, they argue that class-action suits against corporations for violations of international law are likely to complicate diplomatic relations. It will also likely generate pressure on governments from powerful corporations to stop the practice.

Although two decades ago the concept of "Plaintiffs' Diplomacy" was unknown, as Michael Bazyler has shown, it has become a new legal theory thrust upon, and to some extent accepted by, US courts and state legislatures. Relying to a large degree on the Alien Tort Claims Statute of 1789, three categories of "Plaintiffs' Diplomacy" cases have made their way to US courts. The first category of plaintiffs' diplomacy suits includes suits brought against individuals who have committed grave violations against international law in the name of the government. The second were suits brought against corporations that may have violated international law. Lastly, the third category of suits are those supported by Congress in an effort to achieve justice for victims of terrorism and oppression and filed against foreign governments.

The use of the 1789 Alien Torts Claims Act to engage US Courts in such political settlements of moral questions arising from National Socialism and World War II was a compelling reason for German industry to make its offer to create a new German foundation to make payments to surviving forced laborers. German industry sought "legal peace" for its companies in the United States for acts arising from National Socialism and World War II. However, the legal peace we achieved is likely to have little effect as a deterrent to new foreign policies of ethnic cleansing, revived hatreds, or new economic grievances that lead to new injustice.

Despite success in obtaining legal and compensatory resolutions, the effectiveness and incentive(s) of utilizing the Alien Tort Statute in resolving such suits are still undetermined. Essentially, successful plaintiffs' diplomacy

305

suits have relied on governments to negotiate agreements, as was done in the slave and forced labor cases. These governmental agreements, however, have only yielded two outcomes: (1) monetary payments for victims, and (2) legal peace for companies. Neither of the two fully resolves the issues of reconciliation, nor is broad enough to deter future xenophobia, nationalism, or anti-Semitism.

The danger is that the narrow scope of legal peace and monetary payments may even facilitate political leaders' failure to recognize injustices, to develop ways to remember transgressions, or to apologize to surviving victims or their descendents. Only continued research to determine a fact-based history, such as the reports prepared by historical commissions, which are mandated to determine the truth and to promote political dialogue based on accurate histories can act as a barrier to future injustice.

14. Historical Commissions and Remembrance

Much has already been done over the past fifty years. German historians have written world-renowned histories on the Holocaust and the Third Reich. The new German Foundation also seeks to remember the victims of National Socialism, accepts German responsibility for the Holocaust, and provides "a measure of justice" for survivors and heirs through modest but significant payments for former slave and forced laborers.

Both financial assistance and apology were essential in the German effort. One without the other would have been insufficient. No one believed that several thousand dollars could truly compensate former slave and forced laborers for their suffering and loss, but all could agree that such payments added real meaning to the apology. Moreover, these payments provide valuable assistance especially for Eastern European survivors, all of whom are old and many of whom are poor. But the inability of governments to provide full compensation for the wrongs of the past—to do the impossible—need not prevent governments from doing what is needed and possible. In fact, others have addressed the horrible history of the twentieth century as well. France has reported on the role of the Vichy regime with great detail in the Matteoli Report. Also, the Austrian historical commission, chaired by Clemens Jabloner, completed its research and published its final report in 2003.

In the broadest sense, governments that seek reconciliation have the obligation to resolve conflicts and to restore amicable relationships that facilitate acceptance of an undesirable event or the settlement of a quarrel. The ongoing process of reconciliation—apology, compensation, and remembrance—requires the aggressor and the victims to make a commitment to teaching the lessons of an atrocity in order to prevent it from occurring again. The success of our effort to achieve justice for slave and forced labor survivors will be determined by the continued commitment of those countries to open their archives on their World War II policies, to research the actions of governments during the war, and to uncover the truth of injustices inflicted in the name of their people. The international community at the Washington Conference should be held to their declaration about the opening of archives pertaining to the Holocaust. That commitment was to full archival openness on the Holocaust so that the Holocaust was neither to be forgotten nor distorted, and it held that healing is a solemn duty of all who cherish freedom and human dignity. The Washington Declaration was strengthened by the January 2000 Declaration of the Stockholm International Forum on the Holocaust, which also pledged that nations should strengthen international efforts to promote education, remembrance, and research about the Holocaust. Forgetting would continue to be an injustice to the victims.

We have finally found a process to open archives and remove the historical obstacles standing in the way of understanding the past and of entering a future based on respect for human dignity. Although attempts at reconciliation for Holocaust injustices have enabled us to accomplish tremendous feats, there is still much to be done. Over the longer term, it is our hope that young people in the United States and other countries will benefit from education and remembrance of both the Holocaust and other injustices. As such, they will be able to better understand how and why these acts of inhumanity occurred, the scourge of prejudice, what can happen when the rule of law breaks down, as well as the importance of promoting reconciliation among racial, religious, and ethnic groups so that the persecution and violence that marred the twentieth century is not repeated. Consequently, the international community's work of the Task Force for International Cooperation on Holocaust Education, Remembrance, and Research has also begun to take steps to combat the attitudes that foster intolerance, prejudice, and ethnic hatred, which will help to prevent future occurrences of violence and genocide.

The various historical commissions now engaged in researching and reporting on this history need not only conclude their research and publish their reports, but they also need to lead the debate and help shape their own domestic as well as their foreign policy to understand the utter destruction which these historical policies created, and the implications such policies have for the current realities.

15. Apology, Reconciliation, Deterrence

The agenda is crowded with new initiatives to remember the horrors of twentieth-century Europe in order to bring a measure of justice to surviving victims and to find reconciliation among perpetrators and victims. The German Foundation's Future Fund, endowed with DM 700 million, invests in the future by devoting resources to prevention of future human transgressions. The German Future Fund will foster projects among the peoples affected by these events that will continue to preserve the memory of the victims of the Nazi terror. The Future Fund will also work intensively for a more stable, peaceful, and cooperative region. Through Future Fund projects, the Trustees of the German Foundation are dedicated to fighting the continuing evils of intolerance, hatred, xenophobic nationalism, and anti-Semitism that led to the Second World War.

To their credit, Austrian and French leaders did not allow the philosophical and practical questions to prevent them from embarking on the long road to reconciliation. France created the Foundation for the Memory of the Shoah; Austria created the Reconciliation Fund and has made a provision for the Salzburg Seminar to teach tolerance. Both of these new efforts will preserve the victims' memory and fight against new hatreds. All three instruments—apology, compensation, and remembrance—are essential to Holocaust reconciliation efforts, so should it be for other tragedies. Nothing, even financial restraints, should prevent a country from doing what is necessary or feasible to further reconciliation efforts.

Hopefully there will never be another war with the destructive impact of the Second World War, nor will nations wait so long to provide justice for the victims of conflict. One lesson of the September 11 terrorist attack on the United States is that hatred still dominates the policies of aggrieved parties. Hatred can take many forms, and the risk of weapons of mass destruction falling into the hands of terrorists demonstrates the danger we face. Understanding the lessons of the Holocaust is an urgent task. Fighting against hatred and xenophobia today and preserving the hard-won peace after the Cold War is an important agenda for political, business, civil opinion, and moral leaders.

Donald Kagan, in his book *On the Origins of War and the Preservation of Peace* (New York, 1995), argues that modern states, especially those who triumphed in the Cold War, have the greatest interest in preserving peace and are quite different than ancient Greek or Roman cultures that "venerated the military virtues, deprivation, and subordination to authority." He adds that barriers of conscience that can be used to preserve peace now stand in the way of acquiring and maintaining power. Consequently, a sustained effort to develop such barriers of conscience is needed to prevent new hatreds from dominating domestic and foreign policy again. The slave and forced labor executive agreements with the United States will have limited deterrence effect unless these values are strengthened by actions such as those which the Germans, the French, and the Austrians have begun to defeat the scourge of hatred.

While the United States will continue to be a leader in what is necessarily an ongoing effort, other nations are taking important and independent action. As long as respect for human dignity is the guiding principle for respect among nations, as the American President and the German Chancellor agreed, we will fulfill our pledge to give meaning to the words that echo our hope after the Holocaust—"Never Again."

References

Authers, John and Richard Wolffe. 2002. *The Victims' Fortune: Inside the Epic Battle over Debts of the Holocaust*. New York: HarperCollins.

Bazyler, Michael. March 2000. "Nuremberg in America: Litigation of the Holocaust in US Courts." *University of Richmond Law Review* 34, 1.

Baker, James A. 1990. Exchange of letters with Hans-Dietrich Genscher.

Bindenagel, J.D., ed. 1999. *Proceedings, The Washington Conference on Holocaust-Era Assets*. Washington: US Government Printing Office.

Clinton, William J. December 1999. Exchange of letters with Gerhard Schröder.

Gnewuch, Erich. 1993. E. Kogon, H. Langbein, and A Rueckerl, eds., *Nazi Murder: Documentary History of the Use of Poison Gas*, 57–59. New Haven: Yale University Press.

Gregor, Neil. 1998. *Daimler-Benz in the Third Reich*, 194. New Haven: Yale University Press.

Gross, Jan Tomasz. 2001. *Neighbors: The Destruction of the Jewish Community in Jedwabne, Poland*. Princeton: Princeton University Press.

Kagan, Donald. 1995. *On the Origins of War and the Preservation of Peace*. New York: Doubleday.

Kwasniewski, Aleksander. July 10, 2001. Statement in Jedwabne, Poland.

Nicholas, Lynn H. 1995. *The Rape of Europa: The Fate of Europe's Treasures in the Third Reich and Second World War*. New York: Alfred A. Knopf.

Rau, Johannes. December 19, 1999. Statement before Holocaust survivors at Schloss Bellevue, Berlin.

Regeringskansliet. 2000. *Proceedings, The Stockholm International Forum on the Holocaust*. Stockholm.

Report of the Presidential Commission on Holocaust Assets in the United States. 2001. Washington: US Government Printing Office.

Slaughter, Anne-Marie and David Bosco. September/October, 2000. "Plaintiffs' Diplomacy." *Foreign Affairs*.

Von Weizsäcker, Richard. 1985. A *Voice from Germany*. Berlin: Wolf Siedler Verlag.

CHAPTER 14

The Worst is Yet to Come: Abu Ghraib and the Politics of not Apologizing

ELAZAR BARKAN

"To those Iraqis that were mistreated by members of our armed forces, I offer my deepest apology. [...] It was inconsistent with the values of our nation, inconsistent with the teachings of the military, and it was fundamentally un-American."

"There are a lot more photographs and videos that exist. If these are released to the public, obviously it's going to make matters worse."

Donald Rumsfeld warned Congress that "yet-undisclosed images of Iraqi prisoner abuse containing what one lawmaker described as "rape and murder" might touch off a new furor."[1] The images of abused and tortured prisoners were first aired on CBS on April 28, 2004, following two weeks of negotiations with the Bush Administration as the network attempted to "act responsibly" during war. CBS waited for a response before publishing the report. The Bush administration was not surprised by the revelation, yet it was slow to respond. Although the disclosure of abuse led the news, it took President Bush himself two days to make a public statement. He described the news from Abu Ghraib as "abhorrent" and said he felt "deep disgust." But he did not apologize. The defining image of the war in Iraq was no longer the heroic toppling of Saddam's statue during the fall of Baghdad a year earlier, but rather the torture and abuse suffered by prisoners at the hands of US soldiers. As the photographs of prisoners—hooded and wired, naked and stacked in human pyramids, cowering naked in front of vicious dogs and posturing soldiers—flashed on television sets around the world, the outcry quickly became a political embarrassment for the Bush Administration. The demands for apology and resignations mounted. The crisis over Abu Ghraib was a distilled representation of the state of apology in international politics in the post-9/11 atmosphere. Apology has continued to be a successful political tool, even in conservative circles, but its limitations have been particularly evident when confronted by security and safety.

President Bush's initial response introduced the central element in subsequent official American responses, emphasizing that the abuse did "not reflect the nature of the American people," but merely the "actions of a handful of soldiers," and therefore it "should not taint the tens of thousands who serve honorably in Iraq." In an interview on an Arab television, Bush argued that American citizens "are appalled by what they saw, just like people in the Middle East are appalled." The president repeatedly established parity between the perpetrators and the victims, claiming that we are all in it together: "We share the same deep concerns. And we will find the truth . . . the world will see the investigation and justice will be served." Furthermore, he put the onerous task on the "Iraqi citizens [who] must understand that."

The public discussion and demands for apology provided both a political space for critics of the Administration and an opportunity to explore the morality of the war. As important as the bona fide demand for apology was, it was also an opening to demand that the president would admit his general mistakes regarding Iraq. This seemed such a clear case of abuse that under the old notion of "ministerial responsibility"—whereby a leader is responsible for the actions of his subordinates—Bush should have accepted and acknowledged responsibility, and Rumsfeld should have resigned. The mounting pressure to apologize produced another instance of non-apology the following day. Facing reporters at a White House press conference, accompanied by King Abdullah of Jordan, President Bush described a conversation between the two: "I told him I was sorry for the humiliation suffered by Iraqi prisoners and the humiliation suffered by their families." Simultaneously, Bush engaged in the lowest form of apology—namely using the construct of an apology to blame the victim: he was "equally sorry that people seeing these pictures didn't understand the true nature and heart of America." Instead of being sorry for what the American military had inflicted on the prisoners, Bush blamed the audience and particularly the Iraqis who felt injured, faulting them for "not understanding" the real America. Bush had turned what should have been an apology into an indictment. The president ended his comments with further self-adulation: "I also made it clear to His Majesty that the troops we have in Iraq, who are there for security and peace and freedom, are the finest of the fine, fantastic United States' citizens, who represent the very best qualities of America: courage, love of freedom, compassion, and decency."

The non-apology was widely reported and received with scorn in the Arab world. Some of the criticism was focused on the torture and the abuse. In addition, the symbolism of American torture at the Abu Ghraib prison, where some of the worst abuses of the Saddam Hussein regime had taken place, was particularly devastating. The widespread criticism among Arabs of Bush's apology, however, ought not to be surprising. It was part of the overall anti-Americanism—and "anti-Bushism" in particular—in the region. In the words of the Arab League's ambassador in London, Ali Muhsen Hamid, Arab viewers "will not be persuaded [by Bush], because they don't trust the Americans." There is no doubt much truth to Hamid's claim. But this comforting analysis places the responsibility for the so-called failed apology on the Arab audience ("Bush could never apologize adequately") and avoids the analysis of the politics of the apology itself. An alternative perspective was advanced by a former Arab League Ambassador Clovis Maksoud, who argued that a real apology "would have defused the tremendous amount of anger."[2] This Rorschach-like reading of the "Arab world" is important but has its own limitation. The claim that the US credibility in the Arab world has been shredded by the prisoner abuses in Iraq was largely unsubstantiated. Even *before* Abu Ghraib, the United States had no credibility in many Arabs' eyes. The scandal changed very little. A few people, mostly supporters, may have been particularly disappointed. The torture only enhanced Arab criticism of the United States, and Bush's response, at best, did not improve the situation, and at worst, aggravated it.

Domestically, Bush's critics found ample material to latch on to. Susan Sontag pointed out that the "president was shocked and disgusted by the photographs—as if the fault or horror lay in the images, not in what they depict."[3] One could even push it further to say that he was shocked by the revelation, not by the depiction. While this might be true, it was not what Bush said. The crisis was, no doubt, exploited by the presidents' critics. But Abu Ghraib was a real crisis, and none of it was the making of the Opposition.

1. The Minions Respond

The initial public demand was for top officials to issue apologies and shield the President. National Security Adviser Condoleeza Rice apologized on the Al Arabiya television network: "I couldn't be sorrier that some Iraqi prisoners had to suffer from this humiliation" (May 4, 2004) as did Deputy Secretary of State Richard Armitage in an interview with Al Hurra television. Other apologies came from Major General Geoffrey Miller, the commander at Abu Ghraib, and Brigadier General Mark Kimmitt, the spokesman for the American military in Iraq. All of these apologies emphasized the "small number" of soldiers who were involved in the abuses; the offense of these images to American values; and its inconsistency with military norms, as well as the embarrassment and shame for the military.[4] Condoleeza Rice said: "no American wants to be associated with any dehumanizations," which turned the apology into a political hot potato with little regard or focus on the suffering of the victims.[5]

The apologies by the military in Iraq were more explicit than those in Washington. While the apologies were offered for what the soldiers did to Iraqis, much of the text focused on the injury to the American image and interests and on the embarrassment it caused America. If one reads the text of the apologies devoted to the American suffering from the revelations of the torture and abuse, it is not self-evident who the real victims were. Was it the Iraqi prisoners or the American people and military who were shamed? The claim, before any investigation was conducted, that only a small number of soldiers were involved sounded more like an evolving policy of plausible denial than an apology. Clearly, these apologies by minions were insufficient, and the stakes were being raised. The demand in the media was that President Bush, Defense Secretary Donald Rumsfeld, and Secretary of State Colin Powell had to offer the apology if it were to satisfy the critics. There were even reports that Bush was "demanding" explanations from Rumsfeld, the harshest leaked criticism from the President of a government official during the war. Was anyone going to pay the price for what, as we learned in the following weeks, had been explicit policy, not an aberration?[6] Were the lowly soldiers to be left on their own, or were there to be consequences among the "higher-ups" for the widespread abuse? The critics focused on Rumsfeld, and the White House was sending smoke signals of caving in. It was reported that Rumsfeld had come under fire; that he had angered even some of the Administration's Republican supporters in Congress; and that "Bush said he [had] demanded that Rumsfeld give him a full accounting of what happened at the prison."[7] On May 6, 2004, there was an appearance of possible accountability—Rumsfeld was to testify in front of the Senate and House Armed Services committees. Although Congress was angered as much by not being told by Rumsfeld what the Defense department knew about the abuse allegations before they came to light as by the abuse itself, the domestic criticism was nevertheless gaining momentum.

2. Rumsfeld's Smoke Screen

This was high noon for Rumsfeld, and he responded in style. The secretary had briefed some members of Congress on April 28, 2004, just hours before the story broke—which was two weeks after the administration had begun negotiating with CBS over its broadcasting the pictures. As was to be disclosed later, Rumsfeld was in the midst of it all, but he never mentioned the impending crisis to members of Congress. Shutting them out was offensive, and it did not promise a friendly audience. Resisting as long as he could, and only under pressure and innuendoes from the White House, Rumsfeld returned nine days later to testify on Capitol Hill. Aside from the president's, this was the most widely anticipated apology. Rumsfeld's testimony read like a script. He hit all the right buttons: the apology was directed to the Iraqi victims; he offered his "deepest apology," and even went on to acknowledge that: "I failed to recognize how important it was to elevate a matter of such gravity to the highest levels, including the president and the members of Congress." The failure apparently was of public relations not of policies; the guilt seemed to stem more from the implied disrespect to Congress than from the policies that led to the torture and abuse.

Having moved to reestablish his own credibility with Congress, Rumsfeld, consciously or not, raised the expectations regarding the extent of the abuse by referring to images and facts unknown to the public, which were much worse. "It's going to get a good deal more terrible, I'm afraid," Rumsfeld announced.

One can speculate what these images might be, but it is crucial to remember that Rumsfeld's comments came against the background of disclosures that death in custody had occurred and that widespread torture and abuse were in plain sight. In the military language, soldiers were "implicated in the death" of Iraqi prisoners and were to be "charged with aggravated assault." Several soldiers were put on trial. One soldier was charged with "dereliction of duty" and later in the year "sentenced to 60 days of hard labor," but was not discharged from the Marines.[8] Others did receive prison terms. Information disclosed later included alleged incidents of a female prisoner who was sexually humiliated by US military intelligence officers, and a male inmate who was shot at to force him to cooperate.

With the various US authorities in Iraq handling their own investigations, it was entirely unclear who transgressed and in what way. By election time, the military had investigated fifty-eight deaths, of which nine cases were deemed "justifiable homicide, seven homicides, and twenty-one deaths from natural or undetermined causes." (Twenty-one other deaths were not classified.) There were even indictments for murder, and altogether the military was said to investigate 229 cases of abuse, ranging from these deaths to incidents of theft. The FBI, the CIA, and other agencies did not come under public scrutiny, nor did the privatization and outsourcing of security receive much public exposure. Among other "unknown knowns," in the famous Rumsfeld characterization, was the hiding of "as many as 100 'ghost detainees' from the Red Cross" by the CIA.[9] All of this and much more was the result of the policies formulated and approved of by the Defense Department. Rumsfeld, according to any definition of responsibility, was the person in charge. One must trust that Rumsfeld knows the particulars when he says the additional information is "GOING TO MAKE MATTERS WORSE." Indeed, that would apply to almost anything that came from Iraq following the occupation.

As details emerged and further allegations were made, the sado-pornographic nature of the abuse dominated the news. No doubt the "graphic details" provided for an irresistible mix of voyeuristic titillation and repulsion: "They stripped me naked. One of them told me he would rape me. He drew a picture of a woman to my back and makes me stand in shameful position holding my buttocks."[10] A Staff Sergeant, who was the highest-ranking US soldier sentenced for abusing Iraqi prisoners, was punished with an eight-year jail term. He admitted, among other things, to forcing one group of detainees to masturbate publicly and later piled them naked into a human pyramid. If further evidence was needed to the intertwining of politics, culture, and pornography in the abuse scandal, porn web sites were quick to integrate the category of "Iraq prison abuse Abu Ghraib photos," and "Iraq prison sex pictures directories" together with other fetishes, *Playgirl* magazine centerfold links, and so on. The innocuous Google search instantaneously transformed one from the gruesome to web pages of self-described "maniacal photos."[11]

Rumsfeld's apology was unambiguous, but the context was not one of "we made a mistake, and we will not do it again." Rather, it implied that this was a widespread system and "wait until you hear the full story, then you'll really be shocked." Rumsfeld had been fully aware and involved for a long period in the aggressive policies that instigated the abuses at Abu Ghraib. But this was obviously not part of his apology. Indeed, the administration treated and contained the crisis as an aberration, and it vehemently denied that this was a policy. The ingenious (or merely unscrupulous) part was that Rumsfeld and the administration were denying that this was anything but isolated cases perpetrated by individuals, while raising the bar for a political scandal by alluding to even worse evidence: Their strategy involved formally distancing themselves from using the term torture, limiting the apology to abuse, denying that the practice (torture) was widespread, yet simultaneously warning/titillating the public with the promise/threat of worse images. We are left in suspense, with such a high bar and as the voyeuristic urge remains and controls the sense of outrage, we wait for the other shoe to fall.

When Rumsfeld declared in his six long hours of testimony that "these events occurred on my watch. As secretary of defense, I am accountable for them. I take full responsibility," one may be excused for wondering what he meant. Similar to the apology, the total content of "responsibility" was uttering the word. The insincere apology and the abstract responsibility were clearly not matched by action. Furthermore, the minimal compensation for the abused could have been a potential meaningful action if it were done in conjunction with individual responsibility beyond the low-ranking abusers on the floor of the prison. The lack of consequences for anyone higher-up, together with the extensive evidence of a widely implemented policy of abuse from Guantanamo to Afghanistan and Iraq, testifies that this was a cover-up, not to apology.

The extent of the smoke screen was made apparent as the scope of the policy of torture and abuse became public after the apologies. The additional information was not about supplementary photos, but rather pointed to the direct and extensive responsibility of Rumsfeld and others in the Administration: responsibility for policies, not knowledge about abuses.[12] As the conversation and the internal memos were made public, it became clear that the Administration saw the war against terror as a conflict against "a vast international enemy," which operated outside ordinary constraints of international treaties and the rules of war and concluded from that that the situation permitted extralegal policies which, among other things, ignored the Geneva Conventions as "quaint" and "obsolete."[13]

3. Previous Bush Apologies

Bush, as became apparent during his reelection campaign, does not admit responsibility or mistakes. Some say this is his nature. Yet, the controversy over Abu Ghraib was not the first time Bush was called upon to apologize. His track record is sufficiently varied to enable a contextualization of his response to the crisis. Bush's earliest international apology came in February 2001, in the wake of the sinking of a Japanese ship crew by high school fisheries trainees by a US nuclear submarine. The apology was hand delivered by a special US envoy to Japanese Prime Minister Yoshiro Mori in Tokyo, and followed a phone conversation by Bush, in which "the president expressed his regrets and apologized for the accident and said the United States would do all it can to be of assistance to the Japanese government and the Japanese people."[14]

In April 2001, Bush faced his first serious international challenge, which in retrospect can be viewed as a mild form of a tempest in a teapot. A clash (or crash?) between an American surveillance plane and a Chinese fighter jet over the South China Sea resulted in the death of the Chinese pilot and an emergency landing by the American crew on Hainan Island. The Pentagon claimed it was the Chinese pilot who caused the collision. The crew was detained for eleven days; China demanded an apology before it released the crew; and the crisis endangered Sino-American relations, especially the military contacts. The domestic pressure from conservatives was to not submit to the Chinese demands, namely not to apologize in order to gain the release of the crew. American nationalism was matched on the Chinese side by anti-Americanism. Chinese President Jiang Zemin demanded that the United States apologize for the collision, to which Secretary of State Colin Powell declared: "there is nothing to apologize for." But Powell took a further step by saying the United States was "sorry" for the loss of a Chinese pilot's life, while maintaining the no apology stand. The gap between the sides was chipped away on a daily basis, as neither country was interested in prolonging the crisis. The dispute evolved into a translation of various concepts between apology, formal apology, and regret, with comparable Chinese equivalents, subject to all the cultural misunderstandings. Ten days later, the United States issued a "statement of regret," while insisting "there is no apology." The ambiguous space of mistranslation finally allowed both governments to construe the appropriate construct to their own domestic audience, which ended the controversy: the Chinese accepted the apology that the United States claimed never to have given.[15]

In June 2001, the President issued two further "apologies." First Bush apologized (through a spokesperson) for the Secret Service's removal of a Muslim congressional intern from a meeting between Muslim and White House officials. The fiasco displayed more miscommunications through the administration's efforts to present openness to "every religion," which led to "the president apologizes for it on behalf of the White House." (Presumably more formal than a personal apology, perhaps on behalf of the staff, but not quite presidential, one could understand the designation as either.) To add to the confusion, the intern in question was the son of Sami Al-Arian, a controversial South Florida college professor who was later charged with being "a leader"—primarily a fund-raiser—of the terrorist group Palestine Islamic Jihad and spent extended time in jail.[16]

The second "regret," but not apology, came in response to an alleged rape by a US solider stationed at Okinawa. "We express regret, sincere regret," said the new US Ambassador to Japan, Howard Baker, minutes after arriving at Tokyo's Narita Airport. Baker "reiterated an apology for the incident from US President George W. Bush."[17] In part, the crisis resulted from demands in Japan to renegotiate the US military presence in Okinawa. It was only two years later, in the wake of another rape by a US solider, that negotiations were reopened. The allegation (the solider was later found guilty and sentenced to thirty-two months in prison) was part of a series of "incidents" involving US. military personnel. Consequently, the United States was under intense public pressure in Japan and the immediate goal of the US administration was to stop Japanese efforts to revoke the Japan-US Status of Forces Agreement. The sensitivity was high, in part because the Japanese Prime Minister Junichiro Koizumi had just met Bush on his first visit to Washington, a summit that took place under the cloud of the brewing controversy. Whether Bush issued an apology during the summit is uncertain. Although there were certain anonymous quotes to suggest that Bush himself apologized, the *New York Times* reported that the topic was not discussed at the meeting.[18] Despite the public pressure, apology did not figure prominently in the US response. If there was a "regret," it was clearly too muted to have any public impact. These several cases suggest that in his first six months in office, Bush certainly had opportunities to apologize, and in a limited way he did apologize. But when he did, he did it grudgingly. Although he apologized and instructed others to do so in his name, his style left an aura and an impression that he never did.

The next time Bush was involved in a potential political apology was after September 11. In the months following 9/11, increasing pressure and media reports blamed the Saudis for being complicit with the terrorists. This was viewed as a political burden particularly in light of the cozy relationship between the Bush family and Saudi Arabia. Following a conversation between Bush and Prince Abdullah (October 25, 2001), the Saudi Crown Prince said that the President had apologized for the critical reports in the media. Did the president apologize? Prince Abdullah quoted the President as saying he "was sorry." The White House denied an apology was offered but insisted on not contradicting the Saudi statement. The substance of the crisis—US criticism of the Saudi lack of cooperation in fighting terror—was denied by the administration. The apology double act had to appease the Saudis and the President's conservative supporters.

With the war on terror in full swing, and the criticism of US policies widespread, President Bush did not manage to master the art of apology as a shield for a crisis or to pursue international diplomacy. One critical and potentially controversial relationship for the United States was with South

Korea, especially in light of the increasing likelihood that North Koreas possessed nuclear weapons. Therefore, when a US military's armored vehicle caused the deaths of two Korean middle school girls, the potential crisis was significant, though the reasons might not have been. Similar to Okinawa for the Japanese, the presence of American military and the tension with North Korea are continuous sources of Korean public criticism of the United States. As a result of the accident in the summer of 2002, initial calls and demonstrations in Korea for an apology from Bush were largely ignored, though there was an apology from Colin Powell and a trial of the responsible soldiers. It was in the wake of the soldiers' acquittal in late November that South Korean protests escalated, the issue became involved in the Korean presidential campaign, and the United States tried to assuage the pressure by issuing intermediate apologies through the ambassador and the deputy secretary of state, but to no avail. President Bush had to apologize himself. But even when he recognized it as inevitable, he chose to do so through an announcement and a phone call to the Korean President, not in public. By the time he had reportedly apologized, the protest had its own momentum: Korean protesters went on hunger strikes, and the indirect apology was rejected as insufficient. Tens of thousands of Koreans chose to welcome the New Year with a candlelight vigil and to continue the protest. The Korean protest was partially motivated by the comparison to the apology for Okinawa rape crimes: "It is hard to understand why President Bush is being so stingy with offering an immediate, direct, and sincere apology for the deaths of our middle schoolgirls."[19] Although Bush reputedly had apologized for a rape crime by a soldier in Okinawa, it was compared to the earlier apology by President Bill Clinton, who offered "a personal apology" for a series of crimes (including sex attacks) committed by US servicemen in Okinawa, which provided the model the Koreans were seeking. Clinton was quoted to say he was personally ashamed by the incidents that "hurt me in the heart."[20] There is little doubt that the hobbled public response by the United States made its relations with Korea more difficult. The public protest was built on strong opposition to the American forces and general anti-American political sentiments. But these were inflamed in part because of the slow and partial American response.

4. Confined Apologies

One aspect of the centrality of the apology can be gauged by the performance, where it is put on and who gets the best script. President Clinton and even

Prime Minister Blair frequently have been their own main actors; Bush has been more likely either to delegate the script, or report on having acted it out in private. Instead of apologizing himself, the President is reported to have talked to an ambassador who conveys the regrets, or a spokesperson would report of a phone call where an apology was tendered. In the case of the Abu Ghraib scandal, Bush first responded on Arab television. This had the advantage that it kept him at an arm's length from the American public. Even there, far away from the main stage, and despite wide expectations in Washington that the President would apologize during the interviews, he balked at the chance. Bush did not use the word "sorry." This was a double distancing: neither apologize nor face the American public, where the price of admitting guilt, or responsibility, is seen as having a political cost. Washington was abuzz with the anticipated apology, from talking points reputedly provided by the State Department to leaking to the press by senior Administration aides of the recommendations. The disappointed response in Washington, even more than in the Arab media, led Bush to try to make amends in his meeting the next day with King Abdullah II of Jordan. King Abdullah, as a neighboring monarch, was provided as a prop for an Arab world. Although he was clearly not closely related to the Iraqi people, the Kingdom has always been an American ally, and as such could not be viewed as the "other side" by any stretch of the imagination. The King even distanced his country from involvement in the war by rejecting the notion of sending troops or making any direct contribution in Iraq. Despite these shortcomings, a prop is a prop, and this was the best available on hand. But instead of apologizing—performing an act of contrition—Bush reported to the media that he had done so in private. He simply announced that he had expressed his regrets to the king in their private meeting earlier.

The indirect regrets and the parity of regretting the abuse of the prisoners with the regret of the Arab misunderstanding of American culture did not quell the critics. It was left to others to put Humpty Dumpty together again. Powell "confirmed" the apology at a meeting of Arab leaders in Jordan a week later (May 16, 2004): "The President has expressed an apology on behalf of the nation. I will reinforce that apology. We are devastated by what happened at Abu Ghraib. We apologize to those who were abused in such an awful manner." Powell waited for nearly two weeks to issue the apology, taking some pleasure, one might guess, from watching Rumsfeld sweat it out.

In an age of instantaneous communications, these mediating tactics have only limited impact. It could be that the debate over apology is more important to those who demand it than to the rest of society. If so, the lack of apology would be more harmful to those involved in the debate than to the broader political system. Apology in that sense is interest group politics. One might be excused, however, for concluding otherwise from the media reports. If apology is most important to a particular group, we would assume that it would be a win-win situation, because the aggrieved party is assuaged, while others are hardly involved. But a counter-argument has to be considered. If an apology is viewed by Middle America as a form of weakness and if it taints the apologizer with guilt, hiding the apology from this mildly engaged public may be politically wise. If the reports about the large percentages of Americans who believed in patently false information about Iraq are correct (and it would be hard to dismiss it giving Bush's victory in 2004), large segments of the American public are isolated from mainstream news. By avoiding the first person sound bite "I apologize" in numerous crises, Bush may succeed in "hiding" his involvement and responsibility from his supporters. At least he does not force them to confront his contrition by "admitting" the guilt. The seemingly international cost of the constrained, insincere apologies, cannot a priori be said not to have had a political value or not to have been compensated in Middle America.

Distancing is not a Bush monopoly. Even President Clinton, who was a master of contrition and could convey an apology in a convincing manner, chose at times to distance his apology, as he did in the case of slavery, a potentially controversial matter with political consequences. Clinton's most famous apology—during the Monica Lewinsky scandal—had nothing to do with high international polities but was obviously his lowest moment in public office: this was done on prime time and in the United States. Indeed, Clinton can be said to have made a career of contrition. His first famous use of a political apology was in 1981 in Arkansas, when he announced his reelection campaign by saying he was sorry for letting his supporters down earlier in his first term as governor. The apology succeeded, and he was reelected. In the White House, perhaps Clinton's most important use of apology as a political tool was in addressing race issues. One prominent case was offered seemingly less for political reasons and more as a moral apology to the surviving participants of the Tuskegee Syphilis Study. He did it with a formal ceremony at the White House on behalf of the United States government (May 16, 1997). Toward the end of his time in office came the apology to Native Americans, though not strictly by Clinton, but as part of his administration (see Chapter 9). But it was Clinton's apology for slavery that merits comparison to Bush's effort to distance the act of apology. Despite that similarity, the differences were significant. Clinton gave his apology in Uganda on his African tour, where he acknowledged that the United States was wrong to benefit from slavery. Similar to Bush, Clinton stopped short of an explicit apology: "Going back to the time before we were even a nation, European Americans received the fruits of the slave trade," Clinton said. "And we were wrong in that." In addition, Clinton acknowledged that the United States neglected Africa during the Cold War and too often supported ruthless dictators.

Although Bush was prepped for an apology before his interviews on Arab TV, Clinton was widely reported to have considered and rejected the idea of making an official apology to American blacks for slavery. Somehow, policy mavens concluded that a *mea culpa* would distract from real racial healing by alienating white "centrist" voters. In contrast to Bush, "aides" told journalists that Clinton would not apologize. But unexpectedly, as the *Washington Post* reported, Clinton was overcome by the "spirit of the moment" and extemporized an apology. The major papers in the country debated whether it was an apology, whether it went far enough, or perhaps only came close enough, while critics were imputing motives more related to the Lewinsky scandal. But in the larger context and in historical perspective, it seems as though one president could not bring himself to say sorry, even though the stars were perfectly aligned, while the other could not stop himself, despite the belief that doing so was politically unwise. While Bush chose the distant site to get away from a public apology, Clinton seemed to have been eager to sneak the apology through the distant site, because his advisors judged that the home crowd was not ready for it. If Bush has an aversion to apologies or admitting wrongs, Clinton could not resist the temptation. If one could isolate a personal component in all the overly programmed presidential acts, the two presidents' proclivities to accept responsibility were poles apart.

5. Blair's Apologies

On October 13, 2004 Tony Blair, during Prime Minister's Questions in the House of Commons, declared: "I take full responsibility, and indeed apologize, for any information given in good faith that has subsequently turned out to be wrong." This was his most direct apology for any failures related to the Iraqi war. He also stated that he had apologized before, and he was right. Blair as well as others in his cabinet, including the Foreign Secretary Jack Straw, have repeatedly apologized for the much discredited intelligence reports in different venues. However, Blair did not apologize for any policy mistakes: he rejected claims of misrepresenting the intelligence information he had received, and did not apologize for the war itself, nor would he respond in particular to the repeated claim in the British press that the justification for the war was regime change, which is illegal in international law: "What I do not in any way accept is that there was a deception of anyone. I will not apologize for removing Saddam Hussein. I will not apologize for the conflict. I believe it was right then, is right now, and essential for the wider security of that region and the world." During the summer between the investigative report by Lord Hutton (over the dispute with the BBC, which largely cleared the government of wrongdoing) and following the report by Lord Butler, which cleared the government of distorting the intelligence while arguing that Iraq had weapons of mass destruction, the British press was abuzz with demands for an apology, even more intense than during the previous year, when the Hutton inquiry was ongoing. The scrutiny of the potential apology was discussed at length, as was Blair's statement in the fall at the Labor party conference where Blair said he "could apologize," but not that he "did" apologize, as well as reputedly deleting the word "sorry" from his speech, according to pre-circulated briefs to journalists. Tony Blair might have delivered an *apologia*—a justification of his actions—rather than an apology. He did admit to mistakes but did not apologize. This resistance to apologize, however, has not always been the case.

Indeed even earlier in the spring of 2004, when a "mild" British case of prisoners' abuse in Iraq surfaced, Blair was quick to apologize. The fact that the *Daily Mirror*, which exposed the abuse, actually used faked photos to show the abuse brought a quick end to the affair. The abuse itself was quite real, despite the fake photos, even though it was not as egregious as the American case, and was not part of an explicit worldwide policy. In this case Blair's apology was unreserved: "We apologize deeply to anyone who has been mistreated by our soldiers [...] This is totally unacceptable. Those responsible will be punished according to the army disciplinary rules."[21] Although Blair apologized in an interview on French television while in Paris, it was not quite distancing the apology because it was part of the news cycle, at the top of the news, and he certainly made the apology himself. Blair's propensity to apologize has been evident over the years numerous times: from the famous apology for the Irish famine on the 150 years commemoration (his 1997 letter spoke of the "deep scars" although he did not explicitly apologize. No matter, every news outlet described it as an apology) to more minor affairs such as a scandal over A-Levels examination, the mishaps with the millennium dome, an apology over a campaign-money scandal, to the serious miscarriage of justice in the case of the "Guildford four" (who were wrongly convicted of bombing pubs and spent fifteen years in prison before their convictions were overturned in 1989). He even offered internal apologies to his own cabinet (for not formally consulting them before announcing a referendum on the European constitution) and to Gordon Brown, his ever-expectant heir, after Blair's close aide labeled the Chancellor "psychologically flawed."

In offering these and other apologies, Blair has often been successful at achieving his goals, in most cases bringing to an end a scandal or a political controversy, and saving himself and the government a good deal of negative publicity. Much of the public debate has been over the demands for apologies, although it is hard to find critics more derogatory to, or mocking of apologies than the London press. In those cases where the apology was withheld, the public dispute continued. Critics have blamed Blair for insincere apologies. The question then is why did he not apologize in the case of war? (After all, if the apologies were indeed insincere, one should have little scruples in making further apologies.). Is it plausible that his refusal to apologize actually implies that he was sincere in other cases? The insincerity critique would be compatible with the argument that since the Iraq war is ongoing, an apology would force him to resign, and this would come to define his tenure. Even so, Blair did find space to apologize for the prisoners' abuse and for the mistaken intelligence data. Would he go as far as to suggest that had he known about the correct data, Britain would not have joined the war?

6. Routinized Apology

Among the apologies during the war in Iraq, the most prominent and emotional was the direct apology by Richard Clarke, the former head of US counterterrorist on March 24, 2004 given as a testimony in front of the 9/11 commission: "Your government failed you. Those entrusted with protecting you failed you. And I failed you. We tried hard but that doesn't matter, because we failed. And for that failure, I would ask, once all the facts are out, for your understanding and your forgiveness." Clarke's apology, however, was for failures that led to September 11, for which no other leader apologized. Neither was there any apology forthcoming for the war in Iraq. Perhaps as the war was being pursued, it was unrealistic to expect such an apology.

But when it comes to distinct aspects of the war, it was not too much to expect accountability and responsibility. Indeed, Blair apologized, partially for the misleading information, and completely for the abuse of Iraqi prisoners. The debate over whether Bush apologized, the fact that everyone else in the administration did, together with the knowledge that an investigation was going on and that more damning evidence would be exposed contributed to

divert public attention from the scandal. The anticipation for more information, in particular with a delayed military investigation; perhaps the prospect
of bombshells and the contentious case of allegedly missing documents cu-
riously created a lull in the eye of the storm. Possibly, under more tenacious
criticism it would have fanned the fire, but in this case the apology combined
with expectations led to a pause in the scandal.[22] In the medium term, the
most important factor perhaps was the increased insurrection in Iraq, which
distracted attention from the torture and abuse. In the 2004 presidential election campaign the debate never really progressed beyond generalities, so no
attention was devoted to the question of torture. Indeed, the first new cabinet member proposed for the second Bush term was White House counsel
Alberto Gonzales, who was responsible for the infamous "torture memos"
and the policy of declaring the Geneva Convention "quaint" and inapplica-
ble. There was little public criticism of Gonzales' nomination to be Attorney
General.

In the post-9/11 world, security is far more urgent than moral considerations
for most of the public. When essential security considerations collide with
what is viewed as moral obstacles, advocacy of security wins out. As long
as there is a belief that under certain circumstances torture is necessary to
achieve security, the torture can be excused or preferably ignored. The public
is willing to be misled that torture is the exception, not the policy. But getting
away with illegality is not the same as managing the crisis well. Because
President Bush is loathe to admit any errors or to apologize, he overlooks an
important tool that is available to a head of state even more than to others,
where the embodiment of the state in an individual provides for a constructive
use of words to engender goodwill in moments of crisis (see Chapter 5).

The normalization of apology as a diplomatic tool, which has been embraced since the 1990s, has not disappeared. Although even cursory comparison between Bush and his predecessor shows how inept he is in utilizing
apologies, much of his reluctance to apologize may be a result of his character.
Bush has, indeed, shown at least some willingness to apologize. His apologies
during his first term show that he clearly can apologize when necessary, even
if he does it reluctantly, and therefore only occasionally and barely succeeds
in quelling the crisis. Bush has apologized, but has done it so reluctantly that
the process sometimes only aggravated the situation.

This may be analogous to the distinction between genuine and insincere
apologies in American courts. Consider American litigation and the correlation between a successful apology and reduced settlement cost as opposed
to insincere apology and increased cost. It has been shown that apologies

increase the chance for the settlement of a legal dispute, as a first step in righting the wrong, even though the dynamic is complex, and we have to take into account the context, the severity of the injury, and the evidence of responsibility.[23] If the apology includes sympathy but does not acknowledge responsibility, there is at times a negative correlation to settlement of disputes—the situation can become even worse than if no apology was offered at all. The quantitative analysis backs the intuition that insincere apology might only aggravate the anger of the injured party.

Bush's actions fall in this category. The manner of his apologies leaves his audience cold.

To what degree were the differences between Bush, Blair, and Clinton a matter of personality or political ideology? Was Bush's reluctance to apologize a matter of temperament, as was Clinton's enthusiasm? There is little doubt that personality goes a long way to explain the distinctions. However, was there more to it? A manifestation of their divergent worldview was displayed during the presidential debates in Bush's derision of Senator John Kerry's appeal to the global community for partnership and understanding. Bush mocked Kerry for submitting the United States to "a global test." In contrast, both Blair and Clinton shine on the international scene, even more than domestically. At one level, this is related to the polarized view about the international community. The internationalist perspective requires the appearance of equality, and it abhors exceptionalism. Apology constructs parity even where none exists. But Clinton's apologies went beyond the international arena, and conveyed a profound worldview that prefers to be viewed as owning up to mistakes, as showing moral responsibility. This is not to be sanctimonious about Clinton who had more than his share of hypocrisy. There was much truth to the demand that Clinton would stop apologizing for what he did not do and begin taking responsibility for what he did. But for our purposes, it is the eagerness to use the apology as a political tool that is important. Frequent apologies in this sense did not cleanse Clinton, but they did contribute to the public discourse of apologies and, in effect, normalized it.

In contrast, both domestically and internationally, the neorealist rhetoric views apologies as weakness. Internationally, weakness translates into damage to national security. Thus, the opposition to the apologies from the right led to criticism of Bush when he has apologized as in the case of China over the plane crash. On the other hand, Rumsfeld's apology suggests more a differentiated threshold than polarized positions, though these can hide dramatic differences even within a generally shared worldview. If this is true, and there is a strong correlation between a worldview and a propensity to apologize, liberals would be expected to embrace apology in cases when conservatives would resist. This is probably true, broadly speaking. Yet at some level of offense, everyone seems to want to use an apology to attempt and bridge a political conflict. These differences point to more than personality differences. If anything, these might suggest that apology has been tested under fire, and survived. Even at the risk of giving the enemy the pleasure of glee, Rumsfeld and many others apologized for Abu Ghraib. Although we should not exclude the possibility that the "age of apology" would come to an end not because apology would be lacking, rather the opposite might be true, apology may become trite. Apology with no consequences may lose its appeal. While this possibility exists, I do not think it is a likely scenario. Personal relationships seem to have insatiable capacity to consume apologies. It is hard to imagine that public life would not also.

Bush has not earned political capital from his apologies, and is certainly underutilizing apologies to engender good will. They are almost always too late to extinguish criticism. Invariably, one has the sense that it could be done more efficiently. Bush is yet to face a crisis when his own apology would turn the tide of public opinion. His reluctance is possible in part because he governs in a partisan manner and is understood as such. But as Blair, Clinton, and other global leaders have showed, timely apology can earn a leader capital and make life somewhat easier for a government. But liberals have no monopoly on apologies. While Bush was reluctant to apologize, Rumsfeld with his back to the wall, used apology to save his job. Under enormous public pressure, Rumsfeld apologized while simultaneously diverting attention from the truth that was in plain view. His comprehensive apology demonstrated that hard-nosed conservatives can admit fault and apologize. Whether this is a sincere apology, or perhaps cynical, is secondary. It is performed as sincere, and received as such. It confirms that apologies have become a convention, have been routinized, and are expected in the normal course of events. Despite the reluctance to apologize, Rumsfeld's performance shows it can succeed even in conservative circles. Bush may take note.

Apology has come to be equated with accountability. But many apologies are actually aimed at avoiding responsibility. The very notion of acknowledgment in the "War on Terror," as has been pointed out, was used as a way of avoiding accountability and keeping the truth hidden.[24] Because in times of war governments can abuse power to a much greater extent, and given the security risks, they are likely to do so. Political apology may have room even under such circumstances, and most likely in the medium- to long-run will play an important role in helping resolve crises. Given the war on terror and the "unknown *unknowns*," it would seem foolhardy to ignore Rumsfeld's warning that the worst is yet to come. Apologies, it may be anticipated, will only become more frequent under such circumstances.

Notes

1. Jim Garamone, "Rumsfeld Accepts Responsibility for Abu Ghraib," *American Forces Press Service*, May 7, 2004. Edward Epstein, "Rumsfeld Warns About Photos of Worse Abuses; ON THE HILL: Defense Chief Apologizes to Iraqi Victims," *Chronicle Saturday*, May 8, 2004.

2. "Arab World Scorns Bush's TV 'Apology'," *The Guardian*, May 6, 2004. CBS, "Damage Control on Abu Ghraib," May 5, 2004.

3. Susan Sontag, "Regarding the Torture of Others," *The New York Times*, May 23, 2004.

4. "I would like to apologize for our nation and for our military for the small number of soldiers who committed illegal or unauthorized acts here at Abu Ghraib," said General Miller. In "A Prison Tour with Apologetic Generals," *New York Times*, May 6, 2004.

5. "Top US Officials Apologize to Arabs for Prisoner Abuse," *The Washington Post*, May 5, 2004.

6. Seymour M. Hersh, "Chain of Command," *The New Yorker*, May 17, 2004. By far, Hersh's have been the best and most timely reports. The two official reports by the Independent Commission (the Schlesinger Report) and by the military commission, have indicated that the responsibility extends to higher ranks. Schlesinger's commission was appointed by Rumsfeld and reported to him, as well as conducted its news conference at the Pentagon. Its language was appropriately opaque. However, Schlesinger declared that the responsibility goes up the chain of command "all the way to Washington," but he rejected the idea that Rumsfeld should resign because that "would be a boon to all America's enemies." Pointedly, he did not say that Rumsfeld was not responsible. (See Dave Moniz and Donna Leinwand, "Top Officials Played Role in Prison Abuse," *USA Today*, August 24, 2004.) Gonzales' memo (see below) provided even more direct evidence of the responsibility of the Department of Defense and the White House for the abuse.

7. "Bush Reaches Out to Quell Arab Rage at Inmate Abuse; President Reported to Rebuke Rumsfeld," *The Boston Globe*, May 6, 2004.

8. "Main Charge is Reduced in Court-martial," *The San Diego Union-Tribune*, November 6, 2004.

9. "Two More Soldiers Charged with Homicide; IRAQ DEATHS," *Financial Times*, September 29, 2004.

10. "New Details of Prison Abuse Emerge," *Washington Post*, May 21, 2004.

11. For a different framing of the relation to porn and popular culture, see Frank Rich, "It Was the Porn that Made Them Do It," *New York Times*, May 30, 2004.

12. Seymour M. Hersh, "Torture at Abu Ghraib," "Chain of Command," and "The Gray Zone," *The New Yorker*, May 2004.

13. "The Roots of Torture," *Newsweek*, May 24, 2004.

14. "Bush Apologizes for Japanese Trawler's Sinking," See at, http://www.cnn.com/2001/WORLD/asiapcf/east/02/13/japan.substrike.02/.

15. Indira A.R. Lakshmanan, "China Ties and Crew Hang on Semantics," *The Boston Globe*, April 11, 2001.

16. "Professor's Son Ejected from D.C. Meeting," *St. Petersburg Times* (Florida), June 29, 2001; "Washington in Brief," *The Washington Post*, June 30, 2001. At the time of writing, his trial is underway in Tampa, Florida. Al-Arian and three co-defendants are charged in a 51-count indictment with, among other things, operating a criminal enterprise, conspiracy to murder and maim people outside the United States, and conspiracy to provide material support to a terrorist organization.

17. "Alleged Rape Inflames Okinawa Issue," *The Nikkei Weekly* (Japan), July 9, 2001.

18. "Bush Backs Japan's Economic Plans, Sidestepping 2 Disputes," *The New York Times*, July 1, 2001.

19. "Bush Apologizes to Koreans For Killing of 2 Girls by G.I.'s," *New York Times*, November 28, 2002; "Rok Commentary Calls US President Bush's Expression of Regret 'Unsatisfactory'," *Financial Times Information*, December 14, 2002.

20. "Clinton Apologizes for Crimes by Troops," *Mainichi Daily News*, July 23, 2000.

21. "Blair Offers an Apology for Abuses by Soldiers," *The New York Times*, May 10, 2004.

22. "Lull in Iraq Prison Probe Won't Last, Senator Says," *Los Angeles Times*, July 6, 2004.

23. Jennifer K. Robbennolt, "Apologies and Legal Settlement: An Empirical Examination," *Michigan Law Review* 102 (2003): 460.

24. Mark Gibney and Niklaus Steiner, "Apology and the 'War on Terror'," (mss.).

Index

Index

chosen trauma; reactivation of, 129;
   sharing of, 128
clash of ideals, resolving methods, 73–75
clinical commissions, 41–42
coerced virtue, 222
conflict management; procedures of,
   132; traditional Hawaiian process of,
   199
contemporary apology, 108–111;
   examples of, 109–110; religious rituals
   of repentance, link between, 155
Council of State declaration, of past
   mistakes, 272–274
criminal guilt, 164
Crying Father monument, 122, 124–127

D

Danielle Celermajer's examination, of
   Australian apology, 16–17, 26
David Crocker argument, of restorative
   justice, 10–11
democratic reciprocity, means to, 68–71
*Divided Arsenal and The Unsteady
   March,* (book), 217–218, 220

E

ethical imperative, level of, 4
ethics; of responsibility, *see
   Verantwortungsethik;* of ultimate ends,
   see Gesinnungsethik
executive apology, 11

F

forgiveness; conceptual roots of, 83–100;
   mnemonics of, 96
From Madness to Hope report, 42

G

Gaullist "resistancialist" myth, 260
German-Czech declaration, on mutual
   relations and their future
   development, 9

Gesinnungsethik (ethics of ultimate
   ends), 85
Gift, The, (book) 93
Goble's report, on riot commission,
   243
Greenwood residents, 237, 239
group apology, 6; creative application
   of, 27; critics of, 6, 26; Emperor
   Hirohito's letter of apology, 6–7;
   ethical and political considerations
   of, 8–12; Guatemalan Commission
   (1997–1999), 42; National Sorry Day,
   7; negotiating intergroup apologies,
   12–16; of Bishop Desmond Tutu's, 8;
   of Japan's Zen Buddhist community,
   7; of Kevin Gover, 7–8; of President
   Bill Clinton's, 7; of President Jacques
   Chirac's, 7, 23; of Pope John Paul II,
   7; significance of, 9–10

H

historical clarification commissions;
   differences between truth commission
   and, 40; working of, 38–40
Holocaust, reconciliation approach to
   victims of; apology, 289; German
   foundation, 295, 297–299, 308;
   monetary compensation, 289;
   negotiation for reconciliation
   between Germans, 298–299;
   preservation of memory, 289; task
   force for international cooperation on
   holocaust education, 292; 1998
   Washington Conference on assets,
   292
"Ho'oponopono", *see* conflict
   management, traditional Hawaiian
   process of

I

individual mourning, types of; concrete,
   117; developmental, 117
interpersonal apology, elements of;
   expression of attitude of regret and